Coalition of the unWilling and unAble

COALITION OF THE
unWILLING AND unABLE

European Realignment and the
Future of American Geopolitics

John R. Deni

University of Michigan Press
Ann Arbor

First paperback conversion 2022
Copyright 2021 by John R. Deni

For questions or permissions, please contact um.press.perms@umich.edu

Published in the United States of America by
the University of Michigan Press
Manufactured in the United States of America
Printed on acid-free paper

First published in paperback July 2022

A CIP catalog record for this book is available from the British Library.

ISBN 978-0-472-13249-2 (hardcover : alk. paper)
ISBN 978-0-472-12879-2(ebook)

ISBN 978-0-472-03915-9 (paper : alk. paper)

To my parents, John S. and Carole L. Deni

Contents

Digital materials related to this title can be found on the Fulcrum platform via the following citable URL https://doi.org/10.3998/mpub.11473281

List of Figures

List of Tables

Preface and Acknowledgments

According to Winston Churchill, the only thing worse than fighting with allies is fighting without them. This maxim has been at the heart of American national security policy implicitly since the end of World War II and explicitly since the 1990s. In conflicts and crises stretching from the Korean War of the 1950s through the anti-Daesh coalition of the 2010s, the United States has routinely and consistently sought to operate with allies by its side, despite the complications of working with other sovereign states in the application of military force. The primary reasons for this have been to share the material burdens as well as the political risks associated with shedding blood and treasure in defending common interests.

Since the presidency of Bill Clinton, and continuing through those of George W. Bush, Barack Obama, and Donald Trump, operating with allies has been a regular feature of nearly every national security strategy. This is a particularly ironic aspect of American strategy—that the world's most powerful country, with a military that can decisively affect political outcomes practically anywhere on the planet, would consistently try to enlist the help and support of other countries. This approach can be thought of as the "American way of war." Perhaps, though, given that Washington prefers to manage all manner of international security challenges with allies on board, it is more accurate to think of this as the American way of engaging in the world.

More often than not, American leaders aim to enlist the support and assistance of European allies. Historically, Europeans have been willing and able to support the United States for a variety of reasons. First, Europeans have tended to view international security threats in the same light as Americans. A revisionist Russia, a nuclear-armed Iran, and a predatory China are all perceived by Americans *and* Europeans as threatening the international order and "Western" interests. Second, many European allies have a long history of actively engaging the world or once led colonial empires, or both. They therefore typically conceive of their interests in a broader geographic context that looks beyond their immediate neighbors, much as the United States does. Third, European allies have typically had the ability and wherewithal to actively engage the broader world. They have maintained worldwide diplomatic posts and they have built highly capable military forces. Considered together, these factors differentiate America's European allies from those in other regions, such as South Korea, Japan, or Australia. Certainly, these non-European allies have contributed to U.S.-led diplomatic, economic, and military missions and initiatives, but they have not matched the willpower, capability, and capacity exhibited by Washington's most important European allies over the last couple of decades.

The troubling thing is, all of that looks like it is undergoing significant change. For a variety of reasons, I argue that Washington appears likely to face a future in which its most important allies are incapable, have insufficient capacity, or lack the will power to defend and promote collective security interests beyond Europe. Each of the major allies addressed in this book have recently undergone or are undergoing *major* domestic transformation—what is termed "realignment" or "strategic-level" change in the book, beyond the typical ups and down of particular political parties, or the peaks and troughs of the business cycle. These changes will have long-lasting implications affecting the ability of those major allies to act internationally in the way in which they, and Washington, have become accustomed.

The story told in this book in therefore generally a pessimistic one from America's perspective, or at least it certainly turned out more pessimistic than I expected when I began researching it in the summer of 2018. Nonetheless, the largely gloomy tale is tempered in two ways. First, I have identified a small handful of silver linings among the gray clouds on the horizon. It is incumbent on U.S. decision-makers to leverage them. Second, although nearly all of what has unfolded in the major American allies addressed in this book is outside the control of Washington, the United States is not necessarily powerless in *responding* to those unfolding events. By utilizing economic, diplomatic, political, and military tools at its disposal, the U.S. government can try to accentuate the positive trends and mitigate the worst of the negative ones.

One cannot write a book about transatlantic relations these days without addressing the impact of Donald Trump's presidency. More specifically, it is impossible to ignore the fundamental question posed by many Europeans and others since Trump's election in November 2016—is Trump and his nativist, unilateralist, international-organization-bashing approach to American foreign policy a short-term problem, or a longer-term trend? It is important to note that although the populist Trump has seized control of the Republican Party, he has yet to seriously dent Americans' views of its European allies. Public opinion polls still show strong majorities of Americans (regardless of age or party) support NATO, overwhelming bipartisan majorities in both chambers of the U.S. Congress support the alliance, and there remains broad agreement among U.S. international relations scholars and experts that American membership in NATO enhances our national security.

The larger risk, at least in terms of transatlantic relations, is that a kind of decoupling might emerge from Europe's inability or unwillingness to join the United States in defending common values and interests beyond the continent. That is, as European capability, capacity, and willpower dwindle, Europe will play less of a role in affecting political outcomes in geographic regions beyond the Mediterranean basin, the North Sea, or the Baltic region, just as Washington's security focus and its economic interests shift increasingly eastward, toward China.

In many ways, this is the mirror image of what many in Europe perceive today regarding the challenges facing the transatlantic relationship. For the most part, Europeans are worried about how to handle an imminent U.S. withdrawal from Europe. Although, as I mentioned above, this may be possible in a second Trump term, I remain unconvinced that there is sufficient evidence to support this outcome. If anything, Russia's invasion of Ukraine has reinvigorated Washington's interest in European security, evidenced by the reversal of what had been a steadily declining American military presence in Europe. Instead, this book flips the script somewhat in focusing on how Washington can manage the likely—although not predetermined—demise of capacity, capability, and willpower among many of its most important European allies over the next 10 years.

My interest in tackling this subject emerged in the years following Russia's invasion of Ukraine, as European members of NATO began to slowly but steadily increase their defense spending. Since 2014, there have been broad-based defense budget increases on the part of almost all European NATO members, thanks to Moscow's destabilizing, threatening behavior as well as the rise of Daesh in Iraq, Syria, and elsewhere. After many years during which European NATO defense spending had steadily declined, the turnaround was remarkable. However, through the second half of the 2010s it also became increasingly clear that the most significant percentage increases in defense spending were occurring among the newest members of the alliance, especially those in Central and Eastern Europe. Western (to include Italy) and Northern European defense budgets were growing at a far slower rate, rates that were barely keeping up with the demands of resetting and recapitalizing their military forces following many years of operating in Iraq, Afghanistan, and elsewhere. Given that British, French, German, and Italian defense spending together accounts for roughly two-thirds of *all* NATO European defense spending, and given the important role these countries (including Poland) have played in American security policy across the globe, it seemed to me that this inadequate defense investment was going to have long-term implications. When given the opportunity to apply for a year-long sabbatical from my regular duties at the U.S. Army War College, I knew this was the topic I wanted to devote my time to.

As I write this, I have reached the end of that sabbatical period, grateful that I was able to devote an extended period of time to a major research project such as this. The U.S. Army War College—and especially its Strategic Studies Institute—is a rewarding, fulfilling, and fascinating place to work. There, I benefit not simply from an array of expert, insightful, and experienced colleagues but also from the chance to interact with, instruct, and learn from our students. Most of these students are American military officers, but a great many come from other countries as well as from across the U.S. national security enterprise. Engaging with them in the classroom and across the Carlisle Barracks "campus" is one of the highlights of my job.

Some of those students as well as former students who have since graduated from the Army War College were interviewees for my research. I am grateful to them as well as to all of the more than four dozen anonymous military leaders, governmental and intergovernmental officials, journalists, think-tank experts, and academics that agreed to share their knowledge, experiences, and insights with me as I researched this book. I would also like to thank Chris Bolan, Ed Callahan, Judy Dempsey, Jennifer Fuller, Josh Henson, Dominik Jankowski, Pierre Prod'Homme, Chris Mason, Christian Mölling, George Shatzer, Gary Speer, Jerzy Zubr, and two anonymous reviewers for their helpful comments on earlier drafts of one or more chapters of the book, and David Swenson for research assistance. Finally, I'm grateful to Elizabeth Demers and the team at the University of Michigan Press—they were a pleasure to work with through this research project.

I must also thank the most important people in my life—my wife Shuchi and our daughters Mira and Jaya. They have endured my seemingly endless mutterings on European transformation, Brexit, Macron, German productivity, Italian populists, and Polish nightmares about Russia. They are probably as glad to see me complete this project as I am to be bringing it to a close. Together, they are the most important part of my life, and I'm grateful for their support, their encouragement, and their patience and understanding as I labored to complete this book.

Despite all the support and assistance I've received in this effort, the fact remains that any errors or shortcomings herein are mine. Similarly, the views expressed in this book are mine alone, and do not necessarily reflect those of the U.S. Army, the U.S. Department of Defense, or the U.S. Government.

About the Author

Dr. John R. Deni is a Research Professor of Joint, Interagency, Intergovernmental, and Multinational (JIIM) Security Studies at the Strategic Studies Institute, the research arm of the U.S. Army War College, and an Adjunct Professorial Lecturer at the American University's School of International Service. Previously, he worked for eight years as a political advisor for senior U.S. military commanders in Europe. Prior to that, he spent two years as a strategic planner specializing in the military-to-military relationships between the United States and its European allies. While working for the U.S. military in Europe, he was also an adjunct lecturer at Heidelberg University's Institute for Political Science where he taught graduate and undergraduate courses on U.S. foreign and security policy, the North Atlantic Treaty Organization, European security, and alliance theory and practice. Before working in Germany, Professor Deni spent seven years in Washington, D.C. as a consultant specializing in national security issues for the U.S. Departments of Defense, Energy, and State. He completed his undergraduate degree in history and international relations at the College of William & Mary. He holds an MA in U.S. foreign policy from the American University in Washington, D.C., and a PhD in international affairs from George Washington University. He is the author or editor of several books, peer-reviewed monographs and journal articles, book chapters, and essays, all of which can be found at www.johnrdeni.com.

Prologue

The president turned off the secure video teleconference with more force than was really necessary for a touchscreen, wishing she'd instead had an actual handset to fling across the conference room table. The days of slamming down a telephone receiver had passed with her grandparents, and so she was left to vent in some other way. Her frustration shouldn't have been *un*expected though. After all, her advisors had all warned her not to expect much in the way of force contributions from London—and they were right. In fact, the Brits wouldn't add *anything* to the second rotation of peacekeepers in what had euphemistically been named Operation Rapid Recovery.

The notion that this was just a short-term peacekeeping mission had gone out the window early, just after the first large-scale aid convoy sent through the foothills of the Sulaiman mountain range was diverted by way of a GPS hacking operation. The newest generation of GPS satellites were supposed to be more secure than their predecessors, but evidently this failed to prevent somebody—or some group—from spoofing the receivers relied on by most of the nongovernmental aid organizations now operating in the region. The U.S. military had stopped relying on GPS years ago, favoring an integrated suite of sensors and indicators that proved collectively far more secure, albeit expensive as well. Of course, the NGO community—not to mention America's major allies—didn't have a Pentagon-sized budget to keep up with such technological innovations. As a result, aid convoys were now routinely diverted, stolen, held for ransom, or just destroyed by any number of actors rising from the ashes of what *had* been a unitary political entity—the country formerly known as Pakistan.

The Chinese didn't exactly intend for their client Pakistan to break apart, but they couldn't have been too disappointed with the repercussions of the country's demise. Desperate to maintain their slowly but steadily declining geopolitical position relative to India and to make good on the as-yet-unrealized promise of a Chinese-dominated Pacific Century, Beijing had deftly incentivized and cajoled Pakistan's leader in Islamabad into pushing New Delhi just a bit too far. Pakistan's efforts over the last several years had gone beyond the occasional Islamic State of Iraq–orchestrated terrorist attack on an Indian hotel or mall of a generation ago, evolving into more sophisticated cyber assaults on Indian critical infrastructure, fomenting and arming an increasingly violent Muslim separatist movement across India after New Delhi rescinded Kashmir's autonomy, and routinely violating sovereign Indian airspace and sea space. New Delhi historically thought of Pakistan as an ankle-biter—China was the real challenge. However, the domestic political calculus confronting Indian politicians had begun to shift over the last year, and the ruling party found itself under increasing pressure over the rising tide of Pakistani provocations.

As a result, India devoted an increasingly large proportion of attention and resources toward managing the growing tension with Pakistan. Naturally, this prevented New Delhi from focusing on expanding its role, presence, and influence in the Indian Ocean, across Southeast Asia and Oceania, and throughout East and Southern Africa—exactly what Beijing had hoped for.

What the Chinese leadership *didn't* plan for was how quickly the Indians would escalate the conflict with Pakistan, nor for how fragile the Pakistani state would prove. There was still uncertainty over whether, as Islamabad had claimed, India had pulled the nuclear trigger first, despite its no-first-use policy. As expected, New Delhi accused the Pakistanis of being the first to do so. Regardless, in short order the Pakistani government and its highly centralized military enterprise were effectively decapitated. With central authority almost entirely absent, and regional governments eager to either stake their claims to independence or form the nucleus of a new post-Pakistani rump state, the country descended into a humanitarian and political morass. At the same time, terrorist organizations of various stripes, which were previously held on a relatively tight leash by Islamabad, were completely unbound, and they began to build more training camps and other infrastructure and support mechanisms across the former Pakistan.

New Delhi's satisfaction over the decisive end it had brought to Islamabad's campaign of provocation and aggression soon gave way to anxiety over the practical ramifications of an imploding Pakistan. This included the high likelihood that tens of millions of Muslim refugees would flee political instability—not to mention nuclear fallout—by heading south, into India. This is what compelled Indian officials to finally seek the involvement of the international community. A large-scale, short-term humanitarian relief mission was necessary, they argued, to provide food and medical assistance across Pakistan. Only in this way, maintained officials in New Delhi, would a massive refugee crisis be averted, and stability returned, so that a new central government might arise.

In the United States, India's call found receptive ears. Washington was also concerned about the potential impact on India of a collapsed Pakistan, and specifically on India's economic and military power. Eager to keep India in the game as *the* counterbalance to an increasingly aggressive China, the United States agreed to build a coalition of military forces necessary to facilitate the delivery of desperately needed food and medical aid, and to act as a peacekeeping force in key locations throughout Pakistan, thereby facilitating the delivery of aid and stanching the flow of refugees across India's border.

That was several months ago. Given the urgency of India's request, the American interests at stake, and the specialized equipment and skills necessary to operate in a radioactive environment, the United States decided to source the first nine-month rotation of nearly 140,000 peacekeepers largely on its own. A handful of American allies agreed to contribute forces for the first rotation, including the British (one brigade, or about 5,000 troops) and the Germans (also one brigade). It was the French, though, that provided the largest non-American contingent—one enhanced brigade of roughly 8,000 troops. Washington hadn't even bothered to make official requests of the Poles, who remained firmly transfixed by what they perceived as the threat from Russia, even as Moscow's conventional capabilities continued to atrophy with the slow but steady decline in oil prices. Nor had the United States formally approached the Italians, who had largely drawn back from all overseas commitments since 2020, with the notable exception of their nearly decadelong operation trying to bring stability and security to Libya.

Like the Brits, the French would not be extending their deployment beyond the first rotation. Manpower shortfalls remained among the greatest challenges facing both countries' military forces, but more broadly they each also continued to struggle in terms of defense resourcing. The Brits were midway through a multiyear effort to build a new base for their two Dreadnought-class nuclear-powered ballistic missile submarines, having had to vacate facilities in Faslane after Scotland voted for independence in the wake of Brexit. And although prospects for a reboot of the French economy seemed bright in the late 2010s, entrenched interests on both right and left won the struggle for the country's future against upstart centrists. As a result, France remained mired in economic stagnation that severely limited its defense budget and hence any attempt to expand force structure or aggressively pursue advanced military technology.

The lone European ally that appeared to have any significant fiscal wherewithal when it came to defense investment was Germany. Over the last several years, the Germans had successfully leveraged their relative advantages in productivity, labor market flexibility, and industrial automation to widen the gap between their own economic output and that of every other European economy. Berlin's economic dominance had only slowly— but steadily—been transferred into military power. Instead of focusing on capacity, though, German defense investments over the last decade had emphasized capability and readiness, in an effort to keep technological pace with the United States and under the belief that a more capable German military would be less intimidating to the rest of Europe than a *larger* German military. For the purposes of Operation Rapid Recovery, this meant Berlin might be convinced to send a brigade-sized force for the second nine-month rotation but it would be unlikely to do so for a third or fourth rotation, if the need arose.

If Beijing had anything to say about it, there would definitely be a need for additional rotations. Chinese military and intelligence organizations were doing all they could—as quietly as they could—to ensnare the West in what increasingly had the potential to become a quagmire of Vietnam (1964–75) or even Afghanistan (2001–21) proportions. Although the precise modalities and full extent of Chinese involvement wouldn't be clear to the United States and its allies for several more years, evidence was already mounting in the form of advanced capabilities showing up in the hands of nonstate actors across the former Pakistan. In addition to the GPS spoofers, peacekeepers had seen increasing use of adaptive camouflage on 4x4 pickup trucks that made them virtually invisible to optical and thermal detection, and lasers had been used to bring down allied unmanned aerial vehicles (UAVs)—technologies that, aside from the United States and one or two of its European allies, only the Chinese were thought to have.

All of this added up to "peacekeepers" increasingly drawn into peace enforcement and outright maneuver warfare in some instances, well beyond the original mandate of ensuring the safe and secure delivery of humanitarian aid. In the years to come, American presidents would find themselves in the same situation as the current occupant—unable to coax reluctant allies that lacked sufficient capacity or capability in the first place to put their troops in an increasingly deadly and complex situation.

ONE

Introduction

The Enduring Value of Europe

Despite the promise of a "Pacific century," Europe remains a region vital to U.S. security and the American way of life. There are arguably several reasons for this, but the most important of them is the trade relationship between the United States and Europe. The European Union is America's single largest trading partner, accounting for 18.5 percent of all U.S. imports and exports, excluding services. In comparison, China accounts for 16.3 percent.

When services are included, the differences are even greater—the European Union accounts for nearly 24 percent of all U.S. trade in goods and services, while China accounts for just 11.3 percent.[1] The U.S. Department of Commerce estimates that exports of goods and services to the EU supports 2.6 million U.S. jobs, while exports of goods and services to China supports roughly 911,000 U.S. jobs.[2]

In short, it is no exaggeration to say that given the extensive array of trade and investment ties between the United States and Europe, the

---

1. Figures cited are from 2019. If one adds Japan and Korea, the total for East Asia is just under 20 percent. "U.S. Census Bureau, U.S. International Trade in Goods and Services (FT900), Exhibit 20—U.S. Trade in Goods and Services by Selected Countries and Areas—BOP Basis," www.census.gov/foreign-trade/Press-Release/current_press_release/index.html#seasonalgeo

2. As cited by the Office of the U.S. Trade Representative, ustr.gov/countries-regions/europe-middle-east/europe/european-union and ustr.gov/countries-regions/china-mongolia-taiwan/peoples-republic-china

American way of life depends on a stable, secure Europe free from the domination of a single, hostile, protectionist power and both able and willing to defend shared interests and values at home and abroad. In one form or another, this has been the foundational bedrock of American grand strategy, arguably for the last 100 years but certainly since the end of World War II. Through Republican and Democratic administrations, the vast majority of American political leaders, experts in academia and think tanks, and other opinion leaders in the media and elsewhere have consistently held that Europe is vital to American national security. It is possible this assessment could change over the long term, particularly as the preponderance of American trade and investment shifts to the Pacific. However, at least in the short- to midterm—and certainly over the next 10 years, which is the time horizon for this book—the importance of Europe in American grand strategy is unlikely to change.

Reinforcing the material factors at the heart of U.S. interest in a stable, secure Europe is the fact that the United States and Europe share similar values, as well as a similar heritage. The shared values include a commitment to personal liberty, representative forms of government, and the rule of law. And although European emigration to the United States is a fraction of what it once was, decades if not centuries of European arrivals in America continue to define and even shape the transatlantic relationship today.

Together, the combination of material and cultural ties have led to a political, diplomatic, and military relationship that is truly second to none. In rhetoric and practice, the United States views Europe as its partner of first resort in nearly all international contexts, in dealing with state and nonstate adversaries, and in response to challenges and threats in Europe and well beyond. Among other manifestations, this preference for partnership with Europe has been evident through American national security strategies of the last 25 years, which have been remarkably consistent on this central point, differing administrations notwithstanding. From the national security strategy of an American president viewed as decidedly pro-European—Bill Clinton, who led the effort to expand NATO—to that of a president far more dubious toward American commitments in Europe—Donald Trump, who questioned the utility of NATO's mutual defense clauses—the United States continues to view Europe as its most willing and most capable partner in international affairs. Even if the preponderance of American trade and investment shifts to the Pacific in the longer term, the United States will still need like-minded international partners in order to bolster the legitimacy of its foreign, economic, and security policies in the eyes of domestic as well as international audiences. Consequently, Washington will likely remain strongly interested in maintaining and building strong political, diplomatic, economic, and security ties with European partners.

However, there is growing reason for Washington to be concerned. There appears to be a fundamental strategic realignment now under way within Europe. Shifting demographic, economic, political, and military trends among many of America's key partners in Europe—especially but not limited to the United Kingdom, Germany, France, Italy, and Poland— are upending the Europe that Washington thought it knew and which it had become exceedingly comfortable in working with. At the same time, Washington has finally awakened to the great power competition with Russia and China now under way—it needs and wants capable and willing allies by its side in that competition, yet both Moscow and Beijing threaten to exploit for their own purposes the same transformative trends among America's closest and most significant allies in Europe.

This realignment and its exploitation by Russia, China, and possibly other adversaries portends profound implications for the United States. Specifically, the realignment that is unfolding has serious repercussions for U.S. interests in Europe and its approach to international security well beyond the continent. For instance, can a post-Brexit United Kingdom continue to play its historic role as America's right-hand partner in global security? If not, can an increasingly economically powerful Germany fill the gap? Will the promise of France's political rejuvenation fuel its rise economically, providing a much-needed boost to its geopolitical power and influence? Will Italy's ability to exercise both hard and soft power beyond the Mediterranean littoral contract even further? If and when the Russian threat recedes, can Poland be counted on to maintain its commitment to transatlantic solidarity beyond Europe? Understanding this realignment, analyzing its far-reaching implications, leveraging its opportunities, and mitigating its negative consequences are vital for American diplomacy, the U.S. Department of Defense, and U.S. military forces.

If America's rebalancing to the Pacific were more manifest, or if Europe were somehow less important to the United States politically, diplomatically, but especially economically, the strategic realignment now playing out in Europe would be interesting but not exactly compelling. Unfortunately for Washington, at just the moment when it most needs reliable, strong, outward-looking allies to manage the challenge from near-peer competitors like Russia, it instead finds dubious capacity, capability, willpower, and vision among the countries it prefers to partner with, with whom it has partnered and operated extensively, and which are among its closest allies. The following section will address the major trends now unfolding, foreshadowing a more detailed treatment of each in the chapters that follow.

Outlines of the Realignment

The realignment that is the subject of this book is not to be confused with the rise of populism—or what might be more accurately labeled nationalism—in some European countries. Rather, it is a realignment among America's most economically, politically, diplomatically, and militarily powerful allies in Europe—the United Kingdom, Germany, France, and Italy. In addition to being America's most powerful European allies, these countries are of great importance to Washington because they—along with Poland (which has one of the fastest growing economies in Europe)—have long shown a willingness to defend common interests side by side with Americans. The five countries examined in this book have done this repeatedly over the last quarter century in Europe and beyond, across an array of what the U.S. military calls "warfighting domains"—on land, in the air, at sea, in space, in cyberspace—and in other contexts such as in international trade and finance policy.[3]

Could other European allies have been included in this analysis? Possibly, but because of their more limited economic, political, diplomatic, or military power (the Netherlands, Denmark) or their lack of consistent participation in U.S.-led operations and initiatives (Spain, Turkey), they do not carry the same weight when it comes to how change among and within them might affect the pursuit of U.S. interests. In contrast, the changes unfolding among and within the five countries considered in this book are likely to have *profound* implications for how the United States defends and promotes its own interests and those of its allies in Europe and across much of the world.

First among these changes is the United Kingdom's exit from the European Union, also known as Brexit. Most independent analyses hold

---

3. Warfighting domains can most usefully be thought of as "a frame of reference that defines the preparation and conduct of war." See Michael C. Davies and Frank Hoffman, "Joint Force 2020 and the Human Domain: Time for a New Conceptual Framework?," *Small Wars Journal*, June 10, 2013, smallwarsjournal.com/jrnl/art/joint-force-2020-and-the-human-domain-time-for-a-new-conceptual-framework. The U.S. Joint Chiefs of Staff recognize five warfighting domains—air, land, sea, cyber, and space. Throughout this book, though, a slightly broader conceptualization of warfighting domains will be used, including the electromagnetic spectrum and information space.

that Brexit is likely to affect the UK economy negatively, shrinking the economy by roughly 6 percent and increasing both borrowing costs and unemployment over the next several years. The impact of the economic slowdown caused by the COVID-19 pandemic will only magnify the fiscal short-term challenges confronting the United Kingdom.

From a political perspective, and in the worst-case scenario, Scottish nationalists might insist on a new independence referendum so that Scotland—which strongly opposed Brexit—might maintain membership in the EU. If Brexit results in the reimposition of a hard border between the Republic of Ireland and Northern Ireland, and Scotland succeeds in leaving the United Kingdom, it is possible leaders of Northern Ireland might also seek an independence referendum. While the loss of Northern Ireland might not hold strategic consequences for the United Kingdom, there would be serious military operational challenges posed by Scottish independence. Such challenges might not prove insurmountable, but a UK outside the EU that consists of just England and Wales would likely result in a smaller UK defense budget and subsequently a less capable UK military.

Just as the loss of empire took some amount of time to manifest itself in terms of Britain's approach to its national security, so too would the full impact of Brexit take time to become fully appreciated in the way the United Kingdom conceptualizes its national security. For this reason, the United Kingdom is likely to remain outward-looking, maintaining a security horizon beyond Europe, at least in the short run.

Just as the United Kingdom endures another era of decline, Germany is in the midst of an economic and diplomatic resurgence. Chancellor Angela Merkel, now in her fourth term as the country's leader, has positioned Germany as the first among equals when it comes to managing the Eurozone, responding to Putin's Russia, and furthering the decades-old project of European integration. Some critics perceive Merkel as diffident, unwilling to lean forward, and overly pragmatic. Despite this—or perhaps because of it—she has placed Germany on a footing that appears increasingly hegemonic.

From an economic standpoint, no other European country can match Germany in terms of size and strength, despite the economic dislocation caused by COVID-19. Germany's nominal GDP is nearly $4 trillion—the next largest economy in Europe is the United Kingdom, at $2.8 trillion—which accounts for almost one-fifth of total European economic output. Federal budget surpluses, low national unemployment, and reduced public debt paint a picture of a stable, growing economy with good long-term prospects. While Germany faces challenges in terms of recovering from the COVID-19 pandemic, public education, an aging population, infrastructure investment, and fostering an innovation investment climate, the strength of the German economy has placed Berlin in a commanding position. Certainly with regard to the sovereign debt crisis, it is no exaggeration to say that Europe's response—grounded in fiscal austerity—was largely crafted in and led by Berlin.

At the same time, Germany has emerged as the West's leading interlocutor with Putin's Russia. In many respects, this represents a reprise of Germany's historical role as the bridge between the West or at least Western Europe on the one hand and the East, or Russia, on the other. Since the invasion of Ukraine, Germany has been the West's center of diplomatic gravity, formulating a two-track effort comprising diplomatic engagement through the so-called Minsk process and a program of economic sanctions designed to compel changes in Russian behavior over time.

Germany has also led efforts to respond to the largest migratory crisis since the immediate aftermath of World War II. As a result of the devastating civil war in Syria, as well as continued turmoil in Iraq and Afghanistan, a wave of refugees flooded into Europe in 2015. Traveling mostly by boat across the Mediterranean or Aegean Seas into Italy, Greece, Spain, Cyprus, and Malta, 1.3 million refugees applied for asylum in Europe in 2015, four to five times the number in 2014. Germany alone received nearly half a million asylum requests in 2015, the most of any European country that year, far outpacing second-place Hungary (174,000 applications) and third-place Sweden (156,000). For this reason, Merkel and the German government led efforts in late 2015 and early 2016 to arrive at an agreement with Turkey to reduce the flow of asylum-seekers into the European Union.

Although integrating refugees that are granted asylum remains a challenge for Germany as well as for other European countries, the German economy stands to gain a great deal from Berlin's decision to essentially maintain an open-door policy toward asylum-seekers. As noted above, Germany has the most dynamic economy in Europe and, until the COVID-19 pandemic, unemployment was at historic lows—its economy *needs* workers in order to continue growing without significant inflationary pressure. Moreover, Germany has an aging population—if it hopes to maintain its generous system of social welfare, an influx of more youthful laborers would certainly help. For these reasons, and assuming Germany can successfully integrate, educate, and train those granted asylum, the massive influx of refugees in 2015 may have a significant silver lining.

The questions now facing German leaders are whether and how to turn their country's economic might, its soft power, and its diplomatic heft into increased hard power. For the last several years, Germany has obviously been wrestling with these questions. In 2014, Germany's president, foreign minister, and defense minister each argued that it was time for their country to take on greater responsibility in international security. Those important initial rhetorical moves found a more detailed articulation in the 2016 German Defense White Paper, or *Weissbuch*. The White Paper represented a significant step forward in Germany's ongoing transformation to a "normal" power. In particular, the 2016 *Weissbuch* stated German security policy is "guided by interests," which stands in contrast to the emphasis on values evident in the 2006 version.[4]

Additionally, the 2016 White Paper notes for the first time that Germany would be willing to lead coalitions of the willing—or what the White Paper refers to as ad hoc coalitions—outside formal multilateral frameworks like NATO or the EU. Berlin's willingness to "participate in ad hoc cooperation and initiate it with its partners" is a major shift from the past, when Germany was unwilling to lead or participate in such coalitions outside the confines of multilateral institutions and the legitimacy conferred by international sanction.[5]

Nevertheless, even if German leaders and the public they serve become more willing to wield military power in the defense of national or collective interests, it is unclear whether Germany will have the *capacity* or *capability* to do so. Although Berlin has committed to increasing defense spending over the next several years, there are serious questions about both the capabilities and the capacity of German military forces. Readiness issues are perhaps the most serious of those facing the Bundeswehr.[6] In fact, German security policy remains hobbled by a lack of adequate resourcing that no amount of "efficiencies" through multilateral collaboration can overcome.

France faces a dilemma similar to that of Germany in many ways. Rhetorically, it remains committed to a robust role in the world, and Paris maintains a security horizon well beyond the European continent. However, the French economy lacks the dynamism of Germany's, and its security establishment remains obsessed with homeland security following

---

4. White Paper 2016 on German Security Policy and the Future of the Bundeswehr, July 2016, www.planungsamt.bundeswehr.de/portal/a/plgabw/start/grundlagen/weissbuch/!ut/p/z0/04_Sj9CPykssy0xPLMnMz0vMAfIjo8zinSx8QnyMLI2MQjydDAwc3f2MjM3NPYzdQw30g1Pz9AuyHRUBnYeirA!!/

5. White Paper 2016 on German Security Policy and the Future of the Bundeswehr, July 2016.

6. "'No More Missions for Germany's Navy,' Warns Armed Forces Ombudsman," *Deutsche Welle online*, February 11, 2018, p.dw.com/p/2sTQ9

several dramatic terrorist attacks. This has resulted in a strategic retrench-ment of sorts, as relatively static or even declining French military power focuses inward in an effort to secure the homeland first.

The fact that the French economy remains sluggish, hampered by incomplete structural reforms, is somewhat ironic given the immense transformation that has played out in French politics in recent years. The election of centrist Emmanuel Macron as president of the French Repub-lic in 2017 ushered in a new political movement, resulting in nothing less than a fundamental changing of the guard, politically speaking, in Paris's halls of power. In April 2016, then economy minister Macron launched a new political movement—not yet a party—called En Marche (On the Move). Macron's movement appeared directed against the standard pillars of political power in France—the conservatives of the right and the social-ists of the left—as it criticized the system of privilege in France as well as its sclerotic, overly regulated economy.[7]

A year after the centrist movement's founding, the 39-year-old Macron became France's youngest leader since Napoleon Bonaparte. A month later, in June 2017, legislative elections in France were just as stunning—En Marche secured 350 seats, well beyond the 289 necessary to govern alone. Many of the deputies elected—about 75 percent of the legislature—had not served in the previous legislature, which was elected in 2012. The aver-age age of the incoming legislature—roughly 48 years old—was 5 years younger than the average age of the outgoing legislature. The previous legislature included 155 women, or roughly 27 percent of the deputies—in contrast, the 2017 election resulted in 224 female deputies, or about 39 percent of the legislature. Given all of this, it is no exaggeration to say that in the spring and early summer of 2017, France had been seized by a sense of rejuvenation.

Frustratingly, however, that sense of political renewal has yet to be translated into a significant economic reversal of fortune. Despite the best efforts of Macron's administration and its supporters in the new legislature to enact and implement major structural economic reforms, the French economy remains sluggish and will likely be further hampered by the response to COVID-19. Although job growth has increased through the first three years of Macron's tenure, official unemployment has remained high as gross domestic product growth hovers around 1.7 percent. This

7. Elizabeth Bryant, "In France, Maverick Macron Sets His Movement En Marche," *Deutsche Welle*, May 1, 2016, www.dw.com/en/in-france-maverick-macron-sets-his-move ment-en-marche/a-19227953

economic sluggishness has inhibited France's ability to devote increased resources to national and international security.

This has been particularly problematic for France since 2015, when the country was subject to two horrific terrorist attacks—in January, in and near the offices of the satirical publication *Charlie Hebdo*, and in November, in a coordinated series of attacks culminating in a mass shooting at the Bataclan theater. These events compelled the French government to declare a state of emergency and to launch Opération Sentinelle, activating 10,000 soldiers and 4,700 police and gendarmes to protect the public in major French cities. Although the deployed forces have thwarted or contained terrorist attacks, they are preventing a large segment of the French military from focusing on other, arguably more pressing security challenges in Europe and beyond. And given pressure on the French defense budget due to less favorable macroeconomic conditions and the COVID-19 economic slump, it appears unlikely that the French military can play a significantly broader role beyond homeland defense.

Like France in the wake of the 2015 terrorist attacks, Poland has been singularly focused on a very specific security challenge. Of course, the roots of Poland's security obsession date back decades, to the Soviet domination of the Cold War years. Even after the Soviet Union's demise, Warsaw continued to maintain its focus on the security threat to its east. Meanwhile, outside of Poland, many security analysts, government officials, and academics considered Russia a relatively weak, unthreatening state, despite its nuclear weapons. Rife with corruption at every level of government and society, consigned to demographic decline and brain drain, economically and fiscally dependent on resource extraction, and unable to significantly reform its military despite numerous attempts, Russia seemed to lack both the ability and willingness to credibly threaten core Western interests.

All that changed in early 2014, when Russia singlehandedly upended the post–Cold War security order in Europe by invading, occupying, and dismembering a pivotal country, Ukraine, in the heart of the continent. Polish officials likely took little satisfaction in finally convincing their counterparts throughout the rest of Europe that Russia was indeed as threatening and destabilizing as it had long argued, or at least since Moscow's 2008 invasion of Georgia. Nonetheless, Polish allies finally awoke to the reality of Russia's aggressive, opportunistic foreign policy.

As a result, NATO has been thrust back into the business of collective defense, and in many ways Poland is its vanguard. For instance, in order to help redress the underfunding of defense across the continent, Poland is the one of the few allies to have enacted a requirement that the government spend the equivalent of 2 percent of gross domestic product on defense. This has enabled Poland to become one of the few allies to fulfill a politically binding agreement within NATO to achieve more equitable burden-sharing.

Poland has also been aggressive in recapitalizing its military to strengthen its capabilities and capacity against other state actors. Warsaw approved a military modernization plan to spend $37 billion between 2016 and 2025 on acquisition programs such as the Patriot air defense system, helicopters, and long-range artillery. At the same time, Poland has been expanding its military manpower, moving swiftly to create and train a 50,000-strong reservist force that will focus on territorial defense.[8] This mirrors a plan to also add 50,000 personnel to Poland's active duty force. In total, Polish military manpower will eventually reach 200,000, larger than Italy's military.

Finally, Poland has pushed NATO to adopt what it views as a more realistic approach to preparing for a Russian attack. This includes crafting major NATO exercises so that they address territorial defense against a large-scale Russian incursion.

These examples illustrate the robustness of Poland's response to Russia's invasion of Ukraine and its illegal annexation of Crimea, but that robustness is a double-edged sword. On the one hand, Poland is indeed a leader within the alliance in rebuilding NATO's ability to conduct large-scale maneuver warfare against a state adversary. Its role here is made easier by a booming economy—the second-fastest growing in Europe, behind Malta, at just over 5 percent. On the other hand, though, Poland's response evinces a kind of single-mindedness that may prevent it from contributing in any significant way to the defense of allied interests outside of Eastern Europe. In fact, Poland's 2017 Defense Concept clearly noted, "the number one priority [is] the necessity of adequately preparing Poland to defend its own territory."[9]

Poland recognizes it must be a "good ally" by responding to threats beyond Europe and committing both blood and treasure to collective operations.[10] However, given the still limited capabilities and capacity of the

---

8. Justyna Pawlak and Kacper Pempel, "In Training with Poland's Volunteer Militia," *Reuters*, October 18, 2018.

9. Ministry of National Defence, "The Defence Concept of the Republic of Poland," May 2017, 6.

10. Interview with a senior civilian official in the Polish Ministry of Defense, March 2, 2016.

Polish military, particularly when it comes to operations far from Europe, Warsaw is likely to be unable and perhaps unwilling to share increased burdens or take on increased risk. For example, although Poland contributed four F-16s to the anti–Islamic State in Iraq and the Levant coalition, those aircraft were consigned to an intelligence and surveillance role.

In some ways, Italy's situation is similar to that of Poland, insofar as its security horizon is very limited. Where Italy differs significantly though is in the fact that just a few years ago, that horizon was *quite* different. Of Washington's closest defense and security partners in Europe, none are arguably in the midst of a more dramatic change than Italy.

A decade ago, Italy was a major contributor to NATO's operations in Afghanistan, responsible for the western part of the country with a sizable contingent of nearly 4,000 troops as part of the International Security Assistance Force. Before and during that operation, Italy was also a major contributor to post-major-combat operations in Iraq, deploying roughly 2,400 troops from 2003 to 2006, mostly in southern Iraq.

Since the end of major combat operations in Afghanistan, though, Italy has retrenched strategically, as well as militarily. Much of this has been due to the sovereign debt crisis, which struck Italy particularly hard and necessitated dramatic fiscal belt-tightening. This fell hardest on the Italian military's budget, which was utilized in many respects as a bill payer for social safety net programs.

The retrenchment was formally enunciated in Italy's 2015 defense white paper, which made it clear from Rome's perspective that the security horizon had receded. For example, with regard to Italy's immediate neighborhood, it notes that terrorism, transnational uprisings, illegal immigration, militant proselytizing, and energy "make the stability of the Euro-Mediterranean region of vital national interest."[11] Meanwhile, Italian engagement beyond the Euro-Mediterranean will only occur "according to [Italian] resources."[12]

Just as defense budget cuts necessitated a retrenchment of sorts, crises much closer than Afghanistan erupted on Italy's doorstep. Destabilization in Libya following Qaddafi's death, the civil war in Syria and the rise of Daesh, and economic stagnation in sub-Saharan Africa led to a massive wave of refugees flowing across the Mediterranean onto Italian shores. As a result, Italy took in roughly 713,000 migrants from 2014 to 2018. This

---

11. Ministry of Defence (Italy), "White Paper for International Security and Defence," July 2015, 27, www.difesa.it/Primo_Piano/Documents/2015/07_Luglio/White%20book.pdf

12. Ministry of Defence (Italy), "White Paper for International Security and Defence," July 2015, 31.

wave of migrants—and the risk that terrorists might be hidden among them—compelled Italian military and security personnel to refocus on homeland and regional security.

For the moment, Italy remains somewhat committed to stability and security beyond the Euro-Mediterranean—during 2019, it maintained just over 4,600 troops in overseas missions. However, whether Italy actually retains the capabilities and capacity—not to mention the willpower—necessary to sustain any significant military operation or to even project significant deterrent force far from the Euro-Mediterranean is unclear given Italy's relatively flat defense budget over the last several years and strong prospects for deep defense cuts in the coming years.[13]

These challenges in terms of military capability and political willpower are underpinned by several problematic trends in Italy's economy, which will only be worsened by the COVID-19 economic slump. Foremost among these is youth unemployment, which has been exceptionally high since 2008, far higher (40 percent) than Eurozone youth unemployment (22 percent). At the same time, Italian government debt also remains very high—at €2.3 trillion, it is second only to Greece in the Eurozone.[14] Plans to spur growth by reducing taxes and increasing welfare spending—again at the expense of the defense budget[15]—cast more doubt on the likelihood of Italy being able to play a major role in security beyond the Mediterranean. At the same time, Italian political elites remain accommodating toward both Russia and China, largely for trade reasons but also in the hopes of winning investment from these two countries in Italy.[16]

The Sources of State Power— Economics, Demographics, and Ideas

As the preceding section strongly implies, this book proceeds from the assumption that economic power and population—in both quantitative

---

13. "What Italy's Foreign Policy Will Look Like under New Rulers," *Stratfor*, June 18, 2018, worldview.stratfor.com/article/italy-foreign-policy-under-five-star-league

14. Silvia Sciorilli Borrelli, "Salvini Strikes Conciliatory Tone on Migration, Italy's Budget," *Politico*, September 8, 2018, www.politico.eu/article/matteo-salvini-strikes-conciliatory-tone-on-migration-italys-budget/

15. "Italy: Rome Trains Its Sights on Defense Spending Cuts," *Stratfor*, October 4, 2018, worldview.stratfor.com/article/italy-rome-trains-its-sights-defense-spending-cuts.

16. John Follain and Rosalind Mathieson, "Italy Pivots to China in Blow to EU Efforts to Keep Its Distance," *Bloomberg*, October 4, 2018, www.bloomberg.com/news/articles/2018-10-04/italy-pivots-to-china-in-blow-to-eu-efforts-to-keep-its-distance

and qualitative terms—together form the basis of a state's military capability and capacity, or what some scholars refer to as "hard power." This concept is distinct from the notion of "soft power," which refers to the ways and means by which a state uses persuasion and attraction to shape others' preferences and get them to do its bidding.[17] Soft power is based on the attractiveness or appeal of a state's culture, ideals, and policies. In short, soft power aims to persuade, while hard power aims to compel. Typically, hard power is defined by a state's military strength, but a state can employ other hard power tools—such as economic sanctions or diplomatic pressure—to compel through payment or coercion.[18] For the most part, this book will focus on the military components of hard power.

The suggestion that military strength is based on economic power and population is not a particularly bold assumption, and it largely reflects the perspective of realism, which is arguably the dominant theory of international relations or at least of security studies.[19] Realists, such as scholars John Mearsheimer or Robert Gilpin, hold that great powers are great because they build and maintain large, capable military forces, which can only be drawn from large, educated, innovative populations and funded with significant amounts of economic wealth.[20] Economic wealth is predicated upon a strong, growing economy—only a strong, growing economy can yield the revenue, usually in the form of tax receipts, that is necessary to train, equip, maintain, and employ a state's military force.[21] At the same time, a large population is necessary to form the tax base, to staff the military, and to formulate innovation.[22]

---

17. Joseph S. Nye Jr., *Soft Power: The Means to Success in World Politics* (New York: Public Affairs, 2004), 5–15.

18. Joseph S. Nye Jr., "Get Smart: Combining Hard and Soft Power," *Foreign Policy*, July/August 2009. The author argues that hard power is any capability employed by a state to compel another state's behavior through payment or coercion.

19. As Sean Lynn-Jones has noted, there are actually several strains of realism. Their theoretical distinctions are substantive, but they are not particularly useful to delve into here. For the purposes of this book, it suffices to understand that military power's roots in economic strength and population are based generally on realism. Sean M. Lynn-Jones, "Realism and America's Rise: A Review Essay," *International Security* 23, no. 2 (Fall 1998): 157–82.

20. John J. Mearsheimer, *The Tragedy of Great Power Politics* (New York: W. W. Norton, 2001), 60–67; Robert Gilpin, *War and Change in World Politics* (Cambridge: Cambridge University Press, 1981), 65. See also Michael Beckley, "Economic Development and Military Effectiveness," *Journal of Strategic Studies* 33, no. 1 (2010): 43–79.

21. One might argue that the Soviet Union proved a state could have a relatively poor economy and still generate substantial military power. However, the Soviet Union's efforts to maintain that military power ultimately led to its collapse.

22. For a discussion of some of these issues, see Brian Nichiporuk, *Security Dynamics of Demographic Factors* (Santa Monica, CA: RAND Corporation, 2000).

One might argue that other factors are equally imperative elements of military power, such as territory or natural resources. These are indeed important, but they are essentially subsumed by or are constituent parts of the concept of economic power—large amounts of land and natural resources can contribute significantly to a country's wealth and hence to its economic power.[23] Nonetheless, territory and natural resources do not by themselves define economic power, nor do they alone lead to great power status. For example, Saudi Arabia has immense fossil fuel resources, but it is not an economic power in a broad sense, nor does it have any significant extraregional hard power.

Other perspectives hold that military power is about more than simply material resources provided by a strong economy and a large population. Instead, it is ideas about *how* those material resources are used—or what Kenneth Waltz called simply "competence"—that determine which states are more likely to prevail in a conflict and hence which states have more military power.[24] A more holistic understanding of military power therefore might include assessment of strategy, morale, tactics, and leadership. The scholar Stephen Biddle sums this up with the notion of "force employment," or how a state uses its material assets in military operations.[25] Biddle's conceptualization of "successful" force employment—what he calls the "modern system"—is very broad, though. In fact, it is broad enough to essentially encompass the United States and most of its NATO allies, including the five addressed in this book. For this reason, while ideas of how a state uses its military resources undoubtedly form an important variable in determining military power, there is insufficient variance among the countries studied in this book to make addressing it separately a worthwhile pursuit.

Throughout this book, economic power will be assessed in terms of

23. Territorial size is also somewhat correlated with population—in many cases, states that are geographically large also have large populations. See for example China (3rd in territory, 1st in population), India (7th in territory, 2nd in population), the United States (4th in territory, 3rd in population), Brazil (5rh in territory, 6th in population), and Russia (1st in territory, 9th in population). Obviously, there are also major exceptions, such as Canada (2nd in territory, but only 39th in population) and Australia (6th in territory, but only 55th in population).

24. Kenneth Waltz, *Theory of International Politics* (Reading, MA: Addison-Wesley, 1979), 131; Stephen D. Biddle, *Military Power: Explaining Victory and Defeat in Modern Battle* (Princeton: Princeton University Press, 2004). See also Risa A. Brooks and Elizabeth A. Stanley, eds., *Creating Military Power: The Sources of Military Effectiveness* (Palo Alto, CA: Stanford University Press, 2007). This volume addresses how societal factors, political institutions, and pressure from the international arena each shape how a state uses its military resources.

25. Biddle, *Military Power*, 2.

extant gross domestic product (GDP) and the rate of GDP growth (or decline) year after year. In terms of future potential GDP—or what might be considered a state's latent economic power—the book relies on the concept of labor productivity and the important role of advanced technology in increasing that productivity. Improving human capital, such as through a more highly educated workforce, or gaining economies of scale, which create cost advantages, are important contributors to productivity. However, without technological advancements states have a difficult time building and maintaining economic power.[26] Moreover, advanced technology has spillover effects into the security realm, allowing states to increase their relative power by improving their military capabilities. States can also use advanced technology to offset disadvantages in capacity, for example by teaming unmanned drones with human-operated equipment.

By using advanced technology to increase military capacity or capabilities, states essentially convert their economic power into military power. This is not unusual—in fact, converting economic power into military power has been very common throughout history. Significant differentiation exists though in terms of *how much* economic power states convert into hard power, whether and how states convert economic power into hard power *effectively or efficiently, or both*, and the decisions states make on precisely *what kinds of capabilities or capacity, or both*, to pursue.[27] This book will address these modes of differentiation among the United Kingdom, Germany, France, Poland, and Italy explicitly as well as implicitly in order to build a sense of the trends and trajectory of each of them over the coming decade.

The Roots of America's Partnership with Europe

The trends among America's closest European partners outlined above raise critical questions for U.S. national security and especially about the Pentagon, not simply in Europe but also beyond. Somewhat paradoxically, security in Europe has been both an end and a means to other ends for the United States over the last century. Arguably since World War

---

26. Andrea Filippetti and Antonio Peyrache, "Productivity Growth and Catching Up: A Technology Gap Explanation," *International Review of Applied Economics* 31, no. 3 (May 2017): 283–303.

27. Ashley J. Tellis, Janice Bially, Christopher Layne, and Melissa McPherson, *Measuring National Power in the Postindustrial Age* (Santa Monica, CA: RAND Corporation, 2000); 21–22; and Mearsheimer, *Tragedy of Great Power Politics*, 76.

I but certainly since the end of World War II, American grand strategy has been driven by the need to keep the engines of global production and development—especially Western Europe and East Asia—out of the hands of a single, hostile, protectionist power.[28] The well-being of the American people and their way of life depend on the relatively free exchange of goods and services with other developed areas of the globe. Imperial Germany, the Nazis, Imperial Japan, and the Soviet Union each threatened to dominate either the European landmass or East Asia in a way inimical to U.S. trade and commerce.

In response to each of these threats, the United States sent military forces far from American shores, in an effort to prevent the rise of a hostile regional hegemon that could potentially close off U.S. trade and investment and threaten American prosperity. Through three distinct conflicts—World War I, World War II, and the Cold War—waged against these kinds of threats, the United States developed close partnerships with allies in Europe.

During the last of these conflicts—the Cold War, from roughly 1948 until 1991—partnerships with the United Kingdom, Germany, France, and Italy became particularly close.[29] For instance, the United States and an array of European countries forged a treaty-based alliance—the North Atlantic Treaty Organization, or NATO—pledging to come to each other's defense in the event of an attack against any of them. They developed an integrated command and control system as well as rudimentary military standardization—primarily through NATO but also on a bilateral basis—to make their military forces more interoperable. They built intelligence-sharing mechanisms to synthesize threat perceptions. They crafted forums such as the Group of Seven (G7) industrialized democracies to coordinate macroeconomic and trade policies. And they built economic investment tools such as the World Bank and the International Monetary Fund to promote development and stabilize global finance.

During the Cold War the close security partnership with these leading European countries focused, unsurprisingly, on security and stability in Europe. Washington wanted to avoid getting pulled into postcolonial fights in Africa and elsewhere by its European partners, while Europeans were not very interested in getting too deeply involved in America's efforts to fight communists on the Korean Peninsula or in Vietnam.

The close cooperation among Washington and its European allies dur-

---

28. Mearsheimer, *Tragedy of Great Power Politics* 236–37; John Lewis Gaddis, *Strategies of Containment* (Oxford: Oxford University Press, 1982), 91.

29. During the Cold War, Moscow's domination of Poland prevented any serious Polish-American partnership.

ing the Cold War did not simply end with the Soviet Union's demise in 1991 and the fading away of the bipolar structure of international relations. The close partnership and cooperation of the previous several decades had become something of a norm among the transatlantic allies, and the institution of NATO continued to serve their material interests as well.[30] For instance, starting in the early 1990s, global security was convulsed by a series of regional or localized conflicts and crises. This compelled Washington to reassess its own security and that of its allies, leading to the conclusion that most threats to the West would come not from conquering states like the Soviet Union but from destabilizing, failing, and disintegrating ones.[31] As a result, the United States became involved in an array of smaller-scale conflicts, relative to major wars with peer- or near-peer countries such as Russia or China. These included operations of varying intensity and duration against or in Iraq, Bosnia, Somalia, Serbia, Kosovo, Liberia, Afghanistan, Iraq again, Libya, and most recently Syria.

For reasons both political and material, Washington sought to include U.S. allies in military operations, and the allies most able and willing were those in Europe.[32] Regarding the political factors, Washington typically seeks international partners because multinationality in any military operation abroad tends to confer legitimacy on the intervening state among its own domestic audiences, the broader international community, and the host country or target country.[33] Legitimacy in military operations is not always a high priority objective for the United States, but usually Washington makes a significant effort to convince or cajole allies to join it.

The other important reason Washington sought and continues to seek allied contributions when it comes to military operations abroad is that, although the United States retains a large military force, it often needs additional manpower, niche capabilities, or redundancy. Frequently, this material basis for Washington's pursuit of allied partners is lost on non-American observers. They see a robust military force comprised of 1.3 mil-

---

30. Stanley R. Sloan, *NATO, the European Union, and the Atlantic Community: The Transatlantic Bargain Reconsidered* (Lanham, MD: Rowman & Littlefield, 2002).

31. White House, *A National Security Strategy of Engagement and Enlargement*, July 1994, 1; see also White House, *The National Security Strategy of the United States of America*, September 2002, 1.

32. Canada and Australia have also been regular contributors to American-led operations, including those cited above.

33. Katharina Coleman, "The Legitimacy Audience Shapes the Coalition: Lessons from Afghanistan, 2001," *Journal of Intervention and Statebuilding* 11, no. 3 (2017): 339–58. See also Olivier Schmitt, *Allies That Count: Junior Partners in Coalition Warfare* (Washington, DC: Georgetown University Press, 2018) for a discussion on the practical nature of whether and how coalition partners matter on the ground.

lion active duty American service members, with over 860,000 reservists, and think it preposterous that the United States could possibly need the contributions of far smaller allies.

While the United States military undoubtedly remains able to conduct the widest array of military operations—otherwise known as "full spectrum"—manpower in the era of the all-volunteer force in fact remains an issue for Washington, especially given the vast array of challenges confronting American interests worldwide. Foreign troops operating in an American-led coalition may not always take on the riskiest roles, and they can worsen command and control challenges in complex operations, but that does not mean they are not necessary from a material perspective. This was the case in two examples, both counterinsurgencies requiring significant manpower, over the last 15 years—the occupation of Iraq in the mid-2000s and the surge of NATO troops in Afghanistan from 2009–11.[34] During the former, the allied contributions—especially from the United Kingdom and Poland but also including Spain, Italy, the Netherlands, and others—added up to tens of thousands of boots on the ground that did have to be provided by the United States at a time when it was trying to handle two regional conflicts at once.

With regard to the Afghanistan surge just a few years later, American allies contributed roughly 30 percent of the 140,000 troops on the ground fighting the Taliban. It is at least conceptually possible that American forces could have taken the place of the non-U.S. troops in both Iraq and Afghanistan, but from the mid-2000s through the early 2010s U.S. military leaders were very clear that the American military was "stretched" trying to handle wartime requirements in the absence of a military draft.[35] Without tens of thousands of coalition troops on the ground, the already high demands on American service members would have been considerably higher. In sum, non-U.S. military forces played a critical role in these two manpower-intensive counterinsurgency conflicts.

For all the material and political reasons outlined above, U.S. strategy over the last quarter century has called for close partnership in pursuing

---

34. Amy Belasco, "Troop Levels in the Afghan and Iraq Wars, FY2001-FY2012: Cost and Other Potential Issues," CRS Report for Congress, July 2, 2009.

35. For example, see Julian Borger, "US Military Stretched to Breaking Point: Pentagon Report Says Clear Strategy Is Needed, Rate of Deployment 'Cannot Be Sustained'," *Guardian*, January 25, 2006, www.theguardian.com/world/2006/jan/26/usa.iraq; Demetri Sevastopulo, "US Army 'Stretched Thin' by Iraq War," *Financial Times*, February 18, 2008, www.ft.com/content/eb734b9e-de59-11dc-9de3-0000779fd2ac; and "Is the U.S Military Overstretched?," *Voice of America*, October 30, 2009, www.voanews.com/a/a-13-2005-08-18-voa49/391598.html

interests in concert with like-minded countries, especially Europeans. In fact, American national security strategies have been remarkably consistent on this point, through Democratic and Republican administrations. For the most part, American allies in Europe have been both willing and able to participate in American-led coalition operations across nearly all the warfighting domains.

Of course, there have also been obvious challenges in trying to partner with European allies in some instances. For example, Germany rather infamously abstained in the UN Security Council vote to approve a no-fly zone over Libya, and Berlin then opted against contributing any military forces to NATO's efforts to enforce the same.[36] In another example, NATO occasionally had great difficulty in getting its members to send enough helicopters for operations in Afghanistan.[37]

Despite challenges like these, though, European allies have largely stood by Washington's side and delivered both political will and capability when absolutely necessary. This is especially remarkable in the case of both the Iraq War and the Afghanistan War. Regarding the former, Washington largely instigated this conflict, and there were deep divides across Europe and within many allies over the wisdom of deposing Saddam Hussein's government. With regard to the latter, the war in Afghanistan was the result of an attack on the United States—the terrorist attacks of September 11, 2001—not on Europe per se. Despite these facts, though, European allies have sent thousands of their sons and daughters to Iraq and Afghanistan and spent millions and in some cases billions of euros, pounds sterling, kroner, złoty, and lei in the process.

One might argue that large-scale wars involving massed armies is a thing of the past, and so the material contributions of key NATO allies such as those studied in this book may become increasingly less important. Certainly, the character of warfare has changed over the decades. Nonetheless, the demand for Western military manpower has been rising in recent years, not shrinking. This has been due to NATO's reembrace of collective defense and large-scale maneuver warfare, the demands of homeland defense placed on active duty military forces, and even responses to seemingly non-military-related disasters and crises such as the COVID-19 pandemic.

---

36. Perhaps feeling the pressure from Washington and other allies over these decisions, Germany increased its military presence in Afghanistan by up to 300 personnel to free the forces of allies that were participating in the Libyan operation, and Germany allowed the use of military installations on its territory for the intervention in Libya.

37. "NATO's Helo Woes," *Military.com*, November 28, 2007, www.military.com/defensetech/2007/11/28/natos-helo-woes

Realignment's Implications for Washington

The preceding section briefly made the case for why allies matter to Washington when it comes to defending and promoting U.S. and collective interests in Europe and beyond. These reasons have become increasingly salient in recent years as the United States has come to recognize the end of the "unipolar moment" and has turned its strategy toward great power competition with Russia, an acute but short- to medium-term threat, and China, a less acute but longer-term challenge. It is no exaggeration to posit that the American way of war, if one exists, is to rely on allies for political as well as material reasons and especially on allies in Europe, given decades of familiarity, common values, and a shared heritage, and that those allies are as I important today as they have ever been.

Arguably, that "way of war"—that way of defending American and collective interests in Europe and beyond—is under threat like never before, due to the aforementioned realignment currently unfolding. For example, with regard to the United Kingdom, regardless of how long it takes British political leaders to scale back their security horizon, a smaller, less capable UK military is likely to provide only token military forces to any U.S.-led coalition military operations and have a greatly reduced ability to independently project force across time and distance. Such a contribution will be helpful in augmenting political legitimacy, both within the United States as well as internationally, but it will not be of a size large enough to matter in terms of quantity.

The diminution of British military power in combination with an inevitable reconceptualization of Britain's security horizon is likely to ultimately undermine its role as Washington's partner of choice across the globe. Certainly Washington will continue to foster close ties with the United Kingdom, but the relationship will change. The changes are likely to manifest themselves at not merely at the strategic level but also in terms of the military operational level.

With regard to Germany, its economic strength, its first-among-equals position within the EU, and its growing soft power make Berlin an increasingly attractive security cooperation partner. However, the reluctance of Germany's political leaders to make the investments—not to mention the operational commitments—necessary to fulfill their own rhetoric of leadership and responsibility raise serious doubts about whether Berlin can truly be an international security partner to the United States in the way the United Kingdom has been in recent decades. In contrast to the UK, while Germany may be willing rhetorically to step up its commitments and truly take on leadership internationally, the lack of resourcing and other forms of follow through leave Berlin increasingly unable to do so.

In France, political leaders still retain, at least rhetorically, a security horizon beyond Europe. This is evident not simply through published strategies and white papers but also through French engagement diplomatically and politically outside of Europe.[38] However, France's ability and hence willingness to act in partnership with the United States and others in support of its interests elsewhere may be quite limited for the foreseeable future. Limited defense resourcing as well as increased emphasis on homeland security and the Mediterranean littoral mean that while Paris may be interested in exercising influence and power globally, its ability to do so will remain constrained.

In the case of Italy, Rome's unwillingness to play a more significant role internationally as the United States is attempting to increase competitive pressure on Moscow and Beijing is likely to be unwelcome in Washington. At the same time, Italy's limited ability to project military force across time and distance and its limited and fragmented approach to military operations in cyberspace mean it is likely to act as merely a bit player in any major military operations beyond the Mediterranean basin or in the information space. In summary, Italy over the next decade is unlikely to play a major role alongside the United States internationally, as it did in the 1990s and early 2000s.

Finally, with regard to Poland, from Washington's perspective the good news is that Warsaw is likely to be an aggressive proponent of alliance collective defense capabilities in Eastern Europe, pushing itself as well as other allies to counter perceived Russian military advantages through increased defense resourcing, more aggressive exploitation of Russia vulnerabilities in cyberspace, expanded and dynamic allied military posture models, and robust readiness efforts. When it comes to military operations and the application of force beyond Poland's immediate neighborhood, though, the United States cannot expect much more than token contributions from Warsaw. Additionally, Poland's *will* to pursue collective goals and defend common values beyond Eastern Europe will necessarily be very limited.

These are just some of the implications for the United States of the realignment that is under way. In order to compete with near-peers Russia

---

38. For instance, see John Irish and Marine Pennetier, "France Says It Could Help North Korea Denuclearize if It Sees Real Commitment," *Reuters*, October 15, 2018, www.reuters.com/article/us-france-southkorea/france-says-it-could-help-north-korea-denuclearize-if-it-sees-real-commitment-idUSKCN1MP23Q

and China—especially in contexts short of major interstate war—and to ensure it has allies by its side over the next 10 to 20 years, the United States needs to give greater thought *now* to how it can leverage the realignment. Unless it does so, Washington is likely to find itself relying on partners who cannot deliver.[39]

Key questions policymakers in Washington should be asking themselves include what strategy is appropriate for managing the realignment in a way that protects U.S. interests and those of America's allies? How can the United States mitigate the realignment's negative repercussions? What tools should Washington use to leverage the few positive trends under way within the realignment? This book will seek to answer these and other questions related to the most important changes in a generation that are unfolding in Europe—a continent that has been and remains today vital to American national security.

The Way Ahead

The next several chapters will examine in greater detail the nature of the realignment that continues to unfold in the United Kingdom (chapter 2), Germany (chapter 3), France (chapter 4), Italy (chapter 5), and Poland (chapter 6). A great deal of the story is rooted in economics because, together with population, it is a key codeterminant of a country's military power and hence its ability to wield influence and shape outcomes in Europe and beyond.

Of course, economic policy cannot be separated from politics, and so each of these chapters will examine and analyze the most consequential political-military as well as diplomatic decisions and trends in each coun-

---

39. It is theoretically possible that, as European allies become less able and willing to carry their share of the burden, Washington might come to rely more heavily on Asian allies. However, this is highly unlikely for three reasons. First, America's Asian allies generally lack the will to do this. For instance, America's most powerful Asian ally, Japan, still retains a pacifist tendency, while South Korea remains justifiably focused on Korean Peninsula security. Second, America's Asian allies lack the force structure and power projection capabilities and capacity necessary to play a role similar to that played by European allies over the last couple of decades. Australia is a possible exception here, but its military remains small. Third, the weight of history will prevent America's Asian allies from doing more. For example, South Korea, Australia, the Philippines, and Thailand all lack any kind of recent experience as colonial powers, meaning they generally do not have the kinds of historical, linguistic, and cultural ties that France has to West Africa or the United Kingdom has to the subcontinent. Japan of course has the opposite problem—it was a colonial power over much of East and Southeast Asia, which continues to engender resentment today.

try. Throughout, though, the book will attempt to get beyond the electoral politics of the day, to avoid getting bogged down in the weeds of who is up and who is down in each country. Instead, the chapters will distill and analyze the macro trends prevalent in each of the five countries examined in this book.

Chapter 7 will address the implications for the United States of the realignment across Europe. In doing so, it must begin by painting a picture of the geopolitical security landscape facing the United States as well as its allies. Key elements of this landscape include Russia's upending of the security environment in and around Europe; the revisionist trends in China's rise and the threats Beijing poses to the global commons; the new politics and economics of influence trafficking by both Russia and China; the challenges posed by political-military conflict, identity politics, and economic underdevelopment in Africa, the Middle East, and South Asia; the increasing saliency of manmade climate change; and the destabilizing effects of pandemics like COVID-19. These threats and challenges each drive certain policy responses, including military operations on land, at sea, in the air, in space, and throughout cyberspace. Chapter 7 will examine whether Washington can continue to rely on its key European allies in these issue areas or contexts. Finally, this chapter will address ways in which Washington and specifically the Pentagon can best mitigate the negative implications of the realignment while maximizing the few positive trends. Key policy tools addressed in this section will include Washington's trade policy, military-to-military initiatives, foreign military financing and sales, and other cooperative initiatives. The point is, while much of what drives the realignment is out of American control, responding effectively to it *now* is a policy choice that Washington has a great deal of control over. Indeed, it is a choice Washington must make if it hopes to fulfill its strategy of working side by side with like-minded, capable partners as it has for decades.

TWO

Brexit, Austerity, and the Demise of the Special Relationship

On June 23, 2016, the United Kingdom made the most consequential political decision since deciding 45 years prior to join the European Union[1]—it voted, by a slim but clear majority, to leave. Those in favor of leaving the EU won the referendum by 51.9 percent to 48.1 percent. Turnout was somewhat high by recent UK election standards at 71.8 percent.[2] Although the future relationship between the European Union and the United Kingdom remains somewhat opaque at the time of this writing, what is already clear is that the Brexit vote has reduced British economic output and household purchasing power below what they would have been had voters instead chosen to remain inside the EU. The most objective analyses hold that British economic growth will be hampered over the next decade thanks to Brexit, regardless of the specific terms of any future relationship between the United Kingdom and the EU.

A smaller UK economy—and potentially a smaller UK, if Scotland or Northern Ireland were to secede—will have profound implications for the British defense budget and hence for British military capabilities, capacity, and willpower. However, there is strong evidence to suggest that even in

---

1. Christopher Hill, *The Future of British Foreign Policy: Security and Diplomacy in a World after Brexit* (Cambridge: Polity Press, 2019).

2. From 2001 through 2017, turnout in five UK general elections ranged from 59 to 67 percent. See Noel Dempsey, "Turnout at Elections," UK House of Commons briefing paper CBP 8060, July 26, 2017, researchbriefings.files.parliament.uk/documents/CBP-8060/CBP-8060.pdf

the absence of Brexit, the British military is already in an era of decline. This is largely due to austerity measures that were implemented in the wake of the Great Recession, the medium- and long-term implications of which are only now taking shape. For the time being, British strategic willpower—that is, the desire to shape outcomes on distant shores in the pursuit of British and allied interests—remains steadfast, although history suggests that over time the gravitational pull of reduced capabilities and capacity will compel a reconceptualization of Britain's strategic horizon.

This chapter will examine all of these issues in greater detail, starting with the fateful British decision to leave the European Union and the broad economic implications, some of which have already come to pass. The next section will examine the most serious repercussions for UK defense— namely, in the form of a smaller defense budget. The fiscal impact of Brexit will be felt by an already reeling UK military establishment, and the subsequent section will examine how the nearly decadelong period of austerity is leading to a British military that is a shadow of its former self, especially in terms of capacity but also in terms of capability. Whether and how this will lead to a receding British security horizon is the subject of the penultimate section of this chapter, which will draw on historical examples to make the case that London will necessarily reconceptualize UK interests and how it will pursue them through military power. Finally, the chapter will address the United Kingdom's shifting military capabilities, capacity, and willpower in the context of its relationship with the United States.

June 23, 2016

The relatively close referendum results might lead one to conclude that there was much analytical uncertainty over whether Brexit would be beneficial or costly for the United Kingdom. In fact, though, most reputable, relatively independent, expert-level economic analyses both inside and outside the UK indicated quite clearly that costs would outweigh benefits.[3]

---

3. There was one notable exception to this—a study entitled "The Economy after Brexit," which was led by Gerard Lyons (chief economic advisor to then-mayor of London Boris Johnson, a leading advocate for leaving the EU) and Patrick Minford (professor of applied economics at Cardiff University). Lyons and Minford were prominent members of the so-called Economists for Brexit group, now known as the Economists for Free Trade. Their study (www.economistsforfreetrade.com/wp-content/uploads/2017/08/Economists_for_Brexit_ The_Economy_after_Brexit.pdf) argued that UK GDP would rise by 4 percent over the long run thanks to Brexit. However, it was credibly debunked by critics who pointed out that Economists for Brexit relied on the false assumption that countries buy imports only from

Specifically, these analyses pointed to many of the same conclusions—that over time Brexit would reduce the gross domestic product of the UK, reduce household income through slower wage growth, and result in lower tax receipts for the government. There were of course disagreements over the depth of negative repercussions, but there was an unusual degree of consensus that Brexit would add up to a reduction in national wealth and a UK that was demonstrably worse off than if it remained in the EU.

For instance, the London School of Economics and Political Science's Centre for Economic Performance (CEP)[4] released a major study in March 2016, just a few months before the referendum, which assessed the likely impact of Brexit on the UK economy. The CEP acknowledged that the outcome of Brexit would depend to some degree on the policies adopted by the government following withdrawal from the EU. However, it was clear in noting, "lower trade due to reduced integration with EU countries is likely to cost the UK economy far more than is gained from lower contributions to the EU budget."[5]

Specifically, the CEP study concluded that reduced trade and a concomitant reduction in productivity in the UK would mean a loss of 6.3 to 9.5 percent of gross domestic product. Additionally, CEP argued that national wealth would decrease 1.3 to 2.6 percent, resulting in a decline in average household income of between £850 and £1,700 per year.

The Organization for Economic Co-operation and Development (OECD), an intergovernmental organization dedicated to promoting evidence-based policies to improve economic and social well-being, also released a study in advance of the 2016 referendum. It bluntly argued that Brexit "would be a major negative shock to the UK economy."[6] The authors maintained that in the short run—that is, by 2020—higher trade barriers

---

the lowest cost supplier. In fact, consumers and business do not simply buy from the cheapest supplier—a host of other factors affect choice of supplier, including quality, reputation, proximity, and past trading relationships. See, for example, Thomas Sampson, Swati Dhingra, Gianmarco Ottaviano, and John Van Reenen, "Economists for Brexit: A Critique," London School of Economics and Political Science, Centre for Economic Performance, May 2016, cep.lse.ac.uk/pubs/download/brexit06.pdf

4. CEP's Brexit work was funded by the UK Economic and Social Research Council. As a whole the CEP receives less than 5 percent of its funding from the European Union. The EU funding is from the European Research Council for academic projects and not for general funding or consultancy.

5. Swati Dhingra, et al., "The Consequences of Brexit for UK Trade and Living Standards," London School of Economics and Political Science, Centre for Economic Performance, March 2016, cep.lse.ac.uk/pubs/download/brexit02.pdf

6. Rafal Kierzenkowski, et al., "The Economic Consequences of Brexit: A Taxing Decision," OECD Economic Policy Papers, No. 16, April 2016, doi.org/10.1787/5jm0lsvdkf6k-en

and restrictions on labor mobility would reduce gross domestic product by 3 percent, compared to if the UK remained in the EU. In the long run, and under a scenario that the authors argued was neither overly optimistic nor overly pessimistic, by 2030, "structural impacts" in terms of reduced capital availability, immigration, technical progress, and labor productivity would together conspire to reduce GDP by 5 percent versus what would have happened if the UK had remained.

The National Institute of Economic and Social Research (NIESR)[7] also released a study just before the referendum. In May 2016, the NIESR assessed that, through 2030, a UK withdrawal from the EU would result in a GDP of between 1.5 and 3.7 percent lower than if the UK remained. This range is somewhat lower than the CEP and OECD estimates because the NIESR took a more conservative view of the impact of reduced trade on GDP, choosing to assess a narrower range of factors and excluding, for instance, the impact of reduced trade on productivity. When productivity impacts are included, the NIESR estimates increase significantly to a GDP reduction of 7.8 percent.

Finally, the UK government also released a study in April 2016 on the long-term impact of Brexit.[8] It was overseen by George Osbourne, who was then the chancellor of the exchequer (equivalent to a finance minister or treasury secretary), who was clearly in favor of remaining within the EU. This study may therefore appear less objective, given Osbourne's position, but he claimed that the study represented a "serious and sober assessment of the economic facts."[9] The analysis included the best data available to the UK government at the time, and assessed the long-term, 15-year impact of a withdrawal from the EU in three scenarios:

---

7. The National Institute of Economic and Social Research is Britain's longest established independent research institute, founded in 1938. The Institute is independent of all party political interests and is not affiliated with any single university. The NIESR is a charitable organization, and it receives no core funding from government or other sources. Instead, it undertakes research commissioned from a variety of sources, including UK government departments and agencies, British research councils, the European Commission, charitable foundations, and the private sector.

8. HM Treasury, "The Long-Term Economic Impact of EU Membership and the Alternatives," presented to Parliament by the Chancellor of the Exchequer by Command of Her Majesty, Cm 9250, April 2016, assets.publishing.service.gov.uk/government/uploads/system/uploads/attachment_data/file/517415/treasury_analysis_economic_impact_of_eu_membership_web.pdf

9. HM Treasury, "The Long-Term Economic Impact of EU Membership and the Alternatives," 5.

1. Membership of the European Economic Area (EEA), like Norway;
2. A negotiated bilateral agreement, like those of Switzerland, Turkey, or Canada; or
3. Membership of the World Trade Organization without any specific agreement with the EU.

The results of the Treasury's analysis mirrored those of other institutions—namely, that under each scenario, gross domestic product, household wealth, and government tax receipts would all be lower than if the UK voted to remain in the EU. The European Economic Area scenario represented the best case for the UK, with a reduction in GDP of 3.8 percent, a loss of annual household income of £2,600, and a reduction in tax receipts of £20 billion per year. The World Trade Organization scenario—what might today be thought of as "hard Brexit"—resulted in the worst case, with reductions of 7.5 percent of GDP, £5,200 in household income, and £45 billion in tax receipts. The negotiated agreement scenario—what seems most likely today—was barely better, with reductions of 6.2 percent of GDP, £4,300 in household income and £36 billion in tax receipts.

In sum, a number of credible, objective, expert-level assessments all arrived at roughly the same conclusion—that Brexit would damage the UK economy and make most Britons worse off. Table 1 summarizes the analytical assessments of the aforementioned studies regarding GDP specifically, and it provides an average of the same.

In addition to expert-level studies, less academically rigorous but no less objectively relevant surveys of economists reflected an unusually high degree of consensus on the fact that Brexit would damage the UK economy. For instance, in a large survey of UK economists conducted by the Ipsos MORI market research firm, 88 percent concluded that GDP would

TABLE 1. Expected Reductions in Annual UK GDP

	London School of Economics	OECD	National Institute of Economic and Social Research	UK Treasury 2016	Average
Long-term GDP reduced by . . .	7.9 percent[1]	5.0 percent	7.8 percent[2]	6.2 percent[3]	6.72 percent

[1] This figure is an average of the LSE range.
[2] This figure includes the productivity shock.
[3] This figure is based on a negotiated agreement, which is neither the worst case nor the best case scenario.

be negatively impacted in the short run and only 4 percent thought Brexit would benefit GDP over the same period.[10] Over the long run, 72 percent of economists surveyed held that GDP would be negatively impacted, while only 11 percent thought GDP would benefit. Similarly, 73 percent thought that household incomes would drop over the long term.

This degree of consensus among economists in the UK was unusual. It stands in contrast to other public policy questions such as why British recovery from the Great Recession was exceedingly slow, over which there is deep disagreement among economists given the available data.[11]

To some degree, expert analyses had an impact on public attitudes toward Brexit. One of the largest polls conducted in advance of the referendum found that a majority (56 percent) of Britons believed that EU investment in the UK would fall and a plurality (46 percent) believed that UK exports to the EU would decrease. Ironically, though, most Britons believed that despite Brexit's negative macroeconomic repercussions, their own individual standard of living would either stay the same (58 percent) or improve (11 percent).[12]

Brexit's Impact on the UK Defense Budget

Despite what appears to have been some cognitive dissonance on the part of the British public, the mostly consensus view among the experts—that Brexit would harm the UK economy at the macro level as well as the household level—has been borne out so far. According to the National Institute of Economic and Social Research, Brexit is already having an impact on the British economy, primarily through the devaluation of the British pound but also through continued uncertainty over the shape of a future EU-UK relationship.[13] Between June 2016 through April 2020, the

10. "Economists' Views on Brexit," Ipsos-MORI, May 28, 2018, www.ipsos.com/ipsos-mori/en-uk/economists-views-brexit. Six hundred and thirty-nine respondents completed the online survey May 19–27, 2016. Survey invitations were out to nonstudent members of the Royal Economic Society and the Society of Business Economists.

11. Paul Johnson and Ian Mitchell, "The Brexit Vote, Economics, and Economic Policy," *Oxford Review of Economic Policy* 33, no. S1 (2017): S12–S21.

12. "Six in Ten Britons Think Their Standard of Living Won't Be Affected by Brexit," Ipsos-MORI, May 31, 2016, www.ipsos.com/ipsos-mori/en-uk/six-ten-britons-think-their-standard-living-wont-be-affected-brexit. Ipsos MORI interviewed a representative sample of 4,002 British online adults aged 18+ between April 14–25, 2016, with funding from Unbound Philanthropy, an independent private grant-making foundation that works to ensure that migrants and refugees are treated with respect and engage with their new communities.

13. Stephen Clarke, Ilona Serwicka, and L. Alan Winters, "Will Brexit Raise the Cost

pound lost about 16 percent of its value, making imports more expensive for British consumers.[14]

Predictably, Brexit has therefore contributed to an increase in consumer prices and a slowdown in consumption, exclusive of other factors that affect inflation like oil price changes. At the same time, real wages have fallen since Brexit, magnifying the loss of living standards.[15]

The drop in consumer spending has subsequently reduced prospects for significant economic growth in the UK, at least in the next few years.[16] Meanwhile, the COVID-19 pandemic will add an even greater burden on growth prospects in the short run.[17] Excluding the pandemic's impact, the International Monetary Fund had expected the UK's GDP to be 3.5 percent lower by 2021 than it would have been without the Brexit vote.[18] From a slightly broader perspective, the UK economy is already estimated to be as much as 3 percent smaller now than it would have been if the country had voted to remain, mostly as a result of higher inflation and reduced business investment.[19]

of Living?" *National Economic Institute Review*, no. 242, November 2017, doi.org/10.1177%2F002795011724200113; "Prospects for the UK Economy," *National Institute Economic Review*, no. 250, November 2019, https://www.niesr.ac.uk/sites/default/files/UK%20Economy%20Press%20Release%20-NIER%20No250%20November%20-%20Embargoed%20till%2000.01%20Wednesday%2030%20October.pdf

14. Richard Partington, "Pound Gradually Climbs despite Brexit Uncertainty," *Guardian*, September 27, 2018; Adam Taylor, "How Brexit Ravaged the Once-Mighty British Pound," *Washington Post*, August 15, 2019.

15. Anand Menon, Jonathan Portes, and Matthew Bevington, eds., *The Brexit Scorecard* (London: University College London, 2019), 6–7.

16. Phillip Inman, "UK Growth Will Slow to 1.3% amid Brexit Uncertainty—KPMG," *Guardian*, September 10, 2018, www.theguardian.com/business/2018/sep/10/economic-growth-rate-expected-slow-kpmg-report-brexit-uncertainty

17. Ian Hurst et al., *A Preliminary Assessment of the Possible Economic Impact of the Coronavirus Outbreak: Update* (London: National Institute of Economic and Social Research, 2020).

18. See International Monetary Fund, "2017 Article IV Consultation—Press Release, Staff Report, and Statement by the Executive Director for the United Kingdom," IMF Country Report No. 18/42, February 2018; International Monetary Fund, "2018 Article IV Consultation—Press Release, Staff Report, Staff Statement, and Statement by the Executive Director for the United Kingdom," IMF Country Report No. 18/316, November 2018; and International Monetary Fund, "World Economic Outlook," April 2019.

19. Richard Partington, "Brexit Vote Has Cost Each UK Household £900, Says Mark Carney," *Guardian*, May 22, 2018, www.theguardian.com/politics/2018/may/22/brexit-vote-cost-uk-mark-carney-bank-of-england; John Springford, "The Cost of Brexit to September 2018," Centre for European Reform, January 27, 2019, www.cer.eu/sites/default/files/insight_JS_27.1.19_1.pdf; and Fergal O'Brien, "$170 Billion and Counting: The Cost of Brexit for the U.K.," *Bloomberg*, January 10, 2020, www.bloomberg.com/news/articles/2020-01-10/-170-billion-and-counting-the-cost-of-brexit-for-the-u-k

Certainly evidence for this can be seen within the British automotive industry, where investment in 2018 dropped 46.5 percent from the previous year.[20] Elsewhere, it appears Brexit has already prompted several employers to leave the UK and relocate to the continent.[21] And at the level of the average UK household, the impact of the Brexit decision has already meant a real income reduction of £900 per year.[22]

If over the longer run the expert analyses are also proven true, tax revenues will ultimately fall as the UK economy declines somewhat. By one government estimate, depending on the drop in GDP, tax revenues would decrease by £38 billion—reflecting a 5.4 percent fall in GDP—to £66 billion pounds—reflecting a 9.5 percent drop in GDP.[23] Extrapolating from these figures—for which each percentage point drop in GDP means a roughly £7 billion decrease in revenues—it is reasonable to suggest that, given an average estimated 6.72 percent drop in GDP as calculated in the table above, UK government tax revenues would decrease approximately £47 billion, even before the impact of the COVID-19 economic slump. As a reference point, the UK government faced a tax revenue shortfall of £33 billion in 2012 and £33 billion in 2013.[24]

As was the case in 2012 and 2013—and indeed throughout the austerity years—the British government is likely to respond to a revenue shortfall of £47 billion by trimming expenditures. During the austerity years, funding cuts impacted nearly all aspects of the budget. Spending on police forces dropped 17 percent from 2010 levels, road maintenance decreased by more than one-fourth, and support for libraries fell nearly a third.[25] The military was not immune and the UK defense budget decreased by nearly £6.4 billion from the 2009/10 budget year to the 2017/18 budget year.[26]

---

20. Amie Tsang, "U.K. Auto Industry Already Feeling the Brexit Pinch," *New York Times*, January 31, 2019, nyti.ms/2ShLeb3

21. Peter S. Goodman, "U.K. Economy Falters as Brexit Looms: Amsterdam Sees Risks, and Opportunity," *New York Times*, February 11, 2019, nyti.ms/2URjGH5

22. Partington, "Brexit Vote Has Cost Each UK Household £900."

23. Sam Coates and Oliver Wright, "Hard Brexit Could Cost £66bn a Year: Leaked Treasury Papers Reveal Lost Revenue," *Times* (London), October 11, 2016.

24. Szu Ping Chan, "Britain's 'Post-Crisis Hangover' Will Depress Tax Receipts for Years to Come," *Telegraph*, October 16, 2014, www.telegraph.co.uk/finance/economics/11167303/Britains-post-crisis-hangover-will-depress-tax-receipts-for-years-to-come.html

25. Peter S. Goodman, "In Britain, Austerity Is Changing Everything," *New York Times*, May 28, 2018, www.nytimes.com/2018/05/28/world/europe/uk-austerity-poverty.html

26. Noel Dempsey, "UK Defence Expenditure," House of Commons Library briefing paper no. CBP 8175, November 8, 2018, researchbriefings.files.parliament.uk/documents/CBP-8175/CBP-8175.pdf; see also "SIPRI Yearbook 2018 Online," Stockholm International Peace Research Institute, 2018, www.sipri.org/databases/milex

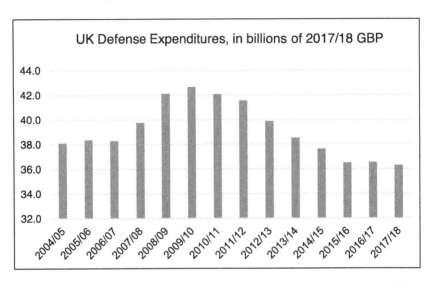

Figure 1. Based on data in Noel Dempsey, "UK Defence Expenditure," House of Commons Library briefing paper no. CBP 8175, November 8, 2018.

At the time of this writing, UK defense spending has fallen in real terms by 18 percent since 2009/10, while military personnel levels have already dropped by 25 percent from 2010 to 2017.[27]

If the annual revenue shortfall brought about by Brexit *is worse than* that endured during the height of the austerity years, the implications for British military capabilities could be quite dramatic. At a minimum, an emergency spending review would likely be called to reexamine defense spending commitments made as a result of the 2015 Strategic Defence and Security Review.[28]

More specifically, UK leaders will likely face very hard choices between trying to maintain as full spectrum a military as possible on the one hand and getting smaller across all remaining capability areas on the other. Admittedly, some key procurement programs, especially those that are closely tied to British national prestige or are critical elements of bilateral cooperation—such as development of a new class of strategic submarines or the Unmanned Combat Air System program with France—are likely to

---

27. Matt Whittaker, "Ending Austerity?," Resolution Foundation, July 2017, www.resolutionfoundation.org/app/uploads/2017/07/Austerity-v2.pdf. See also Dempsey, "UK Defence Expenditure.". Dempsey's figures come from the UK Ministry of Defence.

28. Malcolm Chalmers, "Would a New SDSR Be Needed after a Brexit Vote?," Royal United Services Institute for Defence and Security Studies, Briefing Paper, June 2016.

be top priorities for protection from defense cuts. Similarly, some defense programs—such as the aircraft carriers HMS *Queen Elizabeth* and HMS *Prince of Wales*—endured simply because cancelling them would have cost more in terms of contractual penalties and lost jobs than proceeding with production.[29] Nonetheless, since defense budget cuts are probable in the face of significant revenue shortfalls, the bulk of the cuts will fall on procurement programs and manpower. With regard to the former—which may be deferred, downsized, or even eliminated altogether—targets might include new general purpose frigates,[30] a new main battle tank to replace the Challenger,[31] or helicopter upgrades and replacements.[32]

With regard to manpower, end strength cuts are likely to impact the British ground forces heaviest and worsen the problems of underfilled units in all services.[33] Further personnel cuts also imperil the British Army's ability to project brigade-sized forces for any time period longer than 6–9 months. This is because recent UK military deployments have followed a conventional A-B-C rotation scheme. Under this scheme, one unit is deployed on operations for six to nine months (A), another similar unit is preparing for deployment (B), and a third similar unit is resetting its equipment and personnel (C). This means that for every unit deployed—and assuming an operation of longer than six months in duration—two additional units are necessary in the inventory.

Like the British army, the Royal Marines will be faced with a signifi-

---

29. James Kirkup, "Cancelling Aircraft Carriers Would Have Cost Taxpayers £690 Million," *Telegraph*, November 4, 2010, www.telegraph.co.uk/news/uknews/defence/8111117/Cancelling-aircraft-carriers-would-have-cost-taxpayers-690-million.html; and Richard Norton-Taylor, "BAE Warned Cameron over £5bn Cost of Cancelling Aircraft Carrier Contract," *Guardian*, November 4, 2010, www.theguardian.com/politics/2010/nov/04/bae-cameron-aircraft-carrier-contract

30. Andrew Chuter, "UK Restarts Frigate Competition—but Will Anyone Take Part?," *Defense News*, August 17, 2018, www.defensenews.com/naval/2018/08/17/uk-restarts-frigate-competition-but-will-anyone-take-part/

31. Nicholas Drummond, "The Challenger 2 Life Extension Programme—Is It Worth It?," *UK Land Power* blog, June 23, 2018, uklandpower.com/2018/06/23/the-challenger-2-life-extension-programme-is-it-worth-it/

32. Alan Tovey, "Fears over UK Military Budget as MoD Cuts Back Apache Order," *Telegraph*, June 18, 2017, www.telegraph.co.uk/business/2017/06/18/fears-uk-military-budget-mod-cuts-back-apache-order/

33. "Strength of British Military Falls for Ninth Year," *BBC*, August 16, 2019, https://www.bbc.com/news/uk-49365599; Frances Perraudin, "Numbers in UK Frontline Army Units Down by up to a Third," *Guardian*, April 1, 2019, www.theguardian.com/uk-news/2019/apr/01/numbers-in-uk-frontline-army-units-fall-by-up-to-a-third-figures-reveal?CMP=share_btn_tw; Henry Mance, "UK Armed Forces' Personnel Shortage Is 'Largest in a Decade'," *Financial Times*, April 17, 2018, www.ft.com/content/5ce601e0-4254-11e8-803a-295c97e6fd0b

cant reduction in capability should personnel cuts be necessary. Equipment shortfalls already threaten to eliminate Britain's ability to undertake amphibious landings on hostile shores.[34] In short, budget cuts brought about by lower tax revenues mean the already diminished ground forces—"20 years out of date" according to a recently retired senior military officer—risk losing critical capabilities as well as the ability to project force over time.[35]

Even if most of the UK defense enterprise is somehow fenced off from the worst cuts and the British government maintains the political commitment to base its defense spending on 2 percent of GDP, a lower GDP is likely to mean reduced defense spending in any case. At the end of the Cold War, European[36] NATO member states agreed to spend the equivalent of 2 percent of their GDP on defense. This was intended to ensure a minimum level of burden-sharing among the allies. Since then, the British government has endeavored to maintain defense spending equivalent to at least 2 percent of its GDP. In the mid-2010s, when it looked like London was preparing to drop below this goal due to austerity, intense domestic and international political pressure led to a policy reversal of sorts—the UK government began including in its defense spending figures military pensions, contributions to UN peacekeeping missions, and pensions for retired civilian MoD personnel, all of which pushed it above 2 percent.[37] In any case, the point is that while the 2 percent goal remains important for London, declining GDP means the amount of money the UK government *must* spend to achieve its NATO target declines as well, easing the political challenge of cutting the defense budget in the face of declining tax revenues.

Another potential worst-case outcome of Brexit's impact on the UK

---

34. "Royal Navy Could Lose Its Two Amphibious Assault Ships in Cuts," *Guardian*, October 5, 2017, www.theguardian.com/uk-news/2017/oct/05/royal-navy-could-lose-its-two-amphibious-assault-ships-in-cuts.

35. Ewen MacAskill, "British Forces No Longer Fit for Purpose, Former UK Service Chiefs Warn," *Guardian*, November 14, 2017, www.theguardian.com/politics/2017/nov/14/british-forces-no-longer-fit-for-purpose-former-uk-service-chiefs-warn

36. At the same time, the United States agreed to spend at least the equivalent of 3 percent of its GDP on defense.

37. Ben Farmer, "Obama to Cameron: Maintain UK Defence Spending or Weaken Nato," *Telegraph*, February 10, 2015, www.telegraph.co.uk/news/worldnews/barackobama/11403519/Obama-to-Cameron-maintain-UK-defence-spending-or-weaken-Nato.html; Ami Sedghi, "UK Defence Spending to Be Kept at 2% of GDP," *Guardian*, July 8, 2015, www.theguardian.com/news/datablog/2015/jul/08/uk-defence-spending-to-be-kept-at-2-of-gdp; and House of Commons Defence Committee, "Shifting the Goalposts? Defence Expenditure and the 2% Pledge," HC 494, April 12, 2016, publications.parliament.uk/pa/cm201516/cmselect/cmdfence/494/494.pdf

defense enterprise stems from the potential for constituent nations of the kingdom to secede. Given the strength of support in Scotland for remaining in the EU—Scottish voters favored remaining over leaving, 62 percent to 38 percent—some have speculated that Scotland might seek to leave the United Kingdom and join the EU as an independent state.[38] In fact, immediately after the referendum vote, several polls showed a plurality of Scottish voters in favor of independence. However, by late July 2016 preferences of Scottish citizens had shifted back to more historical norms, with roughly 50 percent opposing independence and about 42 percent favoring it. Nonetheless, in the event of a so-called "hard" Brexit that dramatically disrupts trade between the United Kingdom and the EU, it is possible that a majority of Scots might vote to leave the United Kingdom.

Although Scotland constitutes only 8.3 percent of the UK's population and contributes about the same amount to total UK tax revenues, from both strategic and operational perspectives, Scottish independence could have profound implications for the UK's military capability.[39] Perhaps most important, the secession of Scotland would mean the loss of the UK's only nuclear-capable strategic submarine base. Her Majesty's Naval Base Clyde in Faslane, just west of Glasgow, is home to the core of the UK's submarine fleet, including its strategic nuclear submarines. Faslane's unique attributes—a protected, deep water harbor with easy access to critical lines of communication and trade in the North Atlantic—would be difficult to replicate, not to mention extraordinarily expensive to build elsewhere.[40] In theory, a rump United Kingdom could lease the facilities at Faslane from an independent Scottish government. However, there is a strong antinuclear element in Scottish politics that would instead prefer to see the entire region stripped of any nuclear weapons and related delivery systems, and so a leasing arrangement seems unlikely in the long run.

In addition to the facilities at Faslane, Scotland is home to a number of other important military facilities. Among these is Royal Air Force Station Lossiemouth, one of the largest air stations in the UK and one of only two RAF bases to host Typhoons that are responsible for quick reaction inter-

---

38. David Blagden, "Britain and the World after Brexit," *International Politics* 54 (2017): 1–25.

39. "Scotland in Numbers," *BBC News Online*, November 25, 2013.

40. Hugh Chalmers and Malcolm Chalmers, "Relocation, Relocation, Relocation: Could the UK's Nuclear Force Be Moved after Scottish Independence?" Royal United Services Institute, August 2014, rusi.org/sites/default/files/201408_op_relocation_relocation_relocation.pdf. The authors estimate that the costs to relocate the facilities would be between "£3 billion and £4 billion (at 2012/13 prices), excluding any costs associated with land purchase and clearance."

cepts. The base is also the first in the UK to host the new P-8 maritime surveillance aircraft.

Scotland is also home to significant UK military training facilities. The Defence Training Estate Scotland is composed of an array of individual training locations, including the Cape Wrath training area, home to "the only range in Europe where land, sea and air training activities can be conducted simultaneously and where the Royal Air Force can train using live 1000lb bombs."[41]

Beyond (and before) Brexit

Even before the Brexit referendum of June 2016, the British military was showing signs of significant stress, reduced capability, and limited capacity. This was due to both the austerity program mentioned briefly above and the decade of overseas deployment that preceded and overlapped with it. Regarding the former, the United Kingdom's recovery from the Great Recession, which resulted from the 2008 subprime mortgage crisis in the United States and the related sovereign debt crisis across Europe, was very slow. National income per capita in the UK did not return to precrisis levels until early 2015.[42] Some argue the slow recovery was a direct result of the then-coalition government's decision to pursue austerity policies after 2010 instead of relying primarily on fiscal stimulus.[43] The austerity program had a self-fulfilling character, insofar as it had the effect of slowing economic growth, keeping unemployment high, lowering real wages, and consequently reducing government tax revenues—this in turn slowed deficit reduction efforts, which prompted calls for a prolongation of austerity initiatives. In any case, the continuation of austerity through the mid-2010s had a profound impact on British military capabilities and capacity, well before the Brexit referendum in June 2016.

Among other impacts, austerity accelerated a downward trend in military personnel strength that had been under way since the immediate post–Cold War years. Figure 2 shows total active duty military strength of the

---

41. Ministry of Defence, "The Defence Training Estate," December 12, 2012, www.gov. uk/guidance/defence-infrastructure-organisation-and-the-defence-training-estate#scotland

42. Paul Johnson and Ian Mitchell, "The Brexit Vote, Economics, and Economic Policy," *Oxford Review of Economic Policy* 33, no. S1 (2017): S12–S21.

43. Simon Wren-Lewis, "The Austerity Con," *London Review of Books* 37, no. 4 (February 19, 2015): 9–11, www.lrb.co.uk/v37/n04/simon-wren-lewis/the-austerity-con

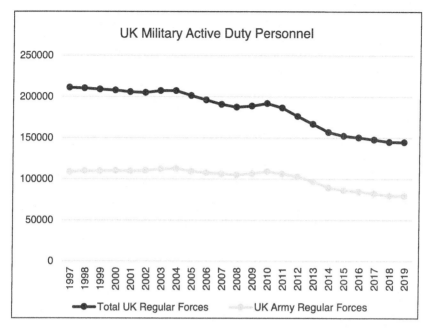

UK Military Active Duty Personnel

Figure 2. Based on data from the UK Ministry of Defence statistical compendia, compiled and plotted by author.

UK military as well as active duty British army personnel for the last two decades.

For almost the entire period depicted in figure 2, UK military manpower has been generally declining. Austerity has meant a smaller, arguably less capable UK military. Undermanning continues to plague the UK armed services, with deficiencies in all of the services.[44] This has been felt most dramatically in the manpower-intensive ground forces.[45] During U.S.-led coalition operations against Iraq in 1991 and again in 2003, the British military was able to field and sustain division-sized mechanized units. Thanks largely to austerity—as well as the overall trend depicted in figure 2—this size of military operation is now impossible for London to pull off.[46]

The other services have felt the pinch of austerity as well from both manpower and capabilities perspectives. For instance, the Royal Navy saw

---

44. *The Military Balance* (London: International Institute for Strategic Studies, 2018), 81.

45. Perraudin, "Numbers in UK Frontline Army Units Down by up to a Third."

46. F. Stephen Larrabee et al., *NATO and the Challenges of Austerity* (Santa Monica, CA: RAND Corporation, 2012), 7.

a slow but steady erosion in the number of platforms available for power projection and naval operations, with some relatively steep decreases during the worst of the austerity years. This improved slightly in 2018, with the addition of the aircraft carrier *Queen Elizabeth*, but it remains to be seen if the Royal Navy's personnel shortages will impact power projection, or whether what remains of the Royal Navy's fleet will end up functioning essentially as little more than a carrier escort fleet.[47]

It is possible in theory for lower numbers of more technologically advanced equipment platforms to be as militarily effective as or even more so than higher numbers of less advanced equipment platforms. Nonetheless, it remains clear that since 1998 and especially since the period of austerity in the late 2000s and early 2010s the loss of manpower and critical platforms such as naval vessels have led to a significant decline in overall British military capabilities.[48] Former U.S. defense secretary Robert Gates made waves in early 2014 when he posited that, given austerity-driven defense cuts, the UK "won't have full spectrum capabilities and the ability to be a full partner as they have been in the past."[49] Others have come to similar conclusions regarding the impact of austerity measures on British military capabilities. According to one study, UK military forces are no longer full spectrum but rather "80 percent spectrum."[50] By another estimate, since the height of London's involvement in NATO's Afghanistan operations, the British military has effectively lost the ability to deploy and sustain itself across time and distance, and it has become instead reliant on the United States to provide necessary enabling capabilities.[51] A former British army chief of the general staff himself foresaw this eventuality, when he noted back in 2011, "An army as small as 80,000 will find itself very hard to operate"[52]—at the time of this writing, British Army end strength is just over 78,000.[53]

47. Jonathan Beale, "The UK's Giant Aircraft Carriers," *BBC News Online*, August 24, 2018, www.bbc.co.uk/news/resources/idt-sh/UK_aircraft_carriers

48. Paul Cornish, "United Kingdom Hard Power: Strategic Ambivalence," in *A Hard Look at Hard Power: Assessing the Defense Capabilities of Key U.S. Allies and Security Partners*, ed. Gary J. Schmitt (Carlisle, PA: U.S. Army War College Press, 2015).

49. "Military Cuts Mean 'No US Partnership,' Robert Gates Warns Britain," *BBC News*, January 16, 2014, www.bbc.com/news/uk-25754870

50. Jan Joel Andersson et al., "Envisioning European Defence: Five Futures," EU Institute for Security Studies, Chaillot Paper No. 137, March 2016.

51. Interview with a U.S. Department of Defense employee based in Europe with extensive knowledge of security cooperation between the U.S. Army and the British army, November 13, 2018.

52. "'Army Cuts Dangerous' Warns Ex-Chief Lord Dannatt," *BBC News Online*, May 28, 2011, www.bbc.com/news/uk-13586499

53. Ministry of Defence, "UK Armed Forces Quarterly Service Personnel Statistics 1 Jan-

More broadly, the UK House of Commons has concluded that many critical capabilities are currently at "the minimum threshold of operational effectiveness,"[54] while one analysis argues that "it will be some time before [UK armed forces] have a credible full-spectrum combat capability against a peer competitor such as Russia."[55] And although the UK Ministry of Defence had proposed a £160 billion 10-year plan for defense capability investment, the National Audit Office recently labeled such goals "unaffordable" and "not sustainable."[56] Much of this is the result of the austerity initiative, which has resulted in a demonstrable decrease in British military capability and power, well before the full impact of Brexit manifests itself across the United Kingdom and through the defense budget specifically.

Do Diminished Capabilities Mean a Diminished Security Horizon?

If the United Kingdom gradually loses key military capabilities and the ability to project force across time and distance, will it eventually have to reduce its national security ambitions? In other words, does a country's inability to shape outcomes through the application of military power necessarily mean that country stops trying to do so? There are good theoretical and historical reasons to think this is the case, at least to some degree, although history also suggests that a recalibrated security horizon typically lags behind a decrease in hard power, sometimes by many years.

Political science, especially realist interpretations that often emphasize the means available to states, tells us that resources can and do play a large role in the setting of defense policy and strategy.[57] This role is not always determinative, as practitioners of American defense strategy and policy

uary 2020," February 20, 2020, assets.publishing.service.gov.uk/government/uploads/system/uploads/attachment_data/file/866842/1_Jan_2020_-_SPS.pdf

54. As cited in *The Military Balance* (2018), 80.

55. *The Military Balance* (2018), 160.

56. National Audit Office, "The Equipment Plan 2018 to 2028," report by the Comptroller and Auditor General, November 5, 2018, www.nao.org.uk/wp-content/uploads/2018/11/The-Equipment-Plan-2018-2028-.pdf

57. See for instance, David Perry, "A Return to Realism: Canadian Defence Policy after the Great Recession," *Defence Studies* 13, no. 3 (2013): 338–60. Regarding cuts in the Canadian defense budget and the related defense policy implications, Perry writes, "The planned renewal of the [Canadian defense strategy] should force a realization that a lower 'level of ambition' for the Canadian military is required in the current budgetary climate." See also Robert J. Art, "Striking the Balance," *International Security* 30, no. 3 (Winter 2005/06): 177–96, who argues that European states are likely to emphasize greater pooling and sharing of dwindling defense resources in order to maintain a strategy of defense autonomy. Finally, see Robert Kagan, "Power and Weakness," *Policy Review*, no. 113 (June/July 2002): 3–28,

know very well.[58] Other factors such as a state's strategic culture, the policy goals or preferences of its leaders or political parties, the economic interests of particular groups within the state, public opinion, and the external threat environment can be important independent variables as well.[59] Nonetheless, the resources available to a state have been shown to have an impact on that state's conception of its role in the world and its willingness to employ military power to achieve its national security goals.

The Netherlands presents a recent, instructive example of how a country's diminished military capabilities can ultimately lead to a receding security horizon. In 2007, the Dutch government published a strategy that outlined the Netherlands' national security interests. Those interests were defined as territorial integrity, economic security through "undisrupted trade," ecological security, public health, and social and political stability.[60] The threats confronting these interests included pandemics, international terrorism, failing states, the proliferation of weapons of mass destruction, and the global drug trade, among others. Although the Dutch government recognized international cooperation and multilateral frameworks were necessary to fulfill all the Netherlands' security interests, the Dutch national security strategy in any event maintained a security horizon well beyond Europe. That is, Dutch interests were conceptualized and articulated in a way that looked beyond Europe, even beyond the Netherlands' Caribbean territories.[61]

Even before the 2007 strategy, there was strong evidence indicating that the Dutch military's ability to safeguard those interests had gradually degraded. The decreased capabilities began as the result of defense budget cuts through the 1990s, as the Dutch and practically every other member of NATO largely cut force structure and manpower. These trends slowed

---

who argues that differing levels of defense capability and capacity have fundamentally shaped American and European national security strategies and defense policies.

58. Rick Berger and Mackenzie Eaglen, "'Hard Choices' and Strategic Insolvency: Where the National Defense Strategy Falls Short," *War on the Rocks*, May 16, 2019, warontherocks. com/2019/05/hard-choices-and-strategic-insolvency-where-the-national-defense-strategy-falls-short/

59. Andrew Moravcsik, "Taking Preferences Seriously: A Liberal Theory of International Politics," *International Organization* 51, no. 4 (Autumn 1997): 513–53; Gary Blackburn, "UK Defence Policy 1957–2015: The Illusion of Choice," *Defence Studies* 15, no. 2 (2015): 85–104; Omar Serrano, *The Domestic Sources of European Foreign Policy: Defence and Enlargement* (Amsterdam: Amsterdam University Press, 2014).

60. Government of the Netherlands, "National Security Strategy and Work Programme, 2007–2008," www.ecfr.eu/page/-/Pays_Bas_-_2007_-_National_Security_and_Work_Programme_2007-2008.pdf

61. Government of the Netherlands, "National Security Strategy and Work Programme, 2007–2008," 35.

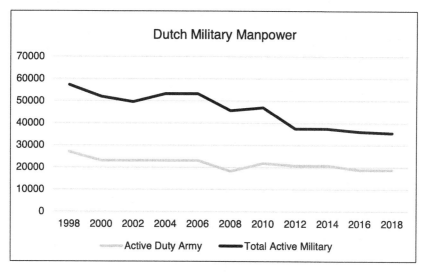

Figure 3. Data from *The Military Balance*, **2018.**

during the early-to-mid 2000s due to demanding operations in Iraq and Afghanistan, but then accelerated as a result of the sovereign debt crisis in the late 2000s and the austerity initiatives that unfolded across most of Europe. In the case of the Netherlands, the Dutch military dropped from 104,000 military personnel in 1990 to 41,000 in 2011; from 181 F-16 Fighting Falcons in 1990 to just 68 in 2011; from 15 frigates and destroyers in 1990 to 6 in 2011; and from 913 tanks in 1990 to none in 2011.[62]

Despite this loss of capability and capacity, the Dutch government maintained a commitment to a global security horizon. In fact, the 2013 national security strategy was rather explicit on this point in noting that although Dutch "influence is limited and is affected by major spending cuts on defence and development cooperation," the Netherlands nevertheless maintains "interests all over the world."[63] Reflecting this, the 2013

62. NATO, "Financial and Economic Data Relating to NATO Defence," press release M-DPC-2(92)100, December 10, 1992; NATO, "Defence Expenditure of NATO Countries (2011–2018)," press release PR/CP(2018)091, July 10, 2018; Marcial Hernandez, "Dutch Hard Power: Choosing Decline," American Enterprise Institute, April 3, 2013, www.aei.org/publication/dutch-hard-power-choosing-decline/; and "Dutch Army to Sell All Leopards and Cougars," Defencetalk.com, April 8, 2011, www.defencetalk.com/dutch-army-to-sell-all-leopards-and-cougars-33370/

63. Dutch Ministry of Foreign Affairs, "International Security Strategy: A Secure Netherlands in a Secure World," June 21, 2013, www.government.nl/binaries/government/documents/policy-notes/2013/06/21/international-security-strategy/ivs-engels.pdf

strategy emphasized arms control, crisis management out of Europe, preventing proliferation of weapons of mass destruction, cyber security, piracy, cross-border crime, terrorism, water and resource scarcity, pandemics, loss of biodiversity, and climate change as threats that could impact Dutch security.

Eventually though, lofty Dutch security objectives could not escape the gravitational pull of diminished capabilities and capacity. The latest Dutch national security strategy, released in 2018, is explicit in noting that "geographically, the strategy focuses more sharply on Europe and the Kingdom."[64] And although the strategy emphasizes the prevention of insecurity wherever possible, the top security threats identified in the strategy—terrorist attacks, cyber threats, undesirable foreign interference and disruption, military threats to Dutch and allied territory, threat to vital economic processes, and the proliferation of weapons of mass destruction— make it clear that emphasis has begun to shift within Dutch strategic and security culture. This is essentially an acknowledgment of the operational reality facing Dutch leaders, who would find it impossible today to simultaneously deploy and sustain a provincial reconstruction team in Afghanistan and deploy and sustain another 1,300 troops elsewhere in the world, as was the case between 2006 and 2010.[65]

The example of the Netherlands—a country that clung to a strategic vision increasingly unsupported by necessary defense investments—may shed light on what might be expected of the United Kingdom as its economic potential shrinks or, in the worst case, its geography shrinks as well. Indeed the United Kingdom has extensive experience itself in the loss of power as well as influence, and its own history—like that of the Netherlands in the last decade or two—proves as well that the reality of decline sets in long before the necessary reconceptualization of a country's role in the world.

In the wake of World War II, the United Kingdom sought to reestablish its costly military presence throughout the world, especially in South Asia, Southeast Asia, and Oceania, even though its economy was in a shambles and Britons themselves were in no mood to endure further fiscal sacri-

---

64. Dutch Ministry of Foreign Affairs, "Working Worldwide for the Security of the Netherlands: An Integrated International Security Strategy 2018–2022," May 14, 2018, www.government.nl/binaries/government/documents/reports/2018/05/14/integrated-international-security-strategy-2018-2022/NL_International_Integrated_Security_Strategy_2018_2022.pdf

65. Marc Bentinck, "Why the Dutch Military Punches Below Its Weight," Carnegie Europe, February 8, 2018, carnegieeurope.eu/strategiceurope/75484

fices. British governing elites believed that Britain's status as a global power *stemmed from* its position across Africa, Asia, and beyond, and were eager to resume the mantle of global power through reestablished military presence around the world.[66] They would soon find, though, that maintaining a global security horizon and the hard power presence that underpinned it were no longer feasible from an economic perspective, in large part due to a decline that arguably began at the end of the nineteenth century or the beginning of the twentieth. It was then that the costs of empire—especially as measured through increasingly expensive power projection military platforms like dreadnought-class battleships[67]—began to exceed the financial and fiscal benefits.[68] However, it was not until the administration of Prime Minister Harold Wilson in the mid-1960s—when a confluence of economic crisis, currency devaluation, domestic political concerns,[69] and ideational factors[70] compelled a difficult decision—that the British fundamentally reconceptualized their role in the world and withdrew from east of Suez. Despite Britain's dissipated hard power, illusions of global influence were hard to shake then, as they are today.

As Brexit appears likely to strike the next body blow to British military capability and capacity, it is unclear when that reality might set in among the British public or its political elites.[71] To some degree, British strategic horizons—or in the words of one analyst, the "strategic rhetoric"—have already shrunk, as judged through strategy documents and official pronouncements,[72] even as the available resources for overseas missions decline further.[73] Even if the first of two planned aircraft carriers fully

---

66. Saki Dockrill, *Britain's Retreat from East of Suez: The Choice between Europe and the World? 1945–1968* (Basingstoke: Palgrave Macmillan, 2002); see also Phillip Darby, *British Defence Policy East of Suez, 1947–68* (Oxford: Oxford University Press, 1973).

67. Dreadnought-class battleships were developed by the United Kingdom in the early 1900s, and were the largest, most advanced naval combatants of the era. They were noteworthy in particular for their thick armor, large caliber weapons, such as 12-inch guns, and steam turbine propulsion, which made them the fastest battleships of the time.

68. David Reynolds, *Britannia Overruled: British Policy and World Power in the Twentieth Century* (London: Pearson Educational, 2016).

69. Jeffrey Pickering, "Politics and 'Black Tuesday': Shifting Power in the Cabinet and the Decision to Withdraw from East of Suez, November 1967–January 1968," *Twentieth Century British History* 13, no 2 (January 1, 2002).

70. David M. McCourt, "What Was Britain's 'East of Suez Role'? Reassessing the Withdrawal, 1964–1968," *Diplomacy & Statecraft* 20, no. 3 (2009).

71. However, there is some reason to think this process may already be under way—see Mark Malloch-Brown, "Is This the End of Global Britain?," *Financial News*, June 28, 2018, www.fnlondon.com/articles/is-this-the-end-of-global-britain-20180628

72. Cornish, "United Kingdom Hard Power," 278.

73. Kevin Knodell, "The British Army Can't Find Enough Soldiers: Who Will Fight the

enters into force in the early 2020s, it is not clear what broad UK foreign or security policy they will support beyond acting as American adjuncts.[74]

If the Dutch example and Britain's own nineteenth and twentieth century experience are any guides, British strategic horizons can be expected to inevitably match the available capabilities and capacity of its military. As that process unfolds over the coming years, there are likely to be serious implications for what role the United Kingdom can play in working with Washington on the most pressing common security challenges.

A Not-So-Special Relationship?

Another era of declining British military power—made worse by Brexit, but already under way thanks to austerity—is very likely to lead to a scaling back of British security horizons. This combination of declining capability, decreasing capacity, and receding willpower will have an impact on the so-called special relationship between London and Washington.

The "special relationship" is a term coined to describe the uniqueness and closeness of the Anglo-American partnership. Most Americans think of the relationship as beginning during World War II, but its origins stem from the late nineteenth century, when leading figures in the United Kingdom and the United States came to see fundamental commonalities that distinguished them from other countries.[75] Increasingly dense networks of economic and cultural ties eventually grew to include a geopolitical confluence of interests. This confluence manifest itself in the World War I but came to even deeper realization in World War II.[76] It was in this crucible of war that the increasingly close government-to-government relationship—characterized by frequent meetings between President Franklin Roosevelt and Prime Minister Winston Churchill, a combined US-UK Joint Chiefs of Staff, and extensive military aid and assistance from Washington to

United Kingdom's Wars?," *National Interest*, January 29, 2017, nationalinterest.org/blog/the-buzz/the-british-army-cant-find-enough-soldiers-19237

74. Christopher Hill, "Turning Back the Clock: The Illusion of a Global Political Role for Britain," in *Brexit and Beyond: Rethinking the Futures of Europe*, ed. Benjamin Martill and Uta Staiger (London: University College London), 2018.

75. Duncan Campbell, *Unlikely Allies: Britain, America and the Victorian Origins of the Special Relationship* (London: Bloomsbury Academic, 2008).

76. On the manifestation of the special relationship in World War I in the field of intelligence sharing, see Jim Beach, "Origins of the Special Intelligence Relationship? Anglo-American Intelligence Co-operation on the Western Front, 1917–18," *Intelligence and National Security* 22, no. 2 (August 2007): 229–49.

London—really took on a uniqueness unparalleled in American national security policy.

Close coordination and cooperation continued through the Cold War, as both London and Washington sought to prevent the spread of communism. Since then, the United States and the United Kingdom have worked closely to keep a unified Germany anchored in Western institutions, to expand NATO, to counter Russian influence and revanchist behavior, and to stem violent extremist ideologies and operations throughout Asia, the Middle East, and Africa. At the operational level, Britain has more officers working within the halls of the Pentagon than any other foreign country,[77] and the United Kingdom remains at the center of the "five-eyes" intelligence sharing effort.[78] In short, the special relationship has grown and deepened, and today it is no exaggeration to say that the United Kingdom is America's closest ally.

Of course, the existence of the special relationship has not meant complete collinearity between U.S. and British interests. For instance, the United Kingdom resisted pressure from Washington to grant independence to British colonies in the wake of World War II, and there was a serious rift between the two countries during the Suez crisis of 1956. Often, the "specialness" has appeared to depend on the personal relationship between the American president and the British prime minister at any given time in history. For example, despite their differing political philosophies, George W. Bush and Tony Blair developed a surprisingly close relationship in the early 2000s, while more recently Theresa May appears to have been spurned—or perhaps burned—in her efforts to bond with Donald J. Trump.[79] However, despite what may appear to be an ebb and flow of

---

77. The Military Personnel Exchange Program (MPEP) places foreign military officers into U.S. billets within the American defense establishment and vice-versa, with an equal number of Americans working in the sending state's military establishment. These personnel are not liaison officers, who function as communications conduits. Rather, they are foreign officer who spend typically two years working as Pentagon or DoD employees. At present, the United Kingdom has roughly 45 MPEP officers—a handful of whom are general or flag officers—working in the U.S. Department of Defense. Among European countries, Germany is in second place with roughly 12 officers in MPEP billets.

78. The Five Eyes arrangement involves the sharing of signals, human, and military intelligence among the United States, the United Kingdom, Canada, Australia, and New Zealand.

79. David Coates and Joel Krieger, *Blair's War* (Cambridge: Polity Press, 2004); Peter Walker, Heather Stewart, and Patrick Wintour, "Theresa May Rebukes Trump as Opposition to State Visit Grows," *Guardian*, November 30, 2017; Daniel Boffey, "Why Does Donald Trump Oppose Theresa May's Brexit Deal?," *Guardian*, November 27, 2018; and Sam Knight, "Theresa May's Impossible Choice," *New Yorker*, July 30, 2018. According to Knight, "After Trump was elected, he and May exchanged phone calls, which she found to be a struggle. The two could not be more different."

relations at the top of the political hierarchy, embedded Anglo-American security cooperation has ensured a remarkable degree of persistence to the special relationship.[80]

The special relationship today is based on not simply material factors such as the military-to-military cooperation outlined above but also on some of the very same nonmaterial factors that helped spawn it, including historical, linguistic, and cultural ties.[81] Typically, the special relationship has been of greater importance to the United Kingdom than to the United States, given the power differential between the two countries and Britain's desire to be seen as a global power.[82] This has been reflected in the degree of attention paid to it by academics as well as pundits on both sides of the Atlantic. In the words of one long-time observer of the relationship, it "is spoken of largely in British accents," and when it is invoked, speakers typically refer to shared history, values, and language.[83]

From the United States' perspective, public opinion polls continue to show that a plurality of Americans view the United Kingdom as the most important foreign partner of the United States.[84] However, it is also clear that the special relationship's primary value for the United States has been based on its military dimensions and, to a lesser degree, on the friendly voice that the UK provided in internal EU deliberations.[85]

The preceding section made the argument that the ability (in the short

---

80. William Wallace and Christopher Phillips, "Reassessing the Special Relationship," *International Affairs* 85, no 2 (March 2009): 263–84.

81. Kristin Archick, "The United Kingdom: Issues for the United States," *CRS Report for Congress*, September 23, 2005; Richard Hodder-Williams, "Reforging the 'Special Relationship': Blair, Clinton and Foreign Policy," in *New Labour's Foreign Policy: A Moral Crusade?*, ed. Richard Little and Mark Wickham-Jones (Manchester: Manchester University Press, 2000), 63–84; Andrew Gamble and Ian Kearns, "Recasting the Special Relationship," in *Progressive Foreign Policy: New Directions for the UK*, ed. David Held and David Mepham (Cambridge: Polity Press, 2007), 116–31.

82. John Dumbrell, *A Special Relationship: Anglo-American Relations in the Cold War and After* (London: Macmillan, 2001).

83. John Dumbrell, "The US–UK Special Relationship: Taking the 21st-Century Temperature," *British Journal of Politics and International Relations* 11, no. 1 (2009): 64–78.

84. Jacob Poushter and Alexandra Castillo, "Americans and Germans Are Worlds Apart in Views of Their Countries' Relationship," Pew Research Center, November 26, 2018, www.pewresearch.org/fact-tank/2018/11/26/americans-and-germans-are-worlds-apart-in-views-of-their-countries-relationship/. Topline data reveals that in September 2018, 21 percent of Americans surveyed said the United Kingdom was the most important partner for American foreign policy, compared to China (18 percent) and Canada (12 percent); no other country reached double digits. In October 2017, the same question yielded similar results, with 20 percent of Americans naming the United Kingdom as the most important foreign partner, 15 percent naming China, and no other country reaching double digits.

85. Graham K Wilson, "Brexit, Trump and the Special Relationship," *British Journal of Politics and International Relations* 19, no. 3 (2017): 543–57.

run) and willingness (in the mid-to-long term) of the United Kingdom to participate in military operations far beyond the British Isles will gradually fade over the next decade, especially as Brexit is implemented and despite the planned entry into service of one or two aircraft carriers. As some of these "material factors" lose their salience in the UK-U.S. relationship, it is unclear whether the nonmaterial factors will be sufficient to sustain the special relationship, the mutual trust, and the degree of diplomatic and political coordination that currently exists between the two countries.

Given these nonmaterial ties as well as extensive trade and investment between the United Kingdom and the United States, which may persist even post-Brexit, it seems unlikely that the special relationship will end precipitously. However, reduced British military capacity and capability as well as a diminished security horizon will ultimately have an impact on the special relationship, primarily because Washington will find it less useful from a military, material perspective.

At a minimum, shrinking British capabilities, capacity, and global ambition will necessarily prevent the United Kingdom from deploying without extensive American assistance and from sustaining any deployment over time. Any U.S.-led military operation that involves the UK military deploying any significant distance from Europe or even the British Isles will very likely need to be extraordinarily limited in duration—perhaps no greater than six to nine months, especially if the United States is not providing significant assistance in terms of enablers like logistics and transportation—or limited in terms of manpower. This will probably mean an end to major British contributions to stability operations—which tend to be manpower intensive and last far longer than six to nine months. At the same time, British political authorities will be more likely to focus relentlessly on identifying exit strategies and mission termination conditions before agreeing to any military commitment.

As a result of all of these changes in the relationship, it is not altogether unrealistic to envision a future UK-U.S. military relationship that looks more like what exists today between the United States and Australia, or even the United States and New Zealand—that is, close coordination on intelligence sharing, but far more limited combined, joint military operations. Certainly, Washington is likely to welcome and encourage *any* UK involvement in joint military operations, since the political legitimacy—both domestic and international—conferred by multilateralism in confronting international crises will remain valuable to any occupant of the White House. However, in this way the United Kingdom will not be terribly distinct from any other prospective member of whatever coalition the United States is trying to assemble. The point is, the less the United Kingdom can contribute in terms of boots on the ground, air wings overhead, vessels at or under the sea, or cyber warriors in the information space, the less value Washington is likely to see in the relationship. Concomitantly, the United States will need to expend greater effort in soliciting operational contributions from—and hence building exceptionally close security cooperation and intelligence sharing mechanisms with—*other* allies and partners.

THREE

Germany's Hegemonic Role in Europe

In contrast to the United Kingdom, the German economy has shown a degree of strength that is the envy of the continent, and it has done so for several years. Specifically, Germany's economy has been characterized by low unemployment, strong manufacturing and services sectors, robust tax revenues, slowly rising wage levels, low inflation, and declining national debt. This economic strength has enabled it to begin bouncing back from the COVID-19-induced recession far more easily than its neighbors. As judged by Germany's embrace of advanced industrial technology and automation, it is likely to remain the leading economy in Europe—by a wide margin—for the foreseeable future.

This economic strength has cast Germany in a role within Europe that could be seen as hegemon*ic*—that is, evincing some of the characteristics of a hegemon but without actually being one. To explain, Germany has used its economic strength to clearly claim the leading position within Europe's macroeconomic issue areas. For instance, Germany fundamentally shaped and drove Europe's response to the sovereign debt crisis, and it was a leading player in negotiations over the EU's response to COVID-19. Outside the realm of macroeconomic policy, though, the story has been quite different. So far, Germany has transformed its economic strength into only a limited political-diplomatic leadership position in Europe, while almost completely eschewing the pursuit of greater hard power or military strength.

This example of an economic hegemon failing to fully pursue political and military hegemony as well is unique in history. John Mearsheimer, one of the foremost scholars of international relations, defines a hegemon as a state that is so powerful that it dominates all other states in its region.[1] Realists like Mearsheimer argue that the self-help nature of the international system virtually compels—or at least strongly incentivizes—states with high levels of latent economic power to parlay it into political and military power. Yet, for reasons that are largely tied to the twentieth-century's world wars and the Holocaust, Germany continues to largely shun serious development of its hard power in land, air, maritime, space, or cyber domains. Given more recent history, though—since the end of the Cold War—there may be reason to think that Germany's views are changing when it comes to hard power and its use in Europe and beyond to defend German as well as Western interests.

Before assessing whether and how German attitudes toward greater involvement in international crises are evolving, this chapter will first lay out the evidence regarding Germany as Europe's economic hegemon. The next section of this chapter will then address how Germany is also using its economic heft in the political-diplomatic realm, at least when it comes to defending collective interests in Europe. In stark contrast, Germany has yet to transform its economic strength into significant hard power, and this chapter will then outline how Germany is lagging in both capability and capacity across multiple domains. The subsequent section of this chapter will examine the interesting case of German willpower to take on greater responsibility internationally, which would most likely require more hard power. As argued in the penultimate section of the chapter, it is possible— perhaps even likely given the views of younger Germans—that over time Germany will grow increasingly willing to become more involved in overseas crises in the defense of common Western interests. The primary questions from Washington's perspective, as addressed in the last section of this chapter, are whether Germany's continued rise will unfold in a way that is sympathetic to U.S. interests and whether the United States can afford to wait as Germany comes to grips with its growing hegemonic power.

Germany as Europe's Economic Hegemon

At the core of Germany's hegemonic position is its economic strength, which remains nearly unrivaled in Europe in terms of depth and breadth. The German economy has been and remains today the envy of many in

---

1. Mearsheimer, *Tragedy of Great Power Politics*, 40.

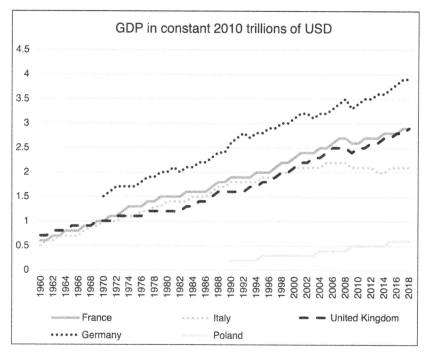

GDP in constant 2010 trillions of USD

Europe, particularly as several European states continue to struggle with the hangover of the Great Recession and the devastating economic impact of the COVID-19 pandemic. Germany today has the largest GDP in Europe by far, it recently had the lowest unemployment rate in a generation, and it maintains a vibrant export-oriented manufacturing base, all of which adds up to an economy that is exceptionally strong relative to its neighbors.

Figure 4 captures GDP in constant 2010 U.S. dollars from the 1960s through 2018. Although France and the United Kingdom largely have managed to maintain economic growth over that lengthy time period—with the notable exception of the Great Recession—it is clear that the German economy remains significantly larger. It is also evident that the German economy returned to pre–Great Recession levels before the British economy.[2] This was mostly due to strong demand in China, which contin-

2. Claire Manibog and Stephen Foley, "The Long and Winding Road to Economic Recovery," *Financial Times* (London), August 10, 2017, www.ft.com/content/c8d1d150-7869-11e7-a3e8-60495fe6ca71

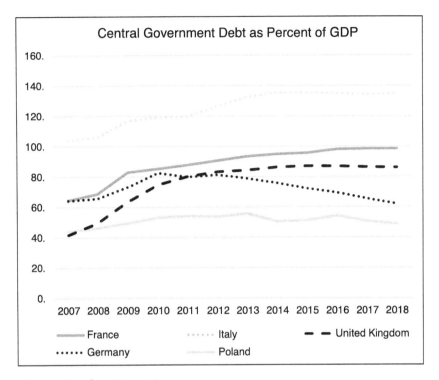

Figure 5. Data from Eurostat.

ued apace during the Great Recession. Elsewhere in Europe, but especially in the worst-hit countries of Cyprus, Greece, Ireland, and Italy, many continue to struggle to find work or survive on greatly reduced incomes even a decade after the debt crisis.[3]

Also in stark contrast to the British, Italian, and most other European economies, Germany has recorded budget surpluses since 2014, the only G7 country to do so. In mid-2018, Germany's budget surplus amounted to 2.9 percent of GDP, the largest since reunification in 1990. In contrast, most of its neighbors run budget *deficits* that are often higher than the 3 percent allowed under EU rules.[4] Germany's surpluses are to a large degree the result of the generally strong economic growth since roughly 2011, resulting in increased tax revenues.

---

3. Peter S. Goodman, "Europe's Economy, after 8-Year Detour, Is Fitfully Back on Track," *New York Times*, April 29, 2016, www.nytimes.com/2016/04/30/business/international/euro zone-economy-q1.html

4. "German Budget Surplus Hits a Record," *Deutsche Welle*, August 25, 2017, p.dw.com/ p/2ioga

The fiscal surpluses have helped Germany pay off its national debt. In 2017, total government debt fell below €2 trillion for the first time in several years. Germany's ratio of public debt to GDP was expected to fall to 60 percent at the end of 2018, from 64.1 percent in 2017.[5] By one estimate, the percentage is set to decline even further over the next five years, assuming growth continues.[6] Figure 5 depicts German government debt as a percentage of its GDP, as well as that for France, Italy, Poland, and the United Kingdom. Clearly, among at least the larger European economies, Germany is an exception, and so far officials in Berlin have resisted calls to cash in on the windfall through tax cuts or major increases in public spending.

At the same time, export-led growth since 2011 put Germany on a track to achieve remarkably low unemployment, even lower than the United States. As seen in figure 6, Germany has had one of the lowest unemployment rates in Europe in recent years. By 2019, unemployment in Germany fell to the lowest level since the country was reunified in 1990. Of course there are significant differences among the federal states within Germany, but overall the labor market has shown remarkable strength in recent years, reflecting the steady, long-term growth trend.[7] This in turn has led to increased consumer confidence and domestic demand, which most recently has shown signs of even surpassing exports as the primary driver of continued economic growth in Germany.[8]

Strong demand for labor has also resulted in an upward trend in real wages and salaries in Germany, which have been outpacing inflation.[9] From 2008 to 2014, disposable income for the average household in Germany increased 15 percent.[10] During the same period and in stark contrast, average household disposable income decreased 4 percent in Italy, 24 percent in Greece, and 22 percent in Cyprus. The medium-term outlook for

---

5. Guy Chazan, "Germany's Record Budget Surplus Triggers Calls for Tax Cuts," *Financial Times*, August 24, 2018, www.ft.com/content/ce744c1e-a784-11e8-8ecf-a7ae1beff35b

6. Sebastian Becker, "Germany's Fiscal Situation," *Deutsche Bank Research*, July 19, 2017, www.dbresearch.com/PROD/RPS_EN-PROD/PROD0000000000447678/Germany%E2%80%99s_fiscal_situation:_Full_employment_and_ze.PDF

7. Oliver Sachgau and Piotr Skolimowski, "Germany's Jobless Rate Drops to Record Low as Economy Booms," *Bloomberg*, January 3, 2018, www.bloomberg.com/news/articles/2018-01-03/german-unemployment-rate-drops-to-record-low-as-economy-booms

8. Michael Nienaber and Holger Hansen, "German Jobless Rate Hits Record Low in May," *Reuters*, May 30, 2018, www.reuters.com/article/us-germany-economy-unemployment/german-jobless-rate-hits-record-low-in-may-idUSKCN1IV0TX

9. Michael Nienaber, "German Real Wages Rise despite Higher Inflation," *Reuters*, September 20, 2018, uk.reuters.com/article/uk-germany-wages/german-real-wages-rise-despite-higher-inflation-idUKKCN1M00UH

10. Goodman, "Europe's Economy, after 8-Year Detour, Is Fitfully Back on Track."

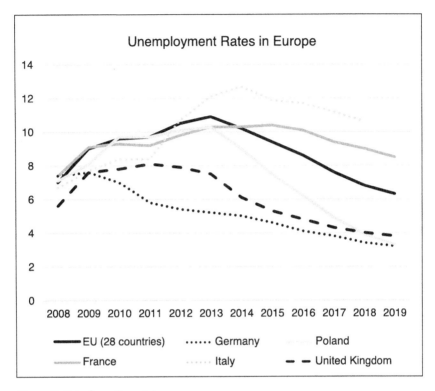

Figure 6. Data from Eurostat.

Germany—that is, over the next five years—is continued growth driven largely by domestic demand and reinforced by a moderately strong export sector. Germany's aggressive approach to recovering from the COVID-19 pandemic slowdown—far more so than its neighbors—should enable it to recover more speedily and maintain growth over the medium term.[11]

Germany's economic success in recent years is not simply due to the availability of export markets in China, which has become a top trade partner for Germany, or increasingly strong domestic demand. Productivity through technological advancement has played an important role as well. Germany is noteworthy for the role that technological advancements—referred to as Total Factor Productivity[12]—have consistently played in

---

11. Silvia Amaro, "Germany Is Vastly Outspending Other Countries with Its Coronavirus Stimulus," *CNBC.com*, April 20, 2020, www.cnbc.com/2020/04/20/coronavirus-germany-vastly-outspends-others-in-stimulus.html

12. Total Factor Productivity (TFP) accounts for all that labor and capital do not when it comes to computing a country's GDP. TFP is basically "everything else," but its primary

accounting for GDP growth since the slowdown of 2012–13. Econo-mists hold that the most important determinants of long-term growth are increased stocks of capital, increased labor inputs such as the num-ber of skilled workers or total hours worked, and technological advance-ment. Of these, there is strong evidence that technological progress and the productivity increases normally associated with it are together the main drivers of long-run growth.[13] This is because the additional output obtained from adding one extra unit of capital or labor, while keeping other inputs constant, will eventually decline. This fundamental princi-ple of economics is known as the law of diminishing returns. As a result of this phenomenon, a country cannot maintain its long-run growth by simply generating more capital for investment or by adding more work-ers. Instead, technological progress is necessary to overcome the law of diminishing returns, and here Germany has done well relative to other mature economies over the last decade.[14]

Germany's European neighbors, particularly France but also the United Kingdom, have had less success in leveraging technological advancement in the pursuit of productivity gains. There are several reasons why these other countries and Europe more broadly have not adapted well to the knowledge-based economy of the future—the so-called Industry 4.0, which is characterized by autonomous robots, cloud computing, the internet of things, and big data, among other technological advances. Beginning in the mid-1990s European economies in general began diverging from the U.S. economy in the level of Total Factor Productivity, mostly due to the inability to invest in and reap the benefits from information and commu-nications technology.[15] This failure has had serious, long-lasting repercus-sions, seen across much of Europe today. Additionally, labor markets across much of the European continent remain excessively regulated, inhibiting firms from achieving the necessary flexibility for the demands of a high-tech economy.

---

components are technological advancements and efficiency gains. So although it is impossible to determine with precision the role that technological advancements *alone* played in improv-ing a country's GDP over the previous year, TFP is a good proxy that approximates the role that technology has played in economic growth.

13. YiLi Chien, "What Drives Long-Run Economic Growth?," *St. Louis Fed On the Econ-omy* blog, Federal Reserve Bank of St. Louis, June 1, 2015 www.stlouisfed.org/on-the-econ omy/2015/june/what-drives-long-run-economic-growth

14. The Conference Board Total Economy Database™ (adjusted version), April 2019, www.conference-board.org/data/economydatabase/total-economy-database-productivity-growthaccounting

15. Marcel P. Timmer et al., "Productivity and Economic Growth in Europe: A Compara-tive Industry Perspective," *International Productivity Monitor* (Spring 2011): 3–23.

However, Germany has been something of an outlier within Europe in these regards. Today, Germany is recognized as one of the global leaders in not simply industrial automation but in related research and development.[16] Indeed, Germany is already the most automated country in Europe, and third in the world behind South Korea and Singapore.[17] Given the commitment of the government in Berlin, German businesses, and German academia to Industry 4.0, Germany is very likely to maintain that leadership position into the future as smart automation—that is, linking the virtual world with the physical world—continues to be adopted throughout manufacturing and industry.[18] Unlike many other European countries, Germany's businesses appear both willing and able to adopt the most advanced automation technologies and techniques, including robots and artificial intelligence.[19]

Of course there is a potential downside to the adoption of technology in the workplace—of 21 advanced economies, German workers are most at risk of having their jobs automated.[20] Viewed from another perspective, though, the growing use of software, connectivity, and analytics will increase the demand for employees with competencies in software development and IT technologies.[21] On a related point, changes in German

---

16. Daniel Küpper et al., "The Factory of the Future," Boston Consulting Group, December 6, 2016, www.bcg.com/en-us/publications/2016/leaning-manufacturing-operations-factory-of-future.aspx

17. Steven Crowe, "10 Most Automated Countries in the World," *Robot Report*, February 7, 2018, www.therobotreport.com/10-automated-countries-in-the-world/

18. Federal Ministry for Economic Affairs and Energy, "What Is Industrie 4.0?," 2018, www.plattform-i40.de/I40/Navigation/EN/Industrie40/WhatIsIndustrie40/what-is-industrie40.html

19. "Embattled German Industrials Pursue the Factory of the Future," *Bloomberg*, June 9, 2017, www.industryweek.com/automation/embattled-german-industrials-pursue-factory-future; Phee Waterfield, "South Korea and Germany Lead 'Automation Index'," *RCR Wireless News*, April 25, 2018, enterpriseiotinsights.com/20180425/channels/news/south-korea-germany-lead-automation-index; Thomas Wagner, "Mehr klicken, weniger schrauben," *Deutschlandradio*, December 11, 2018, www.deutschlandfunk.de/weiterbildung-fuer-industrie-4-0-mehr-klicken-weniger.680.de.html?dram:article_id=435621; Janosch Delcker, "Germany's €3B Plan to Become an AI Powerhouse," *Politico*, November 14, 2018, www.politico.eu/article/germanys-plan-to-become-an-ai-powerhouse/; and Janosch Delcker, "Inside Amazon's German AI Research Program," *Politico*, May 20, 2019, www.politico.eu/article/amazon-germany-artificial-intelligence-inside-secretive-research-program/

20. Germany was actually tied with Austria at 12 percent of workers. South Korea and Estonia were lowest at 6 percent. M. Arntz, T. Gregory, and U. Zierahn, "The Risk of Automation for Jobs in OECD Countries: A Comparative Analysis," OECD Social, Employment and Migration Working Papers, No. 189, OECD Publishing, Paris, 2016, dx.doi.org/10.1787/5jlz9h56dvq7-en

21. Michael Rüssmann, et al., "Industry 4.0: The Future of Productivity and Growth in Manufacturing Industries," Boston Consulting Group, April 9, 2015, www.bcg.com/en-us/

labor laws made over 15 years ago through the Agenda 2010 reform effort significantly weakened the then-stricter labor laws to allow easier hiring and firing of employees and changed the rules to allow for more part-time and temporary work—this has made German companies somewhat more nimble than many of their competitors elsewhere in Europe when it comes to managing labor as an economic input.[22] Although it is possible Agenda 2010 has contributed to limited wage growth in Germany, it seems clear that labor market reforms of the early and mid-2000s will continue to benefit Germany for the foreseeable future.

Whether Germany will have the necessary specialists in its labor force remains something of a question, as does the broader issue of Germany's overall population, which is seen as declining in the long run. Despite a recent massive influx of economic migrants and refugees from the Middle East, North Africa, and South/Central Asia, Germany's population is still projected to decline between now and 2080, as seen in figure 7. The primary reason for the declining population over the next several decades is aging.[23]

This will create additional strains on Germany's welfare state and its economy more broadly, as increasing numbers of people leave the workforce and enter the ranks of the pensioners. This will likely worsen Germany's fiscal situation—with potentially negative consequences for Germany's defense budget—and it remains unclear whether the recent wave of migrants constitute a large enough population bump to make up for what Germany is predicted to lose.

An aging society and anemic fertility rates have long been the subjects of concern among government officials in Germany. Due to dire projections of population decline, policymakers in Berlin have taken steps in recent years to promote childbearing. New policies like paid parental leave of up to €1,800 per month for up to 14 months after childbirth and free or subsidized preschool—in combination with extant policies such as job protection for as long as three years after childbirth—appear to have succeeded in reversing Germany's declining birthrate,[24] even though a causal relationship may be difficult to derive conclusively. Figure 8 shows that

publications/2015/engineered_products_project_business_industry_4_future_productivity_growth_manufacturing_industries.aspx

22. Rebecca Staudenmaier, "German Issues in a Nutshell: 'Agenda 2010'," *Deutsche Welle*, June 6, 2017, p.dw.com/p/2ckuT

23. Michele Catalano and Emilia Pezzolla, "The Effects of Education and Aging in an OLG Model: Long-Run Growth in France, Germany and Italy," *Empirica* 43, no. 4: 757–800.

24. Chris Reiter, "How Germany Is Defusing a Demographic Time Bomb," *Bloomberg*, May 23, 2018, www.bloomberg.com/news/articles/2018-05-23/how-germany-is-defusing-a-demographic-time-bomb

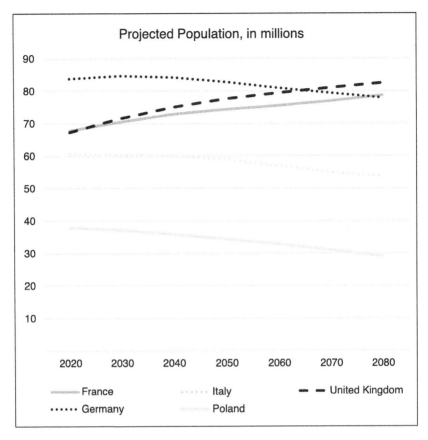

Figure 7. Data from Eurostat.

over the last five years, Germany's fertility rate has been generally trending upward since the Great Recession. It remains to be seen whether these policies, as well as additional migration, will succeed in bending Germany's population trend line upward as well by the middle of the century.

In the meantime though, Germany has been busy employing its economic strength in the service of its policy agenda across the Eurozone.[25] Already Germany has emerged as Europe's indispensable economic power, certainly in finance and fiscal policy, wielding its status as the largest net contributor to the European Union's budget. This was evident most obviously during the sovereign debt crisis of a decade ago. In response to the

_____

25. The "Eurozone" is the name given to the group of 19 members of the European Union that use the euro as their currency—Austria, Belgium, Cyprus, Estonia, Finland, France, Germany, Greece, Ireland, Italy, Latvia, Lithuania, Luxembourg, Malta, the Netherlands, Portugal, Slovakia, Slovenia, and Spain.

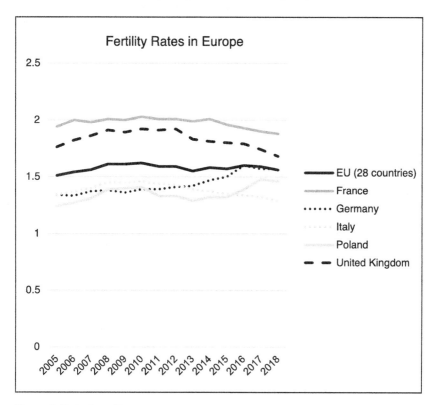

Figure 8. Data from Eurostat.

crisis, Germany—with strong support from the Netherlands and the Nordic EU states—pushed austerity as a central element of the response. So important was Germany's role that the austerity-centered policy response came to be called the "Berlin consensus."[26] Former Finnish prime minister Alexander Stubb was explicit in noting, "Germany has been in the driver's seat through this process, there's no denying it."[27] However, calling the approach a "consensus" does not truly reflect the depths of disagreement in Europe, and not simply among those countries on the receiving end of the budget cutting. For instance, the French government was one of the larger EU member states to favor greater debt forgiveness. Nonetheless, austerity remained the central element of the policy response to the sovereign debt crisis.

Berlin had to tread a fine line, though, between, on the one hand,

26. Neil Irwin, "How Germany Prevailed in the Greek Bailout," *New York Times*, July 29, 2015, nyti.ms/1JR579E

27. Irwin, "How Germany Prevailed in the Greek Bailout."

demanding enough fiscal belt tightening to ensure severely indebted countries did their part to spend less and justify debt restructuring and, on the other hand, demanding too much austerity that consumer demand in Europe—a critical market for German exports—simply collapsed.[28] Put another way, the German government had to find a path that pushed member states to stick to the agreed rules but that also kept the EU and the Euro intact.

Berlin was able to carefully navigate between these extremes in a way that satisfied domestic audiences—thereby justifying German support for EU-financed bailouts—as well as international audiences, principally among EU states—thereby maintaining a consensus approach to the varied challenges faced by the most indebted EU members. Specifically, Berlin enabled the Eurozone recovery plan for Greece by passing emergency legislation to lend €22.4 billion over three years. The German government also successfully argued—against France and the European Central Bank—for the involvement of the International Monetary Fund in the rescue effort. Ultimately, the financial rescue package that was put together in March 2010 was largely the handiwork of the German government as the guarantor of monetary stability.[29] Some argue that Germany in fact helped to cause and prolong the sovereign debt crisis through its trade surpluses with most other members of the EU.[30] While this may be true, the point remains that Germany has dominated European fiscal policy for nearly a decade.

More recently, the same kind of dominance was evident in the response to French president Macron's Eurozone reform proposals. In September 2017, just a few months after his election, Macron unveiled a series of recommendations intended to strengthen the Eurozone and insulate the common currency from future crises. At the core of his presentation were proposals to create an EU finance minister, establish a joint Eurozone budget of hundreds of billions of euros, and institute a body tasked with overseeing bloc-wide economic policy.[31] Berlin's reaction was decidedly cool—"polite

28. George Friedman, "Germany's Role in Europe and the European Debt Crisis," *Stratfor*, January 31, 2012, dworldview.stratfor.com/article/germanys-role-europe-and-european-debt-crisis

29. Brigitte Young and Willi Semmler, "The European Sovereign Debt Crisis: Is Germany to Blame?," *German Politics and Society* 29, no. 1 (Spring 2011): 1–24.

30. Paul Krugman, "Those Depressing Germans," *New York Times*, November 3, 2013, nyti.ms/1hG7D7F; Robert Skidelsky, "Germany's Current-Account Surplus Is Partly to Blame for Eurozone Stagnation," *Guardian*, July 24, 2014, www.theguardian.com/business/2014/jul/24/germany-surplus-part-blame-eurozone-stagnation

31. Lewis Sanders, "How France's Emmanuel Macron Wants to Reform the EU," *Deutsche Welle*, March 16, 2018, p.dw.com/p/2uQnu

silence," in the words of one commentator—to most of these proposals, with German leaders reluctant to sign up for what they regard as mechanisms that would see them transfer more wealth to less prosperous parts of Europe.[32] In the end, German concerns over taking on too much of Europe's risk and too much responsibility for bailing out profligate spenders has meant that Macron's proposals were watered down significantly, mostly on German terms.[33]

Germany as Europe's Diplomatic Hegemon?

Beyond the realm of macroeconomics, Germany is also likely to continue leveraging its economic strength in the service of its political and diplomatic efforts internationally. In terms of the most salient political and diplomatic issues of the day in Europe, Germany plays a leading role if not yet "the" leading role. Berlin does not, for the time being, *dominate* the other states of Europe politically or diplomatically, but it is clear Germany is a vital player when it comes to solving the major political and diplomatic challenges facing Europe.

For example, Germany has become the center of gravity in the West's response to Russia's invasion of Ukraine and its illegal annexation of Crimea.[34] Germany's emergence as the nexus of European decision-making when it comes to responding to the crisis in Ukraine came about as a result of two phenomenon, one domestic, the other international. First, the illegal annexation of Crimea by Moscow in early 2014 shocked the German public, which has for the last 70 years or so held sacred both multilateral frameworks and the rules-based international order. By spring 2014, German public opinion turned against Russia, with a 19 percent increase—from 60 percent to 79 percent—in the number of Germans having an unfavorable view of Russia.[35] The downing of civilian flight MH17 by

32. Isabelle Mateos y Lago and Hans-Werner Sinn, "Should Merkel Embrace Macron's Vision for Eurozone Reform?," *Financial Times*, June 27, 2018, www.ft.com/content/568d5236-786d-11e8-af48-190d103e32a4

33. Steven Erlanger, "Macron Had a Big Plan for Europe: It's Now Falling Apart," *New York Times*, April 19, 2018, nyti.ms/2HazXol; Luke Baker, "Macron's Euro Zone Reforms: Grand Vision Reduced to Pale Imitation," *Reuters*, June 18, 2018, www.reuters.com/article/us-eurozone-france-germany/macrons-euro-zone-reforms-grand-vision-reduced-to-pale-imitation-idUSKBN1JE2KT

34. Wolfgang Koeth, "Leadership Revised: How Did the Ukraine Crisis and the Annexation of Crimea Affirm Germany's Leading Role in EU Foreign Policy?," *Lithuanian Annual Strategic Review* 14 (2015–16): 101–16.

35. "Russia's Global Image Negative amid Crisis in Ukraine," Pew Research Center,

Ukrainian separatists using a Russian-supplied antiaircraft weapon system in July 2014 virtually compelled Berlin's political elites to turn what had largely been rhetoric into action. This was somewhat unexpected, given the role that Germany had long played in relations between the West and Russia—namely, that of a bridge, and the leading advocate for dialog with Moscow. Despite this tradition of *Ostpolitik*, Germany led the effort to enact major sanctions against Russia, convincing reluctant countries like Spain and Italy to jump on board.[36]

The second phenomenon that accounts for Germany's emergence as a leading diplomatic decision-maker within Europe was the *lack* of leadership from either of the other two typical centers of diplomatic and political power in Western Europe, namely London and Paris. Since 2016, UK foreign policy and diplomacy has been largely consumed with Brexit, preventing London from playing a stronger role vis-à-vis Russia over the Ukraine crisis. Even before the referendum, though, London remained decidedly underinvested in European efforts to negotiate an agreement between Ukraine and Russia.[37] At the same time, France has been obsessed with domestic security in the wake of the January 2015 *Charlie Hebdo* attack and the November 2015 Bataclan nightclub attack. Although French president François Hollande was part of the negotiations between Russia and Ukraine, he was obviously a member of the supporting cast as German chancellor—and Russophone—Angela Merkel led the effort to arrive at an agreement.[38] Related to the lack of serious UK or French leadership on this issue was the fact that Washington appeared willing to defer to Germany as well. U.S. leaders were most concerned with maintaining consensus among the major Western powers in responding to Russia, and so Germany became the center of gravity on the diplomatic front. Whatever Merkel (with Hollande by her side) was able to negotiate would likely find a receptive audience in Washington as well as in London.

Germany was also at the center of Europe's response to the refugee crisis stemming from conflicts in Syria and Afghanistan, as well as economic

July 9, 2014, www.pewglobal.org/2014/07/09/russias-global-image-negative-amid-crisis-in-ukraine/

36. "European Foreign Policy Scorecard, 2015," London: European Council on Foreign Relations, January 2015, www.ecfr.eu/page/-/ECFR125_SCORECARD_2015.pdf

37. Con Coughlin, "Britain Is Shamed by Its Impotence over Syria and Ukraine," *Telegraph*, February 11, 2015, www.telegraph.co.uk/news/uknews/defence/11403672/Britain-is-shamed-by-its-impotence-over-Syria-and-Ukraine.html

38. "Can Merkel's Diplomacy Save Europe?," *Der Spiegel Online*, February 14, 2015, www.spiegel.de/international/europe/minsk-deal-represents-and-fragile-opportunity-for-peace-in-ukraine-a-1018326.html

dislocation in sub-Saharan Africa, the Balkans, and North Africa. Well over one million migrants applied for asylum in Europe in 2015, forming the largest migratory flow of humanity since the period immediately after World War II.[39] Germany led the response to the flood of migrants in two ways. First, Merkel essentially opened Germany's doors, declaring that her country would not turn away any refugee who wished to apply for asylum for humanitarian reasons, leaning forward when neither Brussels nor many other European capitals were willing or able to do so.[40]

Second, Merkel took the leading role in negotiating with Turkey to limit migration into Europe. The agreement, concluded in March 2016, required Turkey to take back Syrian migrants who reached Greece illegally in return for the resettling in Europe of Syrian refugees then already in Turkey. The deal also provided for the gradual opening of the Turkish labor market to refugees, the intensification of surveillance of the Aegean Sea through joint naval and aerial operations, and the provision of €3 billion (later increased to €6 billion) in humanitarian and nonhumanitarian aid financed by the EU and its member states. Together, these initiatives reduced so-called irregular migration—essentially, refugees arriving on Greek beaches in less-than-seaworthy boats.[41] The EU also agreed to grant visa-free travel to Turkish citizens, accelerate Ankara's EU membership application, and increase financial aid to help Turkey manage the refugee crisis. The agreement marked a major political victory for Merkel, who had been pursuing Turkish assistance on the migration issue for several months.[42]

Finally, there is also evidence of Germany leveraging its economic heft in the service of political ends in the negotiations over the EU's multi-year budget, known as the Multiannual Financial Framework (MFF). The MFF establishes a seven-year framework that basically governs the EU's annual budget. In discussions on the next MFF—which will cover 2021–27—Germany's Permanent Representative to the EU Michael Clauss

39. "Number of Refugees to Europe Surges to Record 1.3 Million in 2015," Pew Research Center, August 2, 2016, www.pewglobal.org/2016/08/02/number-of-refugees-to-europe-surges-to-record-1-3-million-in-2015/

40. Steven Erlanger, "Migrant Crisis Gives Germany Familiar Role in Another European Drama," *New York Times*, September 2, 2015, nyti.ms/1Q7SWdo

41. Marie Walter-Franke, "Two Years into the EU-Turkey 'Deal': Impact and Challenges of a Turbulent Partnership," Jacques Delors Institut—Berlin, March 15, 2018, www.delorsinstitut.de/2015/wp-content/uploads/2018/03/20180315_Two-years-into-the-EU-Turkey-Deal_Walter-Franke.pdf

42. Matthew Karnitschnig and Jacopo Barigazzi, "EU and Turkey Reach Refugee Deal," *Politico*, March 18, 2016, www.politico.eu/article/eu-and-turkey-finalize-refugee-deal/

noted that Germany's portion of the EU budget might rise to roughly one-quarter of the total, given the loss of the UK's contribution as a result of Brexit. Germany was prepared to do this, but Clauss also made clear Berlin would insist that the member states benefitting most from EU common funding modify their policies appropriately on "other important issues, such as joint burden sharing in the migration issue." Essentially Clauss was saying that Germany would only play its leading role in financing the EU if other countries, especially net recipients of EU funding such as those across most of Eastern Europe, followed policies more in line with Berlin's preferences on issues like migration.[43]

Germany as Europe's Diminutive Military Power

In contrast to the dominance Germany evinces in macroeconomic policy, and the slightly more limited but still vital role it plays in political-diplomatic issue areas important to Europe, German military power has declined dramatically over the last quarter century in terms of capability and capacity. It is no exaggeration to say that during most of the Cold War, the 500,000-strong Bundeswehr formed the backbone of the West's conventional defense against the Soviet Union and its Warsaw Pact allies. The Bundeswehr played the lead role in allied plans to halt or delay a Soviet invasion of the West until additional American reinforcements could arrive from across the Atlantic.

In the early 1990s, as the Cold War ended and the Soviet Union broke apart, Germany joined most of its allies, including the United States, in reducing the size of its military and cashing in on the so-called peace dividend.[44] Germany cut its overall troop strength by 27 percent between 1990 and 1993, even as it assimilated the military of the former East Germany. Further cuts continued throughout the post–Cold War era, including as Germany shifted from a conscript-based military to a professional one starting in 2011.[45]

---

43. Florian Eder, "Brussels Playbook," *Politico*, December 6, 2018, www.politico.eu/news-letter/brussels-playbook/politico-brussels-playbook-presented-by-airbus-eu-splits-on-lgb-tiq-rights-migration-impasse-parliament-vs-austria/.

44. The Conventional Armed Forces in Europe Treaty, which was signed in 1990 and entered into force in 1992, also called for military cuts, but the personnel reductions were part of a political agreement separate from the treaty-mandated cuts in military hardware such as tanks and attack helicopters.

45. The suspension of conscription—which had been in place since 1957—coincided with a plan to reduce personnel strength from 240,000 to 170,000.

The lack of a perceived threat from Russia as well as out-of-area missions in locations such as Kosovo, sub-Saharan Africa, Afghanistan, and off the Horn of Africa also brought about major changes in the capabilities and structure of the German military. As territorial defense became less relevant to the protection of German and allied interests, the German military shed or neglected capabilities less useful in stability operations, crisis management, peacekeeping, logistical support operations, or defense institution-building. These sorts of operations and activities—typically far from Germany and Central Europe—had come to characterize the post–Cold War security environment that Berlin and its allies found themselves engaged in. Therefore, the German military focused on building and maintaining expeditionary capabilities in complex security environments, not on the collective defense tasks of what seemed like a bygone era nor on higher-end cyber or electronic warfare capabilities.

At the same time, two phenomena combined to prevent defense investments that might have helped Germany to maintain adequate capabilities and capacity even during the post–Cold War period. The first was the cost of far-flung operations across the hemisphere over the last 15 years. Wars in places like Afghanistan and Syria were never really Germany's fights, yet Berlin participated out of a sense of allied solidarity and shared security. Such operations across the hemisphere have been expensive—for instance, the mission in Afghanistan cost the German government €8.9 billion, its most expensive post–Cold War overseas mission and roughly half of what Germany has spent on overseas missions from 1992 through 2016.[46] As a result, the Germany defense ministry—like many of its counterparts in Europe—saw current operations funding crowd out other priorities such as acquisition and readiness for collective defense. Without sustained, long-term funding, it is impossible to build an advanced, full-spectrum military force, given the timelines associated with military research, development, procurement, and fielding.

The second phenomenon was defense budget cuts in the wake of the sovereign debt crisis and the Great Recession. In 2010, Finance Minister Wolfgang Schäuble won cabinet approval for defense budget cuts of €8.3 billion from 2011 through 2014—equivalent to about 10 percent of the defense budget—as part of the government's austerity drive.[47] Although these cuts did not all come to fruition, those that were enacted had some

---

46. Frank Bötel, "Überblick: Die 'Armee im Einsatz'," December 15, 2017, www.bundeswehr.de/portal/a/bwde/start/einsaetze/ueberblick/ueberblick

47. James Shotter, "Military Backlash against Defence Cuts Grows," *Financial Times*, February 9, 2011, www.ft.com/content/b3da07e0-3464-11e0-993f-00144feabdc0

serious impacts on the German military's capabilities and capacity.[48] For instance, in addition to the suspension of conscription and reduced end strength previously mentioned, the German army lost a divisional head-quarters in 2013 and had to consolidate its dwindling airborne forces into a single brigade. The air force and navy both also went through downsizing-related restructuring and reorganization. Finally, there were also base closures in Germany and reductions in equipment holdings.

The result is that today the German military labors under debilitating shortcomings across three of the most important metrics for capability and capacity: training and equipment readiness, acquisition, and manning. In terms of identifying readiness shortcomings of the German military, there have been few as blunt as the German Bundestag's commissioner for the military, Hans-Peter Bartels. His reports have included some of the most concerning data points on training and equipment readiness, including the fact that none of Germany's six submarines are seaworthy, pilots are forced to train on privately owned helicopters because of a lack of spare parts for military helicopters, and more than half of Germany's already small fleet of 224 main battle tanks are nonoperational.[49] Moreover, in February 2018, it was reported that just 39 of Germany's 128 Typhoon fighter aircraft were fit for action and there have been recent periods where none of the air force's 14 A400M transport planes are airworthy.[50] In sum, Bartels argues that the Bundeswehr is today "not deployable for collective defense."[51]

Meanwhile, when it comes to acquisition, reforms adopted in 2010 included reductions in some key weapons systems and platforms as well as cuts to research and development.[52] For example, although the number of armored personnel carriers and light armored reconnaissance vehicles was left unchanged, there was a 35 percent cut in the number of main battle tanks and a 45 percent reduction on the number of heavy artillery

48. *The Military Balance, 2014* (London: International Institute for Strategic Studies, 2014), 100.

49. "Limited Number of Weapons in German Military Ready for Action: Report," *Deutsche Welle*, February 27, 2018, p.dw.com/p/2tNlW

50. "German Army Facing 'Big Gaps' as Spending Cuts Bite," *AFP*, February 20, 2018, www.france24.com/en/20180220-german-army-facing-big-gaps-spending-cuts-bite

51. Rick Noack, "Afraid of a Major Conflict? The German Military Is Currently Unavailable," *Washington Post*, January 24, 2018, www.washingtonpost.com/news/world views/wp/2018/01/24/afraid-of-a-major-conflict-the-german-military-is-currently-unavailable/?noredirect=on&utm_term=.f25977b7a83e

52. Patrick Keller, "German Hard Power: Is There a There There?," in *A Hard Look at Hard Power: Assessing the Defense Capabilities of Key U.S. Allies and Security Partners*, ed. Gary J. Schmitt (Carlisle, PA: U.S. Army War College Press, 2015), 95–118.

systems.[53] Additionally, the army reduced the number of combat support helicopters it planned to operate, from 80 to 40. Procurement cuts also affected the air force, including a 21 percent reduction in orders for the Typhoon multirole combat aircraft and a 33 percent reduction in planned orders for the A400M transport aircraft. The navy also saw planned procurement orders cut, such as those for a multirole combat ship that was cut from eight to six. These sorts of decisions have had long-term implications, adversely impacting the character and composition of the military force Germany is able to field *today*.

Finally, in terms of manning, since the shift to a volunteer force in 2011, the German military has struggled with systemic personnel shortages. There simply are not enough volunteers to man all of the billets across the armed forces. Commissioner Bartels reported in early 2018 that as many as 21,000 officer billets were vacant.[54] In some cases, the lack of sufficient training time and limited access to equipment that is all too often in disrepair are pushing some to leave the military prematurely.[55] Furthermore, recent plans to increase military end strength to 200,000 face long odds for two key reasons. The first is the country's long-standing antimilitarist political culture.[56] The second is the strong economy, which has made nonmilitary careers even more attractive.

These shortcomings in manning, acquisition, and readiness imperil Germany's capability and capacity at just the moment when security demands are increasing. Although the dozen-year operation in Afghanistan (2002–14) is no longer the focus of thousands of Bundeswehr troops, a smaller scale operation there continues as do deployments to or operations in Lithuania, Syria, Iraq, Djibouti, Sudan, Mali, and elsewhere.[57] From a capacity perspective the Bundeswehr is stretched to its limit, while from a capability perspective it must now engage in collective defense, peacekeeping, stability operations, *and* cooperative security. In short, the security

53. Bjoern H. Seibert, "A Quiet Revolution," *RUSI Journal* 157, no. 1 (2012): 60–69.

54. "Germany's Lack of Military Readiness 'Dramatic,' Says Bundeswehr Commissioner," *Deutsche Welle*, February 20, 2018, p.dw.com/p/2t0eN

55. Thomas Wiegold, "Schwund beim Eurofighter: Eine Pilotin erklärt ihre Kündigung," *Augen Geradeaus*, May 1, 2018, augengeradeaus.net/2018/05/schwund-beim-eurofighter-eine-pilotin-erklaert-ihre-kuendigung/

56. Barbara Kunz, "The Real Roots of Germany's Defense Spending Problem," *War on the Rocks*, July 24, 2018, warontherocks.com/2018/07/the-real-roots-of-germanys-defense-spending-problem/

57. Germany has 1,300 troops deployed to Afghanistan as part of the post–International Security Assistance Force mission Resolute Support. A full listing of all contributors and personnel levels can be found here: www.nato.int/cps/en/natohq/topics_113694.htm

demands have never been greater for a military force that has never been smaller or less capable.

German policymakers realized relatively quickly following Russia's invasion of Ukraine and its illegal annexation of Crimea in 2014 that the defense reforms and cuts negotiated just a few years prior could not stand in the new security environment. A commitment made to increase defense spending at NATO's September 2014 summit in Wales has meant that German defense spending has increased in real terms every year since then.[58] According to the German ministry of defense, in 2016 the defense budget was €35.1 billion. It increased in 2017 to roughly €37 billion euros and again in 2018 to €38.5 billion. The government's 2019 budget plan called for yet another increase to €42.9 billion, and by 2022 the budget should amount to roughly €43.9 billion.[59] Whether this will remain so in the wake of the COVID-19-related recession is unclear.

Regardless, it is clear defense officials in Germany finally realized that they needed to devote additional resources toward more advanced tools of conflict and warfare, given Russia operations and tactics. For instance, Germany created a military "Cyber and Information Space Command" in April 2017, which has become the sixth service branch of the Bundeswehr.[60]

Institutional adaptations and budgetary increases are significant for a country that has a complex relationship with hard power. However, they are unlikely to turn Germany into a major military power commensurate with its economic and diplomatic strength any time soon. More importantly, the steps taken to date are unlikely to result in a Bundeswehr that is truly capable of being the bulwark behind frontline states like Poland and the Baltics. In terms of funding, by one estimate, just to meet current operational demands would require an increase in the German defense budget of €4 billion per year through 2024.[61] As for the cyber command mentioned above, it is not projected to be at full strength nor completely capable of comprehensive defense in cyberspace until 2021.[62] Whether

---

58. NATO, "Defence Expenditure of NATO Countries (2011–2018)," press release PR/CP(2018)091, July 10, 2018, 6.

59. Bundesministerium der Verteidigung, "Entwicklung und Struktur des Verteidigungshaushalts," www.bmvg.de/de/themen/verteidigungshaushalt/entwicklung-und-struktur-des-verteidigungshaushalts

60. The other branches are the army, navy, air force, joint medical service, and joint support service.

61. Christian Mölling and Torben Schütz, "Verteidigungspolitische Verantwortung: Mehr Geld bedeutet nicht mehr Effizienz," *Deutsche Gesellschaft für Auswärtige Politik*, August 2018.

62. Nina Werkhäuser, "German Army Launches New Cyber Command," *Deutsche Welle*, April 1, 2017, p.dw.com/p/2aTfJ

and how it might *ever* engage in offensive cyber or information operations unilaterally or in coordination with the United States or other allies is an open question that Germans have only recently started to debate.[63] Despite Russia's rampant network attacks—including against the Bundestag—and social media manipulation over the last several years, Germany remains decidedly behind the curve when it comes to cyber and information space operations as well as the very broad strategic objectives that would underpin such operations.[64]

In order to achieve scale for collective defense as well as maximize efficiency in defense spending, the government in Berlin has attempted to leverage its partners throughout Europe by proposing a Framework Nations Concept, which NATO endorsed in 2014.[65] This initiative entails a "framework nation" leading a cluster or group of allies and partners in the development of capabilities or the fielding of larger military formations, or both. With regard to capability development, the framework nation coordinates other participating countries in closing a capability gap, such as in antisubmarine warfare or in advanced combat medicine, which can then be directly applied to an identified but unfulfilled operational requirement or remain as a stand-alone capability ready when necessary. In terms of fielding larger units, the framework nation—typically a larger European state such as Germany, France, or the UK—provides the core of the unit such as logistics and command and control, while smaller allies add their specialized capabilities, such as air defense or engineer units.

The ability to assemble larger multinational formations such as divisions and corps from smaller, disparate national contributions is critical to NATO's ability to deter and repulse the most catastrophic of attacks from the East. However, just as each participating ally makes a sovereign decision to contribute its forces to a German- or French-led multinational formation, there is always the risk that a contributing ally might withdraw its specialized capability at an inopportune moment for any reason, poten-

63. Lewis Sanders, "Germany Creates DARPA-Like Cybersecurity Agency," *Deutsche Welle*, August 29, 2018, p.dw.com/p/33vsA

64. Matthias Schulze, "Germany Develops Offensive Cyber Capabilities without a Coherent Strategy of What to Do with Them," Council on Foreign Relations, December 3, 2018, www.cfr.org/blog/germany-develops-offensive-cyber-capabilities-without-coherent-strategy-what-do-them

65. Claudia Major and Christian Mölling, "The Framework Nations Concept," Stiftung Wissenschaft und Politik (December 2014), www.swp-berlin.org/fileadmin/contents/products/comments/2014C52_mjr_mlg.pdf; Rainer L. Glatz and Martin Zapfe, "Ambitious Framework Nation: Germany in NATO," Stiftung Wissenschaft und Politik, September 2017, www.swp-berlin.org/fileadmin/contents/products/comments/2017C35_glt_zapfe.pdf

tially leaving the larger formation without a critical niche capability. For this reason, when it comes at least to the fielding of larger formations, the Framework Nations Concept can only be viewed as a stop-gap solution to the challenge posed by Russia to NATO's collective defense. For Germany to be able to field divisions and corps *on its own*—which is ultimately required for a serious collective defense response to Russia—Berlin will need to significantly increase defense spending, return to some form of conscription, or perhaps do both.

The Will to Do More?

Capabilities and capacity together form just one-half of a country's decision to use hard power on the battlefield, in cyberspace, or across the airwaves—the other half of course is willpower, and here the picture is decidedly mixed in the case of Germany. On the one hand, German elites—most of the political class, the epistemic community, and other opinion leaders—clearly understand that their country can and should shoulder more international responsibility, including in the area of exercising hard power across all military domains. Evidence for this emerging elite consensus within Germany appeared most clearly during the 2014 Munich Security Conference. During that event, German president Joachim Gauck, Foreign Minister Frank-Walter Steinmeier, and Defense Minister Ursula von der Leyen separately made the case for their country to take on greater responsibility in international security. With regard to conflict prevention, Gauck argued, "Germany should make a more substantial contribution, and it should make it earlier and more decisively if it is to be a good partner."[66] Furthermore, he noted, "Germany must also be ready to do more to guarantee the security that others have provided it with for decades," and with regard to burden sharing, he argued, "at times when the United States cannot keep on providing more and more . . . Germany and its European partners must themselves assume greater responsibility for their security."

Steinmeier picked up on the same theme when he said, " Deutschland muss bereit sein, sich außen- und sicherheitspolitisch früher, entschiedener und substanzieller einzubringen " (Germany must be willing to

---

66. Joachim Gauck, "Germany's Role in the World: Reflections on Responsibility, Norms and Alliances," speech at the opening of the Munich Security Conference, January 31, 2014, www.bundespraesident.de/SharedDocs/Downloads/DE/Reden/2014/01/140131-Muenchner-Sicherheitskonferenz-Englisch.pdf?__blob=publicationFile

engage in foreign and security policy earlier, more decisively and more substantially).[67] When it comes to the use of military force, Steinmeier cautioned against excessive caution, and said essentially that Germany cannot sit on the sidelines: " darf eine Kultur der Zurückhaltung für Deutschland nicht zu einer Kultur des Heraushaltens werden. Deutschland ist zu groß, um Weltpolitik nur von der Außenlinie zu kommentieren" (a culture of restraint for Germany should not become a culture of holding out. Germany is too big to comment on world politics only from the outside).

Finally, von der Leyen also called for Germany to do more, given its size and strength. "Indifference is not an option for Germany," she argued. "As a major economy and a country of significant size we have a strong interest in international peace and stability," said the German defense minister. "Given these facts the Federal Government is prepared to enhance our international responsibility."[68]

Those important rhetorical steps—in what came to be known as the Munich Consensus—found a more detailed articulation in the 2016 *Weissbuch*, or German defense strategy, which repeatedly emphasized the themes of responsibility and leadership. The last time Berlin issued a defense strategy, in 2006, there was a sense of incremental acceptance of Germany's shifting role in the world. The 2006 strategy evinced a willingness to see Germany's role broadened, but an unwillingness to do so outside the confines of multilateralism and the legitimacy conferred by international organizations.

In contrast, the 2016 *Weissbuch* makes clear Germany's willingness to join in ad hoc coalitions in response to collective security crises. The 2016 *Weissbuch* acknowledged what had become an increasingly obvious reality: "Insbesondere Ad-hoc-Kooperationen werden als Instrumente der internationalen Krisen- und Konfliktbewältigung weiter an Bedeutung gewinnen." (Ad hoc cooperation will continue to gain significance as an instrument of international crisis and conflict management).[69] What is perhaps most significant in the 2016 *Weissbuch* is the declaration that Germany would be willing to not simply participate in coalitions of the willing

67. Frank-Walter Steinmeier, *Rede von Außenminister Frank-Walter Steinmeier anlässlich der 50: Münchner Sicherheitskonferenz*, February 1, 2014, www.auswaertiges-amt.de/de/newsroom/140201-bm-muesiko/259554

68. Ursula von der Leyen, speech on the occasion of the 50th Munich Security Conference, January 31, 2014, www.securityconference.de/fileadmin/MSC_/2014/Reden/2014-01-31-Speech-MinDef_von_der_Leyen-MuSeCo.pdf

69. *Weissbuch 2016 zur Sicherheitspolitik und zur Zukunft der Bundeswehr*, July 2016, 81, www.bmvg.de/resource/blob/13708/015be272f8c0098f1537a491676bfc31/weissbuch2016-barrierefrei-data.pdf

but also to *initiate* them. This marked a major departure from the past, in which Germany consistently sought to exercise hard power solely through established multilateral institutions.

The epistemic community, including leading think tanks in Europe and Germany specifically, also agrees that Germany can and should step up its contribution to international security. For instance, scholars at the European Council on Foreign Relations have argued that Germany needs to build a more structured process for coalition-building within Europe for the purposes of international security and that it must be prepared to "foot more of the bill."[70] Meanwhile, scholars at the Stiftung Wissenschaft und Politik have argued that Germany can and should take on more responsibility, but that it will need to increase funding in order to fulfill this goal.[71] Elsewhere, experts at the Deutsche Gesellschaft für Auswärtige Politik have made similar points, including the argument that Germany needs to increase defense spending in order to make good on its own ambitions for greater responsibility.[72]

In contrast to what might be thought of as the opinions of elites, the German public appears to lag somewhat behind. It seems that Germany's lack of serious hard power resources suits most of its public just fine, given their disinterest in crisis management and international conflict. According to a 2018 poll conducted by the Körber Foundation, when asked whether Germany should become more strongly involved in international crises, 55 percent of Germans surveyed said no, while only 41 percent said that Germany should become more strongly involved.[73] These figures were not much changed from 2017, when 52 percent favored restraint, while 43 percent favored greater involvement.

A similar sentiment was evident in a 2017 poll conducted by the Pew Research Center on allied solidarity within Europe. When Pew asked residents of eight NATO member states whether their country should use military force to defend an ally if it got into a serious military conflict with Russia, Germany scored lowest of all. Just 40 percent of Germans

---

70. Josef Janning and Almut Möller, "Leading from the Centre: Germany's New Role in Europe," European Council on Foreign Relations, July 2016.

71. Rainer L. Glatz and Martin Zapfe, "Ambitious Framework Nation: Germany in NATO," Stiftung Wissenschaft und Politik, September 2017, www.swp-berlin.org/filead min/contents/products/comments/2017C35_glt_zapfe.pdf

72. Christian Mölling and Torben Schütz, "Responsible Defense Policy," Deutsche Gesellschaft für Auswärtige Politik, October 11, 2018, dgap.org/en/article/getFullPDF/31396

73. "The Berlin Pulse: German Foreign Policy in Perspective," Körber Stiftung, November 2018, www.koerber-stiftung.de/fileadmin/user_upload/koerber-stiftung/redaktion/the-berlin-pulse/pdf/2018/The-Berlin-Pulse-2018.pdf

answered "yes," while 53 percent said "no."[74] Polling data like this makes Berlin somewhat unwilling to assume the mantle of leadership and responsibility when it comes to developing, maintaining, and wielding hard power across all domains.

However, even if Germany is unwilling today—or put another way, even if German decision-makers are unwilling to get ahead of public opinion—this does not necessarily mean the situation cannot change tomorrow or at some point soon. The Körber Foundation poll referenced earlier found that there was a significant generational difference in responses to the question on whether Germany should show restraint or instead be more involved in international crises. Although just 41 percent of Germans overall believe their country should become more strongly involved in international crises, that number increased to 52 percent among 18–34 year olds. Meanwhile, while 55 percent of Germans overall continue to prefer restraint, just 43 percent of 18 to 34 year olds hold this view. This means there is reason to think that as the older generations—those with firsthand or secondhand knowledge of Germany's tumultuous mid-twentieth-century experience—passes from the scene, public opinion may shift toward greater acceptance of an actively engaged Germany.

Aside from the generational differences of opinion, there are other reasons to think that opinion may continue to evolve in Germany. Over the last quarter century, Germany has demonstrated significant potential for evolution in its strategic culture and in its approach to security issues. During the Cold War, there were several requests for West German participation in Western out-of-area operations and UN peacekeeping operations, but the government refused, claiming that the German constitution forbade the use of military forces for anything but the defense of NATO territory.[75] For instance, in 1992, NATO dispatched its Northern Army Group multinational headquarters to Bosnia to provide command and control of personnel escorting and protecting UN humanitarian relief convoys. However, the German government refused to allow its personnel assigned to the Northern Army Group to go to Bosnia.[76]

---

74. Bruce Stokes, "NATO's Image Improves on Both Sides of Atlantic," Pew Research Center, May 22, 2017, www.pewglobal.org/wp-content/uploads/sites/2/2017/05/Pew-Research-Center-NATO-Report-FINAL-May-23-2017.pdf. The other countries surveyed were Canada, France, the Netherlands, Poland, Spain, the United Kingdom, and the United States.

75. Hanns W. Maull, "Germany and the Use of Force: Still a 'Civilian Power'?," *Survival* 42, no. 2 (2000): 56–80.

76. Martin A. Smith, *NATO in the First Decade after the Cold War* (Dordrecht, the Netherlands: Kluwer Academic Publishers, 2000), 139.

This situation changed dramatically in 1994, when the German constitutional court declared that the constitution did not prohibit participation in multilateral peacekeeping or combat operations, as long as such missions are endorsed by a parliamentary majority.[77] Chancellor Helmut Kohl had already begun dispatching Bundeswehr personnel to participate in a UN stability operation in Somalia and as part of NATO airborne radar crews monitoring a no-fly zone over Bosnia. These actions led to a lawsuit filed by the Social Democrats and the Free Democrats, who ultimately lost when the constitutional court issued its ruling.

Within a year of the constitutional court ruling, the German government—with the Bundestag's vote in support—dispatched Tornado combat jets to Bosnia to support a British-French-Dutch Rapid Reaction Force, the first German combat deployment since 1945.[78] Public opinion had already begun to swing in favor of greater involvement overseas, evidenced by the fact that even Social Democrat and left-leaning Green Party members voted in support of the deployment. Just a year and a half later, the Bundestag went a step further, authorizing by a vote of 499 to 93 the deployment of 2,000 combat-ready ground troops to Bosnia—another post–World War II first.[79] Public opinion was not quite as supportive—in an opinion survey, 51 percent of respondents saw the deployment as "not good," compared with 46 percent in favor.[80] Nevertheless, there remained no serious backlash to the quickly evolving German approach to the application of hard power.

This trend continued when, just a few years later, Germany deployed combat forces to Kosovo in the absence of a UN mandate. Intense diplomatic pressure from the United States on the German government at the time—a left-of-center coalition consisting of the Social Democrats

77. Rick Atkinson, "Court Allows German Troops to Join Missions outside NATO Area," *Washington Post*, July 13, 1994, www.washingtonpost.com/archive/politics/1994/07/13/court-allows-german-troops-to-join-missions-outside-nato-area/e405287e-fc07-4631-b713-6243847e9dd2/?tid=ss_tw&utm_term=.369997e38d5d

78. Mary Williams Walsh, "Edging toward Combat, Germans Boost Bosnia Role," *Los Angeles Times*, July 1, 1995, articles.latimes.com/1995-07-01/news/mn-19197_1_german-troops

79. Alan Cowell, "Germans Plan Combat Troops outside NATO, a Postwar First," *New York Times*, December 14, 1996, nyti.ms/2RbaeQB. The deployment of roughly 1,700 German troops to Somalia in July 1993 was a humanitarian mission under a UN peacekeeping mandate—German troops were sent to distribute aid to Somali civilians, and Chancellor Helmut Kohl maintained that German troops would not be drawn into a combat role. Craig R. Whitney, "German Soldiers Head for Somalia," *New York Times*, July 23, 1993, nyti.ms/2OzG7m0

80. Alan Cowell, "Germans Plan Combat Troops outside NATO."

under the leadership of Gerhard Schröder and the Greens under Joschka Fischer—played a key role in Berlin's decision. Nonetheless, by the late 1990s opinions across the spectrum of elites in Germany as well as that of the public had changed dramatically from earlier in the same decade. This was in no small part due to Schröder's efforts to redefine the debate—and reinterpret German history to some degree—by emphasizing the necessity of Germany taking on greater responsibility to avoid repeating the mistakes of the past.[81]

The operations of the 1990s, which were mostly in and around Europe, paved the way for the even more momentous decision in 2001 to support American-led combat operations in Afghanistan.[82] Sending as many as 4,000 troops thousands of miles away from Germany was truly a watershed in Berlin's approach to international engagement and hard power. Certainly, the decision was made easier by the fact that operations in Afghanistan were carried out in response to the attacks of 9/11 and NATO's subsequent invocation of Article 5. Nevertheless, it is striking that Germany ultimately maintained its commitment to what became the International Security Assistance Force for Afghanistan for over a dozen years, taking responsibility for the north of the country, increasing its contingent to over 5,300 troops and policemen, and sustaining 55 troops killed in action and nearly 250 wounded.

Even more recently, the Bundeswehr's mission in Iraq represents yet another stage in Germany's evolving approach. There, German armed forces were involved in an ongoing conflict supporting the Peshmerga in the Kurdistan region of Iraq, including weapons delivery. For some, this represented "a paradigm change for German defense and security policy."[83]

In sum, German soldiers in recent years have deployed, fought, and died abroad, all without prompting a political backlash at home.[84] Over the last quarter century, German attitudes toward military power, international responsibility, and the appropriate use of the Bundeswehr have changed dramatically. There is no reason to think that additional evolution is not possible. On the contrary, further evolution is likely, given what has unfolded in a relatively short time period, the continuing desire of Ger-

---

81. Alister Miskimmon, "Falling into Line? Kosovo and the Course of German Foreign Policy," *International Affairs*. 85, no. 3 (2009): 561–73.

82. Kate Connolly, "German Troops to Join War Effort in Berlin," *Guardian*, November 6, 2001, www.theguardian.com/world/2001/nov/07/afghanistan.terrorism4

83. Tobias Buck, "German Military: Combat Ready?," *Financial Times*, February 15, 2018, www.ft.com/content/36e2cd40-0fdf-11e8-940e-08320fc2a277

84. Buck, "German Military."

many's leaders to take on more responsibility, and a kind of untapped willingness on the part of the public to be led by German decision-makers in this regard.[85]

America and a New European Hegemon

The preceding sections have painted a picture of Germany as having more latent military *potential* than any other country in Europe today. Berlin looks likely to retain its dominant economic position over the next decade, despite the economic dislocation brought about by the COVID-19 pandemic, far more typical business cycle peaks and troughs, and the potential for longer-term demographic challenges. The primary question from Washington's perspective is whether Germany will turn its latent potential into *actual* military power, with a will to match. In other words, is Germany able and willing to become America's premier international security partner, in ways similar to the so-called "special relationship" between the United States and the United Kingdom over the last several decades?

More broadly, there are also questions over whether German hegemony in Europe— beyond the economic realm—is really in American interests. For the duration of the Cold War, the threat from the Soviet Union kept potential rivals such as Germany and Japan aligned closely with the United States. Somewhat surprisingly, the demise of the Soviet Union did little to change this alignment. Nevertheless, it prompted strategists in the U.S. Department of Defense to contemplate the potential for Germany and Japan to chart a separate course, one that might see them rise as regional hegemons and ultimately challenge U.S. interests. In the immediate aftermath of the Cold War, these concerns were aired through a leaked 1992 draft Defense Planning Guidance, which argued that Washington should prevent the rise of regional hegemons, including Germany.[86]

For the last 30 years, neither Germany nor Japan appear to have actively pursued regional hegemony at the expense of or to the detriment of the United States, or at least they have not done so outside the context of

---

85. Interview with an expert at the American Institute for Contemporary Germany Studies, December 4, 2018.

86. Patrick E. Tyler, "U.S. Strategy Plan Calls for Insuring No Rivals Develop," *New York Times*, March 8, 1992, nyti.ms/2k29HOU. See also Hal Brands, "Choosing Primacy: U.S. Strategy and Global Strategy at the Dawn of the Post–Cold War Era," *Texas National Security Review* 1, no. 2 (February 2018), tnsr.org/2018/02/choosing-primacy-u-s-strategy-global-order-dawn-post-cold-war-era-2/ and Derek Chollet and James Goldgeier, *America between the Wars: From 11/9 to 9/11* (New York: Public Affairs, 2008).

existing security frameworks such as NATO or bilateral alliance arrangements. If three decades of evidence is any indication, it seems that if the aforementioned security frameworks remain intact and continue to serve the interests of Germany and Japan, those countries are unlikely to pursue hegemonic *rivalry* with the United States. This is despite the fact—as argued earlier in this chapter—that Germany has already achieved economic hegemony within Europe. In short, if Germany remains enmeshed in NATO—which appears likely—Germany's rise politically and even militarily need not threaten U.S. interests or those of other American allies.

All of this has made President Donald Trump's pronouncements about Germany and NATO so perplexing and perhaps even self-defeating. As both a candidate for office and during his first few years in office, President Trump repeatedly lambasted Germany on an array of issues such as trade policy and defense burden-sharing while simultaneously questioning the value of NATO and the Article 5 commitment that underpins it. At various points since his inauguration in January 2017, President Trump declared Germany to be a captive of Russia, claimed Berlin owed the United States billions of dollars in defense reimbursements, threatened to pull the United States out of NATO, and essentially undermined the German government by claiming (incorrectly) that its migration policies have led to a spike in crime.[87]

This sort of rhetoric prompted German leaders to pursue European-only solutions to security challenges, made it politically more difficult for German leaders to work with their American counterparts, undermined the very institutional architecture that provides a framework for German security and American leadership in Europe, and prompted "horror" in Berlin over the security risks created by President Trump.[88] Although Germany continues to show little indication of pursuing a form of hegemony in opposition to Washington, President Trump's rhetoric as well as some of his administration's policies risk pushing Berlin in a direction inimical to

---

87. Nahal Toosi, "'Why Germany?' Trump's Strange Fixation Vexes Experts," *Politico*, July 11, 2018, www.politico.com/story/2018/07/11/trump-germany-russia-merkel-714066; Jim Puzzanghera, "Trump Says Merkel Meeting Was 'Great,' Then Blasts Germany for NATO Bills," *Los Angeles Times*, March 18, 2017, www.latimes.com/politics/washington/la-na-essen tial-washington-updates-trump-says-merkel-meeting-was-great-1489845711-htmlstory. html

88. "Trump Takes Aim at Germany and NATO," *Der Spiegel Online*, July 13, 2018, www. spiegel.de/international/world/trump-takes-aim-at-germany-and-nato-a-1218335.html; Damien Sharkov, "Donald Trump Scares Germans More Than Terrorism, Eurozone Crisis, and Climate Change," *Newsweek*, September 6, 2018, www.newsweek.com/donald-trump-scares-germans-more-terrorism-eurozone-crisis-and-climate-change-1109376

U.S. interests. The most plausible scenario in the short run is that Trump's approach and his policies so offend Germans, that Berlin begins to normalize relations with Russia through the pursuit of a rejuvenated Ostpolitik.

If one assumes, though, perhaps somewhat optimistically, that President Trump's words and actions *fail* to do lasting damage and that Germany's unfolding hegemony remains bound within an intergovernmental institutional framework, Germany's role as primus inter pares within Europe will not only avoid harming American interests but it may indeed complement them. Nonetheless, it remains unclear whether Germany has the ability and will to become America's right-hand partner in the defense of common interests in Europe and beyond. Obviously, the German military today lacks the kind of operational capacities and capabilities across land, air, maritime, space, and cyber domains that would make it an ideal— that is, full-spectrum—partner. Moreover, according to one observer, the German military remains imbued "with a culture of restraint."[89] This is derivative of Berlin's extraordinarily limited will to employ what hard power it has. Ultimately, it is possible—given sufficient funding and the continuing evolution of German attitudes toward hard power—that Germany may someday become a UK-like partner in managing and responding to collective challenges. Is the next decade—the time horizon for this book—enough to achieve necessary gains in capabilities and capacity and to convince a somewhat skeptical German public of the necessity of greater involvement? Washington may not be able or willing to wait so long. If it is not, it is likely the United States will need to look to other allies and partners that have and are likely to maintain more full-spectrum capability, moderate capacity, and willpower.

---

89. This remark was made by François Lecointre, chief of the French general staff, as quoted by John Vinocur, "German Lion Emerges from Merkel's Sunset," *Politico*, October 12, 2018, www.politico.eu/article/wolfgang-schauble-german-lion-emerges-from-angela-merkel-sunset/

FOUR

France and the Incomplete Revolution

In contrast to Germany, France has a national security outlook that is similar to that of the United States in many ways. This outlook—as evidenced through France's 2017 Defence and National Security Strategic Review—is so similar in some contexts, such as with regard to the Syrian civil war, that Paris is actually Washington's partner of choice. The French national security community understands and values the role of hard power and a full-spectrum military, including nuclear weapons, to both deter and compel the behavior of state and nonstate actors. Among America's European allies, France is one of the most capable, with a tradition of employing both hard and soft power in the service of broad national security objectives and across a variety of military operational domains on the European continent and well beyond.

However, over the last several years the French military has been overstretched, and it is in need of refitting, recuperation, and reinvestment. The operational demands of homeland defense and missions well beyond Europe over the last five years—coming so soon after the nearly decade-long commitment of thousands of French troops in Afghanistan—have collectively sapped the French military. Compounding the operational stress, French defense budgets were generally on a declining trend for most of the period from 2005 to 2015, resulting in reduced manpower, cuts in force structure, and a lack of ready equipment that are all affecting French capabilities and capacity *today*.

Increased defense resources would go a long way to remedying these problems, allowing the French to increase manpower, address readiness, reinvest in technology, and maintain global ambition. In fact, the French defense budget has started to rebound, but only slightly so. More aggressive investments in defense—the kind necessary to permit Paris to make good on its commitments and maintain a strategic horizon beyond Europe and the Mediterranean—will only be possible if the French government can find firmer fiscal ground, from which increased tax receipts might be channeled into defense coffers.

Recognizing the depth and scope of the malaise that has afflicted the French economy for many years, Emmanuel Macron has attempted to bring about an economic revolution of sorts. Borrowing ideas from both right and left, Macron seeks to break the stalemate between the traditional political forces that have dominated French public policy for decades. Whether Macron can achieve this goal remains to be seen, but his mandate seems clear, thanks to what could be described as a veritable political revolution in 2017. In an era of right- and left-wing populism that has swept across Europe, the centrist Macron and his En Marche political movement rose to power—achieving an absolute majority in the French parliament—on the basis of a promise to fundamentally change the status quo and usher in major economic change. The French electorate has placed a great deal of faith in a relatively untested young leader and his promise of renewal. If he can deliver, the benefits will have significant implications for French national security, the French military, and Western interests. If he cannot, it is highly likely the French economy will remain mired in its malaise, ultimately inhibiting France's ability to fulfill its own objectives and play a role in defending Western interests much beyond Europe.

Before assessing how Macron has fared in his bid to rejuvenate the French economy, this chapter will examine the elections of 2017, positing that the changes ushered in by the electorate amounted to a political revolution. The subsequent section will describe how that political revolution was underwritten by the promise of an economic revolution, and it will examine whether and how Macron is fulfilling this vow. The next section will tie the necessity of economic renewal to French national security, making the case as foreshadowed above that increased defense resourcing would go far in pumping new life into an exhausted, overstretched French military establishment, allowing Paris to make good on its own national security goals as outlined in the 2017 Defence and National Security Strategic Review, and potentially to develop a closer security partnership with the United States. Finally, the last section of this chapter will examine the situation from Washington's perspective. It argues that there are many reasons why a closer security partnership with France makes sense from the view of the United States, but that there are several hurdles standing in the way. Some of the most critical of these—such as the ability to keep pace with advances in military technology necessary for twentieth-century competition and conflict—would be ameliorated with increased French defense spending. In sum, the chapter will argue that Macron's economic revolution is, at best, an unfinished one, and that without it the French military is unlikely to fulfill Paris's broad security ambitions or play a more significant role, in coordination with the United States, in safeguarding and promoting common Western interests in Europe and beyond.

Political Revolution

Over the last few years, France has undergone a political rejuvenation, largely thanks to Emmanuel Macron—a fresh-faced newcomer to politics who had never won elective office before his election as president in 2017—but also due to the failure of the right or left to wrest France from its economic torpor. Macron, the 38-year old economy minister under Socialist president François Hollande, launched a new political movement known as En Marche in April 2016, just a year before the first round of voting in the presidential election.

In August 2016, he formally broke with Hollande, resigning from his ministerial post and campaigning full time. He pledged to rebuild a *"système politique bloqué"* (blocked political system) and go beyond the classic left-right political divide by bringing together *"les progressistes contre les conservateurs"* (the progressives against the conservatives).[1]

Certainly, Macron benefited from serious problems facing the traditional power centers on the right and the left. The conservative candidate, François Fillon, was considered through much of the last half of 2016 to be the most likely to make it into the second round. However, a scandal involving public money paid to his wife and children—whom he hired as parliamentary assistants—for work they never did became his undoing, eating into his support throughout early 2017 and prompting unheeded calls for his withdrawal from the race.[2]

Meanwhile, after President Hollande—in the face of dismal approval

1. Pierre Martin, "Un séisme politique: L'élection présidentielle de 2017," *Commentaire*, no. 158 (2017): 249–64, www.cairn.info/revue-commentaire-2017-2-page-249.htm
2. David Lees, "A Controversial Campaign: François Fillon and the Decline of the Centre-Right in the 2017 Presidential Elections," *Modern & Contemporary France* 25, no. 4 (2017): 391–402.

ratings—finally declared in December 2016 that he would not run again, the divisions within his Socialist Party, which had never really been erased during his term, resurfaced.[3] Through a contentious primary process, the Socialists chose a visionary candidate—Benoît Hamon—over a more pragmatic one—former prime minister Manuel Valls. Burying the hatchet proved practically impossible, given the role that Hamon had previously played in undermining Prime Minister Valls's policy proposals. In fact, Valls ultimately went on to support the candidacy of Macron in the first round. At the same time, Hamon had pressure on his political left thanks to radical candidate Jean-Luc Mélenchon.

All four of these major candidates—Macron, Fillon, Hamon, and Mélenchon—were vying to face far right Front National candidate Marine Le Pen. Le Pen had consistently earned about a quarter of the electorate's support in polls conducted in the weeks and months prior to the first round of voting, thanks in part to her efforts to soften the Front's image and to take on a more populist tone. Given the polling numbers of her four competitors—all less than 25 percent, and generally split fairly evenly—it was widely assumed Le Pen would make it into the second round.

Following the first round of voting on April 23, 2017, it was Macron who actually came out on top with 24 percent of the popular vote. Le Pen performed worse than opinion polls had led most to expect, earning just 21.3 percent. Most of the remaining votes were split between Fillon (20 percent), Mélenchon (19.6 percent), and Hamon (6.4 percent). The second round, between Macron and Le Pen, was held just two weeks later on May 6, 2016. Macron won with just over 66 percent of the vote, a solid victory compared with the far closer second round election in 2012 between Hollande (51.6 percent) and Nicolas Sarkozy (48.3 percent) but not nearly as high as the 82 percent earned by Jacques Chirac in 2002, when the Front last made it to the second round of voting. Turnout was high relative to other recent European elections, but somewhat low by French standards at nearly 75 percent—it was also lower than both the first round in 2017 (78 percent) and the second round in 2012 (80 percent).

Macron's success at the presidential election level was not simply the result of splits within the mainstream political movements of right and left, or just the result of voters choosing the lesser of two evils in the second round, given Le Pen's far right philosophy. Instead, En Marche's success showed that many voters were ready to move beyond the historic right-left

---

3. Yves Mény, "A Tale of Party Primaries and Outsider Candidates: The 2017 French Presidential Election," *French Politics* 15 (2017): 265–78.

divide that had failed to achieve policy success and to bring in a completely new, even untested, political force that promised to challenge the status quo and, as Macron himself argued, move beyond a system that protects the existing order.[4] Macron capitalized on that mood by avoiding entrapment by the right or left, politically or ideologically. According to Benjamin Griveaux, a cofounder of En Marche, "for a century and a half, the left and right in France have tried to apply an ideology to reality. Our approach was the exact opposite. In our intellectual method, we were . . . more pragmatic."[5] Macron could take this more "pragmatic" approach—and in doing so, offend, to varying degrees, the sensibilities of the traditional right and left establishments—because he did not need the institutional scaffolding and the grassroots network of a political party structure to overcome the internally divided and dramatically weakened conservatives and socialists. In contrast, every one of Macron's predecessors, dating back to Charles de Gaulle and the founding of the Fifth French Republic in 1958, had been elected with the solid backing of a major political party. Macron took advantage of the weakness of the traditional parties at a time when the electorate had finally grown sufficiently disillusioned with both right and left.

Macron was able to prove his election was not merely the result of anybody-but-Le-Pen sentiment when just a month after the presidential second round his coattails helped to reconfigure the legislative branch as well. En Marche won 308 seats, more than enough for an outright majority in the 577-seat National Assembly.[6] In alliance with the centrist Democratic Movement party, the two parties held 350 seats, a commanding majority. While it is certainly true that the so-called honeymoon cycle—in which legislative elections that closely follow presidential elections tend to produce a majority supportive of the president[7]—recurred yet again in France, as it did in 2012, 2007, and 2002, En Marche's victory still marked a significant break with the past, as roughly 75 percent of the deputies elected had not served previously. Moreover, the average age of the incoming deputies—about 48 years old—was 5 years younger than the average age

---

4. Emmanuel Macron, *Revolution*, trans. Jonathan Goldberg and Juliette Scott (London: Scribe, 2017), 58–59.

5. Sophie Pedder, *Revolution Française: Emmanuel Macron and the Quest to Reinvent a Nation* (London: Bloomsbury Continuum, 2018), 153.

6. Admittedly, low turnout of 48.7 percent in the first round and 42.6 percent in the second round probably helped Macron, as voters from the mainstream socialists and conservative parties likely sat out.

7. Matthew Soberg Shugart, "The Electoral Cycle and Institutional Sources of Divided Presidential Government," *American Political Science Review* 89, no. 2 (June 1995): 327–43.

of their predecessors. Additionally, the previous legislature included 155 women, or roughly 27 percent of the deputies—in contrast, the 2017 election resulted in 224 female deputies, or about 39 percent of the legislature.

In sum, both the executive and legislative branches had been transformed in large part by En Marche, which went from nonexistence to the dominant political movement in the country in the space of just over 12 months. It is therefore reasonable to argue that the French political landscape itself has been transformed.[8] Today, in contrast to before the 2017 elections, the dominant political cleavage in the country appears to be between those who favor libertarianism and cultural openness on the one hand and those who support authoritarian and anti-immigration policies on the other. A secondary, less robust cleavage has emerged between those that support more classical leftist or socialist positions regarding the economy—represented best by Mélenchon and Hamon—and those that support more neoliberal, pro-business policies—represented by Macron himself.

Some have argued that the "revolution" brought about by Macron was not terribly revolutionary at all, even though Macron tapped politicians from both center-right and center-left for his cabinet and even though he has forged a policy agenda combining probusiness, proenvironment, and socially liberal elements.[9] They further posit that many of Macron's policies are not novel, and that in several respects those policies represent continuity with his predecessors of both the right and the left insofar as those policies tend to be generally neoliberal, probusiness, and socially liberal.

These critiques may have some merit, but they also minimize the manner in which Macron and En Marche essentially vanquished the two most important French political institutions of the last half century or more, namely the Socialists on the one hand and the conservatives under a series of different names on the other.[10] Moreover, if one casts Macron's election into a broader, continental context, En Marche's victories across presidential and legislative elections marked major, rare wins of a centrist, pro-European movement during an era of right- and left-wing populism in Europe. Finally, those that argue Macron and En Marche are not suffi-

---

8. Florent Gougou and Simon Persico, "A New Party System in the Making? The 2017 French Presidential Election," *French Politics* 15, no. 3 (2017): 303–21.

9. Nick Hewlett, "The Phantom Revolution: The Presidential and Parliamentary Elections of 2017," *Modern & Contemporary France* 25, no. 4 (October 2017): 377–90; Raymond Kuhn, "French Revolution? The 2017 Presidential and Parliamentary Elections," *Parliamentary Affairs* 71, no. 3 (2018): 483–500.

10. Verónica Hoyo and William M. Chandler, "Emmanuel Macron Just Won a Majority in France's National Assembly: Here Is Why It Matters," *Washington Post*, June 20, 2017, www.washingtonpost.com/news/monkey-cage/wp/2017/06/20/emmanuel-macron-just-won-a-majority-in-frances-national-assembly-here-is-why-it-matters/?utm_term=.f2f1c25bd8c8

ciently revolutionary dismiss the perspectives of French men and women themselves. Voters appeared convinced Macron and his new party represented something novel—a centrist movement led by a charismatic newcomer who was capable of garnering enough electoral strength to govern by drawing on the right and the left, thereby offering the prospect of truly reinvigorating the French economy.[11]

An Economic Revolution to Match?

As economy minister, Macron gained firsthand insights into the lethargy that has long characterized the French economy—especially its lack of innovation, its labor market inflexibility, and the preferences accorded incumbent companies and captains of industry at the expense of newcomers and disrupters.[12] The political revolution represented by En Marche's campaign and the election were in large part predicated on Macron's commitment to implement an economic revolution. Prior to his victory in May 2017, Macron had promised that addressing the sclerotic French labor code would be his first priority. It was therefore no surprise in summer 2017 when Macron started pushing to make hiring and firing easier, to shift wage negotiations from the industry level to the company level, and place a cap on severance packages awarded by industrial tribunals.

These and other steps were necessary in order to address the well-known, major challenges facing the French economy, including high unemployment coupled with modest growth. Stagnation in the French economy had become something of a self-fulfilling prophecy, as foreign direct investment in France had fallen somewhat over the last decade in comparison to the 2000s.[13] More broadly, the French economy was not particularly competitive globally, ranking just 17th in the World Economic Forum's Global Competitiveness Index, and even that ranking was an exception compared to previous years when France was not within the top 20.[14]

From a comparative perspective, it was also clear that the French

---

11. James Traub, "Macron Has Changed France's Political DNA," *Foreign Policy*, June 5, 2018, foreignpolicy.com/2018/06/05/macron-is-french-for-obama/; Martin, "Un séisme politique."

12. France ranks 84th in the world in terms of its tolerance for entrepreneurial failure. See "The Global Competitiveness Report 2018," reports.weforum.org/global-competitiveness-report-2018/chapter-2-regional-and-country-analysis/

13. Sophie Meunier, "Is France Still Relevant?," *French Politics, Culture & Society* 35, no. 2 (Summer 2017): 59–75.

14. "The Global Competitiveness Report 2018," reports.weforum.org/global-competitiveness-report-2018/chapter-2-regional-and-country-analysis/

economy has long lacked the vitality of its German counterpart. A strong reason for this was the structure of the labor market, which remained unreformed despite periodic attempts by French leaders. In contrast, Germany has gradually liberalized its labor market over the last few decades, including through the decentralization of the wage-setting process from the industry level to the firm level. This localization of wage-setting stands in contrast to France, where although only 11 percent of employees are unionized, 98 percent of employees are covered by collective wage agreements thanks to the extension of union-negotiated wage and work hour regulations industry-wide.[15] As a result of this rigidity in wage-setting as well as other factors, minimum wages have been high relative to productivity.[16] This has subsequently contributed to a growing exodus of French jobs to other countries, some moving elsewhere within the EU to remain inside the Single European Market but with slightly reduced labor costs, and some moving outside the EU to take advantage of even lower wages.[17]

For these reasons—as well as the necessity of showing results before a potential reelection campaign in 2022—Macron sought to tackle France's labor code early in his term. In September 2017, Macron signed the reforms into law as part of a package of executive orders. Although he had a majority in parliament, his administration reasoned it could enact the reforms faster by executive order than if it tried to push the measures through the legislature, which could have taken far longer and might have made it difficult for Macron to show economic results in his first term. In addition to decentralizing wage negotiations, the reforms reduced the risk of legal action against companies that dismiss workers, capped the damages that courts can award for unfair dismissals, and allowed multinational companies to close loss-making plants more easily.[18] In order to maintain a balanced approach, several measures supported by unions were also included, such as keeping oversight of healthcare standards at the sectoral or industry level rather than the company level, requiring union approval for larger companies to modify working hours and conditions, and gaining an increase in severance packages in exchange for the cap on damages.[19]

---

15. OECD, "Employment Outlook 2018: How Does France Compare?" July 2018, www.oecd-ilibrary.org/employment/oecd-employment-outlook-2018_empl_outlook-2018-en

16. Christian Dustmann et al., "From Sick Man of Europe to Economic Superstar: Germany's Resurgent Economy," *Journal of Economic Perspectives* 28, no. 1 (Winter 2014): 167–88, http://dx.doi.org/10.1257/jep.28.1.167

17. Meunier, "Is France Still Relevant?"

18. Nicholas Vinocur, "5 Key Points from Macron's Big Labor Reform," *Politico*, August 31, 2017, www.politico.eu/article/macron-labor-reform-5-key-points/

19. Anne-Sylvaine Chassany, "Emmanuel Macron Pushes through French Labour Law

Nonetheless, and despite outreach efforts on the part of Macron toward major labor unions, protests occurred throughout the late spring and summer 2017. Due to the protests' small size relative to much larger antireform demonstrations in 2016, divisions among the major unions, the decreasing salience of unions in a technology-driven, postindustrial economy,[20] and Macron's perceptions of his electoral mandate, the young president pushed on with the labor code reforms as well as additional measures in 2017, 2018, and 2019, including

- Changes to unemployment insurance;
- The reorganization of apprenticeships and vocational training to address skills shortages, especially in information technology;[21]
- Cuts in the "wealth tax" and the introduction of a lower, flat tax on capital gains, dividends, and interest;[22]
- Increased taxes on retirees;[23]
- Removal of financial and bureaucratic barriers for small businesses;[24]
- Overhauling the costly health care system, including hospital financing; and[25]
- Streamlining the operations of the national railway.[26]

Reforms," *Financial Times*, September 22, 2017, www.ft.com/content/a9ad1728-9f68-11e7-9a86-4d5a475ba4c5; "Macron Signs French Labor Reform Decrees," *Reuters*, September 22, 2017, www.reuters.com/article/us-france-reform-labour/macron-signs-french-labor-reform-decrees-idUSKCN1BX1K7

20. Andrea Garnero, "Why Labor Protests in France Won't Stop Macron's Reforms," *Harvard Business Review*, May 22, 2018, hbr.org/2018/05/why-labor-protests-in-france-wont-stop-macrons-reforms

21. Caroline Pailliez, "You're Hired! France's Macron Targets Apprentices in Labor Market Shake-up," *Reuters*, November 3, 2017, www.reuters.com/article/us-france-reform-apprencticeships/youre-hired-frances-macron-targets-apprentices-in-labor-market-shake-up-idUSKBN1D30Z5

22. Anne-Sylvaine Chassany, "Macron Slashes France's Wealth Tax in Pro-Business Budget," *Financial Times*, October 24, 2017, www.ft.com/content/3d907582-b893-11e7-9bfb-4a9c83ffa852

23. In December 2018, Macron announced he would scale this back by scrapping any increase for pensioners earning less than 2,000 euros per month.

24. Sylvie Corbet, "French President Pushes for New Changes as Criticism Grows," Associated Press, August 22, 2018, apnews.com/37f1ff21598b458aa51ed3dde578b687

25. Corbet, "French President Pushes for New Changes as Criticism Grows.".

26. Reforms included turning SCNF into a joint-stock company, giving its management greater corporate responsibility, phasing out its domestic passenger monopoly starting 2020, and ending generous benefits and pensions for future employees. Luke Baker, "French Parliament Approves SNCF Reform Bill in Breakthrough for Macron," *Reuters*, June 13, 2018, www.reuters.com/article/us-france-reform-vote/french-parliament-approves-sncf-reform-bill-in-breakthrough-for-macron-idUSKBN1J91CU; "Could Striking French Rail Work-

Macron also has plans to take on the structure of the French govern-ment, including by decreasing the number of lawmakers and accelerating the process of making laws.[27] Reforms of the school system are also in the works. Here, Macron hopes to reduce class sizes in underprivileged areas, revamp the French baccalaureate exam to improve standards, and pro-mote research and development in artificial intelligence in select academic institutions.[28]

In sum, Macron's government has clearly been aggressive in pushing long-overdue reforms designed to pull the French economy out of its stu-por, increase productivity, and reduce unemployment. Whether Macron succeeds in rejuvenating the French economy over the long run depends in part on how quickly he can show results in the short run, otherwise the public is likely to lose patience with him and En Marche, as Macron's own advisors have acknowledged.[29]

So how has Macron done so far on the economic front? While some argue that the economy is clearly on the rebound since Macron's election, results have been mixed at best just a few years into Macron's five-year term.[30] Gross domestic product improved by 2.3 percent in 2017 from the previous year, but only by 1.7 percent in 2018 and 1.2 percent in 2019.[31] It is highly likely that the COVID-19 economic slump will reduce annual growth even further, possibly into negative territory.[32]

If the French economy is able to stave off the worst outcomes, low

ers Bring France to a Standstill Once Again?," *The Local*, March 15, 2018, www.thelocal. fr/20180315/can-striking-french-rail-workers-really-paralyse-the-country

27. "Macron Aims to Put Summer Scandal behind Him with New Reform Drive," *France 24*, August 22, 2018, f24.my/3RLt; "French Government Strikes Deal to Cut Lawmakers Number by Almost a Third," *Reuters*, April 4, 2018, www.reuters.com/article/us-france-politics/french-government-strikes-deal-to-cut-lawmakers-number-by-almost-a-third-idUSKCN1HB2AB

28. Ingrid Melander, "'No Kid Left Behind': Macron Tries to Fix France's Education Sys-tem," *Reuters*, July 5, 2018, www.reuters.com/article/us-france-reforms-education/no-kid-left-behind-macron-tries-to-fix-frances-education-system-idUSKBN1JV0MM; "Emmanuel Macron Wants to Change the Beloved Baccalauréat," *Economist*, February 8, 2018, www. economist.com/europe/2018/02/08/emmanuel-macron-wants-to-change-the-beloved-bac calaureate

29. Victor Mallet, "Paris Vows to Extend Labour Reforms despite Gilets Jaunes," *Financial Times*, January 23, 2019, www.ft.com/content/3e2bce58-1e57-11e9-b126-46fc3ad87c65

30. David Schrieberg, "Emmanuel Macron's France Rebounds, yet His Popularity Suf-fers," *Forbes*, February 18, 2018, www.forbes.com/sites/davidschrieberg1/2018/02/18/emmanuel-macrons-france-rebounds-yet-his-popularity-suffers/#1cebcb6f5a40

31. Institut National de la Statistique et des Études Économiques, "Au quatrième trimes tre 2019, le PIB baisse légèrement (−0,1 %)," January 31, 2020, www.insee.fr/fr/statistiques/fichier/version-html/4299215/CNT-T4-2019-PE.pdf

32. Aline Robert, "France's Budget Deficit Could Skyrocket to 7% of GDP in COVID-

GDP growth rates are unlikely to generate the kind of robust job creation necessary to put a serious dent in unemployment levels. Nonetheless, the unemployment rate is down slightly since Macron entered office—from 9.6 percent in July 2017 to 8.4 percent by January 2020. Most promisingly, the unemployment rate is especially lower for 25–49 year olds. However, this could reflect simply a continuing trend that started in early 2015. Since then, when unemployment stood at about 10.5 percent, the numbers have generally improved, albeit slowly, so it is unclear whether the lower unemployment figures are the result of Macron's actions or simply the eventual turn of the business cycle.

Even if Macron can claim credit for the hiring boost and a related increase in confidence within the French business community, purchasing power for the average consumer has remained restrained in recent years. One poll found that 74 percent of the French believed that their purchasing power decreased in 2018, Macron's first full year in office, while just 19 percent believed it remained stable and only 7 percent said it has increased.[33] These perceptions were widely shared among all population groups, regardless of age or social class. According to one analyst, there is a sense in France that Macron has stopped the country's decay, but as of yet "people don't see answers for themselves."[34]

The sense of stagnation at the level of the family unit prompted many, as part of the so-called Yellow Vest movement, to start protesting in late 2018 Macron's plans for an increase in the fuel consumption tax. Macron's government viewed the tax increase as a necessary step toward reducing environmental pollution. In contrast, average citizens—and especially those that rely on driving for their livelihood, such as truck drivers who initially spearheaded the Yellow Vest protests—felt as if they were bearing a disproportionate share of the burden. There was and still is a sense in France that income disparities have grown too large between the wealthier urbanites and the less well-off middle and lower class workers in the smaller towns and rural areas. As a result, the best that can be said of Macron's promise to match the political revolution he and En Marche achieved in 2017 with an economic one is that the work remains unfinished and the outcome highly uncertain.

---

19 Aftermath," *Euractiv*, March 20, 2020, www.euractiv.com/section/economy-jobs/news/frances-budget-deficit-could-skyrocket-to-7-of-gdp-in-covid-19-aftermath/

33. Elabe, "Pouvoir d'achat: Un sentiment de baisse pour 3 Français sur 4," October 31, 2018, elabe.fr/pouvoir-dachat-carburant/. Elabe is an independent research and consultancy firm based in Paris.

34. As quoted in Schrieberg, "Emmanuel Macron's France Rebounds."

Implications for French Security

The question of whether Macron's political revolution is engendering an economic one to match is critical not simply for France's economy and its citizens, but it is also vital for French security and specifically the defense budget. From 2005 through 2015, French defense budgets and force structure fell, threatening the country's ability to project hard power across distance and time. Much of this was the result of France's response to the sovereign debt crisis that struck Europe beginning in late 2009 but which had roots in the global financial crisis of 2007–08.[35] In response to these economic crises, defense budgets were cut in France and in many countries across Europe in order to reduce national debts while safeguarding social safety net programs.

In 2005, France spent roughly €46.1 billion on defense, equivalent to 2.5 percent of its GDP that year—by 2015, that figure, in real terms, had fallen to €37.4 billion, equivalent to 1.8 percent of its GDP that year.[36] Procurement programs were scaled back or stretched out, spurring worries that the French simply would not have enough military systems to remain operationally relevant.[37] Additionally, these cuts prompted alarm within the French defense industry. The leaders of several major defense firms, such as Thales and Dassault, argued that highly skilled jobs, technological innovation, and France's trade balance were all at risk.[38] Finally, tens of thousands of military positions were cut during this 10-year period, as called for in both the 2008 and 2013 Defense White Papers. The former outlined cuts of 54,000 personnel (military and civilian) and the latter added another 24,000 in cuts.

From a strategic horizons perspective, there has also been a retrenching

---

35. It could be argued that defense budget cuts during the early years of this time period were the result of reduced threat perceptions. However, the 2008 *French White Paper on Defence and National Security* warns of "a world not necessarily more dangerous, but certainly less predictable, less stable and more contradictory" than the post–Cold War period. It paints a picture of a "volatile environment" in which French territory and citizens are "vulnerable in new ways."

36. For comparative purposes, defense spending figures cited are in 2010 prices. Source: NATO defense spending figures.

37. Dorothée Fouchaux, "French Hard Power: Living on the Strategic Edge," in *A Hard Look at Hard Power: Assessing the Defense Capabilities of Key U.S. Allies and Security Partners*, ed. Gary J. Schmitt (Carlisle, PA: U.S. Army War College Press, 2015), 173–99.

38. Emmanuel Grasland and Alain Ruello, "Inquiets, les industriels de l'armement demandent audience à l'Elysée," *Les Echos*, March 13, 2013, www.lesechos.fr/13/03/2013/LesEchos/21395-064-ECH_inquiets--les-industriels-de-l-armement-demandent-audience-a-l-elysee.htm

of sorts. The 2013 Defense White Paper was explicit with its emphasis on Africa (especially from the Sahel to Equatorial Africa), Eastern Europe, and the Mediterranean littoral—essentially, "Europe's near environment."[39] Along these same lines, the more recent 2017 Defence and National Security Strategic Review focuses most clearly on the threat of Islamic terrorism, calling for a "clear-sighted approach to priorities based on the geographical proximity of threats and on the interests of our national community."[40] These perspectives stand in contrast to the broader conceptualization of where France should be prepared to exercise its power in the "arc of crisis" outlined in the 2008 Defense White Paper, stretching from Africa's Atlantic Coast to South Asia and the Indian Ocean.[41] The 2013 White Paper also cut in half the 2008 White Paper's goal of being able to deploy and sustain 30,000 troops in a high-intensity, forced entry operation.[42]

Despite the diminution of French capabilities, capacity, and even strategic ambition, France has actually been quite active in projecting hard power internationally in recent years. Deployments have included

- A unilateral intervention in Mali known as Opération Serval from January 2013 through July 2014 involving roughly 4,000 troops, to prevent an Islamist takeover of the country;
- Its follow-on mission, Opération Barkhane, since August 2014 across five countries in the Sahel but with headquarters in Chad, involving 3,500 French troops;
- From December 2013 through October 2016, a unilateral intervention known as Opération Sangari consisting of 2,000 French troops in the Central African Republic, to fight jihadist insurgents;
- Airstrikes in Iraq and Syria as well as artillery support for ground forces and training of Iraqi forces under Opération Chammal, which is part of the broader anti-Daesh coalition, starting in September 2014 and involving only French air and naval forces;
- A relatively small deployment of Special Forces and "intelligence commandos" to Libya in 2016, in conjunction with similar U.S. and UK teams, to conduct operations against Daesh elements.[43]

39. *French White Paper on Defence and National Security* (2013), 53.

40. *Defence and National Security Strategic Review 2017*, 14.

41. *The French White Paper on Defence and National Security* (New York: Odile Jacob, 2008), 41.

42. *French White Paper on Defence and National Security* (2008), 204; *French White Paper on Defence and National Security* (2013), 88.

43. Nathalie Guibert, "La France mène des opérations secrètes en Libye," *Le Monde,*

It is perhaps a sign of Paris's concern over the terrorist threat from abroad and its attachment to the ideal of France as a major international player that these deployments occurred during a period of serious personnel, force structure, and budget cuts. However, the deployments have not been without significant challenges, including a lack of seemingly essential equipment for the modern battlefield, such as advanced bulletproof vests, armored vehicles, and drones.[44] Overseas deployments have also been complicated by the demands of homeland security. In response to the 2015 terrorist attacks, France has deployed up to 10,000 troops at home, or nearly 10 percent of the active duty French Army. Opération Sentinelle—the deployment of French troops at tourist attractions like the Eifel Tower, near religious sites, and on patrol in cities across the country—began in January 2015, in response to the terrorist attack against the satirical weekly *Charlie Hebdo*. Following the November 2015 terrorist attack against the Bataclan concert hall, the operation was reinforced, with greater emphasis placed on more dynamic patrolling rather than static guarding of sensitive sites. This marks the first time since the end of the Cold War that there are as many French troops deployed within metropolitan France—typically 7,000 on patrol any given day, with 3,000 held in reserve—as there are deployed overseas. According to some critics, Sentinelle represents an ineffective response that is more of a show piece than a serious effort to streamline homeland security structures and policies within France.[45] Those same critics also argue the high cost of Sentinelle is unjustified and unsustainable—costs were initially as high as €1 million per day but later fell to an average of €480,000 per day in 2015 and subsequently €397,000 per day in 2016.[46]

Aside from the fiscal costs, Sentinelle and the overseas deployments

---

February 23, 2016, www.lemonde.fr/international/article/2016/02/24/la-france-mene-des-operations-secretes-en-libye_4870605_3210.html

44. Jean-Dominique Merchet, "Au Sahel, l'armée française 'se dépêche d'attendre' ses renforts de materiel," *l'Opinion*, July 18, 2018, www.lopinion.fr/edition/international/sahel-l-armee-francaise-se-depeche-d-attendre-renforts-materiel-157131

45. James McAuley, "In France, Are Soldiers outside the Eiffel Tower and the Louvre Really Worth It?," *Washington Post*, June 4, 2016, www.washingtonpost.com/world/europe/in-france-are-soldiers-outside-the-eiffel-tower-and-the-louve-really-worth-it/2016/06/04/e542f600-2524-11e6-b944-52f7b1793dae_story.html?utm_term=.ae776cfa4c71

46. Interview with an expert on French national security at a Paris-based think tank, February 4, 2019; "Budget de la Défense: L'opération Sentinelle coûte un million d'euros par jour," *LCI*, April 29, 2015, www.lci.fr/france/budget-de-la-defense-loperation-sentinelle-coute-un-million-deuros-par-jour-1199080.html; "Effectifs, coût, efficacité . . . ce qu'il faut savoir sur l'opération Sentinelle," *LCI*, August 9, 2017, www.lci.fr/politique/levallois-militaires-attaques-effectifs-cout-efficacite-ce-qu-il-faut-savoir-sur-l-operation-sentinelle-2060896.html

have resulted in an extraordinarily high operational tempo for French troops. Typically, French troops have conducted a four- to six-month deployment to Africa or elsewhere overseas, then returned for a two-month deployment under Sentinelle, followed by a short period at home station to rest and recover, after which they would be deployed again overseas.[47] This pace has been particularly difficult for the noncommissioned officers, who are typically assigned to high-demand regimental units, meaning they deploy repeatedly.[48] Although the operational tempo for the French army is not very dissimilar from the height of operations in Afghanistan and elsewhere a decade ago,[49] the army is fulfilling its current mission set overseas and domestically with nearly 20,000 fewer soldiers than a decade ago.[50]

Meanwhile, the French navy also saw itself stretched by operational requirements for which it lacked the force structure. In 2015, French naval forces were deployed in five theaters—the North Atlantic, the Baltic Sea, the Mediterranean, the Indian Ocean, and the Gulf of Guinea—even though the navy was configured and sized for simultaneous operations in only two theaters.[51] In late 2014, the French air force—with operations ongoing in Iraq, across the Sahel, and from Djibouti—was said to be operating at 90 percent of capacity after having seen its force structure and infrastructure cut.[52] From 2008, the air force lost 30 percent of its air fleet, six fighter squadrons were disbanded, and eight airbases in France were shuttered.[53] In summary, it is clear that in recent years the French military has endured an exceptionally high operational pace, just as its manpower, force structure, and budgets are smaller than ever.

The question confronting not simply military officials but also the country's political leadership is whether the pace of operations, given the current state of French security forces, is sustainable—and the answer increasingly appears to be "no." "It's absolutely crushing them," according

---

47. Interview with a French field-grade army officer, February 11, 2019; and interview with a U.S. field-grade officer assigned to U.S. European Command, January 15, 2019.

48. Interview with a French field-grade army officer, February 11, 2019.

49. Interview with a French field-grade army officer, April 11, 2019.

50. In 2008, the French army consisted of 133,500 active duty personnel, and by 2019 that number had fallen to 114,450 personnel. For comparison, the French army consisted of 169,000 personnel in 2000. *The Military Balance* (London: International Institute for Strategic Studies, 2008), 118; *The Military Balance* (London: International Institute for Strategic Studies, 2019), 105; and *The Military Balance* (London: International Institute for Strategic Studies, 2000), 58.

51. *The Military Balance* (London: International Institute for Strategic Studies, 2016), 64.

52. *The Military Balance* (2016), 64.

53. Fouchaux, "French Hard Power." 185.

to one observer who has worked closely with the French military.[54] Another expert posits that France is "completely overstretched militarily . . . it's not sustainable"[55] Yet another argues the French are on the cusp of biting off more than they can chew.[56] As a result, morale has been falling and reenlistments have been down.[57] According to a French military report on these issues, "En vérité, la fidélisation constitue un défi de première importance" (In truth, retention is a major challenge).[58]

French military readiness has suffered as well, particularly for conventional maneuver warfare, for which it is underequipped and undertrained, according to France's chief of defense, General François Lecointre.[59] "Nous ne sommes pas en mesure, et nous n'avons pas de scénario prévoyant d'être engagés dans une guerre interétatique massive" (We are not able, and we have no scenario of being engaged in a massive interstate war).[60] Privately, French military officials have claimed that in the event of a major security crisis—such as a Russian incursion into the Baltic States or Poland—they would redeploy forces from places like sub-Saharan Africa.[61] However, this assumes there would be sufficient strategic lift assets at their disposal, a

---

54. Interview with a U.S. field-grade officer assigned to U.S. European Command, January 15, 2019.

55. Interview with an expert on French national security at a Paris-based think tank, February 4, 2019.

56. Interview with a Washington-based U.S. field-grade officer expert on military relations with France, February 28, 2019.

57. Blandine Le Cain, "Pourquoi l'armée a du mal à fidéliser ses troupes," *Le Figaro*, July 10, 2017, www.lefigaro.fr/actualite-france/2017/10/07/01016-20171007ARTFIG00083-pourquoi-l-armee-a-du-mal-a-fideliser-ses-troupes.php; also, interview with a Washington-based U.S. field-grade officer expert on military relations with France, February 28, 2019.

58. Ministère des Armées, "11e rapport thématique du Haut Comité d'évaluation de la condition militaire," June 10, 2017, 7, www.defense.gouv.fr/content/download/514088/8657542/file/11e_RAPPORT_HCECM.pdf

59. Audition du général François Lecointre, chef d'état-major des armées, sur les opérations en cours, Commission de la défense nationale et des forces armées [Hearing of General François Lecointre, Chief of Staff of the Armed Forces, on the ongoing operations, Commission of National Defense and Armed Forces], July 17, 2018, www.assemblee-nationale.fr/15/cr-cdef/17-18/c1718071.asp. In fairness, *many* major Western powers, including France, have been suffering from this same inability to conduct large-scale, high-intensity maneuver warfare, following years of training for stabilization and counterterrorism missions.

60. Audition du général François Lecointre, chef d'état-major des armées, sur le projet de loi de finances pour 2019, Commission de la défense nationale et des forces armées [Hearing of General François Lecointre, Chief of Staff of the Armed Forces, on the draft budget law for 2019, National Defense and Armed Forces Commission], October 18, 2018, www.assemblee-nationale.fr/15/cr-cdef/18-19/c1819015.asp

61. Interview with a U.S. field-grade officer assigned to U.S. European Command, January 15, 2019; interview with a Washington-based U.S. field-grade officer expert on military relations with France, February 28, 2019.

particularly important issue when Paris has relied on the United States, Ukraine, and even Russia to provide strategic airlift for ongoing operations in Africa.[62] Additionally, it ignores the issue of how French troops would fare in a fight—especially one focused on conventional, combined arms maneuver warfare—for which they have not trained. Under the current defense funding law, French forces are supposed to conduct 90 days' worth of general training for combined arms warfare each year—as distinct from more specialized predeployment training—but in 2016 that number was just 72 days, improving slightly to 81 days in 2018.[63] Notably, even the 90 day standard is a cut from previous years—under the preceding defense funding law, covering the period 2009–14, the standard was 120 days.[64]

Just as importantly though, French hopes that they could simply shift troops from Africa to, for example, Eastern Europe with ease in the event of a major crisis overlooks questions regarding the lack of modern, well-maintained equipment across all capabilities—a recurring weakness of the French military.[65] In 2018, major ground forces equipment was operationally ready only 54 percent of the time.[66] Like the high operational tempo of the French military, the lack of sufficient, mission-critical equipment has also begun to affect morale.[67] The low readiness rating of major military equipment reflects not simply the high pace of operations of the military but also the manner and environments in which the equipment has been

---

62. Marine Pennetier, "Russia, Ukraine 'Damocles Sword' Hangs over French Military Deployment," *Reuters*, March 28, 2017, www.reuters.com/article/us-france-defence-report/russia-ukraine-damocles-sword-hangs-over-french-military-deployment-idUSKBN-16Z26N; and James Sheehan, "US Gives Lift to French Forces," *U.S. Army*, February 13, 2019, www.army.mil/article/217360/us_gives_lift_to_french_forces. France's preferred strategic airlift platform—the Airbus A-400M—has been plagued by cost overruns, development challenges, and production delays. See Peggy Hollinger, Tobias Buck, and Laura Pitel, "A400M: The €20bn Military Aircraft That Has Bedevilled Airbus," *Financial Times*, July 3, 2018, www.ft.com/content/b02b65be-7d70-11e8-bc55-50daf11b720d. French strategic airlift challenges received a boost in 2016, when the defence minister announced the planned purchase of four C-130J aircraft, two of which will be configured as refueling aircraft. The first C-130 was delivered in late December 2017. Pierre Tran, "France Places C-130 Order," *Defense News*, February 1, 2016, www.defensenews.com/pentagon/2016/02/01/france-places-c-130-order/

63. Audition du général François Lecointre, chef d'état-major des armées, October 18, 2018.

64. Fouchaux, "French Hard Power."

65. Vincent Lamigeon, "Budget des armées 2019: Qui sont les gagnants?," *l'Opinion*, September 27, 2018, www.challenges.fr/entreprise/defense/budget-des-armees-2019-qui-sont-les-gagnants_615676

66. Audition du général François Lecointre, chef d'état-major des armées, October 18, 2018.

67. Interview with a French field-grade army military officer, February 11, 2019.

used—namely, in the harsh conditions of the Sahel and on the unpaved roads of North, West, and Central Africa.

Given the significant challenges facing the French military, President Hollande decided in 2015 to increase somewhat the defense spending plan, by €3.85 billion for the period 2016–19, and to eliminate planned personnel cuts of around 18,000.[68] However, even this has proven insufficient given the array of security threats the country is facing and the condition of the French military following years of contraction. While a candidate, Macron recognized the magnitude of the problem and campaigned on increased defense spending. However, once he was in office, and in order to remain within EU budget caps, Macron initially announced in mid-2017 that defense would be cut yet again, this time as part of a broader effort to trim €4.9 billion from the central government's budget. Given what the French military had endured over the preceding decade and the relentlessly high pace of operations that showed little sign of abating despite its unsustainability, General Pierre de Villiers, the French chief of the general staff, resigned in protest in mid-2017.[69] This was a highly unusual and unexpected move on the part of de Villiers, who occupied a position of great importance in the French military system. De Villiers's resignation over what he perceived as inadequate defense spending to "guarantee the protection of France and the French people, today and tomorrow, and to sustain the aims of our country" followed very vocal disagreement with the new president, during which the former gave testimony before a parliamentary committee.[70] De Villiers reportedly told the committee, "There is no fat in our army. We are attacking the muscle here—and this as the security situation worsens."[71]

Macron ultimately did announce a defense spending increase of roughly €1.8 billion for 2018, which represented a 5.6 percent increase over 2017

68. *The Military Balance* (London: International Institute for Strategic Studies, 2016), 65; Alessandro Marrone, Olivier De France, and Daniele Fattibene, eds., *Defence Budgets and Cooperation in Europe: Developments, Trends and Drivers,* January 2016, www.iai.it/sites/default/files/pma_report.pdf

69. Rory Mulholland, "Head of French Armed Forces Resigns over Budget Cuts Row with Macron," *Telegraph,* July 19, 2017, www.telegraph.co.uk/news/2017/07/19/head-french-armed-forces-resigns-budget-cuts-row-macron/

70. "Macron Accepts Resignation of French Military Chief," *France 24,* July 19, 2017, f24.my/1W6G

71. Simon Carraud and Michel Rose, "France's Armed Forces Chief Resigns after Clash with Macron over Budget Cuts," *Reuters,* July 19, 2017, www.reuters.com/article/us-france-politics-defence/frances-armed-forces-chief-resigns-after-clash-with-macron-over-budget-cuts-idUSKBN1A40KR

spending levels.[72] Subsequently, and less than a year into his term, Macron announced a new multiyear military spending plan. This was in part tied to the aforementioned Strategic Review, which was launched by Macron in summer 2017 and completed in October of the same year. Although less ambitious than the 2008 or 2013 White Papers, the 2017 Strategic Review provided an important reassessment of France's security ends and means as well as an endorsement of strategic autonomy. Additionally, and perhaps most importantly, the 2017 Strategic Review clearly called for a sustained "national military build-up" in order to achieve France's strategic ambitions over the next decade.[73] Not coincidentally, Macron's government announced it would increase funding for France's armed forces between 2019 and 2025.[74] The multiyear spending plan will be composed of annual increases of €1.7 billion through 2022—the year Macron's term ends—followed by €3 billion per year increases in 2023, 2024, and 2025. Whether the French government will sustain this commitment in a post-COVID-19 economic environment remains highly doubtful. Nonetheless, the increases in defense spending appeared to have had an impact on the quality and quantity of equipment available to troop on overseas missions.[75]

This increase in spending was perceived as necessary not simply to rebuild and modernize conventional equipment stocks and capabilities, to enable more training for a wider range of military contingencies, or to reach the political objective of 2 percent of France's GDP—agreed by all NATO allies—but also to maintain and update France's sea- and air-launched nuclear weapons and related delivery systems. The nuclear deterrent is vital to France's role in Europe and its self-perception as a major international player. Fully funding research, development, and procurement of the new generation of nuclear-powered ballistic-missile submarines, for example, will not be easy, with estimates as high as €4 billion per year in 2018 and 2019 and then €6 billion per year from 2020 to 2025.[76] This modernization process has been slow to get under way, but France

---

72. Anne-Sylvaine Chassany, "France to Increase Military Spending," *Financial Times*, February 8, 2018, www.ft.com/content/fede4e5a-0cb0-11e8-8eb7-42f857ea9f09; and Pierre Tran, "Macron Signs French Military Budget into Law: Here's What the Armed Forces Are Getting," *Defense News*, July 16, 2018, www.defensenews.com/global/europe/2018/07/16/macron-signs-french-military-budget-into-law-heres-what-the-armed-forces-are-getting/

73. *Defence and National Security Strategic Review 2017*, 51, 86.

74. Henry Samuel, "France to Boost Defence Spending in 'Unprecedented' Move to Meet Nato Commitments," *Telegraph*, February 8, 2018, www.telegraph.co.uk/news/2018/02/08/france-boost-defence-spending-unprecedented-move-meet-nato-commitments/

75. Interview with a field-grade French army officer, April 11, 2019.

76. *The Military Balance* (London: International Institute for Strategic Studies, 2018), 74.

remains at least rhetorically committed to maintaining both the sea and air platforms of its nuclear weapons arsenal.[77] At the same time, France put forth a space strategy in 2019 with clear military aspects and it has also prioritized the development of artificial intelligence for the purposes of defense, in order to catch up with the United States, China, and others.[78]

What is somewhat less clear, though, is whether funding for the defense aspects of France's space program, its military artificial intelligence initiative, or its nuclear deterrent will come at the expense of France's conventional capabilities and capacity in air, land, sea, and cyber domains.[79] Without adequate funding for all of these "priorities," Paris will need to make hard choices if it hopes to build a truly full-spectrum military with all of the cyber, information, electronic, and intelligence capabilities necessary for twenty-first century competition and conflict. More broadly, there also remains uncertainty over whether the funding commitments outlined by Macron's government—particularly those after 2022—can be maintained even as the French economy struggles, as the government tries to remain in compliance with EU budget rules, and as COVID-19 implications unfold. For all of these reasons, a true rejuvenation of the French economy is vitally necessary to increase tax receipts, take pressure off the government to rely on the defense budget as a bill payer for maintaining the social safety net, and hence facilitate Paris's national security and defense spending goals.

France and the United States: A New Special Relationship?

In spite of the challenges facing the French military outlined above, France has grown in importance as a security partner for the United States over

---

77. "Thales to Work on French Navy's Future Ballistic Missile Submarine Sonar Tech," *Naval Today*, February 7, 2018, navaltoday.com/2018/02/07/thales-to-work-on-french-navys-future-ballistic-missile-submarine-sonar-tech/; "Here Is the First Image of the French Navy Next Generation SSBN—SNLE 3G," Navy Recognition, October 3, 2018, www.navy-recognition.com/index.php/news/defence-news/2018/october-2018-navy-naval-defense-news/6538-here-is-the-first-image-of-the-french-navy-next-generation-ssbn-snle-3g.html

78. Murielle Delaporte, "From Paris to Orbit: France's New Space Strategy," *Breaking Defense*, January 3, 2019, breakingdefense.com/2019/01/from-paris-to-orbit-frances-new-space-strategy/; "Discours de Florence Parly, ministre des Armées_Intelligence artificielle et defense," April 5, 2019, www.defense.gouv.fr/salle-de-presse/discours/discours-de-florence-parly/discours-de-florence-parly-ministre-des-armees_intelligence-artificielle-et-defense

79. Some experts dispute this notion of a trade-off between conventional and nuclear, arguing for instance that investment in nuclear capabilities directly benefits French air force and naval capabilities. Interview with a French defense expert at a Paris-based think tank, February 25, 2019.

the last several years.[80] In some regions and on some issues—such as with regard to Syria, across Africa, or perhaps on counterterrorism—France is a closer or stronger partner for Washington than the United Kingdom.[81] Given the impact of austerity measures on UK defense as outlined in chapter 2 of this book and the antipathy of President Donald Trump toward Berlin, some argue France is already the most effective global partner of the United States—in terms of capacity, capability, and willpower.[82] From Paris's perspective, a closer transatlantic security partnership would ideally be balanced with the other traditional pillars of French national security strategy, namely the Franco-British axis and the EU's Common Security and Defence Policy anchored by relations with Berlin.[83] Nonetheless, and perhaps with an eye toward the post-Trump era, Paris is certainly keen to build upon its very good and substantive defense and intelligence cooperation with the United States, despite the turbulence brought to transatlantic relations by Trump and even as France continues to pursue strategic autonomy for itself and Europe.[84]

From Washington's perspective, there are several reasons to view a Franco-American "special relationship" as particularly appealing. First, diplomatically and politically, France remains a country with interests beyond Europe, even if its strategic horizon appears to have receded somewhat from a decade ago. Despite its shifting level of ambition, France still maintains the second largest diplomatic network in the world, after the United States. It is the only European country with overseas territories in the Indian Ocean (Réunion, Mayotte, and the French Southern Territories) and the Pacific Ocean (French Polynesia, New Caledonia, and Wallis and Futuna) and with permanent military presences in both. Although far from regions like the South China Sea where great power competition is playing out between China and the United States most obviously, these

---

80. Interview with a former senior civilian employee within the Office of the Secretary of Defense, December 2, 2018; Gorm Rye Olsen, "Transatlantic Cooperation on Terrorism and Islamist Radicalisation in Africa: The Franco-American Axis," *European Security* 27, no. 1 (2018): 41–57.

81. Interview with a U.S. field-grade officer assigned to U.S. European Command, January 15, 2019; Tunku Varadarajan, "Move over Britain, France Is America's 'Special' Friend," *Politico*, April 30, 2018, www.politico.eu/article/macron-trump-may-move-over-britain-france-is-americas-bff-now/

82. Interview with an expert on French national security at a Paris-based think tank, February 4, 2019.

83. Alice Pannier, "France's Defense Partnerships and the Dilemmas of Brexit," German Marshall Fund of the United States, May 30, 2018, www.gmfus.org/publications/frances-defense-partnerships-and-dilemmas-brexit

84. Alexandra de Hoop Scheffer and Martin Quencez, "The U.S.–France Special Relationship: Testing the Macron Method," German Marshall Fund of the United States, April 18, 2018, www.gmfus.org/publications/us-france-special-relationship-after-year-trump

overseas territories shape French perceptions of its interests—particularly in Africa—and also provide tangible means of projecting influence and hard power beyond Europe.[85] The French appear willing to leverage their claim of being an Indian Ocean and Pacific Ocean power as the basis for pressuring China to abide by international law and norms.[86]

Second, the French national security enterprise evinces an extensive and in-depth understanding of what is necessary—in terms of capabilities and capacities—for twenty-first century competition and conflict, even if it as yet *lacks* sufficiency in both. The 2017 Strategic Review calls for a national military build-up unfolding over the next decade to focus specifically on capabilities "that contribute to intelligence, France's role as a framework nation, forcible entry capabilities, and the ability to support long-term engagements."[87] This is a fairly broad conceptualization of the range of military operations. Even though Paris is certainly keen to invest in high-profile, expensive military platforms, which generate jobs as well as national prestige and which are primarily useful against other state actors in conventional conflicts, the French appear to have a vision of future operations that is far more dynamic than "yesterday's war." This is a vision that might include stability operations in developing countries but it might also include offensive cyber operations against state and nonstate actors. For instance, the 2013 Defense White Paper notes that France now considers a large cyber-attack to be an act of war, and the French have placed increasing emphasis on intelligence gathering through drones and other unmanned systems.

Finally, and most broadly, the French remain keenly interested in hard power, and they have the will to use it.[88] According to one longtime observer of European military capabilities, the French are today the most capable of America's partners in Europe, with the ability to deploy and sus-

---

85. Interview with a senior field-grade U.S. officer based in Washington and expert in Franco-American military relations, February 28, 2019.

86. Idrees Ali and Phil Stewart, "In Rare Move, French Warship Passes through Taiwan Strait," *Reuters*, April 25, 2019, www.reuters.com/article/us-taiwan-france-warship-china-exclusive/exclusive-in-rare-move-french-warship-passes-through-taiwan-strait-idUSKCN1S10Q7

87. *Defence and National Security Strategic Review 2017*, 86.

88. Interview with an expert on U.S. and European security at a DC-based think tank, December 4, 2018; interview with a Washington-based U.S. field-grade officer expert on military relations with France, February 28, 2019; Celia Belin and Boris Toucas, "The 'Macron Miracle' Could Transform France into a Global Powerhouse," *National Interest*, April 19, 2018, nationalinterest.org/feature/the-macron-miracle-could-transform-france-global-powerhouse-25477

tain smaller force packages for limited periods of time.[89] Another characterized the French military as having "a warrior mentality," similar to that of the American military.[90] Furthermore, if the French military appears to lack a particular capability necessary for an operation, they are typically blunt with American interlocutors about their need and desire to fill that gap—sometimes in contrast to the British—even if it means buying defense products made in America instead of in France.[91] In summary, the French have shown themselves to have much of the ambition that Washington hopes to find among its leading European partners, including the willingness to defend Western interests in Europe and (somewhat) beyond, to conduct forced entry operations, to act as both coalition teammates and coalition leaders depending on the level of interests at stake, and to do all of this in the air, at sea, on land, and in cyberspace.

Nonetheless, there remain serious impediments to an enhanced security partnership between Paris and Washington. Increased French defense spending—predicated upon a rejuvenated French economy driving increased tax receipts—could help to overcome these, though. First, France lacks sufficient capacity for long-term continuous overseas missions.[92] Increased defense spending could help France overcome difficulties—stemming from the impact of Sentinelle and the requirements of homeland defense—in maintaining longer-term deployments over time and at distance from Europe. In September 2017, General Lecointre noted that the French army had been operating at 30 percent beyond its full capacity for several years, but that the budget trajectory at the time would enable a sustainable operational pace only *by 2030*.[93]

Second, the French have limited offensive cyber capability.[94] Increased defense spending could be critical to enabling Paris to make good on its objectives in the realm of cyber conflict. The 2017 Strategic Review

---

89. Interview with an American civilian employee of U.S. Army Europe with extensive experience in military-to-military programs across Europe, November 13, 2018.

90. Interview with a U.S. field-grade officer assigned to U.S. European Command, January 15, 2019.

91. The French acquisition of C-130J transport aircraft and MQ-9 Reaper drones are good examples of this. Interview with a U.S. field-grade officer assigned to U.S. European Command, January 15, 2019

92. Interview with a senior field-grade U.S. officer based in Washington and expert in Franco-American military relations, February 28, 2019.

93. François Lecointre, "Allocution de Bienvenue," in proceedings from the 15th University of Defense, September 2017, 13, www.universite-defense-2017.org/Data/Sites/8/fich iers/actes-UED-web.pdf?ts=1508251982. Emphasis added.

94. Interview with a Washington-based U.S. field-grade officer expert on military relations with France, February 28, 2019.

acknowledged that France needs both defensive and offensive cyber capabilities, and in early 2019 Defense Minister Florence Parly revealed that France would employ cyber weapons like any other conventional weapon for both offense and defense.[95] Key to this new vision is the development of appropriate doctrine and the recruitment of qualified specialists. France's relatively new military Cyber Command, created in 2017, only recently started the process of crafting a new offensive cyber doctrine. It also has a plan to recruit up to 1,000 additional cyber troops by 2025, but it remains unclear if this objective can be achieved given the scope of other challenges facing the French military.[96]

Third, there is a growing technological divide between U.S. and French military forces. A larger defense budget would permit France to invest in more advanced conventional military platforms, enabling the French military to keep pace and maintain interoperability with the United States and other NATO allies. For example, at present France lacks a fifth-generation jet fighter, which is typically characterized by radar-evading stealth capability, network-centric avionics, and other advanced technologies. Examples of fifth-generation fighters currently include the American-produced F-22 and F-35 and the Chinese-produced J-20. American allies Australia, Belgium, Denmark, Israel, Italy, Japan, the Netherlands, Norway, and the United Kingdom are all currently acquiring the F-35. France relies instead on more dated fourth-generation technology, based on 1970s or 1980s-era designs, in the form of the Rafale fighter jet. Although the French have committed to a €2 billion upgrade program for their Rafale fleet as part of the 2019–25 defense spending law—focused primarily on weapons and radar improvements—the upgraded versions will not begin to appear in the French fleet until 2023 at the earliest and in any case the underlying airframe will still lack more modern design features and stealth technology.[97] Germany and France have explored development of an indigenously produced European next-generation fighter jet—what might be considered a

95. Emmanuelle Lamandé, "Florence Parly, FIC: La France passe à la 'cyber' offensive," *Global Security Mag*, January 2019, www.globalsecuritymag.fr/Florence-Parly-FIC-la-France-passe,20190125,83960.html

96. Christina Mackenzie, "French Defense Chief Touts Offensive Tack in New Cyber Strategy," *Fifth Domain*, January 18, 2019, www.fifthdomain.com/global/europe/2019/01/18/french-defense-chief-touts-offensive-tack-in-new-cyber-strategy/; Emmanuelle Lamandé, "Général Olivier Bonnet de Paillerets, COMCYBER: Le recrutement de cyber-combattants représente un défi colossal pour le ministère des Armées," *Global Security Mag*, February 2019, www.globalsecuritymag.fr/General-Olivier-Bonnet-de,20190201,84178.html

97. Christina Mackenzie, "France Orders $2.3 Billion Upgrade for Rafale Warplanes," *Defense News*, January 14, 2019, www.defensenews.com/global/europe/2019/01/14/france-orders-upgraded-rafale-warplanes-for-23-billion/

sixth-generation aircraft—which would incorporate fifth-generation technologies like stealth but then build upon them by, for instance, including the capability to manage stealthy drones. However, the first deliveries of such an aircraft would not occur until 2035–40 at the earliest.[98] A larger French defense budget might permit more aggressive investment in a project such as this as well as the purchase of American-produced F-35s as a stopgap measure.

Finally, there are only limited routinized ties between the American and French defense establishments. A larger defense budget would permit more intense partnership in security matters between these two entities. The United States and France have only just begun multiyear bilateral command and staff officer exchanges under what Washington calls the Military Personnel Exchange Program.[99] This program provides opportunities for military officers of close U.S. allies to fill specific billets or command positions within the American military establishment, and for U.S. officers to do the same in the military establishments of allies. These kinds of exchanges build extraordinary degrees of interoperability at the staff level, enable two-way learning of practices and procedures, and provide for a depth of networking and relationship development between military staffs that occasional senior officer visits simply cannot replicate. The United Kingdom has been the most robust European partner in this regard, with roughly 35 officers on exchanges with the United States at any given time. With the Germans, the United States has 12 officers exchanged, six with the Italians, five with the Dutch, and one with the Belgians—the U.S.-French exchange is in its infancy, owing primarily to operational demands of the last several years as well as bureaucratic hurdles.

One area in which Washington and Paris have had some success in building more effective defense establishment ties in in terms of intelligence cooperation, but even here there is significant room for improvement. Following the terrorist attacks of 2015 in France, the United States and France initiated intensified intelligence sharing efforts under an initiative called the Lafayette Committee. The committee meets annually and facilitates the exchange of "operational military intelligence."[100] The

---

98. Zachary Keck, "France and Germany Have a Plan to Build a Stealth 6th-Generation Fighter," *National Interest*, June 22, 2018, nationalinterest.org/blog/the-buzz/france-germany-have-plan-build-stealth-6th-generation-26389

99. Interview with an American civilian employee of U.S. Army Europe with extensive experience in military-to-military programs across Europe, November 13, 2018.

100. "Joint Statement of Intent by Mr. Jean-Yves le Drian, Minister of Defence of the French Republic, and the Honorable Ashton Carter, Secretary Of Defense of the United

exchanges have proven very helpful, particularly to French efforts to fight insurgents in Mali and elsewhere in the Sahel.[101] However, the amount of information provided by the United States occasionally overwhelms the French ability to distill and act upon it, and the relationship is struggling to move beyond the tactical and operational.[102]

Not all of the challenges standing in the way of a closer Franco-American security relationship are resolvable simply through additional French defense spending. Other hurdles—such as strengthening cooperation on defense procurement—require different solutions. However, several of the most significant impediments to a "special relationship" between Paris and Washington in national security matters appear responsive to additional funding. Obviously, though, a larger French defense budget depends on expanded tax receipts and hence a larger French economy. President Macron and his En Marche movement have been granted an opportunity to fulfill a mandate for change—whether they are able to seize it and leverage the political revolution of 2017 in the service of a necessary economic one remains uncertain.

States of America," undated, dod.defense.gov/Portals/1/Documents/pubs/Joint-Statement-of-Intent-between-the-US-and-France.pdf

101. Gordon Lubold and Matthew Dalton, "U.S.-French Operation Targeted Elusive North African Militant, U.S. Says," *Wall Street Journal*, November 27, 2016, www.wsj.com/articles/u-s-french-operation-targeted-elusive-north-african-militant-u-s-says-1480276417

102. Interview with a senior field-grade U.S. officer based in Washington and expert in Franco-American military relations, February 28, 2019.

FIVE

The Fall of Italy

For several decades—arguably since the interwar period of 1919–39—Italy has been a part of the so-called big four Western Europe powers, along with the United Kingdom, France, and Germany. Since the end of World War II, these four countries have been the European allies that Washington has most frequently coordinated with in terms of geopolitics, diplomacy, economics, and security policy. The "big four" have accounted for the bulk of geopolitical influence and power among Washington's European allies—that influence and power has been underwritten by the size of their individual economies and populations, the energetic engagement of their diplomats, and the strength of their military establishments. Whether it was for the purposes of precooking a decision to be discussed within the halls of NATO, building a common position within the context of the Group of 20 leading world economies, or preparing to mount a crisis response operation, the size and strength of the Italian economy, population, and military justified Rome's seat at the table.

Relative to the other three major Western European allies, Italy has generally been seen as playing "fourth fiddle," ranking last among the four in terms of economic vitality and hard power resources and capabilities. However, Rome parlayed its relatively limited hard and soft power capabilities and capacity into significant influence and engagement from the end of the Cold War through the 2000s. For example, it was a major player in NATO's operations in the Balkans—admittedly, in part because of its geography—which came to define the alliance and its efforts to reinvent itself after the Soviet Union's demise. It also played a major role in coalition operations in Iraq in the mid-2000s, and in Afghanistan for the duration of NATO's lengthy mission to build security and stability.

All of this—Italy's ambitious pursuit of national and collective interests well beyond Europe and maintaining the capabilities and capacity necessary to do so—began to unravel in the late 2000s, as the global financial crisis struck Italy particularly hard given its massive public debt. Perhaps more accurately, the sovereign debt crisis was the catalyst for great upheaval in not simply Italy's economy but its politics as well, which subsequently had major spillover effects for the ends, ways, and means of Italian national security. For years, the Italian political system had proven largely inept in dealing with the fundamental problems facing the Italian economy. The sovereign debt crisis presented that system with an acute challenge it was utterly incapable of overcoming. Illegal migration, which peaked in late 2015 and early 2016 but which had long afflicted Italy, exacerbated the shortcomings of the government's policies after 2008–09 and became the proverbial straw that broke the camel's back. Ultimately, these twin crises led to a public backlash that resulted in a populist takeover of Italy's government. Since that takeover in 2018, the challenges facing Italy's national security ends, ways, and means have only worsened, amplifying negative trends evident over the last decade. Meanwhile, the longer-term outlook for Italy is grim, thanks to severe demographic challenges, as the population appears likely to shrink and grow older on average, further exacerbating Rome's efforts to maintain and wield both hard and soft power.

This chapter will describe and explain all of these trends, especially how Italy's response to the sovereign debt crisis unfolded and how the migration crisis played a key role in magnifying the scale of ineptitude on the part of mainstream political actors and institutions. It will begin by explaining some of the roots of Italy's economic malaise before turning to examine the role of the sovereign debt crisis in bringing about a *political* crisis within the country. The chapter will also highlight the role of the migration crisis in the middle of the 2010s in providing fuel to populist parties as well as worsening Italy's ongoing demographic challenges. The rejection of mainstream political parties and Italy's turn toward populism appears inevitable in retrospect, given the scale of Italy's challenges and the inability of the center-right or center-left to adequately craft solutions.

The chapter will then address the national security implications of the transformation that has unfolded within Italy over the last several years. In sum, it will argue that Italy has embarked on a trajectory of declining military capabilities and capacity, which has already begun to cause a diminution of Italy's strategic ambition and the receding of its strategic horizon.

Italy's embrace of populism only magnifies the scope of the collapse, as future military budgets are likely to lose ground to social safety net priorities and any available hard power is increasingly focused on homeland missions and shutting down human migration from Africa. Finally, this chapter will examine American interests in Italy's decline, arguing that increasingly diverging viewpoints vis-à-vis the security challenges Washington is most concerned with means the United States is unlikely to rely on Italy for the defense of collective interests, at least beyond the Mediterranean basin.

Italy's Economic Malaise and the Rise of the Populists

In contrast to France—where a centrist political leader beat back a populist challenge—the story of strategic realignment in Italy is one of populism's victory, or rather it is a story *capped by* populism's victory. In the March 2018 Italian national election, two fringe parties came out on top, the first time in a major European country that populists achieved such a victory. The Five Star Movement, an antiestablishment protest party founded on the internet, won roughly 31 percent of the vote, while the League, a Euroskeptic, anti-immigrant party that previously advocated secession of northern Italy, won 17 percent. After three months of political stalemate, the government that emerged in early June 2018 was truly Western Europe's first populist government.

The populist government was relatively short-lived by European standards, but not necessarily by Italian ones. In August 2019, the League backed out of its coalition with the Five Star Movement, hoping to prompt early elections. Instead, the center-left Democratic Party agreed to form a government with the Five Star Movement, forestalling a new election. Although the new government is no longer comprised entirely of populist parties, this does not imply the weakening of populist tendencies in Italian politics—it has become a powerful political force in Italy, as represented by parties both in and out of the government and by elements of both the left and the right.

Populism's rise in Italy is a result of a long-simmering failure of the political system[1] that was then made most acute by an economic or financial crisis and exacerbated further by a migrant crisis that was perceived as fundamentally challenging Italian identity. Financial crises have histori-

---

1. Liza Lanzone and Dwayne Woods, "Riding the Populist Web: Contextualizing the Five Star Movement (M5S) in Italy," *Politics and Governance* 3, no. 2 (2015): 54–64.

cally benefited the electoral outcomes of populist parties, especially those that are right of center.[2] Financial crises give rise to conditions that promote distrust, uncertainty, and dissatisfaction. From a political perspective, these feelings within the citizenry manifest themselves in a crisis of representation. That is, more and more citizens begin to perceive that the traditional political forces or parties do not understand their concerns, do not adequately represent them, and are incapable of solving their problems.[3] These perceptions are seized upon and promoted by political agitators eager to appeal to and identify with "the people" through a nonideological, personalist strategy while demonizing the "elite" establishment or some other "enemy" of the people.[4] In this way, the agitators create new cleavages in society, in an effort to forge a new political majority.

Financial crises are not unique in the sense that they are the only type of exogenous shock that can frustrate the existing political structure and result in a populist uprising. They are also not deterministic—a financial crisis does not *necessarily* lead to a populist uprising. Instead, a shock to or a crisis within the political system, including a financial crisis, can lead to the loosening of ties between citizens and extant political groupings.[5]

The agitators and the populist movements and parties they create often offer potential remedies to the crisis of representation by proffering simplistic or even contradictory solutions to what may be exceedingly complex problems. This is all done in ways that are ideologically unavailable or unseemly to the previously dominant parties of the right or left. For instance, for decades both center-right and center-left political traditions in Italy have embraced European integration, reflecting a broad-based consensus within the Italian public. During its rise to power over the last several years, the Five Star Movement conversely has *opposed* integration, called for Italy to leave the euro, and rejected the austerity measures pushed by the European Commission in response to the sovereign debt crisis.[6] Of course, as economists have pointed out, leaving the euro would

---

2. Manuel Funke and Christoph Trebesch, "Financial Crises and the Populist Right," *DICE Report* 15, no. 4 (December 2017): 6–9.

3. Jan Jagers and Stefaan Walgrave, "Populism as Political Communication Style: An Empirical Study of Political Parties' Discourse in Belgium," *European Journal of Political Research* 46, no. 3 (May 2007): 319–45.

4. Takis S. Pappas, *Populism Emergent: A Framework for Analyzing Its Contexts, Mechanics, and Outcomes*, European University Institute, January 2012.

5. Paul Taggart, "Populism and Representative Politics in Contemporary Europe," *Journal of Political Ideologies* 9, no. 3 (2004): 269–88.

6. The Northern League, now known simply as the League, and in coalition with the Five Star Movement, has also supported leaving the euro.

very likely exacerbate Italian economic challenges, reduce living standards, and make it even harder for Rome to pay off its debt and hence rejuvenate its economy.

Bringing Italy's economy back to life has been the focus of the political class for at least the last two decades. In the 1950s and '60s, Italy's economy surged thanks in large part to strong worldwide demand, which itself was predicated on Italy's cheap labor and inexpensive energy sources. Three factors combined over the subsequent three decades to eat into Italy's competitive edge.[7] First, energy costs for Italian manufacturing rose significantly, thanks in part to the oil crises of the 1970s. Second, labor costs also rose as wage negotiations became centralized across industries and labor productivity flattened. Third, there were insufficient investments made in research and development that, over time, have left the Italian economy too reliant on sectors that were sensitive to low-cost competition from Asia in particular.

On occasion during this 30-year period, the Italian government sought to strengthen competitiveness by devaluing the lira.[8] When Italy joined the Eurozone, the lira's exchange rate became fixed relative to other European currencies, and the lira was of course eventually replaced by the euro. With the disappearance of the lira and the loss of control over exchange rates went Rome's ability to devalue the currency. Unable to manipulate the value of its currency to offset rising domestic labor costs, and in the face of increasing globalization and low-wage competition, Italian growth suffered—since 1999, the Italian economy has grown an average of 0.5 percent per year.

Some attribute this inability to adapt to a reluctance on the part of traditional political parties to admit that Italy was not simply a victim of exogenous forces of globalization and to instead challenge the status quo by, for example, further loosening the labor market through decentralized wage bargaining.[9] Similar to the situation in France, Italian labor unions represent only about 30 percent of all workers, yet collective wage agree-

---

7. Renata Targetti Lenti, "Sviluppo e declino del sistema economico Italiano," *Il Politico* 76, no. 3 (2011): 93–128; and Michael Calingaert, "Italy's Choice: Reform or Stagnation," *Current History* 107, no. 707 (March 2008): 105–11.

8. Although Italy devalued its currency throughout this 30-year period, the two most prominent waves occurred during the mid-1970s and during the early 1990s.

9. Tito Boeri, "Italy's Confidence Crisis: Bad Policies from Bad Politicians," Centre for Economic Policy Research, August 17, 2011, voxeu.org/article/italys-confidence-crisis-bad-policies-bad-politicians; Paolo Manasse and Thomas Manfredi, "Wages, Productivity, and Employment in Italy: Tales from a Distorted Labour Market," Centre for Economic Policy Research, April 19, 2014, voxeu.org/article/wages-productivity-and-employment-italy.

ments cover roughly 97 percent of all workers.[10] This has meant that over time, productivity and salaries have become misaligned—in short, salaries have increased in Italy while productivity has not.

Others attribute the main cause of Italy's economic malaise to a long-term inability to invest in information and communications technology, including but not limited to the so-called Industry 4.0, referenced in chapter 3. It is further argued that the blame for this failure to embrace technological change lies mostly at the firm level, where family and crony connections—rather than merit—govern the selection and promotion of managers.[11]

Another analysis finds that the long-term lack of reforms in not just the labor market but also credit and product markets have combined to suffocate innovation, which has led to low productivity. Subsequently, wages became decoupled from both productivity and demand conditions in the marketplace. This created within Italy a "competitive gap."[12]

Still others argue that Italy's many smaller, privately owned firms lacked the capital necessary to invest in advanced technology, which would promote productivity gains.[13] Unable to pay outright for research and development, and unable to finance those costs through equity sales, privately held Italian firms found themselves at a competitive disadvantage. Other disincentives prevented adequate investment in training for Italian workers and managers, further exacerbating the problem. The result was that for many years Italy saw persistently rising unit labor costs, stagnating incomes, a widening competitiveness gap, and anemic growth, certainly relative to its Eurozone peers.[14] In hindsight, it is clear that the conditions were ripe for an exogenous, systemic shock to cause major political upheaval, prompting Italian voters to finally lose patience with mainstream parties and institutions in which they had long ago lost confidence.

---

10. Alessio Terzi, "An Italian Job: The Need for Collective Wage Bargaining Reform," Bruegel, July 6, 2016, bruegel.org/wp-content/uploads/2016/07/pc_2016_11-2.pdf

11. Francesco Lippi and Fabiano Schivardi, "Corporate Control and Executive Selection," *Quantitative Economics* 5, no. 2 (July 2014): 417–56; Bruno Pellegrino and Luigi Zingales, "Diagnosing the Italian Disease," *NBER Working Paper Series*, October 2017.

12. Paolo Manasse, "The Roots of the Italian Stagnation," Centre for Economic Policy Research, June 19, 2013, voxeu.org/article/roots-italian-stagnation

13. Matteo Bugamelli, Luigi Cannari, Francesca Lotti, and Silvia Magri, "Il gap innovativo del sistema produttivo italiano: Radici e possibili rimedi," *Banca d'Italia, Questioni di Economia e Finanza*, no. 121, April 2012, www.bancaditalia.it/pubblicazioni/qef/2012-0121/QEF_121.pdf?language_id=1

14. "Italy: Selected Issues," International Monetary Fund, IMF Country Report No. 11/176, July 2011, www.imf.org/external/pubs/ft/scr/2011/cr11176.pdf; "Italy: Selected Issues," International Monetary Fund, IMF Country Report No. 17/238, July 2017, www.imf.org/~/media/Files/Publications/CR/2017/cr17238.ashx.

Italy and the Sovereign Debt Crisis

The many factors outlined in the previous section help to explain why, when the sovereign debt crisis hit Europe, Italy was affected perhaps worse than most. Low productivity leading to low growth made Italy appear increasingly unable to repay its massive debt, especially as the costs of financing that debt rose precipitously in the late 2000s. Despite agreeing to the European Union's Stability and Growth Pact—which completely entered into force by early 1999, limits annual budget deficits to 3 percent of GDP, and limits total sovereign debt to 60 percent of GDP—Italy routinely violated its terms in the 2000s. It was able to get away with this thanks, in part, to the convergence of interest rates across the Eurozone, which was brought about through monetary union—that is, the creation of the euro in 1999. The convergence of interest rates facilitated by the euro's debut meant it was much cheaper for Italy to borrow, and as a result both government and private debt grew during the 2000s. By 2010, Italy's public (government) debt amounted to nearly 130 percent of GDP, far larger than the UK, France, or Germany, and increasingly dangerous given the size of the Italian economy and the related impact a default would have throughout the Eurozone.

As long as Italy could continue borrowing at relatively low cost—by offering, for example, a 5 or 6 percent return on its 10-year government bonds—the situation would be manageable. However, the global financial crisis that began in the United States in late 2007 prompted international investors to repatriate their funds.[15] This had a widespread impact, reflecting increased aversion to risk playing out globally, but it was particularly negative for countries that had grown increasingly reliant on external sources of debt, especially countries like Ireland but also including Italy. Just a few months after the crisis started—that is, beginning in March 2008 and continuing through January 2009—the global crisis began to have more unevenly distributed, country-specific ramifications. The bond yield for European countries began to rise (or not) in relation to perceptions regarding the weakness of that country's own financial sector. Any news of financial distress in a European country would cause bond yields to rise for that country, on the expectation of government-funded bailouts and reduced GDP there.[16]

Later in 2009, the crisis began to reduce tax revenues across several

---

15. Philip R. Lane, "The European Sovereign Debt Crisis," *Journal of Economic Perspectives* 26, no. 3 (Summer 2012): 49–68.

16. Ashoka Mody, Damiano Sandri, and Refet S. Gürkaynak, "The Eurozone Crisis: How

European countries, thereby pushing up deficit-to-GDP ratios, which further spooked investors. By late spring 2010, as Greek bond yields began to rise significantly, Athens required a bailout. Soon thereafter, Ireland faced the same bond yield phenomenon, and eventually required a bailout (November 2010) as well. Portugal followed in May 2011. It was shortly after that—in mid-2011—that the debt crisis really hit Italy. The reckoning that Italian politicians had hoped to forestall became inevitable, and the Italian government was forced to ingest some bitter medicine over the next several years.

In immediate response to the crisis, the government of Prime Minister Silvio Berlusconi instituted austerity measures designed to rein in Italy's budget deficit. This first occurred in June 2011, but bond yields still rose, to an 11-year record high of 5.77 percent.[17] Another austerity initiative was unveiled in September 2011, but it too failed to contain investor concerns. Once again, bond yields rose, this time over 7 percent, past the point at which Greece, Ireland, and Portugal had sought bailouts. As other European countries and the European Central Bank demanded additional austerity measures and sweeping economic reforms as the price for further assistance—and as Berlusconi appeared increasingly unwilling and unable to deliver them—the prime minister's coalition partners began to peel away. This prompted a promise from Berlusconi to resign in November 2011 once a new budget was passed.[18] Within hours of passing the new budget, Berlusconi submitted his resignation, ending an era in Italian politics and marking the first major political casualty of the sovereign debt crisis.[19]

The reform measures passed during Berlusconi's last months and days in office included a pledge to raise €15 billion from selling off state assets, the privatization of some local services, an increase in the retirement age from 65 to 67 by 2026, and a loosening of the power of guilds over professional accreditation. Other measures included generating over €60 billion in savings through a mix of tax increases and spending cuts.[20]

Banks and Sovereigns Came to Be Joined at the Hip," *Economic Policy* 27, no. 70 (April 2012): 199, 201–30.

17. Valentina Za, "Italy Key Bond Yield Soars to 11-yr High at Auction," *Reuters*, July 28, 2011, www.reuters.com/article/italy-bond-idUSLDE76R0UT20110728

18. Anthony Faiola, "Italy's Berlusconi Agrees to Resign," *Washington Post*, November 9, 2011, www.washingtonpost.com/world/europe/italys-berlusconi-faces-crucial-vote-amid-mounting-debt-crisis/2011/11/08/gIQAkZBWzM_story.html?utm_term=.03a608728613

19. Rachel Donadio and Elisabetta Povoledo, "Berlusconi Steps Down, and Italy Pulses with Change," *New York Times*, November 12, 2011, nyti.ms/2llPTIM; Hada Messia, "Italy Approves Austerity, Berlusconi Resigns," *CNN Online*, November 13, 2011, money.cnn.com/2011/11/12/news/economy/italy_austerity.cnnw/index.htm

20. "What Are Italy's Fresh Austerity Measures?," *Telegraph*, November 11, 2011, www.

Although these steps—including Berlusconi's resignation—were enough to forestall a catastrophic crisis in Italy and across the Eurozone, they proved insufficient to satisfy the demands of investors and EU officials who wanted to see further austerity and the demands of Italian citizens who wanted more done to stimulate the economy. Achieving both of these objectives would prove practically impossible for the Italian governments that followed in Berlusconi's footsteps, beginning first with the technocratic government of Mario Monti.

In early December 2011, just weeks after Berlusconi succeeded in shepherding the aforementioned budget deal and austerity package through the Italian parliament as his last official act, Monti introduced yet additional austerity measures: another €30 billion package comprising €13 billion in spending cuts, €12 billion in property tax increases, a new tax on luxury goods, a crackdown on tax evasion, a liberalization of business opening hours, and further cuts to local governments.[21]

In part as a result of the spending cuts and tax increases, the Italian economy slumped into its worst recession since World War II and then barely returned to growth territory in 2014, as seen in figure 9. Hundreds of thousands of companies, many of them small businesses, went out of business, and industrial output fell by 25 percent. Unsurprisingly, unemployment began to rise as well, as seen in figure 10. This problem was especially acute among younger workers, who lacked the generous job security protections of the older generation.

Throughout its 16-month tenure, the Monti government vigorously defended the necessity of the austerity measures, arguing that they ultimately kept Italy within the Eurozone and most likely saved the euro.[22] Nonetheless, the technocrat Monti clearly recognized the risks of unmitigated belt-tightening measures, including as seen through the rising unemployment rate. Early in his tenure, during a January 2012 summit with Germany's Angela Merkel, Monti warned openly that sacrifices alone would not pull Italy out of its debt problem, and that a refusal of European

---

telegraph.co.uk/finance/financialcrisis/8883485/What-are-Italys-fresh-austerity-measures. html

21. Giuseppe Fonte, "Italy PM Unveils Sweeping Austerity Package," *Reuters*, December 3, 2011, www.reuters.com/article/us-italy/italy-pm-unveils-sweeping-austerity-package-idUSTRE7B20I220111204

22. Emma Rowley, "Italy's Austerity May Have Saved the Euro, Says Mario Monti," *Telegraph*, November 17, 2012, www.telegraph.co.uk/finance/financialcrisis/9685373/Italys-austerity-may-have-saved-the-euro-says-Mario-Monti.html; "Italy's Monti Defends Austerity Measures," *Wall Street Journal*, December 11, 2012, www.wsj.com/articles/SB10001424127 8873240240045781732737951595 46

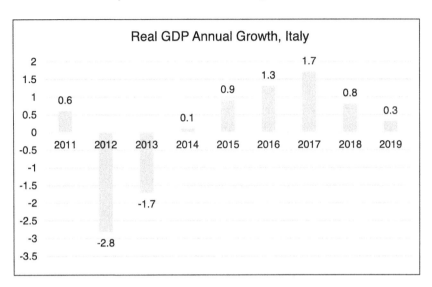

Figure 9. Data from Eurostat.

institutions to assist in stimulating the economy of Italy and other strug-gling European states—for example, by lowering interest rates—would engender "a protest against Europe," and that voters would "flee into the arms of the populists."[23]

Although Monti's actions as prime minister had gained the confidence of his peers throughout European capitals, he held less sway with Italian voters. The general election of February 2013 saw Monti soundly beaten in what many interpreted as a rejection of austerity by the electorate. After two months of political paralysis and backroom negotiation, center-left politician Enrico Letta of the Democratic Party took power, in a grand coalition including Berlusconi's party as well as centrists like Monti.[24] Letta vowed to bring back economic growth by focusing less on austerity and more on reducing unemployment.

During his first months in power, Letta struggled to bring about real reform and implement his agenda. His proposals to introduce a new elec-toral law, to eliminate conflicting powers between different levels of the government, to reduce political stalemate by removing the Senate's power to vote no confidence in the government, to lower taxes on families and

23. Nicolas Kulish, "Monti, in Berlin, Calls for Growth Policies in Europe," *New York Times*, January 11, 2012, nyti.ms/2V0JL6N

24. Rachel Donadio, "President of Italy Nominates Center-Left Official as Premier," *New York Times*, April 24, 2013, nyti.ms/17RdeQN

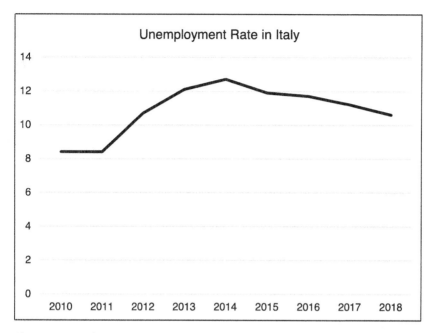

Figure 10. Data from Eurostat.

companies, and to reduce unemployment by increasing public investment struggled to gain traction thanks to coalition infighting.[25] Meanwhile, though, Italian bond yields stabilized, and the bottoming out of the recession appeared imminent, even though unemployment had worsened and Italy's debt-to-GDP ratio had not substantially improved.

Unfortunately for Letta, the electorate, the Italian business community, and his own center-left party had little patience. In February 2014, Matteo Renzi replaced Letta as both leader of the Democratic Party and of the Italian government, again in coalition with center-right parties and centrists. In many ways, Renzi picked up where Letta left off, advocating dramatic reforms, including constitutional changes that would bring about a substantial decrease in the membership and power of the Italian Senate and strengthen the power of ruling parties by making their majorities in the parliament more stable. Although Renzi's government reforms passed the parliament in various votes conducted from fall 2015 through spring 2016, when put to the test of a referendum in December 2016 they were

25. James Mackenzie, "Italian PM Letta Wins Confidence Votes, Vows Reforms," *Reuters*, December 11, 2013, www.reuters.com/article/us-italy-politics-idUSBRE9BA0D220131211

soundly rejected, 59 percent to 41. This prompted Renzi to resign, becoming the fourth prime minister in five years to do so in what amounted to a victory for populist parties—who strongly opposed the changes—and a rebuke of the ruling elite.[26]

Italy and the Migration Crisis of 2015

Just as Matteo Renzi was pushing his reform package, a migration crisis unfolded across all of Europe. Triggered by the ongoing civil war in Syria as well as armed conflict in parts of Iraq and Afghanistan—but magnified by economic migrants from sub-Saharan Africa, North Africa, and the Balkans—the human flow peaked across Europe in late 2015 and early 2016. In 2015, roughly 1 million refugees and migrants arrived in Europe, of which about 150,000 traveled by sea to Italy.[27] This came on the heels of an even larger influx of refugees and migrants into Italy in 2014, when over 170,000 arrived by sea—roughly 60 percent of all arrivals in Europe that year. The number of refugee and migrant arrivals in 2016 was even higher, at over 180,000. These years—2014, 2015, and 2016—represented dramatic increases over the 61,600 refugees and migrants who entered Italy in 2013. Many more refugees and migrants—over 119,000—arrived in Italy in 2017, but the trend since 2016 has been downward. In fact, just over 23,000 arrived in Italy in 2018 and roughly 11,000 in 2019.

The refugee and migrant crisis of the middle of the last decade acted as an accelerant to the rise of populist parties in Italy, which seized on the issue as a threat to Italian identity and security. One survey found that 59 percent of Italians believed their identity was disappearing, while only 22 percent disagreed.[28] Among other methodologies, populist parties craft identity narratives designed to characterize immigration as an invasion or out of control. Those same narratives cast migrants as economic, cultural, and security threats; as part of a largely Islamic religio-cultural threat; or simply as the "other." Finally, populist party narratives portray governing elites as out of touch and unable to control the country's borders, while

26. Stephanie Kirchgaessner, "Italian PM Matteo Renzi Resigns after Referendum Defeat," *Guardian*, December 5, 2016, www.theguardian.com/world/2016/dec/04/matteo-renzis-future-in-the-balance-amid-high-turnout-in-italy-referendum

27. UN Refugee Agency, online Italy portal, data2.unhcr.org/en/situations/mediterranean/location/5205

28. Tim Dixon et al., "Attitudes towards National Identity, Immigration and Refugees in Italy," *More in Common*, July 2018, www.thesocialchangeinitiative.org/wp-content/uploads/2018/07/Italy-EN-Final_Digital.compressed.pdf

mainstream political parties are accused of having failed to protect national interests and identity.[29]

The exploitation of the immigration crisis by populist parties came at a particularly sensitive time, given the demographic challenges facing Italy over the last decade. Like several European countries, Italy has had an aging population and a low birth rate. In 2019, for example, the growth of Italy's elderly population continued in both absolute and relative terms, while the birth rate remained anemic at 1.29 children per woman and the number of live births reached a new low point of 435,000 (142,000 fewer than a decade before and the lowest number since 1918).[30] Magnifying the challenge is the fact that Italy has not allowed in nearly enough migrants to compensate for its substantial natural population decrease. As a result, by 2080, Italy's population is projected to decrease from its current level of just over 60.4 million to 53.7 million.[31] Although the fertility rate may increase to roughly 1.59 children per woman by 2065, this number is still well below what is deemed a minimum replacement level in developed countries of 2.1 children per woman. By 2080, Italy's natural population loss will be similar to that of Germany (almost 19 million), but in terms of cumulative net migration Italy will only gain around 11.8 million immigrants, while Germany will gain almost 14.4 million in immigrant population.[32] Unless it moves to embrace immigration in the face of natural population loss, the median age in Italy will be 50.6 years by 2080, higher than the expected EU average of 46.6 years and the third oldest expected in Europe (behind Portugal and Cyprus). However, given fresh memories of the magnitude of the crisis of 2015–16 and the willingness of populists to exploit it for electoral gain, such a shift in policy seems exceptionally unlikely over the next decade.

29. Ruth Wodak, *The Politics of Fear: What Right-Wing Populist Discourses Mean* (London: SAGE Publications, 2015); Tim Dixon et al., "Attitudes towards National Identity, Immigration and Refugees in Italy," *More in Common*, July 2018, www.thesocialchangeinitiative.org/wp-content/uploads/2018/07/Italy-EN-Final_Digital.compressed.pdf; Ayhan Kaya and Ayşe Tecmen, "Europe versus Islam? Right-Wing Populist Discourse and the Construction of a Civilizational Identity," *Review of Faith & International Affairs* 17, no. 1 (February 2019): 49–64; Luca Ozzano, "Religion, Cleavages, and Right-Wing Populist Parties: The Italian Case," *Review of Faith & International Affairs* 17, no. 1 (February 2019): 65–77.

30. Istat (Italian National Institute of Statistics), "Indicatori Demografici," February 11, 2020, www.istat.it/it/files//2020/02/Indicatori-demografici_2019.pdf

31. Istat (Italian National Institute of Statistics), "The Demographic Future of the Country," April 26, 2017, www.istat.it/it/files//2017/04/Demographic-projections.pdf

32. Eurostat, "People in the EU—Population Projections," November/December 2017, ec.europa.eu/eurostat/statistics-explained/index.php?title=People_in_the_EU_-_population_projections#Population_projections

The Demise of the Italian Political Mainstream

In late 2016, even though the worst months of the immigration crisis appeared to be behind the country, the unfolding implications as well as the failure of Renzi's reform efforts prompted fears among Italy's ruling elite of a populist victory in any hastily called general election. This led Italy's president, Sergio Mattarella, to ask Foreign Minister Paolo Gentiloni to form a government following Renzi's resignation.[33] Gentiloni was from Renzi's own Democratic Party, and so he was expected to pursue the same agenda as his predecessor at the head of a broad-based, left-of-center coalition. In fact, Gentiloni did achieve some electoral reforms, including changes that would have about one-third of lawmakers elected under a first-past-the-post system and two-thirds on a proportional basis while also establishing minimum thresholds to enter parliament of 3 percent of the national vote for single parties and of 10 percent for coalitions.[34] These reforms were strongly opposed by populist parties such as the Five Star Movement, primarily because it had long disparaged coalitions in Italian politics and hence perceived the changes as being aimed at keeping populist parties out of power.

Somewhat surprisingly, the Democratic Party managed to serve out its full term, although it took three prime ministers to do so, and national elections were held as expected in the first half of 2018. In the run up to the vote, Berlusconi's center-right coalition—including the anti-immigrant League party—was expected to get the biggest share of the vote, although it would probably fall short of an overall majority. Meanwhile, the center-left coalition, led once again by Renzi and the Democratic Party, was expected to garner just a quarter of the vote, and the populist Five Star Movement was predicted to earn the most votes of any single party, at 30 percent.[35]

By early 2018, many thought the Italian economy had shown signs of sufficient improvement over the previous two years—as exemplified by GDP growth, seen in figure 2—and was certainly in better shape than during the depths of the 2011 crisis and the recession that followed. As a result, the appetite for further austerity measures or even the continuation of existing measures diminished in Italy, and especially within the ruling

33. Angela Dewan, Livia Borghese, and Milena Veselinovic, "Italy's Foreign Minister Gentiloni Appointed Prime Minister-Designate," *CNN Online*, December 11, 2016, www.cnn.com/2016/12/11/europe/italy-prime-minister-gentiloni-appointed/index.html

34. Alvise Armellini, "Italy Parliament Approves New Election Law ahead of Next Year's Vote," *Deutsche Presse-Agentur*, October 26, 2017.

35. "Italy Heads for Fresh Elections: Italian Politics," *Economist*, December 29, 2017.

Democratic Party-led coalition of left-leaning parties.[36] Nonetheless, as the election approached unemployment remained stubbornly high during Gentiloni's tenure, still above 11 percent nationally and much higher for younger workers. Moreover, Italy's debt-to-GDP ratio barely had budged at roughly 130 percent by late 2017, and the economic growth rate—while positive—was still too low to have a serious impact on unemployment.

At the same time, immigration policy became a major issue once again, just months before the election. Even though the worst of the mid-2010s refugee crisis had ebbed by 2017, as described above, Gentiloni resurrected intense emotion surrounding this topic late that year in an effort to pass a law that would have given citizenship automatically to children born in Italy to immigrants. This proposal was ultimately abandoned—after it became clear to Gentiloni that his efforts would not succeed—but it nonetheless served to motivate the political base of the right-wing parties, including the League, as well as populist parties more broadly.

As a result, and as noted earlier in this chapter, populist parties came out on top in the March 2018 election, capturing roughly 50 percent of the votes cast. The biggest winner, perhaps unsurprisingly, was the Five Star Movement and its leader Luigi Di Maio. In May 2018, the coalition government was unveiled, led by Prime Minister Giuseppe Conte, a little-known lawyer and academic with no prior government experience, Di Maio as the labor and economic development minister, and League leader Matteo Salvini as interior minister. Although the two populist parties dropped a previous proposal to pull Italy out of the Eurozone, the new government's platform included generous increases in unemployment benefits, cracking down on immigration, eliminating planned increases in sales taxes and fuel taxes, abolishing the increase in the retirement age, and eschewing austerity in favor of fiscal stimulus as a means of expanding GDP and hence reducing public debt through increased tax receipts.[37] All told, the proposals outlined in the coalition agreement amounted to €125 billion in new government spending and only €500 million in budget cuts.[38]

---

36. Giulia Segreti, "Italy Eases Austerity as Economy Picks Up," *Financial Times*, April 12, 2015; Pierangelo Isernia and Gianluca Piccolino, "Italians Are Tired of Living under Austerity: That Could Be a Big Problem for Europe." *Washington Post*, July 25, 2018, www.washingtonpost.com/news/monkey-cage/wp/2018/07/25/italians-are-tired-of-living-under-austerity-that-could-be-a-big-problem-for-europe/?noredirect=on&utm_term=.46d60ddeeb77

37. "Contratto di governo Lega-M5s: ecco il testo," *L'Espresso*, May 18, 2018, espresso.repubblica.it/palazzo/2018/05/18/news/contratto-di-governo-lega-m5s-ecco-il-testo-definitivo-1.322214

38. Jason Horowitz, "Italy's Populist Parties Agree on a Common Agenda to Govern," *New York Times*, May 18, 2018, nyti.ms/2IycQRk

European Union institutions—not to mention bond markets—reacted negatively to the Conte government's plans for aggressive stimulus efforts coupled with loosened or completely abandoned austerity measures. As a result, the new government came under pressure to take a somewhat more balanced approach, and in doing so placed the defense budget in the crosshairs. While almost all other European countries have increased defense spending since 2015, Italy is something of an outlier. In late 2018, the government announced defense cuts of roughly €450 million, largely to finance social welfare spending and tax cuts.[39] Along the same lines, the government began a reassessment of Italy's overseas commitments in places like Afghanistan, where Italy has maintained a contingent of roughly 900 troops as part of Operation Resolute Support, the NATO training mission. More broadly, the government has expressed interest in a rapprochement with Moscow that includes easing economic sanctions, which it is hoped will revive Italian exports to Russia as well as facilitate Russian cooperation on crises in Libya and Syria that have resulted in refugee flows into Italy.[40] In sum, the populism spawned by Italy's ineffective political mainstream and triggered by the unprecedented migration crisis has led to a continuation of defense budget cuts, which appear to have already affected Italy's strategic horizon and its willingness to engage beyond the Mediterranean. The next section will examine these changes in greater detail.

The Impact of Austerity on Italian National Security

Efforts in Italy to target the defense budget as a bill-payer for increased social welfare spending and tax cuts will undoubtedly have an impact on the capabilities and capacity of the Italian military over the next decade. Most of the budget cuts are likely to come in the form of delayed purchases of numerous acquisition and modernization programs, such as helicopters for the navy and army, upgrades to Tornado fighter jets flown by the air force, tactical air and missile defense systems, and the F-35 fighter jet. However, years of austerity and a stagnant Italian economy have *already* taken a heavy toll on the Italian military's capabilities and capacity. This section will describe and explain the diminution of the Italian military over the last

39. Tom Kington, "Italy Plans to Slash Half a Billion Dollars from Defense in 2019," *Defense News*, October 24, 2018, www.defensenews.com/global/europe/2018/10/24/italy-plans-to-slash-a-billion-dollars-from-defense-in-2019/

40. "What Italy's Foreign Policy Will Look Like under New Rulers," *Stratfor*, June 18, 2018, worldview.stratfor.com/article/italy-foreign-policy-under-five-star-league

decade and the concomitant shrinking of Italy's strategic horizon, as well as the challenges facing the Italian defense establishment amid the rise of populism and Rome's continuing efforts to rein in the massive public debt.

Over a decade ago, and as guided by the Italian Defense White Paper of 2002, Italy maintained a strategic horizon similar in many ways to the other medium-size powers studied in this book. Italian national security policy was focused first on the defense of Italy and, secondarily, on the security of the Euro-Atlantic area—in other words, Italy's NATO allies. Beyond these top two priorities, Rome listed "management of international crises" as its third mission area, with Italy playing the role of coalition lead or contributing member in a variety of missions across the globe.[41]

The 2002 Defense White Paper justifiably boasted of Italy's impressive implementation of military operations in this third mission area, noting that Italy was third in the world—behind the United States and the United Kingdom—when it came to overall military contributions to multinational peacekeeping, stabilization, policing, and international assistance operations.[42] These operations included support for United Nations missions in

- Western Sahara (MINURSO);
- Lebanon (UNIFIL);
- Iraq/Kuwait (UNIKOM);
- India/Pakistan (UNMO GIP);
- Kosovo (UNMIK);
- Ethiopia/Eritrea (UNMEE); and
- the Democratic Republic of Congo (UNOMC).

At the same time, Italy also participated in a variety of other international missions, including:

- the Stabilization Force (SFOR) in Bosnia-Herzegovina;
- the Temporary International Presence in the city of Hebron, Israel;
- the Kosovo Force (KFOR);
- Amber Fox in the former Yugoslav Republic of Macedonia; and
- Operation Enduring Freedom in Afghanistan.

---

41. For example, in 2005, Italy commanded four multinational military operations: in Afghanistan, Bosnia, Kosovo, and Albania, while participating in a variety of others.

42. Ministero Della Difesa, "Libro Bianco 2002," www.difesa.it/Approfondimenti/ArchivioApprofondimenti/Libro_Bianco/Pagine/Parte_II.aspx

Additionally, Italy was a major contributor to the postinvasion occupation of Iraq starting in 2003. The Italian contingent was deployed in Iraq from June of that year until November 2006 and numbered 2,600 troops at its peak. This force comprised mechanized infantry, helicopters, and Carabinieri national police, serving primarily in southern Iraq, near An Nasiriyah, as part of the British-led multinational division, later known as Multinational Division—Southeast.[43] Even after the withdrawal of major combat forces, Italy maintained nearly 100 trainers in Iraq as part of the NATO Training Mission—Iraq, including providing the mission's deputy commander. Additionally, through what the Italians call Operation Prima Parthica, Italy has maintained since October 2014 roughly 1,500 troops in Iraq, Kuwait, Bahrain, Qatar, and the United Arab Emirates performing training, advise-and-assist missions, and staff level activities within the multinational anti-ISIL coalition.[44]

An even larger deployment of Italian forces occurred from 2003–2014 in Afghanistan, as part of the International Security Assistance Force. Italian forces led the provincial reconstruction team in Herat, Afghanistan's third largest city, and commanded NATO's Regional Command West. Italian troop totals in Afghanistan peaked at about 3,800 in 2010, as part of the surge.

Throughout all of the operations and missions outlined above, it is certainly true that Italian politicians on both the right and the left sought to avoid placing Italian troops in situations or regions—for instance, in the more volatile south and east of Afghanistan—where casualties would have been more likely. In other words, Italian troops only rarely took on the riskiest missions or assignments across most of the deployments noted above. Nonetheless, Italian forces were in harm's way and Rome therefore appears to have played a major role in advancing Western interests and in promoting international security and stability over the two decades or so prior to 2008–09. For instance, in 2006 Italy maintained a total of 10,500 troops deployed abroad—a post–World War II record for Italy, which like Germany and Japan had shifted its views on extraterritorial use of its mili-

43. Stephen A. Carney, *Allied Participation in Operation Iraqi Freedom* (Washington, DC: Center for Military History, 2011), 68–69.

44. "Italy," Operation Inherent Resolve website, March 16, 2016, www.inherentresolve. mil/About-CJTF-OIR/Coalition/Coalition-Display/Article/695631/italy/; Italian Ministry of Defence, "Iraq—Prima Parthica Operation/Inherent Resolve," 2016, www.esercito.difesa. it/en/Operations/international-operations/Pagine/Iraq-Prima-Parthica-Operation.aspx; and Amanda Lapo, "Italy: Renewed Focus on Overseas Deployments," *IISS Military Balance Blog*, April 9, 2018, www.iiss.org/blogs/military-balance/2018/04/italy-renewed-focus-overseas-deployments

tary only gradually. Of course there are a variety of ways in which countries promote their own interests and those of their allies—such as through
international diplomacy or economic and humanitarian assistance—but in
terms of putting military forces on the ground to achieve security goals,
Italy was a clear leader not just among Western countries but even globally.

The sovereign debt crisis changed all of that, marking the beginning
of what would become a gradual unraveling of Italian hard power capacity and capabilities—ultimately, Italian willpower to engage internationally
would begin to flag as well. In the immediate wake of the crisis, the Italian defense establishment endured a series of budgetary, personnel, and
force structure cuts, mostly in an effort to forestall reductions in social
welfare programs. Procurement, modernization, overseas operations, and
research and development were all hit hard.[45] Training was also reduced
significantly, down 69 percent from 2006 to 2011.[46] The budget cuts are
depicted in figure 11, while the personnel and force structure cuts in every
service and across nearly every capability area are depicted in table 2. In
figure 11, there appears to be an uptick in defense spending starting in
2016, which might have represented the long hoped for bottoming out of
defense budget cuts in Italy. However, this uptick is largely accounted for
by one-time bonus payments to Italian military personnel in 2016 as well
as the Carabinieri's absorption of part of the State Forestry Corps, under a
reorganization of government services.[47] As a result, what appears to be an
increase in defense spending in reality left all the Italian military's underlying problems virtually unaltered.

At first glance, the trends evident in the Italian defense budget and the
resulting implications over the last decade were not terribly different from
the impact of debt-induced budget cutting as described in earlier chapters

45. "Italy Hit with 10 Percent Defense Cuts," *UPI*, May 28, 2010, upi.com/3292098; Tom
Kington, "Italy Delays Vehicle, Helicopter Buys," *Defense News*, July 9, 2012, rpdefense.over-
blog.com/article-italy-delays-vehicle-helicopter-buys-107954200.html; Craig Whitlock,
"NATO Allies Grapple with Shrinking Defense Budgets," *Washington Post*, January 29, 2012,
www.washingtonpost.com/world/national-security/nato-allies-grapple-with-shrinking-
defense-budgets/2012/01/20/gIQAKBg5aQ_story.html?utm_term=.60c5dd8cf3ac; Gary J.
Schmitt, "Italian Hard Power: Ambitions and Fiscal Realities," in *A Hard Look at Hard Power:
Assessing the Defense Capabilities of Key U.S. Allies and Security Partners*, ed. Gary J. Schmitt
(Carlisle, PA: U.S. Army War College Press, 2015).

46. "The Impact of the Financial Crisis on European Defence," Directorate-General for
External Policies of the Union, European Parliament, April 2011, www.europarl.europa.eu/
document/activities/cont/201106/20110623ATT22406/20110623ATT22406EN.pdf

47. Giovanni Martinelli, "Bilancio della difesa 2016: Quando le apparenze Ingannano,"
Analisi Difesa, no. 172, February 2016, www.analisidifesa.it/wp-content/uploads/2016/02/
bil2016.pdf; Giovanni Martinelli, "Il bilancio della Difesa," *Analisi Difesa*, no. 184, February
2017, www.analisidifesa.it/wp-content/uploads/2017/02/bildif17.pdf

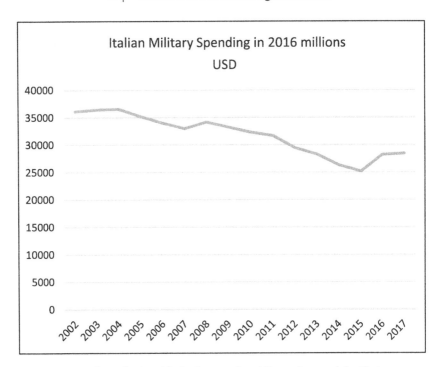

Figure 11. Data from the Stockholm International Peace Research Institute.

on the United Kingdom and France. However, because Italy was already spending less per capita on defense than its European peers and due to the *degree* of belt-tightening necessary to forestall a debt-induced crash of the Italian economy, the cuts resulted in especially dramatic changes. As a result, according to one observer, the Italian army today "cannot be considered in the first tier of European land forces."[48] Another notes that the heavy maneuver warfare capabilities of the Italian military have completely atrophied.[49] Relatively less draconian cuts to the navy and air force have been largely based on the desire to maintain the ability to project power across the Mediterranean in order to manage the refugee crisis of the last decade.

The ongoing drawdown in funding, personnel, equipment, and infrastructure was ultimately, and perhaps inevitably, reflected in a strategic

---

48. Interview with an American civilian employee of U.S. Army Europe with extensive experience in military-to-military programs across Europe, November 13, 2018.

49. Interview with a U.S. field-grade officer based in Washington who works on U.S.-Italy military-to-military relations, March 4, 2019.

retrenchment as well. This was formally enunciated in Italy's 2015 defense white paper, the first such strategic defense document since 2002. The 2015 version cast itself as an extension of its predecessor, but in reality the new defense strategy took a noticeably different approach to Italy's security horizon. While both documents placed emphasis on the Italian homeland and the Euro-Atlantic region as Rome's top priorities, the 2015 white paper indicated that Italy would refocus its international engagement more clearly on its own neighborhood.[50] For example, with regard to Italy's immediate vicinity, the 2015 white paper noted that contemporary security challenges "make the stability of the Euro-Mediterranean region of *vital national interest.*"[51] In contrast, the 2002 white paper casts the Mediterranean region slightly differently—as having "a higher strategic value."[52]

TABLE 2. Italian Military Personnel and Equipment

	2009	2019
Active duty army	108,300	99,950
Active duty navy	34,000	30,000
Active duty air force	42,935	41,100
Mechanized and rapid reaction brigades	14	9
Mountain infantry brigades	2.5	2
rtillery brigades	1	1
ir defense brigades	1	0.75
Engineer brigades	1	1
Aviation brigades	1	1
Main battle tanks	320	200
Infantry fighting vehicles	254	428
Armored personnel carriers, tracked	1,752	361
Armored personnel carriers, wheeled	617	428
Artillery	931	1,018
Army attack helicopters	60	36
Army support helicopters	21	14
Army utility helicopters	148	143
Submarines	6	8
Surface combatants	26	18
Air force combat aircraft	245	211
Air force UAVs	6	14

50. Daniel Keohane, "The Defense Policies of Italy and Poland: A Comparison," Center for Security Studies, ETH Zurich, no. 219, December 2017; Andrea Gilli, Alessandro R Ungaro, and Alessandro Marrone, "The Italian White Paper for International Security and Defence," *RUSI Journal* 160, no. 6 (2015): 34–41.

51. Italian Ministry of Defence, "White Paper for International Security and Defence," July 2015, 27, www.difesa.it/Primo_Piano/Documents/2015/07_Luglio/White%20book.pdf. Emphasis added.

52. Italian Ministry of Defence, "Libro Bianco 2002," 2002, www.difesa.it/Content/librobianco2002/Pagine/default.aspx. In the original, "Il Mediterraneo, con i suoi forti squilibri

In terms of identifying threats, there was a clear shift from the 2002 white paper, which focused more on weapons of mass destruction, to the 2015 white paper, which emphasized resource scarcity, terrorism, cyber-attacks, and crime.[53] Moreover, with regard to engagements and military missions outside the Mediterranean littoral, the 2015 white paper noted that Italian military activity beyond the Euro-Mediterranean region would only occur "according to [Italian] resources."[54] This reflects Italy's desire to maintain its multilateral institutional commitments yet limit those same commitments beyond the Mediterranean.[55] Finally, the 2015 white paper also called for still more cuts to capability and capacity, among them additional personnel reductions of 40,000 by January 2025, resulting in an end strength of 150,000 across all services. Reducing the geographic scope for military action as well as the capacity to conduct the same was somewhat paradoxical, given the fact that the 2015 white paper was far more explicit—relative to the 2002 white paper and an even earlier 1985 white paper—in its treatment of hard power as not merely legitimate but also highly useful in achieving national security interests.

Given the shift in emphasis evident in the 2015 white paper, there has been a concomitant and progressive reduction of Italian military personnel deployed beyond the Mediterranean and specifically in Afghanistan, Iraq, and Kuwait that continues to unfold today. Most broadly, from a high point of roughly 10,000 troops deployed overseas in 2006, Italy had just over 4,600 troops deployed overseas in 2019.[56] Most recently, Italy reduced its contribution to NATO's Resolute Support mission in Afghanistan from 1,037 to roughly 800 personnel, and it is possible Rome may draw down all of its forces sooner rather than later, especially if the United States also begins to withdraw.[57] Meanwhile, Italy's Operation Prima Parthica, which

---

economici tra nord e sud, i suoi molteplici conflitti e tensioni, la sua centralità come via di comunicazione economica, civile e militare, ha assunto una valenza strategica sempre più alta."

53. Fabrizio Coticchia, Andrea Locatelli, and Francesco N. Moro, "Renew or Reload? Continuity and Change in Italian Defence Policy," EUI Working Paper RSCAS 2016/01, Robert Schuman Centre for Advanced Studies, January 2016, 8.

54. Italian Ministry of Defence, "White Paper for International Security and Defence," July 2015, 31, www.difesa.it/Primo_Piano/Documents/2015/07_Luglio/White%20book.pdf

55. Ester Sabatino, "The Innovations of the Italian White Paper: Defence Policy Reform," Istituto Affari Internazionali, Working Paper 17/34, December 2017, www.iai.it/sites/default/files/iaiwp1734.pdf; and interview with a field-grade U.S. officer based in Europe with extensive knowledge of U.S.-Italian military-to-military ties, March 20, 2019.

56. *The Military Balance* (London: International Institute for Strategic Studies, 2019), 123.

57. Interview with a field-grade U.S. officer based in Europe with extensive knowledge of U.S.-Italian military-to-military ties, March 20, 2019; Interview with a field-grade Italian military officer based in Rome, March 3, 2019; "Italian Troops to Remain in Afghani-

is tied to NATO's training mission in Iraq and Kuwait, will see the withdrawal of 700 troops and the reconfiguration of its air component.

Together, the diminished capability and capacity of Italy's military and the receding security horizon of Italian grand strategy mean that Rome is focusing what hard power resources *are* available on North Africa and the Sahel, while also trying to maintain commitments to far less risky observer missions in places like Lebanon and Kosovo. This multiyear trend has been further reinforced by the imperatives of Italy's vibrant populist movement.[58] For instance, recent efforts to expand or establish military missions in countries such as Niger, Mali, and Mauritania have been driven almost entirely by the desire to wield military power as a tool in ameliorating the conditions that spur refugee migration northward, toward the Mediterranean and into Italy.[59]

With regard to this more limited geographic scope of where Italy *is* willing to employ hard power, the 2015 white paper noted rather explicitly that Italy would be capable of and willing to lead full-spectrum operations. However, even the more limited concept of a "regional full spectrum" military power[60] appears unrealizable for at least four reasons. First, austerity-induced cuts have already resulted in the atrophying of Italian maneuver warfare capabilities, and Italy will struggle to get back into this business given popular views of the threats—namely, terrorism and migration—facing the country.[61] Tanks, artillery, and armored personnel carriers are appropriate tools to use against other state military forces, and currently Italian citizens and politicians do not perceive significant threats from other states.

Second, it seems clear that budgetary trends point toward still additional cuts in military budgets and personnel, primarily to safeguard the social safety net.[62] The 2019 defense budget of €21.4 billion was nomi-

---

stan Pending Consultation with Allies—Official," *Kuwait News Agency*, February 22, 2019, www.kuna.net.kw/ArticlePrintPage.aspx?id=2779078&language=ar#; "Gli italiani lasceranno l'Afghanistan dopo la pace tra Trump e i talebani," *Analisi Difesa*, January 29, 2019, www.analisidifesa.it/2019/01/gli-italiani-lasceranno-lafghanistan-dopo-la-pace-tra-trump-e-i-talebani/

58. Interview with a field-grade U.S. officer based in Europe with extensive knowledge of U.S.-Italian military-to-military ties, March 20, 2019.

59. Interview with a field-grade Italian military officer based in Rome, March 3, 2019.

60. Pietro Batacchi, "Il Libro Bianco 2015," *Rivista Italiana Difesa*, as cited in Andrea Gilli, Alessandro R Ungaro, and Alessandro Marrone, "The Italian White Paper for International Security and Defence," *RUSI Journal* 160, no. 6 (2015): 34–41.

61. Interview with a field-grade U.S. officer based in Washington who works on U.S.-Italy military-to-military relations, March 4, 2019.

62. "Italy Minister Says Defence Spending Set to Fall Further Next Year," *Reuters*, July 26,

nally higher than the 2018 budget of €20.9 billion, but additional funding was entirely due to a significant increase in personnel costs that was partially offset by a reduction in procurement.[63] In fact, procurement funding in 2019 was cut by roughly 19 percent from 2018 level. Moreover, the demands of responding to the COVID-19 pandemic, which hit Italy hard, will place even greater pressure on the Italian defense budget in the coming years. This does not bode well for Italian military capabilities and its efforts to remain full spectrum.

Third, Italy's capabilities in cyber and related information operations are limited at best. Although Italy promulgated a National Strategic Framework for Cyberspace Security[64] and an accompanying implementation plan in December 2013, will make its Joint Headquarters for Cyber Operations[65] fully operational in 2019, and regularly participates in NATO and EU cyber exercises,[66] resourcing remains limited. A recent proposal to carve out a special fund—valued at €3 million—for cyber operations and equipment over the period 2019–21 pales in comparison to a French effort to do the same from 2019 to 2025 valued at €1.6 *billion*. Additionally, senior Italian defense officials have suggested that increased funding for cyber may only come at the expense of Italy's conventional forces.[67]

Finally, the government appears increasingly devoted to the concept of a "dual-use" military—one that is capable of both traditional military operations and of providing substantial support to civilian authorities in the event of natural disasters, in response to terrorist attacks, to provide day-to-day security, or even for garbage collection.[68] The ongoing Operazione Strade Sicure is a good example of this—over 7,000 Italian troops are deployed today on the streets of Italy, protecting tourist sites and other

2018, uk.reuters.com/article/uk-italy-nato-spending/italy-minister-says-defence-spending-set-to-fall-further-next-year-idUKKBN1KG20X

63. Giovanni Martinelli, "Il Bilancio Difesa 2019," *Analisi Difesa*, February 25, 2019, www.analisidifesa.it/2019/02/il-bilancio-difesa-2019/

64. Presidency of the Council of Ministers, "National Strategic Framework for Cyberspace Security," December 2013, www.sicurezzanazionale.gov.it/sisr.nsf/wp-content/uploads/2014/02/italian-national-strategic-framework-for-cyberspace-security.pdf

65. "Italy and Cyber Defense," *SLDinfo.com*, May 8, 2018, sldinfo.com/2018/05/italy-and-cyber-defense/

66. Melissa Hathaway et al., "Italy: Cyber Readiness at a Glance," Potomac Institute for Policy Studies, November 2016, www.potomacinstitute.org/images/CRI/PIPS_CRI_Italy.pdf

67. Francesco Bussoletti, "L'Italia in futuro potrebbe avere una Forza Armata cyber," *Difesa & Sicurezza*, September 27, 2018, www.difesaesicurezza.com/cyber/litalia-in-futuro-potrebbe-avere-una-forza-armata-cyber/

68. "Italy Army Clearing Naples Rubbish," *BBC*, May 9, 2011, www.bbc.com/news/world-europe-13330152

popular locations across the country, similar to France's *Operation Senti-nelle*.[69] This dual use trend is having significantly negative implications for Italian military readiness, just as it is in France.[70] Perhaps more importantly, in combination with the gradual drawdown in Italian missions abroad and the loss of both capacity and capability, it is sapping morale in a military force that already struggles to attract and retain young recruits—in some units, the average age of the soldiers (not the typically older officers) is 38. Given Italy's demographic challenges outlined earlier—specifically, its aging population, declining birthrate, and antipathy toward migrants—the long-term outlook for the Italian military as a full-spectrum force with sufficient capacity to matter operationally is not positive.

Italian air and naval forces may fare somewhat better in the coming years, relative to the ground forces. This is largely because the air and naval services rely on procurement programs and related industries that are important sources of employment within Italy, and because they are capable of playing a more direct role in detecting, monitoring, and interdicting migrant flows and human trafficking. However, Italy's ability to retain and broaden the capabilities, capacity, and willpower to engage in high-end military conflict and competition, stability operations, asymmetric operations, or unconventional operations such as cyber even within the Mediterranean basin is highly suspect, given Italy's debt-driven defense budget reductions over the last several years, the impact of the COVID-19 pandemic on Italy's fiscal balance, and strong prospects for further defense cuts in the coming years.[71] This is especially so given the fact that Italian government debt remains very high, second only to Greece in the Euro-zone.[72] On top of all of this, Italy's embrace of political populism will likely result in an even greater application of the brakes when it comes to overseas commitments and international engagements beyond the country's immediate neighborhood.[73]

---

69. Italian Ministry of Defence, "Operation Strade Sicure (Safe Streets)," www.difesa.it/ EN/Operations/NationalOperation/Pagine/OperationStradeSicure.aspx

70. Interview with a field-grade U.S. officer based in Europe with extensive knowledge of U.S.-Italian military-to-military ties, March 20, 2019.

71. "What Italy's Foreign Policy Will Look Like under New Rulers," *Stratfor*, June 18, 2018, worldview.stratfor.com/article/italy-foreign-policy-under-five-star-league; "Italy: Rome Trains Its Sights on Defense Spending Cuts," *Stratfor*, October 4, 2018, worldview. stratfor.com/article/italy-rome-trains-its-sights-defense-spending-cuts

72. Silvia Sciorilli Borrelli, "Salvini Strikes Conciliatory Tone on Migration, Italy's Budget," *Politico*, September 8, 2018, www.politico.eu/article/matteo-salvini-strikes-conciliatory-tone-on-migration-italys-budget/

73. For example, see "Elisabetta Trenta: 'Entro un anno le truppe italiane via dall'Afghanistan,' Moavero risponde: 'Non ne ha parlato con me'," *Huffington Post*, Janu-

Washington's Approach to an Ally in Decline

The strategic transformation that Italy has undergone and the probable future trends outlined above cast serious doubt on the likelihood of Rome being able to play a major role in security beyond the Mediterranean or in unconventional military realms such as cyber or space operations. From Washington's perspective, this is problematic given the strong role that Italy has played internationally over the last quarter century. In contrast to Germany, which struggled to embrace the use of hard power abroad since the end of the Cold War, Italy had shown itself somewhat more able and largely willing to employ its military in direct support of both collective and national interests. As noted at the beginning of this chapter, Washington had long perceived Italy as part of the "big four" allies of Western Europe, with the economic heft, military power, and political consensus—despite its many post–World War II governments—necessary to wield influence and project power far beyond Europe. Italy increasingly does not appear to belong in such a grouping.

At the same time, Italy is generally ambivalent—at least in a security context—toward Washington's main challenges, namely the short-term, acute threat from Russia and the much longer, systemic rivalry with China. In fact, it may be more accurate to say that while France and to some degree Germany are less concerned with the challenges from Russia and China, Italy actively *disagrees* with Washington's perspective. Italian political elites have in recent years evinced a remarkably accommodating attitude toward both Russia and China, largely for trade reasons and specifically in the hopes of winning investment from these two countries in Italy.[74] For example, Italian leaders have pushed for the elimination of sanctions on Russia over its invasion of Ukraine and have characterized Russia not as a threat but rather an economic partner.[75] To some degree, such attitudes toward Russia reflect Italian public opinion, of which 53 percent would prefer a

---

ary 29, 2019, www.huffingtonpost.it/2019/01/28/ministero-della-difesa-entro-un-anno-il-contingente-italiano-si-ritirera-dallafghanistan_a_23654932/

74. John Follain and Rosalind Mathieson, "Italy Pivots to China in Blow to EU Efforts to Keep Its Distance," *Bloomberg*, October 4, 2018, www.bloomberg.com/news/articles/2018-10-04/italy-pivots-to-china-in-blow-to-eu-efforts-to-keep-its-distance; Tom Kington, "Italy's New Defense Minister Commits to F-35, Butts Heads with France," *Defense News*, June 29, 2018, www.defensenews.com/global/europe/2018/06/29/italys-new-defense-minister-commits-to-f-35-butts-heads-with-france/

75. "Italian Leader Urges End to EU Sanctions on Russia during Moscow Visit," *Radio Free Europe/Radio Liberty*, October 25, 2018, www.rferl.org/a/italian-prime-minister-conte-urges-end-eu-sanctions-russia-moscow-visit-putin/29562701.html; Kington, "Italy's New Defense Minister Commits to F-35.".

reduction or elimination of sanctions, while only 38 percent want sanctions to be maintained and just 9 percent want them to be strengthened.[76]

With regard to China, despite reported interagency disagreements,[77] Italy has been a leader within Western Europe in its openness to Chinese investments, including in critical infrastructure. From 2000 to 2015, Italy was Europe's second-largest recipient of Chinese investment, behind only the United Kingdom.[78] More recently, government leaders in Italy have actively and openly cultivated Chinese investment across Italy, including in Beijing's controversial Belt and Road Initiative and as part of Beijing's "Made in China 2025" industrial dominance policy.[79] The Italian government has established a China Task Force to promote cooperation in the areas of trade, finance, investment, research and development, and cooperation in third countries, ensuring that Italy can position itself as a "privileged partner" within Europe.[80] For its part, Beijing has carefully used its economic investments to cultivate and maximize political impact and influence.[81]

Washington has expressed concern over the political and diplomatic costs that increased and especially close cooperation between Rome and Beijing might ultimately impose on Italy, not to mention the national security risks that it may entail. Nonetheless, Rome appears likely to push ahead with a deepening of its relationship with—and growing dependence upon—China. Arguably, Italian attitudes toward both China and Russia have long differed somewhat from those of Washington, but it seems clear now that Rome is not prepared to play a significant role in the strategic greater power competition that has been unfolding.

---

76. "Gli italiani e la politica estera," Istituto Affari Internazionali, October 2017, 23–24, www.iai.it/sites/default/files/laps-iai_2017.pdf

77. Paul Taylor, "Salvini's Sophia Soapbox: Why Rome May Pull the Plug on the EU's Military Mission in the Mediterranean," *Politico*, March 12, 2019, www.politico.eu/article/italy-matteo-salvini-sophia-soapbox/

78. Thilo Hanemann and Mikko Huotari, "A New Record Year for Chinese Outbound Investment in Europe," Mercator Institute for China Studies, February 2016, 7, www.merics.org/sites/default/files/2018-07/COFDI_2016_web.pdf

79. Jason Horowitz and Jack Ewing, "Italy May Split with Allies and Open Its Ports to China's Building Push," *New York Times*, March 6, 2019, nyti.ms/2TEJMjW; Lucrezia Poggetti, "Italy Charts Risky Course with China-Friendly Policy," Mercator Institute for China Studies, October 11, 2018, www.merics.org/en/blog/italy-charts-risky-course-china-friendly-policy

80. Ministry of Economic Development, "MISE: Costituita la Task Force Cina," August 20, 2018, www.mise.gov.it/index.php/it/194-comunicati-stampa/2038553-il-mise-lancia-la-task-force-cina

81. James Reilly, "China's Economic Statecraft in Europe," *Asia Europe Journal* 15 (2017): 173–85.

For these reasons, Washington will likely need to place less emphasis on its relationship with Italy as a partner in defending and promoting collective as well as U.S. interests. It is possible that American and Italian interests in places like North Africa and the Sahel may continue to coincide, and so further cooperation and coordination may be productive in those regions. Since the limited Italian operations in these geographic areas are accomplished without much reliance on the United States, though, most of the cooperation and coordination is likely to occur at the political and diplomatic levels. This is just as well, given diminished Italian military capabilities and what may eventually become reduced U.S. concern over maintaining interoperability with Italian military forces. In any case, it seems likely that Washington may no longer view Italy as a member of the so-called big four, at least when it comes to geopolitical and security affairs. Instead, it is increasingly possible that some other country may supplant Italy's role as "fourth fiddle," a country with a much faster growing economy necessary to support modernization, readiness, and capacity, a country with a demonstrated commitment to hard power, and a country with an increasingly close relationship with Washington—namely, Poland.

SIX

Poland as Europe's Economic
(and Military) Tiger?

In contrast to Italy, and in fact to almost all of the rest of European NATO, Poland has maintained and even increased its defense spending through-out the last decade. The sovereign debt crisis had relatively little impact on the Polish economy, helping Warsaw to avoid painful decisions about spending priorities and fiscal belt-tightening. The decade of economic growth—which was essentially unique across Europe—as well as a legal commitment to maintain defense spending, has allowed Poland to imple-ment a major military modernization and expansion program. This effort was given significant impetus following Russia's invasion of Ukraine in 2014, spurring the Poles to redouble their efforts to further profession-alize their military, get rid of Soviet-era legacy equipment, and pursue self-sufficiency in national defense. By some estimates, Poland already has one of the most powerful militaries in the world.[1] Nonetheless, it is in the midst of building a larger, more technologically advanced, and more lethal military force, one that is unquestionably oriented toward territo-rial defense against Russia.

Poland's ability to pursue advanced modernization and acquisition pro-grams, to expand and maintain a military manpower pipeline necessary to operate that equipment, and to increase its military readiness through

1. "2019 Military Strength Ranking," *GlobalFirepower.com*, 2019, www.globalfirepower.com/countries-listing.asp; and, Jeremy Bender, "Ranked: The World's 20 Strongest Mili-taries," *Business Insider*, April 21, 2016, www.businessinsider.com/these-are-the-worlds-20-strongest-militaries-ranked-2016-4.

large-scale training efforts requires a consistent funding stream over many years. Warsaw has facilitated this by passing into law a requirement to spend the equivalent of a fixed percentage of its GDP on defense, and by passing multiyear defense spending laws.

However, this commitment to defense spending is further predicated on two key variables. The first is a growing economy. Although the Polish economy has recently been among the fastest growing in Europe, that trajectory may not be sustainable over the next decade. The second variable is demography, and here too there are serious questions about what Poland's population will look like in the years to come.

Even if Poland's economy remains strong, and essentially underwrites the ongoing transformation of Polish hard power, and even if Poland's demographic situation improves, there remains the question of whether Warsaw will be interested in defending common interests beyond northeastern Europe. Today, Poland is focused for obvious reasons on the Russian threat, but of course Western interests of varying degrees of importance are threatened elsewhere in Europe, across the Middle East, in Africa, in the Indian Ocean, and East Asia. Leaving aside questions of its capability and capacity, it is unclear whether Warsaw will have the willpower necessary to stand with the United States and other allies in defending collective interests beyond northeastern Europe.

This chapter will begin by assessing whether and how Poland has become Europe's economic tiger. It will especially focus on how Poland avoided the worst of the sovereign debt crisis, enabling it to become one of the fastest growing economies in Europe in recent years. The following section will address Poland's efforts to turn its economic strength into hard power. Among other topics, this section will explain the primary driver behind Poland's hard power pursuits—namely, the threat from Russia, and especially its increasing militarization of Kaliningrad. This section will also outline how Poland is responding to that threat in terms of a renewed focus on territorial defense in its military acquisitions and defense planning. Next, this chapter will assess whether Poland's trajectory of increased defense investments is sustainable over time. Two key variables are examined in this section—Poland's economic outlook and its demographic development—as well as the implications for Poland's national security should likely trends hold true. Finally, the chapter ends with a section devoted to how Washington might perceive and react to a future Poland that is something less than the "tiger" it appears to be today.

Europe's Economic Tiger?

Poland's growth rate in 2019 was, by the standards of the European Union and the developed world, astounding. At 4.1 percent growth over 2018 in real terms, Poland had the sixth-highest GDP growth rate in Europe—behind Ireland (5.5), Hungary (4.9), Malta (4.4), Estonia (4.3), and Serbia (4.2). Most of this was driven by domestic demand, especially strong private consumption, public investment, and a sizeable build-up of business inventories.[2] The year prior, Poland's GDP growth rate was even more impressive at 5.3 percent, ranking third highest in Europe. These strong economic growth rates are not particularly novel. For much of the last decade, Poland has been among the strongest economies in Europe, and it can boast of having one of the longest stretches of continuous economic expansion in the world, ongoing for over 25 years. During the height of the Great Recession, in 2009, Poland was one of only three European countries *not* in recession.[3] Poland's growth rate certainly fell during the Great Recession, but even at its low point, the Polish economy managed to maintain a real GDP growth rate of 2.8 percent in 2009 (see figure 12).

How did Poland achieve this? Several factors explain Poland's success. First, Poland had a strong base from which to manage the challenges associated with the Great Recession. During the 1990s, Poland implemented an array of transformative reforms that fundamentally changed the structure of the economy and made Poland an attractive destination for foreign investment.[4] These reforms were known as "shock therapy" and involved the rapid withdrawal of the state from the economy—most notably, price controls were removed, state subsidies were slashed, and the Polish currency was made convertible with other global currencies. Although highly disruptive in the short run, shock therapy in Poland had the effect of keeping hyperinflation at bay while building a market economy, and in Poland's case this led to rapid transition from a command economy to market capi-

---

2. European Commission, "European Economic Forecast," Institutional Paper 096, February 2019, 24.

3. Albania and Kosovo were the others. Eurostat, "Real GDP Growth Rate—Volume," data as of March 21, 2019, ec.europa.eu/eurostat/tgm/table.do?tab=table&init=1&plugin=1&language=en&pcode=tec00115

4. "Republic of Poland: 2018 Article IV Consultation," International Monetary Fund, Country Report No. 19/37, February 2019, 4, www.imf.org/~/media/Files/Publications/CR/2019/cr1937.ashx

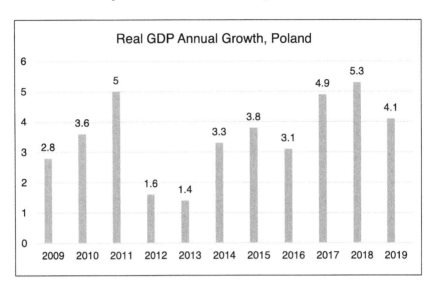

Figure 12. Data from Eurostat.

talism.[5] Additionally, in 1999 Poland's government enacted a debt ceiling rule that was later added to its constitution—under its terms, Poland's government debt cannot exceed 60 percent of its GDP.[6] These and other reforms of the 1990s led to impressive economic performance through most of the 2000s, ultimately allowing Poland to catch up to the more advanced economies of Western Europe in terms of GDP per capita and making the Polish economy more resilient to the Great Recession challenges faced at the end of that decade.[7]

Second, Poland has received substantial inflows of EU funds. From when it joined the EU in 2004 through 2006, Poland received €22.5 billion in EU funding.[8] More than half the projects funded were in basic infrastructure, including the construction or modernization of over 3,700

5. Thomas W. Hall and John E. Elliott, "Poland and Russia One Decade after Shock Therapy," *Journal of Economic Issues* 33, no. 2 (1999): 305–14; Matthew Kaminski, "The Weekend Interview with Leszek Balcerowicz: The Anti-Bernanke," *Wall Street Journal*, December 15, 2012, A15.

6. Victor Lledó, et al., *Fiscal Rules at a Glance*, International Monetary Fund, March 2017, 62, www.imf.org/external/datamapper/fiscalrules/Fiscal%20Rules%20at%20a%20 Glance%20-%20Background%20Paper.pdf

7. OECD, "OECD Economic Surveys: Poland 2014," OECD Publishing, dx.doi. org/10.1787/eco_surveys-pol-2014-en

8. European Commission, "European Cohesion Policy in Poland," ec.europa.eu/regional_ policy/sources/docgener/informat/country2009/pl_en.pdf

kilometers of road and over 200 kilometers of highway. EU funding during this period also paid to upgrade 350 kilometers of railroad tracks. At the same time, the EU also funded over 15,000 projects in support of small and medium-sized enterprises, such as microloans extended to more than 8,800 companies and credit guarantees issued to nearly 7,500 companies. For the EU budget period 2007–13, Poland received just over €67 billion, making it the largest recipient by far of EU funding—in comparison, Spain was a distant second during this same time period, receiving about €36 billion.[9] For the budget period 2014–20, Poland again received the largest amount of EU funding at just over €86 billion.[10] The biggest share—roughly €28 billion—of the 2014–20 funding was dedicated to building transportation and energy infrastructures. Approximately €14 billion promoted the competitiveness of small and medium-sized enterprises, while €11.6 billion was spent on developing Poland's low-carbon economy. These tens of billions of dollars have provided a significant expansionary impulse to the Polish economy at a time when most other governments in Europe were forced to engage in relentless belt-tightening and austerity measures.

Third, the government depreciated the Polish currency—the zloty—substantially against the euro. Over the course of 2008, the zloty fell by about 35 percent relative to the euro, recovering only very gradually starting in February 2009 when the government and central bank in Warsaw announced they would begin to take steps to prevent further devaluation.[11] In any case, the fall of the zloty made Polish exports far more competitive abroad while reinforcing preexisting domestic demand trends for Polish-produced goods inside Poland, as imports became more expensive.[12]

Fourth, the structure of Poland's economy—given its stage of development and transition from decades of communist mismanagement—helped to foster a kind of immunity to the contagion that unfolded during the

---

9. Data taken from European Commission webpage, "European Structural and Investment Funds—Data," cohesiondata.ec.europa.eu/2007-2013/2007-2013-EU-payments-by-Member-State-with-filter-/9gce-zjcr, and European Commission, "European Cohesion Policy in Spain," ec.europa.eu/regional_policy/sources/docgener/informat/country2009/es_en.pdf

10. European Commission, "European Structural and Investment Funds—Poland," April 2016.

11. OECD, "OECD Economic Surveys: Poland 2010," OECD Publishing, 27–8, 10.1787/eco_surveys-pol-2010-en; Matthew O'Brien, "The Big Secret of Poland's Economic Success—and What It Means for Us," *Atlantic*, December 17, 2012, www.theatlantic.com/business/archive/2012/12/the-big-secret-of-polands-economic-success-and-what-it-means-for-us/266347/

12. OECD, "OECD Economic Surveys: Poland 2010," OECD Publishing, 26, 10.1787/eco_surveys-pol-2010-en.

sovereign debt crisis.[13] For instance, Poland's economy during the 2000s was not very dependent on business and consumer credit. At the same time, there was an absence in Poland of high-risk financial instruments in the banking sector, such as securities based on U.S. subprime mortgages. Moreover, the Polish economy was not nearly as reliant on export markets and instead was driven largely by domestic demand. All of these things gave Poland an additional layer of insulation against the global crisis.

Finally, just before the worst of the Great Recession hit, the Polish government implemented key changes to its banking regulatory structure, improving what was generally regarded as an effective system. In 2008, the new Polish Financial Supervision Commission was created, and the transition to this new banking supervisory architecture was relatively smooth. In addition to effectively overseeing existing regulations, the Financial Supervision Commission went even further to implement a variety of additional proactive measures to preserve financial sector stability during the sovereign debt crisis, including tightening capital requirements for banks.[14] These steps strengthened the resiliency of the Polish banking sector as the debt crisis and subsequent recession unfolded.

For all of these reasons, the Polish government weathered the sovereign debt crisis and the Great Recession far better than nearly all other European countries. This meant Poland was able to essentially avoid the difficult trade-off faced by most of its neighbors between adequately resourcing national security requirements on the one hand and protecting the social safety net of its citizens on the other. As the next section of this chapter makes clear, this enabled Poland to begin an unprecedented buildup of both its defense capabilities and its defense capacity.

Transforming Economic Strength into Hard Power

Over the last five to eight years, Poland has leveraged its hard-won economic strength and its robust economy to build up its defense capacity and capabilities. Its efforts in this regard have been reinforced by two fac-

---

13. Maria Drozdowicz-Bieć, "Reasons Why Poland Avoided the 2007–2009 Recession," Research Institute for Economic Development, Warsaw School of Economics, 2011, ssl-kolegia.sgh.waw.pl/pl/KAE/struktura/IRG/publikacje/Documents/pim86_2.pdf

14. International Monetary Fund, "Republic of Poland: Detailed Assessment of Observance of Basel Core Principles for Effective Banking Supervision," IMF Country Report No. 12/232, August 2012, www.imf.org/external/pubs/ft/scr/2012/cr12232.pdf; and OECD, "OECD Economic Surveys: Poland 2012," OECD Publishing, 11, dx.doi.org/10.1787/eco_surveys-pol-2012-en

tors. First, Warsaw has benefited from the fact that demanding military operations in Iraq and Afghanistan have largely ended, freeing up defense budget resources that previously were consumed by current operations. Second, Poland has a legal requirement to spend at least the equivalent of a fixed percentage of its GDP on defense. In May 2001, Poland adopted the "Act on the Restructuring, Technical Modernization, and the Financing of the Armed Forces of the Polish Republic," which initially established the minimum defense spending level as equivalent to 1.95 percent of GDP. Modifications to that law in 2017 pushed the percentage up to 2 percent for 2018 and 2019, and 2.1 percent for 2020—by 2030, the level will be even higher, at 2.5 percent.[15]

The legal requirement to spend money on defense, the end of costly far-flung operations, and the robust Polish economy have led to a dramatic effort to increase Polish military capabilities and capacity, most of which has been aimed at defending the country from Russia. Before examining the details of *how* Poland has been building up its defense and deterrence against Russia and *what* it has been investing in, it makes sense to consider *why* Warsaw has chosen this path.

For obvious historical reasons, most Poles perceive an existential threat emanating from Russia. This is not just the result of Poland's subjugation at the hands of Moscow during the Cold War, but also a historically based imperative that has essentially become part of Polish DNA. For well over a century—from the late 1700s until the end of World War I—the Polish state effectively ceased to exist as an independent political entity, partitioned by Russia, Prussia, and Austria.[16] Thanks in part to President Woodrow Wilson, who included an independent Poland among his Fourteen Points for an enduring peace in Europe following World War I,[17] Poland enjoyed a rebirth politically and culturally beginning in 1919. However, this was short-lived, and Poland was invaded again in 1939—this time by Nazi Germany as well as Stalin's Russia—and partitioned once more. When World War II ended, Poland was essentially subjugated and occu-

---

15. "Ustawa o przebudowie i modernizacji technicznej oraz finansowaniu Sił Zbrojnych Rzeczypospolitej Polskiej," originally passed May 25, 2001 and subsequently amended, www.lexlege.pl/ustawa-o-przebudowie-i-modernizacji-technicznej-oraz-finansowaniu-sil-zbrojnych-rzeczypospolitej-polskiej

16. The short-lived Duchy of Warsaw, which was essentially a satellite of Napoleonic France, lasted from 1807 until 1815, when it was divided and subsumed by Austria and Russia.

17. Wilson's 13th Point reads, "An independent Polish state should be erected which should include the territories inhabited by indisputably Polish populations, which should be assured a free and secure access to the sea, and whose political and economic independence and territorial integrity should be guaranteed by international covenant."

pied by the Soviet Union, which maintained tens of thousands of troops in Poland until the early 1990s.

For the last nearly 30 years, and since the end of the Cold War, the demise of the Warsaw Pact, and the withdrawal of occupying Soviet troops, Poland has been once again independent. This is the longest period of true Polish independence since the eighteenth century. Although now anchored in the West through membership in the European Union and in NATO, Poles retain a great deal of concern toward the threat posed by Russia in particular. Public opinion surveys regularly find that Poles see Russia's power and influence as the top international security threat.[18]

Beyond current threat perceptions, Poles have long been concerned with the potential for Russian revanchism in the wake of a post–Cold War settlement that essentially saw Moscow's influence and power recede from Central and Eastern Europe. Russia's invasion of Ukraine and illegal annexation of Crimea in early 2014 only amplified Warsaw's existing anxiety.[19] Notably, Poland is one of the few member states of NATO to border Russian territory, along with Norway, Estonia, Latvia, and Lithuania. Specifically, Poland shares a 130 mile border with Kaliningrad, an 86 square mile Russian exclave on the Baltic Sea surrounded entirely by Poland and Lithuania. Kaliningrad is arguably the most militarized piece of land in Europe, home to significant naval, air, and ground combat forces of the Russian military. The Russian Baltic Sea fleet is based in Kaliningrad, comprising dozens of surface combatants and submarines, most of which operate out of Russia's only year-round ice-free port on the Baltic. Kaliningrad is also home to two Russian naval airbases as well as the Yantar shipyard. The Russian Army's 11th Corps is also based in Kaliningrad, including several combat and combat support units such as a motorized rifle brigade, a motorized rifle regiment, a naval infantry brigade, an artillery brigade, a surface-to-surface missile brigade, and a surface-to-air missile regiment.[20]

---

18. Jacob Poushter and Christine Huang, "Climate Change Still Seen as the Top Global Threat, but Cyberattacks a Rising Concern," Pew Research Center, February 10, 2019, www.pewglobal.org/2019/02/10/climate-change-still-seen-as-the-top-global-threat-but-cyberattacks-a-rising-concern/#table. Other European countries surveyed included France, Germany, Greece, Hungary, Italy, the Netherlands, Spain, Sweden, and the United Kingdom; Katie Simmons, Bruce Stokes, and Jacob Poushter, "NATO Publics Blame Russia for Ukrainian Crisis, but Reluctant to Provide Military Aid," Pew Research Center, June 10, 2015, www.pewglobal.org/2015/06/10/nato-publics-blame-russia-for-ukrainian-crisis-but-reluctant-to-provide-military-aid/

19. Interview with a Polish expert on transatlantic relations and national security at a Warsaw-based think tank, April 26, 2019.

20. Gudrun Persson, ed., *Russian Military Capability in a Ten-Year Perspective—2016*, report number FOI-R-4326-SE, Swedish Defence Research Agency, December 2016, www.foi.se/

In recent years, Russia has been gradually building up its military capabilities in Kaliningrad even beyond the aforementioned. For instance, Russia has recently deployed the SS-26 Iskander, a nuclear-capable missile with a range of more than 250 miles, to Kaliningrad, and it has upgraded a number of weapons storage bunkers there as well.[21] Additionally, Moscow has deployed the S-400 air defense system to Kaliningrad, as well as its most advanced electronic warfare capabilities.[22] In 2016, Russia also assigned to the Baltic Sea fleet in Kaliningrad two vessels equipped with the advanced antiship KALIBR cruise missile system.[23] All of this has naturally led to an increase in active duty military personnel assigned to Kaliningrad—by one estimate, Russian troop levels have increased by nearly 50 percent in recent years.[24]

Some argue that many of the new weapon systems Russia has placed in Kaliningrad are not as capable as Moscow would like the West and others to believe.[25] Yet even if Russia is exaggerating the capabilities of its military systems deployed in Kaliningrad and elsewhere for the purposes of deterrence or arms sales abroad, Moscow has nonetheless also engaged in a variety of destabilizing activities in and around northeastern Europe that

rest-api/report/FOI-R--4326--SE; and Catherine Harris and Frederick W. Kagan, *Russia's Military Posture: Ground Forces Order of Battle*, Institute for the Study of War and the Critical Threats Project at the American Enterprise Institute, March 2018, www.understandingwar.org/sites/default/files/Russian%20Ground%20Forces%20OOB_ISW%20CTP_0.pdf

21. "New Russia Missiles in Kaliningrad Are Answer to U.S. Shield: Lawmaker," *Reuters*, November 21, 2016, www.reuters.com/article/us-russia-missiles-kaliningrad-idUSK-BN13G0W9; Patrick Tucker, "Russia Building Up Military Sites on Poland's Border before Trump-Putin Meeting," *Defense One*, July 9, 2018, www.defenseone.com/technology/2018/07/satellite-photos-show-new-activity-russias-military-exclave-kaliningrad/149531/; and James Stavridis, "Putin's Big Military Buildup Is behind NATO Lines," *Bloomberg*, October 20, 2018, www.bloomberg.com/opinion/articles/2018-10-20/putin-s-big-military-buildup-is-behind-nato-lines

22. Oren Liebermann, Frederik Pleitgen, and Vasco Cotovio, "New Satellite Images Suggest Military Buildup in Russia's Strategic Baltic Enclave," *CNN Online*, October 17, 2018, www.cnn.com/2018/10/17/europe/russia-kaliningrad-military-buildup-intl/index.html; and Roger McDermott, "Moscow Deploys Latest Electronic Warfare Systems in Kaliningrad," *Eurasia Daily Monitor* 15, no. 174 (December 11, 2018), jamestown.org/program/moscow-deploys-latest-electronic-warfare-systems-in-kaliningrad/

23. "Russian Military Power," *Defense Intelligence Agency*, DIA-11-1704-161, 2017.

24. Ben Hodges, Janusz Bugajski, and Peter B. Doran, "Securing the Suwałki Corridor," Center for European Policy Analysis, July 2018, 37, docs.wixstatic.com/ugd/644196_e63598001eb54f8387b10bc0b30c5873.pdf.

25. "Russian A2/AD Capability Overrated," Swedish Defence Research Agency, March 4, 2019, www.foi.se/en/foi/news-and-pressroom/news/2019-03-04-russian-a2-ad-capability-overrated.html; and Robert Dalsjo, Michael Jonsson, Christofer Berglund, "Don't Believe the Russian Hype," *Foreign Policy*, March 7, 2019, foreignpolicy.com/2019/03/07/dont-believe-the-russian-hype-a2-ad-missiles-sweden-kaliningrad-baltic-states-annexation-nato/

have served to intimidate Poland and its neighbors. Russian fighter jets, bombers, and both manned and unmanned reconnaissance aircraft routinely violate the airspace of Poland as well as NATO allies and partners in northeastern Europe, frequently without activating their transponders, which allow ground-based radar to detect, locate, and identify aircraft.[26] At the same time, Russia has regularly conducted large-scale "strategic" exercises as well as more frequent no-notice or short-notice exercises involving thousands and sometimes tens of thousands of troops, scores of fighter jets, and hundreds of armored vehicles in its Western Military District, of which Kaliningrad is a part.[27] The short- or no-notice exercises are typically indistinguishable from preparations for an actual military attack against Russia's neighbors, and they often catch U.S. military officials by surprise.[28] This is particularly worrisome, since some argue that Russia used exercises as cover or preparation for invasions of Georgia in 2008 and Ukraine in 2014.[29]

For all of the reasons outlined above—not to mention the geography of Europe, which has seen Polish territory used essentially as the invasion route for militaries moving east or west—Poland appears to have plenty of rationale for focusing on security in its immediate neighborhood. Indeed, the 2017 Polish Defence Concept made it clear that "the aggressive policy of the Russian Federation" is the primary threat or challenge facing Poland.[30] From Warsaw's perspective, the main goal of Russian aggression

26. "Rosyjskie śmigłowce wtargnęły nad Polskę i . . . cisza. Nic się nie stało?" *Kresy24. pl*, April 18, 2016, kresy24.pl/rosyjskie-smiglowce-wtargnely-nad-polske-i-cisza-nic-sie-nie-stalo/9; "Rosyjskie drony wlatują do Polski," *Gazeta Olsztyńska*, December 9, 2016, gazetaol sztynska.pl/a/404138,Rosyjskie-drony-wlatuja-do-Polski.html; "From the Baltic to Alaska: More Russian Air Provocations Reported," Warsaw Institute, January 30, 2019, warsawin stitute.org/baltic-alaska-russian-air-provocations-reported/; and "Estonia Says Russian Plane Again Violates Airspace," *Radio Free Europe/Radio Liberty*, June 21, 2018, www.rferl.org/a/estonia-russian-plane-violates-airspace/29310815.html

27. Juliusz Sabak, "Unexpected Russian Air Force Exercise in the Kaliningrad Area," *Defense24.com*, November 2, 2015, www.defence24.com/unexpected-russian-air-force-exer cise-in-the-kaliningrad-area.

28. "US Nato General Fears Rapid Russian Troop Deployments," *BBC Online*, June 20, 2016, www.bbc.com/news/world-europe-36575180

29. Markus Ekström, "Rysk operativ-strategisk övningsverksamhet under 2009 och 2010," FOI-R-3022-SE, Swedish Defence Research Agency, October 2010, 11, www.foi.se/report-search/pdf?fileName=D%3A%5CReportSearch%5CFiles%5C7775772f-4c82-45ec-b9c4-a816a6f38281.pdf; and Michael Birnbaum and David Filipov, "Russia Held a Big Military Exercise This Week: Here's Why the U.S. Is Paying Attention," *Washington Post*, September 23, 2017, https://www.washingtonpost.com/world/europe/russia-held-a-big-military-exercise-this-week-heres-why-the-us-is-paying-attention/2017/09/23/3a0d37ea-9a36-11e7-af6a-6555caaeb8dc_story.html?utm_term=.48e57df151b6

30. Ministry of National Defence, "The Defence Concept of the Republic of Poland," May

"is to create a new international order based on the so called 'concert of powers.'"[31] Given how Poland has fared over the last couple of centuries at the hands of more powerful regional actors such as Germany, Austro-Hungary, and Russia, it is obvious that any moves toward another concert of power in Europe is perceived as a grave, existential threat to Poland.

More specifically, the 2017 Defence Concept pointed at Russia's invasions of Georgia in 2008 and of Ukraine in 2014 as evidence of Moscow's desire to "destabilize the internal order of other states and to question their territorial integrity by openly violating international law."[32] Warsaw also specifically highlighted Russian actions below the threshold of conventional armed conflict—so as to forestall a full-throated Western response—and Moscow's use of proxies to achieve the same objectives, even as Russia engages in a vast program of conventional and strategic military modernization. Finally, the Defence Concept makes it clear that Warsaw views Russia as "the main source of instability in NATO's eastern neighbourhood" by "stimulating political conflicts, corrupting the elites of those states, and striving to gain control over weak state governance."[33]

This conceptualization of Polish security stands somewhat in contrast to the Polish Defense Strategy of 2009 and the subsequent Polish National Security White Paper of 2013. The 2009 strategy cast Polish security in broad terms—"threats to Poland's security are closely related to global threats"—and sought a balance between collective defense and crisis management.[34] It noted that although the risk of large-scale armed conflict had dramatically fallen, the threat of regional or localized conflicts remained, and it highlighted conflict-prone developments in the post-Soviet space, disputes in the Balkans, and tensions between the West and the Muslim world, especially in the Middle East. This reflected Poland's extant operations at the time, including in Iraq and Afghanistan, as well as unease generated by Russia's 2008 invasion of Georgia.

The 2013 National Security White Paper cast Poland's security in similarly balanced terms. On a global level, it noted the increasingly important role of the BRIC countries (Brazil, Russia, India, and China), the rise of influential regional players like Turkey and Iran, the threats posed by failed

2017, 23, www.gov.pl/documents/2756541/2758012/korp_web_13_06_2017.pdf/09790104-c721-da67-f0bd-f600344f8ccb

31. Ministry of National Defence, "The Defence Concept of the Republic of Poland," 23.

32. Ministry of National Defence, "The Defence Concept of the Republic of Poland," 24.

33. Ministry of National Defence, "The Defence Concept of the Republic of Poland," 25.

34. Ministry of National Defence, "Defense Strategy of the Republic of Poland," 2009, 5, http://www.files.ethz.ch/isn/156791/Poland%202009.pdf

states, and the proliferation of weapons of mass destruction and related delivery systems. Moreover, it highlighted the challenges posed by transnational terrorism, cyber-attacks, international organized crime, corruption, climate change, and demographic issues. However, it also noted explicitly that Poland's security hinged on relations between Russia and the West, and it speculated that Russia was likely to seek security at the expense of its neighbors.[35] The rhetorical shift from the balanced approach prior to Russia's upending of the European security order in early 2014 to a more explicitly regional emphasis following the invasion of Ukraine has been made tangible through Polish defense acquisitions and defense planning.

Defense Acquisitions

In terms of acquisitions, since Russia's illegal annexation of Crimea, Warsaw has invested in military platforms that give a clear indication of the emphasis on territorial defense against a conventional military foe. Boosts in defense spending in the last several years—including the 2017 decision to invest an additional $55 billion over the next decade or more—have favored the ground forces and territorial defense missions at the expense of the Polish navy and more expeditionary capabilities.[36] The Polish army is expected to nearly double in size, and Poland plans to restore divisions as tactical combat units, rather than merely administrative entities.[37] Moreover, Poland is in the process of creating an entirely new service branch—the Territorial Defence Forces—which will consist of roughly 53,000 troops and function as a sort of national guard force spread throughout the country.[38] Within the ground forces there is increasing emphasis on

---

35. Polish National Security Bureau, "White Paper on National Security of the Republic of Poland," 2013, 126, www.bbn.gov.pl/download/1/20897/WhiteBookNationalSecurityPL2013.pdf

36. Lidia Kelly, "Poland to Spend $55 Billion More on Defense amid Russia Fears," *Reuters*, August 23, 2017, www.businessinsider.com/r-poland-to-allocate-additional-55-billion-on-defense-by-2032-deputy-minister-2017-8; interview with a Polish expert on transatlantic relations and national security at a Warsaw-based think tank, April 26, 2019.

37. Ministry of National Defence, "The Defence Concept of the Republic of Poland," May 2017, 47.

38. Interview with a senior civilian official within the Polish Defence Ministry, March 2, 2016; Kelly, "Poland to Spend $55 Billion More on Defense amid Russia Fears" ; Matthew Day, "Poland to Establish 46,000-strong National Guard in the Face of War in Eastern Ukraine," *Telegraph*, January 25, 2016, www.telegraph.co.uk/news/worldnews/europe/poland/12120761/Poland-to-establish-46000-strong-national-guard-in-the-face-of-war-in-eastern-Ukraine.html; and Remigiusz Wilk, "Polish Territorial Defence Force Expanded to 53,000 Personnel," *Jane's Defence Weekly*, November 17, 2016.

greater lethality. For example, instead of expanding airborne infantry, more resources will be funneled toward artillery and precision-guided rockets, military engineers, and assault helicopters.

More broadly, modernization of Poland's armed forces is desperately needed, given the continuing reliance on aging, less reliable Soviet-era platforms, such as the T-72 and T-80 main battle tanks, the BMP-3 infantry fighting vehicle, and MiG-29 fighter jets.[39] Poland is attempting to modernize or acquire several combat systems all at the same time, which presents major fiscal and management challenges that may prevent Poland from achieving its goals as quickly as it would like.[40] Among other investments, in 2018 Poland signed the largest arms acquisition deal in its history, agreeing to spend $4.75 billion to acquire two U.S.-made Patriot air and missile defense system batteries by 2022.[41] Warsaw also announced plans to purchase a new multirole fifth-generation combat aircraft, such as the F-35, to replace its Soviet-era fighter jets.[42] Other, nearly simultaneous modernization programs include[43]

- the Narew short-range air-defense system to defend against drones as well as other threats;
- the Wisła medium-range air and missile defense system to defend against manned and unmanned aerial attacks as well as tactical short-range ballistic and cruise missiles;
- the Gryf medium-range tactical unmanned aerial vehicle program;
- the Ważka short-range unmanned aerial vehicle program, primarily for use in urbanized areas and equipped with an opto-electronic head that allows observation day or night;
- the Flame comprehensive reconnaissance aircraft program;

39. Interview with a U.S. field-grade officer based in Washington who works on U.S.-Poland military-to-military relations, April 5, 2019.

40. Interview with a Polish expert on transatlantic relations and national security at a Warsaw-based think tank, April 26, 2019; and interview with an expert on Polish national security and strategy at a think tank in Warsaw, May 1, 2019.

41. Lidia Kelly, "Poland Signs $4.75 Billion Deal for U.S. Patriot Missile System Facing Russia," *Reuters*, March 28, 2018, www.reuters.com/article/us-raytheon-poland-patriot/poland-signs-4-75-billion-deal-for-u-s-patriot-missile-system-facing-russia-idUSK BN1H417S

42. Daniel Darling, "Poland's Harpia Fighter Acquisition Program Tops Project Queue," *Defense and Security Monitor*, March 12, 2019, dsm.forecastinternational.com/wordpress/2019/03/12/polands-harpia-fighter-acquisition-program-tops-project-queue/

43. Ministry of National Defense, "Plan Modernizacji Technicznej—mapa drogowa rozwoju Wojska Polskiego," February 28, 2019, www.gov.pl/web/obrona-narodowa/plan-modernizacji-technicznej-mapa-drogowa-rozwoju-wojska-polskiego; Remigiusz Wilk, "Poland Unveils Military Acquisition Road Map," *Jane's Defence Weekly*, November 21, 2018.

- the Municipal coastal defense ship program;
- the Regina 155 mm artillery program;
- the Rak 120 mm self-propelled mortar program;
- the Homar multiple rocket launcher system, capable of striking targets at ranges of 70 to 300 km;
- the Hust antitank guided missile launchers program;
- the Borsuk modular tracked infantry fighting vehicle program;
- the Mustang high-mobility trucks and passenger car program;
- an anti-submarine warfare helicopter with a combat search-and-rescue capability; and
- a nearly $800 million program to acquire more advanced cryptographic and IT equipment for cyber operations.[44]

While it is also true that the government is planning on acquiring other defense platforms and capabilities that are not necessarily focused on territorial defense—such as the Orka submarine replacement program—these initiatives routinely appear at the bottom of defense priorities or have been otherwise slow to develop as funding is siphoned toward other priorities.[45] Indeed, some experts claim Poland does not even need naval capacity beyond perhaps coastal defense, given the emphasis on territorial defense and the likelihood that most Polish navy assets would be destroyed by Russian precision munitions in the opening hours and days of a conflict.[46]

Regardless of the warfighting domain—air, sea, land, space, or cyber—several of Poland's defense acquisition priorities require extensive research, development, testing, or lengthy contractual or manufacturing timelines. In order to acquire these types of defense capabilities, a long-term "programmatic" approach is typically necessary. Some have criticized this type of approach—known in the United States as the "program of record" process—as too slow to meet the operational demands of twenty-first-century

---

44. Ministry of National Defense, "3 miliardy złotych na cyberbezpieczeństwo," February 28, 2019, www.gov.pl/web/obrona-narodowa/3-miliardy-zlotych-na-cyberbezpieczenstwo

45. Interview with a Polish defense and national security expert at a Warsaw-based think tank, April 15, 2019; interview with an expert on Polish national security and strategy at a think tank in Warsaw, May 1, 2019; and "Poland's ORKA Submarine Competition Limping Along," *Submarine Matters*, September 27, 2018, gentleseas.blogspot.com/2018/09/polands-orka-submarine-competition.html

46. "Czy Polska potrzebuje Marynarki Wojennej?," *Polskie Radio*, July 5, 2018, www.polskieradio.pl/7/4399/Artykul/2164295,Czy-Polska-potrzebuje-Marynarki-Wojennej; and Maksymilian Dura, "Dlaczego Polska potrzebuje Marynarki Wojennej?," *Defence24*, August 15, 2016, www.defence24.pl/dlaczego-polska-potrzebuje-marynarki-wojennej

conflict and competition.[47] However, a programmatic approach enables a defense establishment to effectively manage acquisition programs. A key factor in such an approach is the availability of consistent, long-term fiscal resources, and here Poland has a clear advantage over many of its European allies in the form of a broad-based political consensus as well as a legal requirement to maintain and even increase defense spending over time.[48]

Defense Planning

In terms of defense planning since 2014, Poland's 2017 Defence Concept is explicit in noting that "the Land and Air Forces remain the key elements of the Polish defense."[49] Even the Polish navy is cast, at least in part, in the role of defending land—"the Navy will also play a significant role by defending our coastline and denying enemy supremacy over the southern Baltic Sea." Furthermore, Polish infrastructure and force posture have recently emphasized territorial defense against Russia, shifting from the border with Germany and toward the border with Russia (Kaliningrad) and Belarus, all in an effort to be better positioned in the event of a worst-case scenario. Poland has already relocated two Leopard 2 main battle tank battalions from Zagan—55 kilometers from the German border—to Wesola, just east of Warsaw and the Vistula River and roughly 180 kilometers from the Belarusian border.[50] Additionally, Poland will locate a planned fourth army division east of the Vistula, near the town of Siedice and roughly 100 kilometers from the Belarusian border.[51]

More broadly, while NATO and the Article 5 security guarantee at its heart remain the bedrock of Polish defense planning, since 2014 Poland has pursued additional security through bi- and multilateral frameworks. For instance, Warsaw has sought greater cooperation with Germany and France through the Weimar Triangle grouping, including in terms of arms

---

47. Michèle A. Flournoy and Robert P. Lyons III, "Sustaining and Enhancing the US Military's Technology Edge," *Strategic Studies Quarterly* 10, no. 2 (Summer 2016): 3–13.

48. Interview with a Polish defense and national security expert at a Warsaw-based think tank, April 15, 2019.

49. Ministry of National Defence, "The Defence Concept of the Republic of Poland," May 2017, 46.

50. Remigiusz Wilk, "Poland Relocates Leopard 2A5 Tanks to the East," *Jane's Defence Weekly*, April 20, 2017.

51. Nicholas Fiorenza, "Poland Gives Details of New, Fourth Division," *Jane's Defence Weekly*, September 10, 2018.

acquisition programs.[52] At the same time, Poland has also advanced military cooperation, including in arms procurement, exercises, and the creation of combined military command and force structures, among the so-called Visegrad Group—the Czech Republic, Hungary, Poland, and Slovakia.[53] Slightly more broadly, Poland was a cofounder—along with Romania—of the Bucharest 9 (B9), which also includes Bulgaria, Estonia, Hungary, Latvia, Lithuania, the Slovak Republic, and the Czech Republic. The purpose of the B9 is to promote dialogue and common perspectives on security matters facing Central and Eastern Europe.

In terms of bilateral relationships, in recent years Poland has sought closer defense or security ties with Sweden[54] and the United Kingdom,[55] among others. However, from Warsaw's perspective no bilateral relationship is more important than that with the United States, given its role as the West's security guarantor, divisions within NATO over threat perceptions, Warsaw's chafing at Germany's dominance of the EU, and Polish anxiety toward French-led defense integration within Europe. Building on close ties forged through Polish participation in U.S.-led coalitions in Iraq, Afghanistan, and elsewhere, Warsaw has sought to become Washington's strategic partner within Central/Eastern Europe. In the last several years, Poland has played host to rotational deployments of American armored brigade combat teams and U.S. Air Force detachments. Poland also hosts an American-operated SM-3 missile defense interceptor site, which is part of the United States' European Phased Adaptive Approach and embedded within NATO's ballistic missile defense system. Since 2017, Poland has also hosted an American-led NATO Enhanced Forward Presence bat-

---

52. Aaron Mehta, "Poland Wants to Play in Franco-German Tank Program," *Defense News*, August 3, 2016, www.defensenews.com/industry/2016/08/03/poland-wants-to-play-in-franco-german-tank-program/; Brooks Tigner, "National Calls Growing for Stronger EU Military and Defence Policies," *Jane's Defence Weekly*, August 31, 2016; and Barbara Bodalska, "Germany and Poland to Explore Revived 'Weimar Triangle'," *Euractiv*, January 18, 2018, www.euractiv.com/section/future-eu/news/germany-and-poland-to-explore-revived-wei mar-triangle/

53. Jaroslaw Adamowski, "Poland Launches Effort To Help Arm E. European Allies," *Defense News*, October 4, 2015, www.defensenews.com/2015/10/04/poland-launches-effort-to-help-arm-e-european-allies/; and Patrick Tucker, "Poland Is Preparing for 15 Years of Rising Tension with Russia," *Defense One*, June 1, 2017, www.defenseone.com/technol ogy/2017/06/poland-preparing-15-years-rising-tension-russia/138337/

54. "Poland and Sweden Expand the Military Cooperation," *Defense24*, September 15, 2015, www.defence24.com/geopolitics/poland-and-sweden-expand-the-military-coopera tion

55. Annabelle Dickson, "Poland and UK to Sign Joint Defense Treaty as May Visits Warsaw," *Politico*, December 12, 2017, www.politico.eu/article/poland-uk-defense-treaty-as-may-visits-warsaw/

tlegroup. Warsaw has sought to facilitate the U.S. presence in Poland by spending significant amounts of money on joint use military infrastructure projects as well as offering up to $2 billion in order to support a permanent presence—versus rotational—of U.S. combat forces in Poland.[56] Although a permanent presence is unlikely in the short run, in 2019 Poland and the United States signed a joint declaration to expand the U.S. rotational presence in Poland by roughly 1,000 troops.[57] That same declaration also included an expansion of Special Operations Forces cooperation between Poland and the United States—specifically, the United States committed to establishing "special operations forces capability in Poland to support air, ground, and maritime operations."[58] This comes on top of long-standing cooperation between U.S. and Polish Special Operations Forces, dating to the mid-1990s.[59]

While pursuing greater internationalization of its security challenges through multinational, multilateral, and bilateral frameworks and partnerships, Poland has also adapted its defense planning by recalibrating the training readiness focus of its military forces. During the 2000s and early 2010s, when Poland sent forces to Iraq and Afghanistan, training readiness for Polish forces understandably emphasized counterinsurgency, counterterrorism, peacekeeping, and stability operations.[60] Since 2014

---

56. Interview with two civilian defense experts assigned to U.S. European Command, August 9, 2016; Edyta Żemła and Kamil Turecki, "Poland Offers US up to $2B for Permanent Military Base," *Politico*, May 27, 2018, www.politico.eu/article/nato-poland-offers-us-up-to-2-billion-for-permanent-american-military-base/; and Jennifer Jacobs et al., "Poland and U.S. Closing In on Deal to Build 'Fort Trump,' Sources Say," *Bloomberg*, April 16, 2019, www.bloomberg.com/news/articles/2019-04-16/poles-and-u-s-said-to-close-in-on-deal-to-build-fort-trump

57. White House, "Joint Declaration on Defense Cooperation regarding United States Force Posture in the Republic of Poland," June 12, 2019, www.whitehouse.gov/briefings-statements/joint-declaration-defense-cooperation-regarding-united-states-force-posture-republic-poland/

58. White House, "Joint Declaration on Defense Cooperation."

59. Jim Garamone, "U.S., Poland Sign Special Ops Memo of Understanding," American Forces Press Service, February 19, 2009, archive.defense.gov/news/newsarticle.aspx?id=53141. For examples of more recent U.S.-Polish Special Operations Forces cooperation, see Elizabeth Pena, "US, Polish SOF Enhance Abilities through Culmination Exercise," U.S. Air Force Public Affairs, January 2, 2019, www.af.mil/News/Article-Display/Article/1723242/us-polish-sof-enhance-abilities-through-culmination-exercise/, and Kyle Rempfer, "Green Berets Train Polish, Latvian Resistance Units in West Virginia," *Army Times*, July 8, 2019, www.armytimes.com/news/your-army/2019/07/08/green-berets-train-polish-latvian-resistance-units-in-west-virginia/

60. For instance, see Sean C. Finch, "U.S. Army Europe Soldiers Help Train Polish Troops for Deployment to Iraq," U.S. Army Europe Public Affairs Office, December 19, 2007, www.army.mil/article/151608/us_army_europe_soldiers_help_train_polish_troops_for_deployment_to_iraq

though—when large-scale NATO involvement in Afghanistan ended, and when Russian forces invaded Ukraine—training readiness has justifiably shifted to territorial defense, particularly for large-scale maneuver unit training involving corps and divisions.[61] For instance, in 2016, Poland led and hosted one of largest post–Cold War exercises NATO allies have ever conducted—Exercise Anakonda 16. For ten days, 31,000 troops from more than 20 countries participated in the exercise at the Drawsko Pomorskie training area in northwestern Poland as well as six other locations across the country.[62] Their objective was to exercise and integrate Polish national command and force structures into allied, joint, and multinational environments, as well as to exercise elements of the NATO Response Force in improving their rapid deployment procedures and multinational cohesion.

Is Poland's Trajectory Sustainable?

Poland is in the middle of trying to turn its envious economic performance over the last decade into an impressive array of hard power capabilities and capacities. The fundamental question facing the country is whether it can sustain this trajectory. Given the political consensus that exists among all major political parties on the need to invest more in national security and modernize the armed forces,[63] the answer depends in large measure on the future of the Polish economy and the country's demographic trends.

In terms of the economic outlook for Poland, although the country has been Europe's economic tiger—as noted earlier, Poland's growth rate in recent years has been greater than 4 percent per year—the short-run future outlook is not as positive. A tighter labor market and somewhat higher inflation rates are likely to be the primary culprits.[64] Together, these two factors will probably push down private consumption, which was a major factor in Poland's strong growth through the middle of the

61. Interview with a Polish civilian employee of the Ministry of Defense and a Polish field-grade military officer assigned to the General Staff, March 2, 2016.

62. "Polish-Led Exercise Anakonda 2016 a Huge Success," SHAPE Public Affairs Office, June 17, 2016, shape.nato.int/2016/polishled-exercise-anakonda-2016-a-huge-success

63. Interview with a Polish defense and national security expert at a Warsaw-based think tank, April 15, 2019; interview with a Polish expert on transatlantic relations and national security at a Warsaw-based think tank, April 26, 2019; interview with an expert on Polish national security and strategy at a think tank in Warsaw, May 1, 2019; interview with a civilian defense policy expert at the Polish mission to NATO, May 17, 2019.

64. European Commission, "European Economic Forecast," Institutional Paper 096, February 2019, 24, ec.europa.eu/info/sites/info/files/economy-finance/ip096_en.pdf

2010s. External demand is not expected to make up for the decline in domestic demand.

In the medium term, the Polish economy is expected to grow at an average rate of about 2.8 percent per year.[65] This is a strong growth rate by European standards, but if the growth rate slips slightly, the country's economic performance may not be enough to sustain Poland's defense spending plans.[66] Assuming the Polish economy grows at roughly 2.8 percent per year in the midterm, defense spending as a percentage of total government expenditures is likely to remain fairly steady. However, if the Polish economic growth rate slips slightly, Poland's defense budget will gradually begin to consume a higher and higher percentage of Poland's overall government expenditures.

To solve this challenge, Poland could increase borrowing and take on more debt. However, recall that Poland's government is obligated by Polish law to limit debt to below 60 percent of GDP and it is limited by the European Union to keep its annual budget deficit below 3 percent of GDP. Under current expectations, Poland's debt will hover between 44 and 48 percent of GDP and its annual budget deficit will be between 1.3 and 2.1 percent. Therefore, there appears to be some "headroom" for Poland to deficit spend and take on greater debt to support its defense spending goals if its economy performs slightly worse than anticipated. Otherwise, Poland's defense budget may begin to consume other parts of the Polish federal budget, such as social welfare. This could cause a revision to the defense spending law and ultimately compel Poland to reduce its long-term defense budget plans.

If Poland's economy performs poorly in the medium term, it will likely be the result of three factors. First, private investment is expected to remain sluggish and this will likely have a dampening effect on Polish growth, especially as EU funding is expected to decline in the future.[67] Poland lags behind the European Union average when it comes to the percentage of firms carrying out some type of investment and when it comes to invest-

---

65. "Poland," *Economist: Intelligence Unit*, August 16, 2018, country.eiu.com/report_dl.asp?mode=fi&fi=CF_CFPL_MAIN_20180801T000000_0005_CSV.CSV

66. Interview with a civilian defense policy advisor at the Polish mission to NATO, May 17, 2019.

67. "EIB Group Survey on Investment and Investment Finance Country Overview: Poland," European Investment Bank (EIB), 2018, www.eib.org/attachments/efs/eibis_2018_poland_en.pdf. EU funds are expected to decline for two reasons—first, Poland's economic success over the last several years means it no longer needs as much assistance, and second, officials in Brussels and in several EU member states have viewed Poland's rightward shift politically under the Law and Justice (PiS) party as endangering civil right and the rule of law.

ment per employee. This is ironic given that 44 percent of Polish firms see replacement of existing infrastructure, equipment, or machinery as their main priority for investment, which is higher than the EU average of 33 percent. This appears to imply that Polish firms know they need to invest in order to modernize and increase productivity but are unable or unwilling to do so. Most Polish firms blame their reluctance to invest for the long term on the lack of skilled labor—more on this below—and uncertainty about the future.[68]

Second, Poland is expected to show very limited productivity gains in the years ahead, unless the government can relinquish control over several areas of the economy that it currently dominates as well as spur a stronger embrace of Industry 4.0 initiatives by private Polish firms across the entire economy. Government ownership is high in banking, insurance, energy, and transport, and the main Warsaw stock index is dominated by state-owned enterprises.[69] The most significant productivity gains in the Polish economy for the period 2005–16 occurred within foreign-owned firms—both state-owned enterprises and private domestic firms had far lower productivity gains during this period.[70] Foreign-owned firms were more likely to leverage technology, and hence to deliver more efficient outcomes.

With regard to Industry 4.0 initiatives, or what Poles refer to as Przemysłu 4.0, these technologies include manufacturing automation and robotics, big data, cloud computing, and the internet of things, to name a few. Small and medium-size enterprises in Poland have lacked even an *awareness* of these technologies, and the complexity of legislating the development of mechanisms to support small and medium-size enterprises financially has not helped either.[71] In order to overcome these challenges, in 2016 the Polish government initiated a "Future Industry Platform" that was meant to make financing available to public and private firms throughout Poland so that they could embrace digital transformation. Whether this will succeed has yet to be seen, but in any case Warsaw faces an uphill struggle given the significant gap between Polish firms and those elsewhere in Europe when

---

68. "EIB Group Survey on Investment and Investment Finance Country Overview: Poland," European Investment Bank (EIB), 2018, 8, www.eib.org/attachments/efs/eibis_2018_poland_en.pdf

69. "Republic of Poland: 2018 Article IV Consultation," International Monetary Fund, Country Report No. 19/37, February 2019, 17, www.imf.org/~/media/Files/Publications/CR/2019/cr1937.ashx

70. "Republic of Poland: Selected Issues," International Monetary Fund, Country Report No. 19/38, February 2019, www.imf.org/~/media/Files/Publications/CR/2019/cr1938.ashx

71. European Commission, "Poland: 'Initiative for Polish Industry 4.0—The Future Industry Platform'," February 2018.

it comes to promoting technologically based productivity—Poland ranks twenty-fourth out of 28 European economies in terms of embracing the digital economy,[72] and its degree of roboticization is well below both the EU average and the Central European average.[73]

Third, and perhaps most important, Poland has a shrinking working-age population. Polish fertility rates are among the weakest in the developed world.[74] In 2014, the fertility rate in Poland was 1.32 children per woman, fifth lowest in the EU, ahead of just Spain (1.31), Cyprus (1.31), Greece (1.29), and Portugal (1.23).[75] The rate fell even lower in 2015, to 1.31 children per woman, ahead of just Portugal (1.30) that year. The year 2016 saw a slight improvement, to 1.38, and by 2017 the rate had increased to 1.48. However, this rate was still below the European average of 1.58, and below the rates of France (1.89), the United Kingdom (1.73), and even Germany (1.56).

Recently enacted policies designed to promote childbirth may have helped here. In April 2016, the Polish government launched the "Family 500+" program. The centerpiece of the program is a tax-free cash payment of 500 złotys per month—equivalent to one-third of the net minimum wage per month—for every second and subsequent child under the age of 18. Similar payments for a first child were previously also offered just to very low-income families, but in July 2019 the payments for a first child were extended to *all* families regardless of income.[76] Moreover, the benefits were granted to *all* eligible children, not just those born after the program was introduced. By one estimate, almost 2.5 million Polish families were taking advantage of this benefit by September 2018, at a cost of about 24 billion złotys, or more than 1 percent of Poland's GDP.[77] Other reforms enacted over the last decade include a lengthening of parental leave time for childcare and making it easier to get children into preschool and kindergarten.

---

72. European Commission, "Digital Economy and Society Index (DESI) 2018 Country Report Poland," 2018, ec.europa.eu/newsroom/dae/document.cfm?doc_id=52233

73. "Polish Manufacturers Embrace Industry 4.0," *Industry Europe*, September 17, 2018, industryeurope.com/pl/

74. OECD, "OECD Economic Surveys: Poland 2014," OECD Publishing, 15, dx.doi.org/10.1787/eco_surveys-pol-2014-en

75. Eurostat, "Fertility Rates by Age," data as of April 3, 2019, ec.europa.eu/eurostat/data/database

76. "Ruling Party Presents Five Major Proposals for 2019 Election Year," Polish Press Agency, February 23, 2019, www.pap.pl/en/news/news%2C410195%2Cpoland-stake-2019-campaign-ruling-party-leader.html

77. Monika Pronczuk, "Ruling Party Hopes Child Benefit Scheme Will Woo Poland's Voters in Biala Podlaska," *Financial Times*, February 5, 2019, www.ft.com/content/bde47e98-22e8-11e9-8ce6-5db4543da632

Nonetheless, long-term projections show Poland's population declining over the coming decades. Part of the decline stems from the emigration of younger Poles in the years since Poland joined the European Union. When Poles were offered the opportunity to work elsewhere in Europe, particularly Western Europe, many of them took it, largely to take advantage of higher wages and to escape what was then a relatively high unemployment rate in Poland.[78] By one estimate, roughly 1.2 million Poles left their homeland to work elsewhere in the EU between 2004 and 2014.[79]

To make up for these emigrants, Poland could allow increased immigration, but Warsaw has a mixed record here. On the one hand Poland resisted accepting any refugees from Syria, Iraq, and elsewhere at the height of the migration crisis just a few years ago, but on the other hand it *has* accepted roughly one million Ukrainians fleeing Crimea, violence in the Donbas, and economic dislocation across Ukraine.[80] Many of these Ukrainians work in Poland, often on seasonal contracts, and they have proven invaluable to Poland's recent economic success, given the number of Poles that have left for Western Europe.[81] However, EU efforts to ease travel restrictions on Ukrainians will make it easier for them to work—perhaps only illegally—across all of Europe. This will mean that many Ukrainians will not stay in Poland and instead continue on to other EU countries. For all of the reasons described above, Poland's population is expected to begin aging at a very fast pace,[82] and by 2080 Poland's population is expected to be roughly 10 million fewer than it was in 2015, as depicted in figure 2.

One way to mitigate the impact of a declining population on the broader economy is by increasing labor utilization—that is, getting more Poles to take jobs in the economy.[83] In 2017, roughly 71 percent of the

---

78. Mihaela Simionescu, Yuriy Bilan, and Grzegorz Mentel, "Economic Effects of Migration from Poland to the UK," *Amfiteatru Economic* 19, no. 46 (2017): 757–70.

79. Wiktor Szary, "Poland Counts the Cost of Losing Millions of Its Workers," *Reuters,* December 5, 2014, uk.reuters.com/article/uk-europe-demographics-poland/poland-counts-the-cost-of-losing-millions-of-its-workers-idUKKCN0JJ0KT20141205

80. Yaroslav Trofimov, "Turning Muslims Away, Poland Welcomes Ukrainians," *Wall Street Journal,* March 26, 2019, www.wsj.com/articles/turning-muslims-away-poland-welcomes-ukrainians-11553598000; Frey Lindsay, "Ukrainian Immigrants Give the Polish Government an Out on Refugees," *Forbes,* September 19, 2018; Jo Harper, "Poland Fears Economic Hit as EU Opens Door to Ukrainians," *Deutsche Welle,* January 30, 2018, p.dw.com/p/2rln29

81. Michał Strzałkowski, "Poland Seeks to Protect Its Ukrainian Connection," *Euractiv,* February 22, 2019, www.euractiv.com/section/europe-s-east/news/poland-seeks-to-protect-its-ukrainian-connection/.

82. OECD, "OECD Economic Surveys: Poland 2014," OECD Publishing, 15, dx.doi.org/10.1787/eco_surveys-pol-2014-en

83. A related method of increasing labor utilization is to increase the *number of hours*

eligible workforce aged 20–64 were employed in Poland.[84] This figure is slightly higher than either France (70.6 percent) or Italy (62 percent), but below the EU average (72.2 percent), the United Kingdom (78 percent), and Germany (79 percent). However, the aforementioned social welfare policies designed to promote childbirth as well as a reduction in the age before workers can claim a pension mean that it is more likely Poland will actually see *lower* labor force participation in the coming years.[85]

The broad economic impact of Poland's demographic challenges will be exacerbated by the productivity problems cited previously. As noted earlier in this book, GDP growth occurs through increased productivity or through higher rates of labor utilization, or both. If Poland cannot increase worker productivity, especially in sectors where it faces a considerable gap with its EU partners such as in mining, agriculture, manufacturing, and energy, *and* it has fewer workers, the inevitable result will be declining or at least stagnating economic output and living standards, especially relative to the rest of Europe.

The implications of all of this for Poland's defense and national security could be significant. Specifically, it is likely that Poland's demographic and related economic challenges will impact its hard power in at least two ways—by creating a fiscal crunch, and by creating military capacity issues. First, with regard to the fiscal challenges, a slow-growing, static, or perhaps even declining Polish economy means reduced income tax receipts, at least relative to inflation. At the same time, the aging Polish population is likely to place increasing demands on the government for social and health services. As suggested earlier, the government could be placed in the position of having to cap or reduce the defense budget in order to devote more spending to social services and healthcare. Second, with regard to military capacity, a low birth rate and a shrinking population will necessarily make it more difficult to increase the size of the military as well as find the

worked by each worker. However, Polish workers already work more hours per year than British, French, German, Italian, or even American workers, according to the OECD.

84. Eurostat, "Employment Rate by Sex, Age Group 20–64," data as of August 17, 2018, ec.europa.eu/eurostat/tgm/table.do?tab=table&init=1&language=en&pcode=t2020_10&plugin=1

85. Iga Magda, Aneta Kiełczewska, and Nicola Brandt, "The 'Family 500+' Child Allowance and Female Labour Supply in Poland," Institute for Structural Research, IBS Working Paper 01/2018, March 2018, ibs.org.pl//app/uploads/2018/03/IBS_Working_Paper_01_2018.pdf. The authors estimate that "up to 103 thousand women did not participate in the labour market in the 1st half of 2017 due to the" new child benefits (12). On lowering the retirement age, see Marcin Goettig, "Polish Cut in Retirement Age Comes into Force, Bucking European Trend," *Reuters*, October 1, 2017, www.reuters.com/article/us-poland-pension/polish-cut-in-retirement-age-comes-into-force-bucking-european-trend-idUSKCN1C60Z6

digital natives who are necessary to operate ever more advanced military equipment Poland is aiming to acquire. This means that Polish military capacity—especially in the manpower-intensive ground forces—may not meet the political goals established by Poland's leaders.

America's Future Relationship with an Increasingly Lethargic Tiger

This chapter began by arguing that Poland has become the economic tiger of Europe, and that Poland is attempting to use its economic strength to establish itself as a leading, if still second-tier, military power within Europe. If Poland's economic trajectory and hence its military expansion are sustainable, it is possible that over the next decade Warsaw might join the ranks of the so-called Big Four within Europe—by displacing Italy, for instance—or become important enough to justify expansion of the infor-mal grouping into a "Big Five." Operationally, at least when viewed from Washington's perspective, such an outcome would mark the point at which the United States could rely upon Poland to do much more than simply act as a speed bump for invading Russians or play the role of first responders for the Baltic States. However, there are two serious impediments to this outcome.

The first is tied to Polish capabilities and capacity. Certainly Warsaw has put into place an impressive pipeline of military force structure initia-tives and defense modernization and acquisition programs that should—assuming Poland can overcome the challenges of managing so many moving pieces—bring about marked improvement in the capabilities and capacity of the Polish military over the coming years. However, the dura-bility of these improvements appears limited at best. As argued in the pre-vious section, the Polish economy looks unlikely to repeat the gains of the middle-to-late 2010s thanks to long-term productivity shortcomings, and Poland's demographic challenges will both compound an expected economic slowdown and frustrate Warsaw's efforts to bulk up its military capacity. These issues will make it exceedingly difficult for Poland to build a defense enterprise that can both defend itself from Russia *and* contribute to Western security beyond northeastern Europe.

The second impediment is related to Warsaw's willpower. Poland remains unquestionably focused on the Russian threat, for good reason. Although Russia is a declining power across a variety of measures,[86] War-

---

86. John R. Deni, ed., *Current Russia Military Affairs: Assessing and Countering Russian*

saw perceives that Russia presents an acute short-term threat due to Moscow's revisionist tendencies and its predisposition to take on greater risk in international security.[87] Given this sway that Russia holds over Polish interests, it will be nearly impossible for American policymakers to convince their Polish counterparts to devote resources or significant attention to security challenges elsewhere, even if the capacity and capability challenges cited above do not materialize. Poles remain fixated on territorial defense in northeastern Europe, and expeditionary operations farther afield hold little if any appeal given where most Poles perceive Polish interests at risk.[88]

Many years of involvement in U.S.-led coalitions in Iraq and Afghanistan have had little impact on the strategic culture of Poland, despite the lip service paid to allied solidarity in rhetoric as well as in strategy documents like Poland's 2017 Defence Concept.[89] Poland's involvement in U.S.-led coalition operations in Iraq and Afghanistan was driven not by any imperative to transform authoritarian societies but rather by a desire to be viewed as a reliable ally and thereby build political capital, which could then be exchanged for security and other benefits in northeastern Europe.[90] Poland's policies were guided by an almost transactional mindset, one in which some degree of support for alliance security across Southern Europe and for Washington's agenda outside northeastern Europe

Strategy, Operational Planning, and Modernization (Carlisle, PA: U.S. Army War College Press, 2018), ssi.armywarcollege.edu/pubs/download.cfm?q=1385

87. Sumit Ganguly, John R. Deni, R. Evan Ellis, and Nathan P. Freier, "History Begins (Again) for the Pentagon," Foreign Policy Research Institute, February 22, 2018, www.fpri.org/2018/02/history-begins-pentagon/; and interview with a civilian defense policy advisor at the Polish mission to NATO, May 17, 2019.

88. Interview with a Polish defense and national security expert at a Warsaw-based think tank, April 15, 2019; interview with an American civilian employee of U.S. Army Europe with extensive experience in military-to-military programs across Europe, November 13, 2018; and interview with a former senior civilian employee within the Office of the Secretary of Defense, December 2, 2018.

89. In contrast, operations in Iraq and Afghanistan had a major impact on the Polish military, highlighting equipment, training, and force structure shortcomings and establishing a primary rationale for the major modernization and capacity improvements now under way. Interview with an expert on Polish national security and strategy at a think tank in Warsaw, May 1, 2019.

90. Interview with an expert on Polish national security and strategy at a think tank in Warsaw, May 1, 2019; Rachel Dicke et al., "NATO Burden-Sharing in Libya: Understanding the Contributions of Norway, Spain and Poland to the War Effort," *Polish Quarterly of International Affairs* 22, no. 4 (2013): 29–53; Laura Chappell, "Poland in Transition: Implications for a European Security and Defence Policy," *Contemporary Security Policy* 31, no. 2 (2010): 225–48; Jacek Lubecki, "Poland in Iraq: The Politics of the Decision," *Polish Review* 50, no. 1 (2005): 69–92; Matthew Rhodes, "Central Europe and Iraq: Balance, Bandwagon, or Bridge?," *Orbis* 48, no. 3 (2004): 423–36; and David H. Dunn, "Poland: America's New Model Ally," *Defence Studies* 2, no. 2 (2002): 63–86.

would lead to arms deals, increased or more permanent U.S. deployments to Poland, more Western European support for deployments in Eastern Europe, political support for Warsaw's hardline response to Russian provocations, and turning a blind eye to the increasingly poor quality of Polish democracy.[91]

In the post-Crimea security environment, if Poland *does* contribute resources to meeting a security challenge beyond northeastern Europe, it will likely do so only in exchange for security benefits *in* northeastern Europe. Poland's involvement with the anti-ISIL coalition is emblematic of this. For nearly two years, Washington sought a Polish contribution to the coalition. Only in 2016, after Warsaw had received assurances from the United States that its rotational presence of forces in Poland would be enhanced, did the Polish government decide to make a contribution to the coalition.[92] Even then, Poland's contribution was relatively small—four F-16s that were limited to a reconnaissance role and several dozen Special Operations Forces personnel to assist with training on the ground. This reflects what has occasionally been called the Komorowski Doctrine, named after former President Bronisław Komorowski who promulgated a change in approach even prior to Crimea.[93] The Komorowski Doctrine, announced in 2013, called on Poland to avoid far flung expeditionary operations and instead to focus on developing a self-sufficiency when it comes to territorial defense. The overly transactional approach also has contributed to a sense among some U.S. policymakers and government officials that Poland is one of America's most difficult allies to work with.[94]

It is possible that military operations in cyberspace may be a way of drawing Poland into a broader conceptualization of defending and promoting Western interests beyond the geographic bounds of northeastern

91. Interview with a Polish expert on transatlantic relations and national security at a Warsaw-based think tank, April 26, 2019; interview with an expert on Polish national security and strategy at a think tank in Warsaw, May 1, 2019; and Fredrik Doeser and Joakim Eidenfalk, "Using Strategic Culture to Understand Participation in Expeditionary Operations: Australia, Poland, and the Coalition against the Islamic State," *Contemporary Security Policy* 40, no. 1 (2019): 4–29. The authors also argue that a secondary reason for Polish participation in expeditionary operations is to gain operational experience for Polish military forces that might then benefit Poland's territorial defense efforts.

92. Fredrik Doeser, "Historical Experiences, Strategic Culture, and Strategic Behavior: Poland in the Anti-ISIS Coalition," *Defence Studies* 18, no. 4 (2018): 454–73.

93. "President: No More Far-Off Military Missions," Polish Press Agency, August 15, 2019, www.prezydent.pl/en/president-komorowski/news/art,485,president-no-more-far-off-military-missions.html

94. Interview with a former senior civilian employee within the Office of the Secretary of Defense, December 2, 2018; interview with a former civilian political advisor to U.S. military forces in Europe, June 16, 2017.

Europe.[95] Obviously, Russia has been very involved in the cyber domain over the last several years, yet cyber is also a realm in which other countries—such as China and North Korea—have sought to attack Western interests, including in Europe. Poland's cyber capacity and capabilities are very limited, and it remains unclear whether cyber efforts can successfully compete in Poland's modernization program with far more visible and seemingly more impactful programs such as armored vehicles, fighter jets, helicopters, and air defense systems.[96] Moreover, although Poland's 2014 National Security Strategy calls for the development of offensive cyber capabilities, there are no indications that Warsaw has made significant progress toward this objective.[97] Nonetheless, if Poland can develop the capabilities and capacity to conduct offensive as well as defensive cyber operations, Washington may be able to convince Warsaw to take on a larger role in the pursuit of Western interests beyond northeastern Europe, at least in the cyber domain.

It is also possible that the salience of the Russian threat may decrease over the next decade in the eyes of Poles, permitting decision-makers in Warsaw greater latitude in determining where and how to apply Polish hard power. Already there is some evidence that the threat of Russians rolling through Ukraine and into Poland is not as prominent in the minds of Poles as it was in 2014 or 2015, adversely affecting today's military recruitment efforts in Poland.[98] Nonetheless, the question that U.S. policymakers will need to ponder as they assess the degree to which Poland can and will contribute to the security of Western interests beyond northeastern Europe is whether the contribution that Poland might make is worth the effort to gain Warsaw's participation.

---

95. Interview with civilian defense policy advisor at the Polish mission to NATO, May 17, 2019.

96. Interview with a Polish expert on transatlantic relations and national security at a Warsaw-based think tank, April 26, 2019.

97. "National Security Strategy of the Republic of Poland," 2014, 32.

98. Interview with a U.S. field-grade officer based in Washington who works on U.S.-Poland military-to-military relations, April 5, 2019.

SEVEN

The American Response

The preceding chapters have made the case that there are an array of strategic level changes that have unfolded or that continue to unfold among several of America's most important allies in Europe. These changes are going to have a profound impact on the ability and willingness of those allies to play important roles as partners with the United States in defending and promoting common interests and collective security in the decade to come. In short, the constellation of major European allies that the United States has relied upon over the last 15 years across air, land, sea, cyber, and space domains will not look the same in the late 2020s.

In the case of the United Kingdom, the unfolding Brexit and the austerity that preceded it have already greatly diminished the capacity and capabilities of British armed forces. Economic and political factors—including the COVID-19 recession and the potential secession of Scotland—are likely to advance the UK military along a continued trajectory of reduced hard power, despite a growing population. It is true that Britain's security horizon remains expansive, but as its capacity and capabilities continue to decline history suggests London's strategic ambition will as well, potentially undermining the so-called special relationship with the United States.

Germany appears to be in the opposite situation—it is reluctant to convert its impressive latent power into hard power, but it has the potential for significant change in this regard over time. Germany's economic strength is well established, and given extant indicators of productivity and the degree of automation across its economy it is likely that the country will remain

Europe's economic hegemon over the next decade, even as it navigates the peaks and troughs of the business cycle and as it faces demographic headwinds. Its hesitancy to embrace the role of political hegemon—much less a military one—has the potential to evolve significantly, though, considering how far Berlin has shifted over the last quarter century in its approach toward the use of force. Even if this is so, the speed of that evolution remains an open question.

France, like the United Kingdom, has a growing population and it still retains a broad security horizon, despite its recent emphasis on homeland defense. Moreover, in recent years and in certain security contexts, Paris has already become a closer, more important ally than London—in many respects, it seems poised to displace the United Kingdom as Washington's "special relationship" partner in Europe. However, the French economy remains hobbled by an austerity hangover and even longer-term structural problems that President Emmanuel Macron's and En Marche's political revolution has yet to successfully and completely ameliorate, especially considering the impact of the COVID-19 recession. The signs of stress on France's hard power assets have already manifest themselves, and the French military remains overstretched by significant operational demands at home and in Africa.

Italy combines the worst trends outlined above. Its population is aging and declining. Its economy nearly imploded during the sovereign debt crisis, has stagnated since then due to an insufficient level of reform and long lingering productivity shortcomings, and confronts a painful postpandemic recovery in the coming years. Italy's economic problems were magnified by the migration crisis of the mid-2010s, which ushered in Western Europe's first populist government. Meanwhile, Italian military power has contracted significantly thanks to fiscal belt-tightening over many years, thereby matching what appears to be a receding security horizon and a contraction of Italy's role in the world, as recently redefined by populist political forces.

Poland has the potential to displace Italy as a leading economic, political, and military power in Europe, becoming the fourth of the "Big Four." Thanks to earlier reforms and limited exposure to global financial currents, Poland managed to avoid recession and hence dramatic defense budget cuts at the height of the sovereign debt crisis and the Great Recession. Since then, the Polish economy has been among the fastest growing on the continent, allowing leaders in Warsaw to begin turning economic strength into hard power through an ambitious—perhaps too ambitious—military modernization and expansion effort. However, what brought Poland to this point will not succeed in furthering its long-term objectives, as its economy looks likely to slow down and as its population contracts over time.

All of this presents a major challenge to American grand strategy, which has long favored reliance on allies—especially those in Europe—to help shoulder political, diplomatic, and military burdens. If its most important European allies are incapable of wielding power, unable to muster the willpower to do so, or lacking the capacity for sustained engagement, this bodes poorly for Washington's efforts to promote U.S. as well as allied security and interests in Europe and beyond. However, the United States is not completely helpless in this regard—it can wield policy tools that might build upon the few silver linings noted in the preceding chapters while mitigating the worst aspects of the strategic transformations that have played out or that are continuing to unfold.

This chapter will examine what tools Washington has at its disposal, and how it might use them to accentuate the positive trends, as few as they may be, while managing the negative ones. Before doing that, the chapter will first examine the security environment in Europe and beyond to identify the key threats to U.S. and Western interests, all in an effort to answer the question of what Washington expects of its allies. The chapter will next try to identify how and where U.S. allies might figure into meeting the major security challenges of the next decade. Finally, the last section of this chapter will attempt to identify the most effective and efficient tools for the United States to wield in encouraging and enabling its most important European allies to shoulder more of the burden. Many of these tools are military or security policy ones, but some are not, and so this section of the chapter will also address diplomatic and economic or trade policy levers that Washington might utilize.

The Strategic and Geopolitical Environment of the Next Decade

Over the last several years, a new broad-based consensus has emerged among leading U.S. politicians, foreign policy thinkers, policy-oriented academics, think tank experts, and other opinion leaders that the United States has spent much of the last two decades overly focused on the challenge posed by transnational violent extremist groups.[1] The focus on this

---

1. Jim Garamone, "Dunford Describes U.S. Great Power Competition with Russia, China," *Defense.gov*, March 21, 2019, dod.defense.gov/News/Article/Article/1791811/dunford-describes-us-great-power-competition-with-russia-china/; Robert Malley and Jon Finer, "The Long Shadow of 9/11: How Counterterrorism Warps U.S. Foreign Policy," *For-*

particular threat made sense in the context of the 9/11 attacks of 2001 and during a period of what many perceived as unchallenged American hegemony. However, attempting to identify and eliminate transnational terrorists worldwide, depose regimes willing to provide safe havens, and return stability and security to conflict-wracked societies in places like Iraq and Afghanistan has resulted in a lack of attention devoted to other, arguably more profound challenges. Principal among these other challenges has been great power competition on the part of Russia and China.

Russia is a declining state along a number of common measures, including those relied upon in this book. Demographically, despite government efforts to increase childbearing, Russia continues to face both short-term challenges and a long-term declining population.[2] The United Nations estimates that Russia's population in 2050 will be roughly 132 million people, versus nearly 144 million today.[3] From a macroeconomic perspective, the Russian economy remains tied to resource extraction,[4] corruption continues to plague most aspects of private, public, and business life,[5] and the massive size of the state in the economy will continue to act as a major impediment to stronger growth.[6] For these reasons, and especially in light of the collapse of oil demand in 2020 due to the global COVID-19-induced slowdown, Russia's economy is likely to grow only very slowly into the mid-2020s.

Militarily, though, Russia's efforts at reform and improved capabilities

eign Policy, July/August 2018, www.foreignaffairs.com/articles/2018-06-14/long-shadow-911; A. Trevor Thrall and Erik Goepner, "Step Back: Lessons for U.S. Foreign Policy from the Failed War on Terror," CATO Institute, Policy Analysis No. 814, June 26, 2017, www.cato.org/publications/policy-analysis/step-back-lessons-us-foreign-policy-failed-war-terror

2. Matthew Luxmoore, "Rising Mortality Rates Challenge Russia's Efforts to Kick-Start Population Growth," *Radio Free Europe/Radio Liberty*, April 4, 2019, www.rferl.org/a/rising-mortality-rates-challenge-population-growth-decline-putin-demographics/29861882.html; "Russia's Population Declines in 2018 for First Time in a Decade," *Moscow Times*, December 21, 2018, www.themoscowtimes.com/2018/12/21/russias-population-declines-2018-first-time-in-decade-a63926; "Birth Rate Hits 10-Year Low in Russia," *Moscow Times*, January 29, 2018, www.themoscowtimes.com/2018/01/29/birth-rate-hits-10-year-low-russia-a60321; and Tom Balmforth, "Another Worrying Sign for Russia's Dire Demographics," *Radio Free Europe/Radio Liberty*, September 27, 2017, www.rferl.org/a/russia-population-decline-labor-oreshkin/28760413.html

3. "Urban and Rural Population: Russian Federation," UN World Urbanization Prospects 2018, population.un.org/wup/Country-Profiles/

4. Katsuya Ito, "Dutch Disease and Russia," *International Economics* 151, no. C (2017): 66–70.

5. Noah Buckley, "Corruption and Power in Russia," Foreign Policy Research Institute, April 2018, www.fpri.org/wp-content/uploads/2018/04/buckley.pdf

6. Gabriel Di Bella, Oksana Dynnikova, and Slavi Slavov, "The Russian State's Size and Its Footprint: Have They Increased?," *IMF Working Paper*, WP/19/53, March 2, 2019.

have yielded some serious results over the last decade, mostly in the wake of the Georgia War. Although successful in terms of achieving a political outcome acceptable to Moscow, Russia's war in Georgia in 2008 revealed several capability and readiness shortcomings, even though units from Russia's North Caucasus Military District—which formed the bulk of the forces involved in the war—had some of the most combat-experienced troops in Russia.[7] In particular, Russia's lack of advanced night vision devices, reactive vehicle armor, advanced radios, advanced body armor and helmets, and advanced fire control systems meant that Georgian forces—most of which *had* all of these capabilities—inflicted more damage than they suffered.[8] Moreover, the lack of drones, counterbattery radars, satellite imagery for intelligence planning, precision guided munitions, and electronic warfare capabilities all degraded and inhibited Russia's efforts. Finally, Russian tactics reflected traditional, outdated Soviet models of maneuver and engagement; Russian operations relied excessively on poorly trained conscripts; and Russian military personnel policies revealed that even top-line military units needed significant personnel augmentation to fight.[9]

Since the Georgia War, many of these shortcomings have been addressed through a military reform effort known as the "New Look." Funneling more money into modern equipment, decreasing reliance on conscripts, trimming the officer corps, increasing mobility by focusing on brigade-sized forces versus larger divisions, and more effectively employing unconventional capabilities such as information and cyber operations were all hallmarks of the post-Georgia reform effort. Certainly Moscow's post-2008 reforms remain somewhat hampered by corruption, inefficiencies inherent in the Russian economy and defense sector specifically, and the impact of post-Crimea sanctions imposed by the West, but the Russian military today is far more capable than that which overwhelmed Georgia through sheer magnitude of force in August 2008.[10]

Evidence for this increased capability was seen in Crimea beginning in

7. Michael Kofman, "The August War, Ten Years On: A Retrospective on the Russo-Georgian War," *War on the Rocks*, August 17, 2018, warontherocks.com/2018/08/the-august-war-ten-years-on-a-retrospective-on-the-russo-georgian-war/

8. Ariel Cohen and Robert Hamilton, *The Russian Military and the Georgia War: Lessons and Implications* (Carlisle, PA: U.S. Army War College Press, 2011), 28, 33.

9. Lionel Beehner et al., "Analyzing the Russian Way of War: Evidence from the 2008 Conflict with Georgia," Modern War Institute at West Point, March 20, 2018, 50–1, mwi.usma.edu/wp-content/uploads/2018/03/Analyzing-the-Russian-Way-of-War.pdf

10. Fredrik Westerlund, "Force or Modernization?" in *Current Russia Military Affairs: Assessing and Countering Russian Strategy, Operational Planning, and Modernization*, ed. John R. Deni (Carlisle, PA: U.S. Army War College Press, 2018), 35–39.

spring 2014 as well as in Syria starting in September 2015, which marked the first expeditionary Russian military operation since the end of the Cold War. Although fluctuating oil prices—and the related impact on Russia's fiscal situation—have prevented Moscow from accomplishing as much in terms of reform and modernization as quickly as it would have liked, the Russian operations in Ukraine and Syria provide evidence of a military force that is significantly more capable than it was a decade ago from a qualitative point of view. The changes have been most evident in terms of more professional personnel, new command and control systems, more advanced communications equipment, significantly improved situational awareness, greater distribution of precision weapons across all branches, and more modern weapons in general.[11] The U.S. Defense Intelligence Agency assessed that, as a result of ongoing Russian reforms, the Russian military "is on the rise," smaller but more mobile and nearly able to conduct the full range of military operations.[12]

This far more capable military is increasingly placed in the service of Moscow's revisionist foreign policy. One prominent scholar refers to this as "heavy metal diplomacy," in which both the use and threatened use of the military serve the broader interests of Russian national security policy in dividing, distracting, and deterring the West from challenging Russia, especially in what Moscow perceives as its zone of privileged interest.[13] Despite a quarter century of Western attempts to engage Russia, pull it into the global economy, reduce tensions by cutting military forces across Europe, and bury the acrimony of the Cold War, political dynamics within Russia continue to incentivize Moscow toward a zero-sum approach with the West. Historically—and based in large measure on Russia's particular geography—Russians have associated territory with security. Russian politicians—and before them, Soviet politicians, and before them, Czarist politicians—are skilled at exploiting that association and the attendant demonization of the "other" across the vast borderlands for political and

---

11. Anton Lavrov, "Russian Military Reforms from Georgia to Syria," CSIS, November 2018, csis-prod.s3.amazonaws.com/s3fs-public/publication/181106_RussiaSyria_WEB_v2.pdf

12. Defense Intelligence Agency, "Russia Military Power: Building a Military to Support Great Power Aspirations," 2017, www.dia.mil/Portals/27/Documents/News/Military%20Power%20Publications/Russia%20Military%20Power%20Report%202017.pdf?ver=2017-06-28-144235-937

13. Mark Galeotti, "Heavy Metal Diplomacy: Russia's Political Use of Its Military in Europe since 2014," European Council on Foreign Relations, December 19, 2016, www.ecfr.eu/page/-/Heavy_Metal_Diplomacy_Final_2.pdf

sometimes material gain.[14] Given the challenges Russia faces from China in the Far East, Moscow's approach may ultimately prove counterproductive to Russian interests over the long term, just as Russian power and the ability to control events across its borders recede. Nevertheless, it seems clear that at least in the short run Russia presents an acute threat to U.S. and Western interests across Europe and beyond thanks to Moscow's wide-ranging nuclear arsenal and its ability and willingness to destabilize Europe through occupation, intimidation, and covert action.

If Moscow represents an acute short-term threat, the most likely long-term threat confronting the United States is China. Europe also faces a long-term threat from China, even if some European capitals prefer not to acknowledge this just yet. The conventional wisdom holds that China is on an inexorable rise and is hence likely to dominate the twenty-first century economically and perhaps politically and militarily, yet some scholars do not subscribe to this perspective on China's trajectory. They argue that its models of governance and development cannot continue without some eventual upheaval, or that its demographic trends paint a picture of an aging society that will increasingly lose ground to neighboring India, or both. For some or all of these reasons, they conclude that China is already on a path toward relative economic stagnation, increased social tension, and political decline.[15]

If the China "decliners" are correct, then perhaps the West has little to worry about and any efforts to confront the long-term challenge presented by Beijing are actually a waste of time and effort. However, between now and the point at which China eventually declines, the United States and its allies will nonetheless face an array of threats stemming from Beijing's efforts to wield its newfound power and slow or reverse its decline. More alarmingly, if the decliners are *wrong* and China has not already peaked economically and hence politically and militarily, the same array of threats exist and are only likely to become more intense. In such a scenario, the defense of Western interests will require a far clearer collectively agreed road map than currently exists.

---

14. For a discussion of the forces shaping Russian foreign policy, see John R. Deni, *NATO and Article 5: The Transatlantic Alliance and the Twenty-First-Century Challenges of Collective Defense* (Lanham, MD: Rowman and Littlefield, 2017), 37–72.

15. David Shambaugh, *China's Future* (Cambridge: Polity Press, 2016); Collin Meisel and Jonathan D. Moyer, "Preparing for China's Rapid Rise and Decline," *War on the Rocks*, April 15, 2019, warontherocks.com/2019/04/preparing-for-chinas-rapid-rise-and-decline/; and "Ageing Tigers, Hidden Dragons," *Voice of Asia*, no. 3, September 2017, www2.deloitte.com/insights/us/en/economy/voice-of-asia/sept-2017/demographics-ageing-tigers-hidden-dragons.html

There are many indicators that China has in fact *not* peaked economically, militarily, or politically and is instead engaged in a significant, occasionally aggressive effort to build and wield hard power commensurate with its expanding economic heft. Washington has long been convinced that China seeks to become the preeminent power in the massive Indo-Pacific region, and there is plenty of evidence that this is Beijing's goal. Most obviously, President Xi Jinping's "China Dream" concept articulates a long-standing national aspiration of restoring China's status as a powerful and prosperous nation with a strong military.[16]

In order to achieve these goals, Beijing continues to funnel its growing economic wealth into ever increasing defense budgets aimed at dramatic military modernization efforts. The latest modernization push aims to have the Chinese military match the U.S. military in terms of technological capabilities by 2035. The intent of defense modernization, according to Chinese military strategy documents, is for the Chinese military to fight and win wars, deter potential adversaries, and secure Chinese national interests overseas.[17] The Chinese are also placing increased emphasis on maritime and information domains, offensive air operations, long-distance mobility operations, and space and cyber operations.

Even as China pursues these objectives, there are signs it has *already made* substantial progress to date. For instance, Beijing currently has two deployable aircraft carriers, allowing it to project power beyond its coast and neighboring seas, and it has begun building a third.[18] In terms of advanced air power, China is the only other country besides the United States to have developed and deployed a fifth-generation jet fighter—the J-20.[19] The Chinese are researching and probably developing directed energy weapons and transmission jamming equipment for use against sat-

16. "What Does Xi Jinping's China Dream Mean?" *BBC Online*, June 6, 2013, www.bbc. com/news/world-asia-china-22726375; Office of the Secretary of Defense, "Annual Report to Congress: Military and Security Developments Involving the People's Republic of China 2019," May 2, 2019, media.defense.gov/2019/May/02/2002127082/-1/-1/1/2019_CHINA_MILITARY_POWER_REPORT.pdf

17. Office of the Secretary of Defense, "Annual Report to Congress: Military and Security Developments Involving the People's Republic of China 2019," May 2, 2019, media.defense.gov/2019/May/02/2002127082/-1/-1/1/2019_CHINA_MILITARY_POWER_REPORT.pdf

18. Robert Burns, "Pentagon: Chinese Carrier Likely to Join Naval Fleet in 2019," Associated Press, May 2, 2019, apnews.com/9a514cd09c58435ab323efa52638473f; Greg Torode and Ben Blanchard, "Exclusive: Images Show Construction on China's Third and Largest Aircraft Carrier—Analysts," *Reuters*, May 7, 2019, www.reuters.com/article/us-china-military-carrier-exclusive/exclusive-analysts-images-show-construction-on-chinas-third-and-largest-aircraft-carrier-idUSKCN1SD0CP

19. Anthony Capaccio, "China's Stealth Jet May Be Ready This Year, U.S. Commander

ellites in orbit above Earth, and Beijing already has a proven antisatellite missile capability.[20] Additionally, the Chinese military is capable of projecting power—although not yet sustaining it—as far away as the Arctic, and most broadly Chinese leaders have been clear about their desire to build a "world class" military.[21]

All of the aforementioned initiatives and programs—focused on building modern military forces capable of conducting operations across a variety of domains—might sound benign enough, the stuff of any country's plan to ensure its security in a chaotic world. However, China's unique challenge to the West—whether it is on a downward trajectory over the coming decade or an upward one—lies in the *manner* in which Beijing employs its growing power as well as the *scale* of China's potential influence.

Already there is evidence China is willing to use its power in ways that flaunt commonly held norms, ignore international law, and violate the sovereignty of its neighbors. Take for example China's approach toward the disputed islands and atolls in the South China Sea. For many years, China has claimed sovereignty over almost the entirety of the South China Sea, an area rich in natural resources and fossil fuels. To counter China's sweeping territorial claims, the government of the Philippines—a treaty ally of the United States—accused Beijing of violating the UN Convention on the Law of the Sea, to which China is a signatory. In 2013, Manila brought a case before the Permanent Court of Arbitration at The Hague, in accordance with the Law of the Sea. In 2016, the Court ruled in favor of the Philippines in almost all matters of the case, finding that "China had violated the Philippines' sovereign rights in its exclusive economic zone by interfering with Philippine fishing and petroleum exploration, constructing artificial islands, and failing to prevent Chinese fishermen from fishing in the [Philippines'] zone."[22] China has had similar disputes over South China Sea islands and territory with Vietnam, Malaysia, and Taiwan, yet it

Says," *Bloomberg*, May 1, 2019, www.bloomberg.com/news/articles/2019-05-01/china-s-stealth-jet-may-be-ready-this-year-u-s-commander-says?srnd=politics-vp

20. Carin Zissis, "China's Anti-Satellite Test," Council on Foreign Relations, February 22, 2007, www.cfr.org/backgrounder/chinas-anti-satellite-test; Defense Intelligence Agency, "China Military Power: Modernizing a Force to Fight and Win," 2019, 43, www.dia.mil/Portals/27/Documents/News/Military%20Power%20Publications/China_Military_Power_FINAL_5MB_20190103.pdf; and Office of the Secretary of Defense, "Annual Report to Congress: Military and Security Developments Involving the People's Republic of China 2019," May 2, 2019, 50–51, media.defense.gov/2019/May/02/2002127082/-1/-1/1/2019_CHINA_MILITARY_POWER_REPORT.pdf

21. Kathrin Hille, "China's Army Redoubles Modernisation Effort," *Financial Times*, January 28, 2019, www.ft.com/content/b255a1c0-1e69-11e9-b126-46fc3ad87c65

22. Permanent Court of Arbitration, "Press Release: The South China Sea Arbitration

has refused to relinquish its claims or modify its behavior. On the contrary, Beijing has deepened these disputes by constructing military infrastructure such as harbor facilities and airstrips on several South China Sea islands claimed by more than one country.

These disputes matter not simply to U.S. allies in the immediate vicinity, such as the Philippines and Thailand, or to just Washington's other Asian allies such as Japan and South Korea. They also matter to Europe, primarily because of the massive volume of world trade that passes through the South China Sea in any given year. Germany alone sent $117 billion in exports through the South China Sea in 2016, or roughly 9 percent of the value of all German exports.[23] That same year, France and the United Kingdom each sent $42 billion in exports, which represented 8.6 percent of all French exports and just over 10 percent of all British exports for 2016. In contrast, the United States shipped just 5.7 percent of the value of its exports through the South China Sea in 2016. Of course China is more dependent on the flow of trade through the South China Sea than any European or North American country, so it would not appear to be in Beijing's interest to see trade through it disrupted. Nonetheless, misunderstanding or miscalculation could lead to conflict. If the South China Sea or the important Malacca or Lombok straits that connect to it were made inaccessible, European trade would be dealt a serious blow, potentially affecting the jobs and income of millions of European citizens, given that roughly one in four of Germany's 45 million workers depends on exports.[24] So far, there is some early evidence that European countries are becoming increasingly willing to exercise hard power to defend norms and lines of communication in the Indo-Pacific.[25]

China has similarly violated international norms in its relentless pur-

(The Republic of the Philippines v. the People's Republic of China," July 12, 2016, pcacases. com/web/sendAttach/1801

23. China Power Team, "How Much Trade Transits the South China Sea?," CSIS, August 2, 2017, updated October 27, 2017, chinapower.csis.org/much-trade-transits-south-china-sea/; World Integrated Trade Solution, "Product Exports by Country and Region 2016," World Bank, wits.worldbank.org/CountryProfile/en/Country/USA/Year/2016/TradeFlow/Export/Partner/all/Product/Total

24. "Germany in World Trade," Federation of German Industry, June 27, 2016, english. bdi.eu/article/news/germany-in-world-trade/

25. Wendy Wu, "European Militaries 'Will Do More to Counter Assertive China' in Indo-Pacific," *South China Morning Post*, March 19, 2019, www.scmp.com/news/china/diplomacy/article/3002319/european-militaries-will-do-more-counter-assertive-china-indo; "How Will France's Growing Naval Presence in Asia Affect Its China Ties?," *World Politics Review*, June 3, 2019, www.worldpoliticsreview.com/trend-lines/27908/how-will-france-s-growing-naval-presence-in-asia-affect-its-china-ties

suit of technological modernization of its economy. Its government has engaged in systematic economic espionage and intellectual property theft on a massive scale for many years, all in an effort to boost Chinese companies, many of which have been or remain state-owned or state-affiliated.[26] Beijing leverages a veritable army of domestic computer hackers, traditional spies overseas, and corrupt corporate insiders in U.S. and other companies to steal that which it cannot develop indigenously.[27] In many instances, the state-directed economic espionage and intellectual property theft—described as "methodical, persistent, and well-resourced"—is funneled directly into Chinese military advancements in areas such as radiation hardened integrated circuits, accelerometers, gyroscopes, space communications, military communication jamming equipment, aviation technologies, and antisubmarine warfare.[28]

Increasingly, the United States is not alone in viewing China's approach as at least somewhat malevolent, especially when it comes to cyber espionage and intellectual property theft.[29] German companies have become alarmed at the degree and scope of Beijing's predatory behavior, its subsidizing of Chinese companies, and its discriminatory treatment of foreign companies, referring to China as a "systemic competitor."[30] Across Europe, economists and other experts have become increasingly concerned about China's efforts to systematically steal trade secrets from EU member states.[31] Thanks to prodding from the United States—as well as a 2017 Chi-

---

26. Lingling Wei and Bob Davis, "How China Systematically Pries Technology from U.S. Companies," *Wall Street Journal*, September 26, 2018, www.wsj.com/articles/how-china-systematically-pries-technology-from-u-s-companies-1537972066

27. Del Quentin Wilber, "China 'Has Taken the Gloves Off' in its Thefts of U.S. Technology Secrets," *Los Angeles Times*, November 16, 2018, www.latimes.com/politics/la-na-pol-china-economic-espionage-20181116-story.html; Jim Sciutto, "'The Shadow War': How a Chinese Spy Stole Some of the Pentagon's Most Sensitive Secrets," *CNN*, May 14, 2019, www.cnn.com/2019/05/14/politics/shadow-war-chinese-spy/index.html

28. Office of the Secretary of Defense, "Annual Report to Congress: Military and Security Developments Involving the People's Republic of China 2019," May 2, 2019, 103–4, media.defense.gov/2019/May/02/2002127082/-1/-1/1/2019_CHINA_MILITARY_POWER_REPORT.pdf

29. Matthew Karnitschnig, "For NATO, China Is the New Russia," *Politico*, April 4, 2019, www.politico.eu/article/for-nato-china-is-the-new-russia/

30. "Partner and Systemic Competitor—How Do We Deal with China's State-Controlled Economy?" German Federation of Industry, January 10, 2019, english.bdi.eu/media/publications/#/publication/news/china-partner-and-systemic-competitor

31. Zak Doffman, "China's Spies Accused of Stealing EU Tech Secrets, Just as China and EU Agree Stronger Ties," *Forbes*, April 11, 2019, www.forbes.com/sites/zakdoffman/2019/04/11/chinese-spies-accused-of-major-european-ip-theft-just-as-china-and-europe-agree-stronger-ties/#1af64e0d70f4; "ifo Umfrage: Direktinvestitionen aus China werden kritischer betrachtet als die anderer Länder," ifo Institut, May 20, 2019, www.cesifo-

nese law requiring organizations and citizens to support national security investigations—many in Europe have grown anxious over Beijing's ability to leverage and exploit Chinese telecommunications companies like Huawei and ZTE for China's national security benefit.[32] At the intergovernmental level, the European Union previously viewed China as a potential "strategic partner" in maintaining global trade rules and in other aspects.[33] Today, though, that perspective is gradually evolving, as the EU recognizes it needs a more balanced approach, including by recognizing that China is a "systemic rival" in some contexts.[34]

Beijing has perhaps sensed the shifting tone. To burnish its otherwise poor image and distract from its malign activities, Beijing has begun cultivating a wide variety of influencers and advocates across the continent who, among other things, downplay the security threat posed by China and gloss over Beijing's human rights record.[35] In Brussels alone, the Chinese company Huawei has a lobbying staff of 10 and an annual budget of $2.2 million, all in an effort to dispel any security or espionage concerns.[36]

While China and Russia are very different sorts of challenges, what they have in common for the United States and its European allies is the fact that they are likely to each pursue strategic competition with the West in ways that approach but avoid crossing the threshold of NATO's Article 5 clause on mutual defense assistance. Although not unimaginable, a massive,

---

group.de/de/ifoHome/presse/Pressemitteilungen/Pressemitteilungen-Archiv/2019/Q2/pm_20190520_china.html

32. For example, Beijing could exploit embedded electronic "backdoors" that would provide unauthorized access to private and personal data. Jonathan Stearns and Alexander Weber, "China Threat to Telecoms Cited in EU Parliament Draft Resolution," *Bloomberg*, March 11, 2019, www.bloomberg.com/news/articles/2019-03-11/china-threat-to-telecoms-cited-in-eu-parliament-draft-resolution-jt4gae79

33. European Commission, "Joint Communication to the European Parliament and the Council: Elements for a New EU Strategy on China," June 22, 2016, eeas.europa.eu/archives/docs/china/docs/joint_communication_to_the_european_parliament_and_the_council_-_elements_for_a_new_eu_strategy_on_china.pdf

34. Laurence Norman, "EU, in Major Shift, Moves to Confront China's Growing Assertiveness," *Wall Street Journal*, March 13, 2019, www.wsj.com/articles/eu-in-major-shift-moves-to-confront-chinas-growing-assertiveness-11552417033; European Commission, "Joint Communication to the European Parliament, the European Council and the Council: EU-China—a Strategic Outlook," March 12, 2019, ec.europa.eu/commission/sites/beta-political/files/communication-eu-china-a-strategic-outlook.pdf

35. Peter Martin and Alan Crawford, "China's Influence Digs Deep into Europe's Political Landscape," *Bloomberg*, April 3, 2019, www.bloomberg.com/news/articles/2019-04-03/china-s-influence-digs-deep-into-europe-s-political-landscape

36. Alexander Fanta, "Chinas fleißigster Lobbyist: Wie Huawei um seine Rolle im 5G-Ausbau kämpft," Netzpolitik.org, February 8, 2019, netzpolitik.org/2019/chinas-fleissigster-lobbyist-wie-huawei-um-seine-rolle-im-5g-ausbau-kaempft/

conventional and potentially nuclear confrontation with China or Russia is unlikely. What is far more likely are an unending array of relatively small yet provocative initiatives on land, at sea, in the air, in space, across media of all forms, in the cyber realm, and even in boardrooms and stock markets designed to gain leverage and influence at the expense of the United States and its allies. Maintaining the Western way of life in economic, political, social, legal, and cultural terms will require adroitly wielding hard and soft power iteratively vis-à-vis China and Russia, but Washington still faces many hurdles in convincing its European allies of the nature of the competition at hand and the best ways to go about responding to it.[37]

At the same time, other threats and challenges will remain, requiring the West to figuratively chew gum and walk simultaneously. Chief among these will be counterterrorism, especially in places like Africa and the Middle East where transnational terrorist groups take advantage of safe havens. While devoting more attention and resources to great power competition, the United States and its allies must also adequately, effectively, and efficiently address the residual counterterrorist threat. This threat is not existential, certainly not in the way the near-peer competition from China or Russia could become, but it is a serious one. Although ISIL may no longer control territory in the Middle East the way it did just a few years ago, the threat it poses there, in Africa, and in Europe remains significant, at least in the short run. Meanwhile, al-Qaida maintains a nearly worldwide network of affiliates interested in planning and carrying out attacks against the United States and its allies. Despite battlefield and key personnel losses, a tightening of border and travel restrictions, and increasingly difficult efforts to fundraise, it is unlikely ISIL or al-Qaida will simply fade away over time. Instead, it is possible they will undergo metamorphoses, rebrand themselves, splinter, or merge with other like-minded, transnational movements, given that the underlying reasons for their development have not disappeared.[38] Poor, unresponsive governance; unrepresentative governments; disaffected, unemployed youth; and Islam's clash with modernity remain fixtures of life across North Africa, sub-Saharan Africa, and the Middle East.

---

37. See, for example, Noah Barkin, "The U.S. Is Losing Europe in Its Battle with China," *Atlantic*, June 4, 2019, www.theatlantic.com/international/archive/2019/06/united-states-needs-europe-against-china/590887/. For an example of how the United States failed to convince Europe, see Matthew Yglesias, "How a Chinese Infrastructure Bank Turned into a Diplomatic Fiasco for America," *Vox*, April 1, 2015, www.vox.com/2015/4/1/8311921/asian-infrastructure-investment-bank

38. "National Strategy for Counterterrorism of the United States of America," October 2018, www.whitehouse.gov/wp-content/uploads/2018/10/NSCT.pdf

Additionally, the proliferation of technology related to weapons of mass destruction remains a major security challenge for the West. Iran and North Korea represent the two most significant problems in this regard. The former has explicitly declared its desire to upend the security environment of its particular region and it maintains extensive ties to transnational terrorist groups, while the latter has done its best to destabilize Northeast Asia and seems willing to sell "almost any of its military hardware if the price is right."[39]

Finally, large-scale sociopolitical instability and conflict—including that stemming from or exacerbated by climate change or pandemics like COVID-19—will remain a threat to U.S. interests. Humanitarian motivations occasionally drive Western intervention in foreign internal crises, but a more common scenario for Western intervention is that of a crisis generating cross-border effects that impact the security or stability of American allies, especially those in Europe.[40]

No political leaders on either side of the Atlantic have any desire to repeat the lengthy, inconclusive stability operation in Afghanistan, but other imperatives may compel intervention in such a conflict again over the next decade. The Syrian civil war provides a good example of a case in which Western apprehension and hesitation arguably worsened the crisis, from which hundreds of thousands of civilians fled as refugees. This led to the largest refugee flow into and across Europe since World War II, with attendant political, social, and economic implications for many American allies in Europe, including those described earlier in this book. Had the Syrian civil war *not* erupted just as the West was winding down the bulk of its involvement in Afghanistan, it is possible the United States and its leading European allies would have become far more engaged earlier in Syria. Eventually, as memories of deployments to Afghanistan fade, Western willingness to intervene in foreign domestic conflicts will increase.[41]

---

39. An unnamed senior U.S. intelligence official, as quoted by Harry J. Kazianis, "US Intelligence Officials: North Korea Will Sell Nuclear Tech to Iran," *The Hill*, June 29, 2018, thehill.com/opinion/national-security/392868-us-intelligence-officials-next-fear-north-korea-will-sell-nuclear. See also Daniel Salisbury, "Will North Korea Sell Its Nuclear Technology?," *The Conversation*, September 25, 2017, theconversation.com/will-north-korea-sell-its-nuclear-technology-83562

40. Christopher S. Chivvas, *Toppling Qaddafi: Libya and the Limits of Liberal Intervention* (Cambridge: Cambridge University Press, 2014); Philip Hammond, *Framing Post–Cold War Conflicts: The Media and International Intervention* (Manchester: Manchester University Press, 2007); and Jon Western, *Selling Intervention and War: The Presidency, the Media, and the American Public* (Baltimore: Johns Hopkins University Press, 2005).

41. The nearly two-decade military commitment in Afghanistan may linger in the collective consciousness for some time, but one factor that is likely to help it fade from Western and

What Does Washington Want of Its Allies?

Most broadly, Washington wants to share the burdens of defending commonly held interests, and it prefers to do so with Europeans. In rhetoric and practice, the United States views Europe as its partner of first resort in nearly all international contexts. Rhetorically, the preference for partnership with Europe has been evident through American National Security Strategies and National Defense Strategies of the last 25 years, which have been remarkably consistent on this central point. From an American president seen as decidedly pro-European—Bill Clinton, who led the effort to expand NATO—to that of a president far less inclined to favor alliances of any sort—Donald Trump, who suggested the United States withdraw from NATO—Washington continues to view Europe as home to its most willing and most capable partners in international affairs.[42] From a practical perspective, European countries have been among the first Washington engages when soliciting partners for any number of security challenges, from large-scale stability operations in South Asia, to counterterrorism operations in the Middle East and North Africa, to economic sanctions against Russia for its invasion of Ukraine. There is a broad consensus across Washington and throughout the country that America's allies are an important and significant comparative advantage it has over rivals such as China and Russia, which do not enjoy the benefits of similarly like-minded allied states, outside of some rare exceptions such as Cuba or Syria, in the case of Russia. Certainly convincing and cajoling allies to pursue particular courses of action in international affairs is never easy. Even more difficult—from both political and operational perspectives—is actually fighting side by side with allies against a common foe, as the U.S. Army's exhaustive study of the Iraq War made clear. It describes coalition operations as useful from a political perspective, but largely unsuccessful otherwise, primarily because allies did not send enough troops or because they limited the scope of those troops' operations, or both.[43] Nevertheless, allies can and do provide critical political legitimacy at home and abroad, operational capacity

American memories is that the war was fought entirely by professional military forces, not the conscripts of the Cold War era. For this reason, the wars in Iraq and Afghanistan have not had the American-society-wide impact of the Vietnam War, for instance.

42. *National Security Strategy of the United States of America*, December 2017. The strategy notes, "The United States is safer when Europe . . . can help defend our shared interests and ideals" (48).

43. Joel D. Rayburn and Frank K. Sobchak, eds., *The U.S. Army in the Iraq War—Volume 1: Invasion—Insurgency—Civil War, 2003–2006* (Carlisle, PA: U.S. Army War College Press, 2019); and Joel D. Rayburn and Frank K. Sobchak, eds., *The U.S. Army in the Iraq War—*

to take the load off of American resources, unique or redundant capabilities, and logistical and related support that enable far-flung engagement.

Countering great power intimidation and coercion, bringing stability and security to war-torn developing countries, and conducting counterterrorism missions near and far requires deep reserves of national power. Today, those reserves are threatened by the inability of Western societies to address persistent structural problems that would make Western economies relatively stronger than those of its adversaries. Roughly a decade ago, Chairman of the Joint Chiefs of Staff Admiral Michael Mullen captured the essence of this notion when he argued that the greatest threat to U.S. security was the national debt.[44] Of course this was before Russia's invasion of Ukraine, China's militarization of islands in the South China Sea, and the rise of ISIL. Nonetheless, the point remains a valid one even today—the United States and its closest allies in Europe need political and other solutions to the persistent structural problems afflicting each of their economies and societies. This is the surest way to increase their relative economic strength, their resilience in the face of setbacks and shocks, their comparative advantages over other states and modes of governance, and their international soft power vis-à-vis China and Russia.[45]

This book has made clear that some of Washington's most important allies have yet to adequately address—or even *begin* to address—longstanding, widely acknowledged challenges. If they can—and this obviously remains an open question—they stand a good chance of reinvigorating and reviving their national power, relative to competitors. They will subsequently need to channel that power through a multifaceted set of policy tools if they hope to address the most pressing national security challenge of the day.

Economic and financial policy tools are obviously important, and have proven so in dealing with several of the aforementioned security challenges. Sanctions of various sorts are foremost among the economic tools at the West's disposal. Since the terrorist attacks of 9/11, the United States and leading allies in Europe have made aggressive, widespread, and ultimately successful use of sanctions to cut off terrorist financing and to coerce Iran

---

Volume 2: *Surge and Withdrawal, 2007–2011* (Carlisle, PA: U.S. Army War College Press, 2019).

44. "Mullen: Debt Is Top National Security Threat," *CNN*, August 27, 2010, www.cnn.com/2010/US/08/27/debt.security.mullen/index.html

45. For a similar argument, see Micah Zenko, "America's Military Is Nostalgic for World Wars," *Foreign Policy*, March 13, 2018, foreignpolicy.com/2018/03/13/americas-military-is-nostalgic-for-great-power-wars/

and North Korea.[46] Even the *threat* of sanctions today can shape international relations and compel changes in national decision-making.[47]

Other economic and financial tools include establishing standards for foreign direct investment. In the United States, an interagency entity known as the Committee on Foreign Investment in the United States reviews proposed foreign direct investments and transactions for national security implications. Some U.S. allies in Europe have similar screening mechanisms, but the EU itself has only recently established an investment screening framework.[48] Ultimately, it should provide member states and the European Commission with a mechanism for more coherent investment screening. However, this framework does not unify foreign direct investment screening mechanisms already in place in some EU member states nor does it require member states to establish such mechanisms. Efforts to coordinate foreign direct investment screening not just within Europe but across the Atlantic are becoming increasingly important as a means of protecting Western interests—especially in terms of critical infrastructure and sensitive technologies—in the face of aggressive, large-scale sovereign investment on the part of the Chinese government. The Belt and Road Initiative is the most obvious manifestation of Beijing's efforts to literally build influence abroad. In addition to China, Russia has attempted to vertically integrate the energy supply chain, which would increase its ability to wield energy as a tool of influence across Europe.

In addition to economic and financial tools, development assistance is another potent mechanism for defending common Western interests from the array of threats outlined above.[49] The United States and its leading European allies have robust development assistance budgets and programs, devoting money to improve governance, infrastructure, education, nutrition, and an array of other priorities in an effort to strengthen societies and build stability. In fact, the European Union carries a heavier share of the burden here than the United States—for example, in 2017, the EU con-

---

46. Jill Jermano, "Economic and Financial Sanctions in U.S. National Security Strategy," *PRISM* 7, no. 4 (November 2018), cco.ndu.edu/Portals/96/Documents/prism/prism7_4/181204_Jermano_PDF.pdf?ver=2018-12-04-161236-650

47. Michael B. Greenwald, "To Manage Great Power Competition, America Needs a New Economic Patriot Act," *Diplomat*, April 17, 2019, thediplomat.com/2019/04/to-manage-great-power-competition-america-needs-a-new-economic-patriot-act/

48. European Parliament, "Regulation of the European Parliament and of the Council Establishing a Framework for the Screening of Foreign Direct Investments into the Union," February 20, 2019, https://www.consilium.europa.eu/media/38347/pe00072-en18.pdf

49. Vin Gupta and Vanessa Kerry, "Foreign Aid Makes America Safer," *Foreign Policy*, April 11, 2018, foreignpolicy.com/2018/04/11/foreign-aid-makes-america-safer/

tributed roughly $85 billion on overseas development assistance, while the United States spent just over $35 billion.[50] During its next budget cycle, the EU plans to increase foreign assistance even further.[51] Foreign aid to developing countries can, among things, encourage those countries to avoid dependency on China.[52]

Although the use of development assistance or economic and financial tools by major American allies in Europe helps to share some of the burden of defending common interests and mitigating security challenges, the United States obviously remains keenly interested in allies contributing their hard power capabilities and capacity as well. Typically for domestic political reasons, American allies are not always as responsive—or as pliable—as Washington would prefer.[53] Nonetheless, from the coalition to remove Saddam Hussein's forces from Kuwait three decades ago to the anti-ISIL coalition of just a few years ago, the United States prefers to wield hard power in the defense of national and common interests in coalition with its European allies. Conceptually, the United States relies upon its allies as one of three essential pillars—along with force posture and defense modernization—to "provide the capabilities and agility required to prevail in conflict and preserve peace through strength."[54] American allies are deemed so critical to U.S. interests that they are viewed as the "backbone of global security."[55]

Over time, and as the limits of American power became more obvious through lengthy wars in Iraq and Afghanistan, Washington has become increasingly comfortable with—and desirous of—managing risk by relying

---

50. European Commission, "EU Remains the World's Leading Donor of Development Assistance: €75.7 Billion in 2017," October 4, 2018, ec.europa.eu/europeaid/news-and-events/eu-remains-worlds-leading-donor-development-assistance-eu757-billion-2017_en; OECD, "Development Aid Stable in 2017 with More Sent to Poorest Countries," April 9, 2018, www.oecd.org/development/financing-sustainable-development/development-finance-data/ODA-2017-detailed-summary.pdf

51. Benjamin Fox, "EU Unveils Increased Foreign Aid Budget for 2021–27," *Euractiv.com*, June 14, 2018, www.euractiv.com/section/global-europe/news/eu-unveils-increased-foreign-aid-budget-for-2021-27/

52. Sam Parker and Gabrielle Chefitz, "China's Debtbook Diplomacy: How China Is Turning Bad Loans into Strategic Investments," *Diplomat*, May 30, 2018, thediplomat.com/2018/06/chinas-debtbook-diplomacy-how-china-is-turning-bad-loans-into-strategic-investments

53. Stéfanie von Hlatky, *American Allies in Times of War: The Great Asymmetry* (Oxford: Oxford University Press, 2013).

54. U.S. Department of Defense, *Summary of the 2018 National Defense Strategy of the United States of America*, January 2018, 1.

55. U.S. Department of Defense, *Summary of the 2018 National Defense Strategy*, 2.

on allies to share more of the defense and security burden.[56] Functionally, this translates into a desire on the part of Washington for its major European allies to be capable of conducting military operations across the spectrum of conflict—from high intensity maneuver warfare operations, to medium intensity stability operations or peace enforcement, to low intensity and covert operations. Of course, the United States has very different expectations for allies with smaller or less capable militaries—such as Bulgaria, Norway, or Hungary. In these cases, the United States as well as NATO have promoted the notion of niche capability development or the creation of multinational military formations, or both. The Czech Republic's focus on nuclear/chemical/biological/radiological weapon defense capability is a example of the former, while the South-Eastern Europe Brigade—comprised of smaller units from Albania, Bulgaria, Greece, North Macedonia, Romania, and Turkey—exemplifies the latter.[57] Initiatives such as these allow *all* allies to play a role in providing security for themselves and their allies, ameliorating the burden-sharing dilemmas that are inevitable in an organization such as NATO.

However, with regard to those allies that have relatively greater capability and capacity—such as those studied in this book—Washington wants and indeed needs them to be able to conduct military operations across the land, air, sea, cyber, space, electromagnetic, and information domains, in both conventional and special operations formations. Notably, this includes *offensive* cyber operations, which are becoming increasingly necessary to counter, deter, and disrupt seemingly relentless Russian and Chinese cyber-attacks and cyber espionage.[58] On this last point, European queasiness over offensive cyber operations leading to escalatory spirals is probably unfounded.[59]

---

56. Interview with a former senior civilian employee within the Office of the Secretary of Defense, December 2, 2018.

57. Martin Michelot and Milan Šuplata, "Defence and Industrial Policy in Slovakia and the Czech Republic: Drivers, Stakeholders, Influence," Armament Industry European Research Group, December 2016, www.iris-france.org/wp-content/uploads/2016/12/Ares-Group-12-Policy-Paper-Slovakia-and-Czech-Republic-dec2016.pdf

58. Ellen Nakashima, "U.S. Cyber Command Operation Disrupted Internet Access of Russian Troll Factory on Day of 2018 Midterms," *Washington Post*, February 27, 2019, https://www.washingtonpost.com/world/national-security/us-cyber-command-operation-disrupted-internet-access-of-russian-troll-factory-on-day-of-2018-midterms/2019/02/2 6/1827fc9e-36d6-11e9-af5b-b51b7ff322e9_story.html?utm_term=.c294869a8c30; Patrick Tucker, "NATO Getting More Aggressive on Offensive Cyber," *Defense One*, May 24, 2019, www.defenseone.com/technology/2019/05/nato-getting-more-aggressive-offensive-cyber/157270/?oref=d-river

59. Erica D. Borghard, "What a U.S. Operation against Russian Trolls Predicts about

From a geographic perspective, Washington obviously wants European allies to be capable of acting militarily within their own neighborhood as well as projecting force well beyond Europe.[60] This entails the ability and capacity to deploy and sustain military forces to northeastern Europe in order to deter Russian adventurism.[61] More broadly, it also entails using naval, air, and other hard power assets to defend Western interests in the Arctic, which is quickly becoming a venue for great power competition.[62] It also means being able to deploy forces off the Horn of Africa to combat smuggling and piracy, or to the South China Sea to defend the global commons and international norms.[63]

Additionally, Washington is clearly looking to Europe to bear more of the security burden throughout the African continent—including through wielding hard power—as U.S. priorities and focus shift to great power competition vis-à-vis Russia and China.[64] In particular, Washington hopes to rely increasingly on its European allies to "degrade terrorists; build the capability required to counter violent extremism, human trafficking, trans-national criminal activity, and illegal arms trade with limited outside assistance; and limit the malign influence of non-African powers" such as China.[65]

Escalation in Cyberspace," *War on the Rocks*, March 22, 2019, warontherocks.com/2019/03/what-a-u-s-operation-against-russian-trolls-predicts-about-escalation-in-cyberspace/

60. Efforts on the part of the United States to convince countries to join its coalitions against Iraq starting in 2003, in Afghanistan throughout the 2000s, and against the Islamic State in Iraq and the Levant during the last decade, are well known.

61. For example, the Washington has pushed Italy to make at least some contribution to NATO's Enhanced Forward Presence mission in northeastern Europe. Interview with a field-grade U.S. officer based in Washington who works on U.S.-Italy military-to-military relations, March 4, 2019.

62. David Auerswald, "China's Multifaceted Arctic Strategy," *War on the Rocks*, May 24, 2019, warontherocks.com/2019/05/chinas-multifaceted-arctic-strategy/

63. Edward R. Lucas, "Countering the 'Unholy Alliance': The United States' Efforts to Combat Piracy and Violent Extremism in the Western Indian Ocean, 2001–2014," paper presented to the International Studies Association International Conference, Hong Kong, June 15, 2017, web.isanet.org/Web/Conferences/HKU2017-s/Archive/81cdbb71-5fb2-4a9d-9428-9f6a32db2ed1.pdf; interview with a senior field-grade U.S. officer based in Washington and expert in Franco-American military relations, February 28, 2019; and Bill Hayton, "How Europe Can Make a Difference in the South China Sea," *Berlin Policy Journal*, February 7, 2019, berlinpolicyjournal.com/how-europe-can-make-a-difference-in-the-south-china-sea/

64. Alexandra de Hoop Scheffer and Martin Quencez, "U.S. 'Burden-Shifting' Strategy in Africa Validates France's Ambition for Greater European Strategic Autonomy," German Marshall Fund of the United States, January 23, 2019, www.gmfus.org/blog/2019/01/23/us-burden-shifting-strategy-africa-validates-frances-ambition-greater-european

65. U.S. Department of Defense, *Summary of the 2018 National Defense Strategy*, January 2018, 9.

U.S. Policy Tools

If U.S. national security strategy depends even to a limited degree on Washington's most capable, most powerful allies to shoulder the burden, this book has made the argument that this strategy is at risk of failing, given the shifting constellation of major European allies and the likelihood that Washington could be faced with a combination of unwilling and incapable allies a decade from now. The options for the United States in such a situation are limited. Obviously, Washington does not have the ability to *control* how its major European allies will address the strategic shifts that have played out over the last five to 10 years or are continuing to unfold, nor does it have the ability to *dictate* desired outcomes.

Nonetheless, Washington is not entirely without some degree of influence. In fact, there are several policy tools at Washington's disposal that could help to accentuate what few positive trends exist among its major European allies while also mitigating the many negative ones. This section will outline those opportunities, offering an array of options that policymakers throughout Washington should consider to strengthen the allies upon which its own security and strategy depend.

Expand Transatlantic Free Trade

Many of the negative trends among America's major European allies outlined in this book stem from economic weakness, and one of the underlying assumptions of this book—as well as the dominant theories of international relations such as neorealism—is that economic strength and resilience, along with demographics, form the bedrock of a state's military power. For these reasons, the United States should seize on available opportunities to build economic strength in concert with Europe. One way of doing this would be to expand free trade with Europe. Free trade has a proven track records of enriching societies and reducing poverty in the long run even as it makes some groups within those societies worse off in the short run.[66]

Barriers to trade between the United States and Europe are already relatively low, thanks to membership by both sides in the World Trade Organization and thanks to previous transatlantic trade agreements. Nonetheless, in early 2013, the United States and the EU began negotiations to reduce

---

66. World Bank Group and World Trade Organization, "Trade and Poverty Reduction: New Evidence of Impacts in Developing Countries," 2018, documents.worldbank.org/curated/en/968461544478747599/pdf/132833-REVISED-TradePovertyWBWTONew.pdf

remaining tariffs as well as nontariff barriers through a Transatlantic Trade and Investment Partnership (TTIP), which would have been the largest bilateral trade and investment agreement ever negotiated. By some estimates, TTIP could have raised GDP 0.5 percent higher each year for the EU and 0.4 percent higher each year for the United States.[67] Furthermore, TTIP could have raised wages for both high- and low-skilled workers by 0.5 percent in the EU, 0.3 percent for high-skilled workers in the United States, and 0.4 percent for low-skilled workers in the United States. Total exports were expected to increase for both the EU (by 8.2 percent) and the United States (by 11.3 percent), as well as total imports (7.4 percent and 4.6 percent, respectively).

Some of these potential gains do not sound impressive, but given the size of the U.S. and European economies, small percentage swings in GDP or total exports can have major implications for employment. For instance, estimates for TTIP-related job creation in the United States were as high as 750,000, while estimated gains in Europe ranged from as few as 102,000 jobs to as many as 1.35 million.[68]

The rise of populism in the West—and populists' electoral success in the United States, Poland, Italy, and elsewhere in the mid- and late 2010s—make any serious reembrace of free trade difficult, at least in the short run.[69] If the populist wave in the West crests and begins to recede, it is possible that renewed negotiations toward TTIP might begin in the early 2020s. In the meantime, another economic policy tool the United States should pursue—again, in coordination with its European allies—is the strengthening of the World Trade Organization (WTO). As the world's second largest exporter of goods and services—behind China—the United States depends on the WTO system. Its rules and procedures cover 98

---

67. Jacques Pelkmans et al., "The Impact of TTIP: The Underlying Economic Model and Comparisons," Centre for European Policy Studies, no. 93, October 2014, www.ceps.eu/system/files/No%2093%20Appraisal%20of%20IA%20on%20TTIP.pdf; European Commission, "Trade SIA on the Transatlantic Trade and Investment Partnership (TTIP) between the EU and the USA," May 2016, www.trade-sia.com/ttip/wp-content/uploads/sites/6/2014/02/TSIA-TTIP-draft-Interim-Technical-Report.pdf

68. "TTIP and the Fifty States: Jobs and Growth from Coast to Coast," Atlantic Council of the United States, the Bertelsmann Foundation, and the British Embassy in Washington, 2013, 2, www.atlanticcouncil.org/images/publications/TTIP_and_the_50_States_WEB.pdf; "TTIP and Jobs," European Parliament's Directorate-General for Internal Policies, 2016, 42, www.europarl.europa.eu/RegData/etudes/STUD/2016/578984/IPOL_STU(2016)578984_EN.pdf

69. Jack Ewing, "A Populist Win Could Dull Europe's Appetite for Free Trade," *New York Times*, May 22, 2019, nyti.ms/2VGn7k1; Douglas A. Irwin, "Trade under Trump: What He's Done So Far—and What He'll Do Next," *Foreign Affairs*, November 6, 2018, www.foreignaffairs.com/articles/2018-11-06/trade-under-trump

percent of global trade, creating a fairer system that provides U.S. and European companies with lower tariffs around the world and significantly less discrimination, protectionism, and predatory pricing than would otherwise be possible. When disagreements arise—and they inevitably do in international trade—the WTO's dispute resolution system defuses the potential for an international trade war, provides restitution when serious rules violations occur, and allows aggrieved parties to retaliate within the rules of the system. However, the United States and its European allies could do much to protect and strengthen their own economies by pushing to address shortcomings and weaknesses in WTO practices. For instance, WTO dispute resolution takes considerable time, during which trade rule violations can continue unabated. Moreover, the WTO does not explicitly include labor standards—doing so would help to level the playing field for Western workers vis-à-vis their counterparts in China and elsewhere.

Expand National Security Information Sharing

There is always a risk in increasing intelligence sharing with foreign partners that doing so will put sensitive sources and methods at risk. However, the more intelligence that is shared between the United States and its European partners, the better the odds that those partners will develop perspectives similar to Washington's on security threats and appropriate responses.[70] American intelligence analysts are increasingly "writing for release"—that is, crafting intelligence analysis that is planned from initiation to be shared with an ally or partner.[71] This is usually far more efficient than try to declassify an existing intelligence product, and it means the United States can share information on a timelier basis. Nonetheless, there is more that can be done to ensure the United States and its key allies are on the same page. Steps to increase intelligence sharing might include inviting other countries to participate in the Five Eyes arrangement. This arrangement consists of the United States, Australia, Canada, New Zealand, and the United Kingdom, and it has roots in the close security relationship forged by these countries in World War II. Since then, the arrangement has become a vitally important mechanism for the sharing

---

70. Interview with an American civilian employee of U.S. Army Europe with extensive experience in military-to-military programs across Europe, November 13, 2018.

71. Interview with a senior field-grade U.S. officer based in Washington and expert in Franco-American military relations, February 28, 2019; Godfrey Garner and Patrick McGlynn, *Intelligence Analysis Fundamentals* (Boca Raton, FL: CRC Press, 2019), 83.

of both raw intelligence data—primarily signals intelligence—and interpreted intelligence analysis among the five participants.

Of all the European allies discussed in this book, it makes most sense to invite Germany to participate in the Five Eyes arrangement. Germany is very likely to be America's most powerful ally by the end of the 2020s, at least economically and politically, yet its will to both invest in hard power resources and wield those resources may be lacking. Expanding Five Eyes by including Germany could help in at least three ways. First, the United States could leverage Five Eyes membership as a carrot to incentivize Berlin's fulfillment of readiness and defense investment targets. Second, by exposing German leaders to more security-related information, especially on the exploitative challenges posed by China in Europe, it may help persuade them of the necessity of fulfilling the Munich consensus and shouldering more responsibility in the defense of common interests. Third, inviting Germany into the Five Eyes program may help to convey to its leaders and its public the strength of Washington's (and London's and Ottawa's) desire to see Berlin take on greater responsibility as a major international actor. In this way, it might help to finally compel Berlin to stop hiding behind the mistaken notion that its allies fear a powerful Germany.

Increased intelligence sharing by the Five Eyes countries with Germany is already occurring in some limited circumstances. For example, in the case of China's aggressive economic espionage, the Five Eyes countries have begun sharing more intelligence on China with Germany as well as France and Japan.[72] Five Eyes intelligence sharing coordination with Germany has also reportedly occurred with regard to Russian influence operations in Europe. However, formally including Germany in the Five Eyes arrangement would enable even closer coordination. For its part, Berlin has reportedly expressed interest in joining.[73]

The United States might also try to convince France to join the Five Eyes arrangement—and especially if it invites Germany—given Paris's willingness to wield hard power and its still broad conceptualization of its interests in Europe and beyond. This topic has in fact been discussed by policymakers in Washington and Paris, yet the French seems more interested in a special bilateral relationship with the United States, even if it

---

72. Noah Barkin, "Five Eyes Intelligence Alliance Builds Coalition to Counter China," *Reuters*, October 12, 2018, www.reuters.com/article/us-china-fiveeyes/exclusive-five-eyes-intelligence-alliance-builds-coalition-to-counter-china-idUSKCN1MM0GH

73. Adam Martin, "NSA: Germany Was 'a Little Grumpy' about Being Left Out of Spying Club," *New Yorker*, November 2, 2013, nymag.com/intelligencer/2013/11/nsa-germany-insulted-it-got-left-out-of-spying.html?gtm=top

remains largely focused on the operational level.[74] Moreover, the French government already shares intelligence data with the Five Eyes countries, building on an agreement with the United States dating from 2013–14.[75] The more recent "Lafayette Initiative," described in chapter 4, entails in-depth U.S.-French intelligence data sharing, mostly on operational matters and the fight against terrorism in the Levant and Africa. Making France a formal member of the Five Eyes arrangement would help to shift the intelligence-sharing relationships among these countries toward a more strategic outlook, promote closer coordination on dealing with China and Russia, and possibly assist France in more effectively digesting all of the raw intelligence data it already receives from the United States by giving Paris access to more refined intelligence analysis products.

Take Interim Steps to Fill the Capabilities Gap

As the preceding chapters in this book made clear, several allies are likely to shed hard power capabilities over the coming years, despite broad-based defense spending increases in Europe. Until defense spending increases become more robust and until long lead-time procurement programs can meet the needs of depleted military forces, those allies are likely to lose the ability to operate side by side with American forces in at least some capability areas.

There are several steps the United States could take in order to maintain transatlantic interoperability and the know-how necessary to operate technologically advanced military equipment across the spectrum of conflict. First, the United States should expand the training of foreign officers on American military platforms. Washington has some experience offering this option to European allies. For example, British pilots have been sent to the United States since 2012 to train on the P-8 Poseidon maritime patrol aircraft, well before London committed to buying the airframe in 2016 and before the Royal Air Force took delivery of any P-8s in 2019.[76] Expanding

---

74. Interview with a former senior political appointee within the U.S. Department of Defense, July 23, 2019.

75. Interview with a senior field-grade U.S. officer based in Washington and expert in Franco-American military relations, February 28, 2019; interview with a former senior civilian employee within the Office of the Secretary of Defense, December 2, 2018; and Pierre Tran, "French Official Details Intelligence-Sharing Relationship with Five Eyes," *Defense News*, February 5, 2018, www.defensenews.com/global/europe/2018/02/05/french-official-details-intelligence-sharing-relationship-with-five-eyes/

76. Hope Hodge Seck, "British Pilots Look Forward to Flying P-8 Sub-Hunter in UK,"

similar options for close European allies could help to maintain the skill sets and knowledge necessary for military units of different countries to operate side by side, as well as encourage the purchase of interoperable equipment.

Second, the United States should place greater emphasis on achieving jointness within allied militaries. Certainly, there are serious shortcomings in the scope and depth of jointness within the U.S. military, but in many respects the Americans are far ahead of allies in this regard. For example, Italian military services are very stove-piped and often they compete strenuously with one another for resources, as was seen in the case of the F-35.[77] Increased jointness within allied militaries would allow them to spend more efficiently, build up capabilities more quickly, and operate more effectively with the United States and NATO.

Third, Washington should lead the creation of a clearinghouse for defense acquisition best practices. This capability could be situated under or within NATO, or it could be located within the U.S. Department of Defense. Regardless, the objective would be to assist allies in the *process* of defense acquisition by connecting communities of practice with centers of excellence and academia. Newer allies, especially countries such as Poland, lack the know-how to effectively and efficiently implement and manage multiyear, high-tech military procurement efforts.[78] Even those allies with more experience in such defense acquisition activities could stand to learn how other countries achieve their objectives in this regard.

Build German Willpower by Relying on R2P

Of all the countries studied in this book, Germany represents the greatest opportunity for Washington, given its uniquely strong economic fundamentals. However, the most significant challenge in leveraging Germany's strength in the defense of common interests is the fact that Berlin's willpower is limited, at least in the short run. As noted in chapter 3, there are strong differences of opinion among different generations in Germany—younger Germans tend to support greater engagement and involvement

Military.com, July 14, 2016, www.military.com/daily-news/2016/07/14/british-pilots-look-forward-to-flying-p8-sub-hunter-in-uk.html

77. Interview with a field-grade U.S. officer based in Europe with extensive knowledge of U.S.-Italian military-to-military ties, March 20, 2019.

78. Interview a Polish expert on transatlantic relations and national security at a Warsaw-based think tank, April 26, 2019.

by Germany in the world, including in terms of hard power, while older Germans tend to support a more reserved approach by Berlin. It is likely to take another decade or more before leaders in Berlin perceive that they can act with greater leeway in foreign affairs. One way to encourage the process of building willpower among German politicians, especially in terms of exercising military power beyond Europe,[79] would be for the United States to emphasize the importance of "responsibility" in international affairs, and of the concomitant need for Berlin to play a leading role in this regard.

The concept of the responsibility to protect (R2P) has become increasingly important in shaping and framing German decisions when it comes to national security policy. A little more than a generation ago, as Yugoslavia descended into chaos, Germans shed their Cold War era nearsightedness and learned that what happened in places like Bosnia and Kosovo could have a significant impact on Germany's economy, society, and security. That lesson has recently been relearned by another generation of Germans thanks to the disastrous Syrian civil war and the resulting refugee crisis. At the height of the crisis, German chancellor Angela Merkel gave voice to what millions of her fellow citizens perceived: "In many regions war and terror prevail. States disintegrate. For many years we have read about this. We have heard about it. We have seen it on TV. But we had not yet sufficiently understood that what happens in Aleppo and Mosul can affect Essen or Stuttgart. We have to face that now."[80]

Given Germany's twentieth-century history, it is understandable that German political culture remains governed by restraint when it comes to international engagement, especially involving hard power. Two decades ago, Chancellor Gerhard Schröder and his foreign minister, Joschka Fischer, convinced the German public to send combat forces to Kosovo by emphasizing the necessity of Germany making right its historical mistakes and of avoiding repeating mistakes of the past.[81] As a result, the German Bundestag approved the deployment of 8,500 troops to Kosovo, making Germany the largest single provider of forces. Since then, German politicians have come to see R2P as a burgeoning international norm as well as a moral principle.

79. Missions beyond Europe are arguably the most difficult to motivate the German public and politicians to support. Interview with a civilian strategist within the Germany Ministry of Defence, September 13, 2018.

80. As quoted in Karl Vick and Simon Shuster, "Chancellor of the Free World," *Time*, December 2015, time.com/time-person-of-the-year-2015-angela-merkel/

81. Lars Brozus (with Jessica von Farkas), "Germany and R2P: Common but Differentiated Responsibility?," in *The Responsibility to Protect: From Evasive to Reluctant Action?*, ed. Malte Brosig (Johannesburg: Hanns Seidel Foundation, 2012), 53–69.

This line of argumentation is not guaranteed to succeed, though. For example, Germany was unwilling to vote in favor of a UN-sanctioned intervention in Libya on the eve of what looked to become a major humanitarian disaster in Benghazi in 2011. Nevertheless, relying on notions of Germany's responsibility to uphold international law, protect innocent civilians, and prevent atrocities could encourage greater German involvement in managing and responding to security challenges near and far. This in turn could spur greater German attention on the operational requirements of intervening with hard power in an expeditionary context, providing the rationale and justification for increased German investment in military capabilities designed to project force across time and distance.

Explain the Requirement

For several years, conventional wisdom has held that Western efforts at strategic messaging, information warfare, psychological warfare, and the like are woeful compared to those of Russia, China, and insurgent groups around the world.[82] In part, this is because U.S. and Western societies are open and free, and because their efforts typically focus on propagating the truth and on building transparency, which are both necessarily more time-consuming and challenging to achieve. In contrast, Russia, China, other autocracies, and even nonstate actors appear to act with an efficiency that the West cannot match. They often employ obfuscation in an effort to distract, counter Western information sources, and create a disorienting environment in which it becomes difficult to discern truth.[83]

In addition to these sorts of "built-in" or systemic hurdles faced by the United States and its allies, Western efforts to effectively utilize information to achieve national security objectives are hampered by inadequate institutions and ineffective content. With regard to the former, it is unclear

---

82. See, for instance, Emilio J. Iasiello, "Russia's Improved Information Operations: From Georgia to Crimea," *Parameters* 47, no. 2 (2017): 51–63. See also Joseph Nye, "Protecting Democracy in an Era of Cyber Information War," *Governance in an Emerging New World*, November 13, 2018, www.hoover.org/research/protecting-democracy-era-cyber-information-war.

83. Alexey Kovalev and Matthew Bodner, "The Secrets of Russia's Propaganda War, Revealed," *Moscow Times*, March 1, 2017, www.themoscowtimes.com/2017/03/01/welcome-to-russian-psychological-warfare-operations-101-a57301; Olga Oliker, "Russian Influence and Unconventional Warfare Operations in the 'Grey Zone': Lessons from Ukraine," statement before the Senate Armed Services Committee Subcommittee on Emerging Threats and Capabilities, March 29, 2017, www.armed-services.senate.gov/imo/media/doc/Oliker_03-29-17.pdf

whether the United States has the institutional tools in place to achieve unity of effort in an effective and efficient way. Calls to bring back the U.S. Information Agency—which was dismantled in the late 1990s—have been controversial.[84] Nonetheless, current efforts to influence foreign public opinion and disrupt foreign efforts to do the same are stove-piped across the U.S. government, with little visible unity of effort among or even sometimes within federal departments. One way of fixing this would be to create an institutional tool or mechanism to better coordinate activities, with the necessary funding and authority to compel action across the federal bureaucracy. The State Department has attempted to do something like this with the creation in 2016 of its Global Engagements Center, the purpose of which is to direct, lead, synchronize, integrate, and coordinate the efforts of the U.S. government to recognize, understand, expose, and counter foreign state and foreign nonstate propaganda and disinformation efforts. However, the Global Engagements Center has faced significant funding, staffing, leadership, and mandate challenges in recent years, and it is unclear if it has the ability, the will, or the independence to fulfill its mandate.[85]

Having the right institutional tools in place is only half the challenge, though—an effective strategy with appropriate content is necessary as well. With regard to the messaging content, it seems clear the United States can and should do more to shape public opinion when it comes to capability and capacity development on the part of its European partners. Issuing threats to pull out of NATO unless more allies reach the alliance's 2 percent defense spending goal is ineffective and often counterproductive.[86]

84. For examples of the disparate viewpoints over reviving USIA, see Will DuVal and Adam Maisel, "It's Time to Bring Back This Cold War Agency and Stop Ceding the Propaganda War to Russia," Modern War Institute, August 15, 2017, mwi.usma.edu/time-bring-back-cold-war-agency-stop-ceding-propaganda-war-russia/, and Matthew Armstrong, "No, We Do Not Need to Revive the U.S. Information Agency," *War on the Rocks*, November 12, 2015, warontherocks.com/2015/11/no-we-do-not-need-to-revive-the-u-s-information-agency/

85. Nahal Toosi, "Tillerson Spurns $80 Million to Counter ISIS, Russian Propaganda," *Politico*, August 2, 2017, www.politico.com/story/2017/08/02/tillerson-isis-russia-propaganda-241218; Patrick Tucker, "Analysts Are Quitting the State Department's Anti-Propaganda Team," *DefenseOne*, September 12, 2017, www.defenseone.com/technology/2017/09/analysts-are-quitting-state-departments-anti-propaganda-team/140936/; Gardiner Harris, "State Dept. Was Granted $120 Million to Fight Russian Meddling: It Has Spent $0," *New York Time*, March 4, 2018, nyti.ms/2FQ9TLb; Robbie Gramer and Elias Groll, "With New Appointment, State Department Ramps Up War against Foreign Propaganda," *Foreign Policy*, February 7, 2019, foreignpolicy.com/2019/02/07/with-new-appointment-state-department-ramps-up-war-against-foreign-propaganda/

86. "Munich Security Conference Chief: Trump Pushes Germany toward Russia and

Instead, what is necessary is a more effective explanation of the capability and capacity requirements that exist among key U.S. allies in Europe, the tangible and intangible benefits for European citizens that fulfilling those requirements brings, and the risks associated with doing less.

Strengthen French Capabilities by Emphasizing Sovereignty

East and Southeast Asia are not normally regions of the world that decision-makers in Paris consider vital to French national security. For this reason, French military leaders remain largely focused on protecting French interests far closer to home, and on homeland security of metropolitan France in particular. However, France is the only European country with a permanent military presence in both the Indian and Pacific Oceans. It uses that presence to maintain security in and around its territories there, comprised primarily of Mayotte and Réunion in the southwestern Indian Ocean, and New Caledonia and Wallis and Futuna in the southwestern Pacific Ocean.

Just as the responsibility to atone for past mistakes lies close to the heart of German strategic culture, so too do sovereignty and autonomous strategic action play central roles in guiding and shaping French security policy.[87] Washington can leverage these imperatives in French strategic culture to encourage greater French military engagement through and in defense of sea lines of communication across the Indian and Pacific Oceans. Paris may be amenable to increasing its military presence and engagement in both regions, as there is reason to think that France would like to expand logistical support facilities there over the long run.[88] Since 2014, French forces have conducted freedom of navigation operations in the South China Sea, in an effort to push back on Chinese militarization of disputed islands. More recently France has shown a willingness to push back on other Chinese maritime claims.[89] Nonetheless, greater involvement and increased,

China," *Euractiv*, September 4, 2018, www.euractiv.com/section/global-europe/news/munich-security-conference-chief-trump-pushes-germany-toward-russia-and-china/; and interview with a German think tank expert on Europe security and transatlantic relations, May 9, 2019.

87. French security policy is also significantly driven by the desire to promote human rights and democracy abroad.

88. Interview with a U.S. field-grade officer assigned to U.S. European Command, January 15, 2019.

89. Idrees Ali and Phil Stewart, "In Rare Move, French Warship Passes through Taiwan Strait," *Reuters*, April 25, 2019, www.reuters.com/article/us-taiwan-france-warship-china-exclusive/exclusive-in-rare-move-french-warship-passes-through-taiwan-strait-idUSKCN1S10Q7

persistent presence on the part of French forces would help to share the burden of defending common interests in the Asia-Pacific.[90] Moreover, encouraging greater French involvement in these regions would help to spur Paris to remain invested in major power projection platforms.

Leverage Italy's Desire for Prestige

Chapter 5 of this book made the argument that Italy has arguably declined the most of all major U.S. allies in Europe over the last decade, in terms of its economic, military, and diplomatic power and influence. The inability or unwillingness, or both, of its political class to address long-standing, well-known structural problems in its economy were exacerbated by the sovereign debt crisis and the migration crisis. As a result, populist influence has grown significantly there, pulling Italy onto a path of even greater withdrawal from most overseas engagements.

Many Italian leaders—especially those in the national security enterprise—are well aware of these dynamics, and they are eager to reverse them as a means of not simply protecting Italian and collective interests but also to safeguard and promote Italian prestige. Italians leaders are especially sensitive to any hint that they are being excluded from U.S. discussions and decision-making with other "major" European states such as France, Germany, and the UK.[91] Washington should leverage Rome's strong desire for prestige in order to keep Italians striving for capability and capacity. This might be accomplished by convening so-called "quint" meetings—an informal grouping of major alliance powers that normally consists of the United States, France, Germany, the United Kingdom, and Italy—that include Poland or Spain, thereby signaling that Italy's role is perhaps not as significant as it once was. It could also be accomplished by guiding the Italians toward taking more of a leadership role for the alliance in the central Mediterranean. Of course, Washington must be careful in leveraging Italy's desire for prestige and leadership in these ways, lest it

---

90. Wesley Rahn, "South China Sea: France and Britain Join the US to Oppose China," *Deutsche Welle*, June 27, 2018, p.dw.com/p/30OQx; "French Navy Frigate Conducts FONOP in South China Sea," *Navy Recognition*, March 23, 2018, www.navyrecognition.com/index. php/news/defence-news/2018/march-2018-navy-naval-defense-news/6081-french-navy-frigate-conducts-fonop-in-south-china-sea.html

91. Interview with a field-grade U.S. officer based in Washington who works on U.S.-Italy military-to-military relations, March 4, 2019.

appear to others—especially America's smaller allies and those that are not aligned—that Europe is run by a "cabal" of leading capitals, an arrangement that Moscow has been pursuing since the end of the Cold War.

Use Force Posture to Build the Future German-U.S. Military Relationship

The outlook for the German economy over the long run is one of the few positive trends foreseen in this book. In almost every other instance, the large European economies are not expected to perform robustly in the coming decade, even if they can bounce back from the COVID-19 economic slump. Germany's success may hinge on its relatively flexible labor market, the investments German industry has made in advanced manufacturing technology and automation, and the broader outlook for German labor productivity. Admittedly, the picture is complicated somewhat by German demographic trends, which are not positive. Nonetheless, over the long run, and through the usual peaks and troughs of the business cycle, the German economy looks to be the strongest in Europe.

This should provide Germany with significant potential for investment in defense capabilities and capacity. Without a growing economy, Berlin is surely not going to build up its military strength, but *with* a growing economy Germany at least has a chance to avoid choosing between guns *or* butter, as many of its neighbors likely will be forced to do. At least in the short run, German leaders are more likely to choose to increase capabilities and readiness instead of dramatically increasing capacity. Even though Germany's readiness and capability shortcomings are so significant, Berlin is likely to conclude that its neighbors will find a more capable German military less threatening than a *larger* German military.

The United States can help to cultivate German capability development, military readiness, and security cooperation burden-sharing across all services but especially air, land, cyber, and special operations forces by maintaining and even building upon its forward-stationed presence in Germany. Forward-stationed U.S. military forces in Germany—which include U.S. Army units, U.S. Air Force units, special operations forces, and cyber forces—comprise one of the best ways to expose German counterparts to advanced military technology, to share best practices on train-and-equip security cooperation, to build interoperability, to maintain readiness for multinational operations, and to shape the national security policy preferences of German leaders.[92] Forward stationing also has significant fiscal, readiness, morale, and political-military benefits relative to stateside basing for U.S. forces.[93]

Embrace Divisions of Labor

Although Washington prefers having as many partners on board as possible in confronting global challenges, it is clear that most of its European partners will face diminished capacity and capability over the next decade, especially the United Kingdom, Italy, and Poland, and potentially France. Germany is the only one of the five countries addressed in this book that has significant latent power, but its willingness to tap into this for increased hard power capabilities and capacity remains a serious question. Over the last three decades, Washington's approach has typically focused on asking these and other allies and partners to participate robustly in operations near and far. This has helped to build international legitimacy, maintain allied solidarity, and spread burdens and risks, but it has come at a high cost on several scores. First, it has led to European militaries spreading themselves too thin in many instances, unable to conduct operations across the world *while also* maintaining readiness and investing in modernization. Second, the fact that European militaries have become so overstretched means that the risk of mission failure has increased. And third, these two factors together have meant there is even greater pressure on already stretched U.S. capabilities in areas such as strategic lift, command and control, intelligence, surveillance, and reconnaissance, and other critical enablers that are necessary to facilitate allied/partner deployments and operations.

Rather than continuing to cajole allies with less capacity and capability to do more and more, Washington should consider embracing a division of labor with those allies that clearly cannot build, sustain, and operate globally or even regionally. For instance, if Macron's economic revolution does not come to fruition and French military capabilities and capacity remain limited over the next decade, Washington should stop demanding more than the French are capable of delivering. Instead, the United States

---

92. Interview with a civilian NATO expert in the German Ministry of Defence, September 11, 2018; interview with a European security expert at Johns Hopkins University, December 4, 2018.

93. John R. Deni, *Rotational Deployments vs. Forward Stationing: How Can the Army Achieve Assurance and Deterrence Efficiently and Effectively?* (Carlisle, PA: U.S. Army War College Press, 2017).

ought to encourage France to focus its limited capabilities and capacity on Africa and the Middle East. To some degree Washington has already been encouraging France to lead in these regions, willingly facilitating French-led operations across sub-Saharan Africa for example.[94] At the same time, though, the United States has also pressured France to participate in NATO operations in northeastern Europe. Washington should stop this—again, assuming Macron's economic revolution does not deliver—and allow the French to concentrate what limited capabilities and capacity they may have over the next decade on Africa and the Middle East.

In a similar way, Washington ought to stop requesting Polish support for operations outside of northeastern Europe. Instead, Poland ought to be recognized and empowered as NATO's "first responder" across all of Eastern Europe, particularly in a land context.

Meanwhile, the Italians ought to be asked to focus on refining and reinforcing their role in the Mediterranean as NATO's lead for southern flank security, as well as on spearheading and coordinating development assistance and the strengthening of civil society in North Africa. This may require Washington to provide greater political support for Rome's efforts in Libya and, more broadly, a more coherent U.S. approach to the central Mediterranean. American efforts to date have been hampered to some degree by the fact that the Mediterranean falls along a "seam" between U.S. combatant commands—European Command (EUCOM) and Africa Command (AFRICOM)—which oversee American military operations and related activities in their respective areas of responsibility.[95] AFRICOM is responsible for U.S. military activity in Libya and 12 miles off of Libya's cost, but from that point northward EUCOM has responsibility for the rest of the Mediterranean. This split in responsibility along a major transit route for migrants, traffickers, and others complicates efforts by the United States to support allies such as Italy.

Washington should ask the United Kingdom to focus on reinforcing the Poles in northeastern Europe in the air and at sea. Additionally, the United Kingdom ought to be pressed to focus on countering both Russia and China in the Arctic. This might mean a further diminishment of

---

94. Quentin Lopinot, "What Does 'European Defense' Look Like? The Answer Might Be in the Sahel," *War on the Rocks*, March 19, 2019, warontherocks.com/2019/03/what-does-european-defense-look-like-the-answer-might-be-in-the-sahel/

95. Seams between geographic combatant command have long created challenges for American diplomacy—prominent examples of challenging seams include that between Israel (EUCOM) and all of its Arab neighbors (CENTCOM), and between Pakistan (CENTCOM) and India (INDOPACOM).

the British army's capabilities and capacity as relatively more resources are devoted to the Royal Navy and the Royal Air Force, but it would allow London to retain in the short run a vision of itself as an extracontinental power, even as it inevitably shrinks from that role in reality.

Finally, the United States might consider asking European allies to expand or make increased use of their deployable paramilitary police forces for more international security tasks, instead of tasking active duty combat forces, which are under increasing demand. These kinds of forces—such as Italy's Carabinieri—have played an important role in humanitarian and postconflict stabilization.[96] Given the rise of hybrid war and asymmetric military operations, paramilitary forces are arguably better suited than active duty troops for many modern security challenges and contingencies. Expanding their capacity and their remit would lessen the burden on active duty European manpower that is already stretched thin.

Certainly, embracing a division of labor along the lines suggested above means weakening the sense of "solidarity" that NATO and several allies including the United States often value—that is, having as many allies as possible contribute to addressing a security challenge that is most acute for merely a handful, like the threat Russia poses in northeastern Europe. Additionally, it could worsen the risk-sharing imbalance that was evident within the alliance during Afghanistan operations, in which some allies were willing to take on missions that were more likely to generate casualties while other allies simply were not. However, the reality is that token contributions of often caveat-laden forces provide minimal benefit beyond the rhetorical, they burden allied military enterprises with unsustainable requirements, they complicate operations when multinationality is pushed below the brigade level, and they do little to spur increased defense investment.

Rely on Multilateral, Intergovernmental Frameworks

Although the United Kingdom and France have historically been more willing to wield hard power abroad in the absence of a mandate approved by the United Nations or NATO, for example, most American allies in Europe prefer the imprimatur of an intergovernmental organization before exercising military force abroad. This is especially so for Italy and

---

96. Elisabeth Braw, "For Not-Quite-Wars, Italy Has a Useful Alternative to Traditional Troops," *Defense One*, April 16, 2018, www.defenseone.com/ideas/2018/04/todays-not-quite-wars-italy-has-alternative-traditional-troops/147457/

Germany. With regard to the former, Article 11 of the Italian constitution explicitly bans the use of military power for resolving disputes.[97] Rome has nonetheless wielded military force abroad many times over the last couple of decades by relying on its commitment to institutional multilateralism as a primary rationale. So long as the United Nations, NATO, the European Union, or some other intergovernmental organization has provided its approval, Italian prime ministers have typically succeeded in obtaining parliamentary and public approval for the use of force.

Germany is similar in many ways, despite the fact that the 2016 *Weissbuch*, or defense white paper, appeared to open the door to German participation in and initiation of coalitions of the willing, as discussed in chapter 3. In 1994, the German constitutional court found that as long as the Bundestag gave prior approval, the German government could use the Bundeswehr abroad in the context of German obligations under international treaties, such as those establishing the UN or NATO. Subsequent constitutional court cases on the use of the Bundeswehr abroad have led scholars to refer to it as a parliamentary army or military.[98] Given the vitally important role of the Bundestag in authorizing *any* deployment of German forces, an international mandate can greatly assist in providing the justification for German involvement and hence approval of the deployment. So important is an intergovernmental blessing that, in some cases, the German government's request for approval or renewal of a deployment mandate has been explicitly conditioned on the persistence or renewal of UN Security Council approval.[99]

For these reasons, Washington should endeavor to continue using NATO and other intergovernmental organizations as the frameworks for the exercise of hard power abroad, instead of relying on more informal "coalitions of the willing." Relying on NATO as a "toolbox" of potential coalition partners is not problem-free. Many countries in Europe resent being thought of as "tools" wielded by Washington without much regard for national interests beyond America's. Meanwhile, Washington sometimes finds working through the alliance onerous and cumbersome when it comes to military operations.

97. Constitution of the Italian Republic, 6–7, www.senato.it/documenti/repository/istituzione/costituzione_inglese.pdf

98. Russell A. Miller, "Germany's Basic Law and the Use of Force," *Indiana Journal of Global Legal Studies* 17, no. 2 (Summer 2010): 197–206.

99. Anne Peters, "Between Military Deployment and Democracy: Use of Force under the German Constitution," *Journal on the Use of Force and International Law* 5, no. 2 (2018): 246–94.

Despite these problems, using intergovernmental frameworks provides more benefits than costs. Countries such as Italy and Germany are more likely to participate if NATO is the vehicle for action, domestic audiences and especially the U.S. Congress see military action abroad as more legitimate when it is blessed by an intergovernmental organization, and America is seen as less of a lone ranger by foreign audiences. Moreover, NATO provides established mechanisms for command and control, communications, and standard operating procedures that would otherwise need to be erected from scratch in more informal coalitions of the willing.

Negotiate a New Burden-Sharing Bargain

Burden-sharing debates between the United States and its European allies are as old as the alliance itself. In recent years, but especially since the election of Donald Trump in 2016, American political leaders have regularly berated European allies—in public and in private—over their meager military budgets, in an effort to garner more contributions to the common defense. Despite those increasingly shrill appeals—and in some instances, *because* they were made by President Trump—most European allies have failed to meet agreed-upon levels of defense spending or related capability targets. As was made clear in several chapters in this book, the burden-sharing imbalance—at least as perceived by Washington—is likely to become *worse* in the coming decade, as European economies prove unable to sustain robust defense budgets.

In order to incentivize commitments to defense spending, Washington should give up on the heated rhetoric and strategically destabilizing threats to leave the alliance without greater burden-sharing on the part of Europe allies. Instead, the United States should offer a new burden-sharing bargain to its major European allies. The bargain ought to focus on obtaining defense-spending commitments and capability targets from European allies such as those addressed in this book in exchange for applying a wider definition to the notion of "defense burden-sharing."

Specifically, in exchange for meeting defense spending commitments and capability targets, Washington ought to agree to expand the notion of defense burden-sharing to include broader security spending as well. This broader conceptualization might include dual-use infrastructure spending by European allies—after all, it is European roads, shipping ports, airports, and railroads that U.S. and other allied forces would rely on in the event of a military crisis in northeastern Europe or elsewhere on the continent. It makes sense to include spending on this sort of infrastructure—assuming it meets certain criteria regarding military suitability—in what a European ally contributes to the common defense. Additionally, given the importance of foreign assistance, development aid, and security assistance such as military training in *preventing* conflicts before they erupt, Washington ought to include European spending in these areas within a broadened definition of "security burden-sharing."

Begin Procurement Programs by Thinking Interoperability

The United States and its European allies can significantly reduce the cost of military procurement if they research, develop, produce, or purchase hardware together. Combined research, development, testing, and production also inherently build military interoperability, making it easier to operate side by side. While these realities are widely known by all of the allies, changing the practices associated with research, development, and procurement has proven very difficult.

Part of the challenge here lies in intellectual property rights and which country or company retains ownership when multiple players are involved. NATO has experience dealing with and managing this—specifically in the context of the alliance's Science for Peace initiative—but the issue still manages to create impediments in the minds and in the practices of allies with significant defense manufacturers. Additionally, some experts have theorized that irreconcilable differences among participating purchasing countries over the necessary specifications or capabilities of the finished armament or product and over delivery timeline requirements contribute significantly to the inability of countries to successfully implement multinational defense procurement programs.[100] This "too many cooks" phenomenon is often cited as a reason for the F-35's high cost, slow development, and ongoing maintenance challenges, for example.[101]

Assuming allies can surmount the legal issues involved and arrive at

---

100. Vesa Kanniainen and Juha-Matti Lehtonen, "Joint Procurements in Building National Defence: Why Are There So Few?," Helsinki Center of Economic Research, Discussion Paper No. 427, March 2018, helda.helsinki.fi/bitstream/handle/10138/233583/HECER-DP427.pdf?sequence=1&isAllowed=y

101. Sydney J. Freedberg Jr., "FVL Helicopters: How to Avoid F-35 Snafu," *Breaking Defense*, September 8, 2014, breakingdefense.com/2014/09/fvl-helicopters-how-to-avoid-f-35-snafu/; Valerie Insinna, "Inside America's Dysfunctional Trillion-Dollar Fighter-Jet Program," *New York Times*, August 21, 2019, www.nytimes.com/2019/08/21/magazine/f35-joint-strike-fighter-program.html

agreement on when and what should be procured, there is still a broader, almost cultural challenge for Washington to overcome. U.S. policymakers and decision-makers still do not have a predisposition to build multinational cooperation and armaments interoperability into procurements programs *from the outset.*[102] The U.S. Defense Department has in place guidance that would appear to prioritize multinationality in armaments procurement. DoD Directive 5000.01 requires program managers to "pursue international armaments cooperation to the maximum extent feasible."[103] The same directive mandates that "systems, units, and forces . . . shall effectively interoperate with other U.S. Forces and coalition partners."[104] Moreover, the directive prioritizes the use of cooperative development programs with one or more allied nations over a new joint Component or Government Agency development program, or a new DoD Component-unique development program.[105]

With this sort of guidance in place, it is therefore ironic that current practice does not always measure up. Instead of leading when it comes to the necessity of building multinationality and interopability into procurement practices and procedures, Washington is more often reacting. Changing this culture will require time and effort, but it is the sort of transformation that is achievable over a period of years. Certainly the U.S. defense industry may raise concerns, perhaps based in the intellectual property issues described above. However, defense spending can be a powerful, market-shaping incentive, and American defense companies are likely to adapt as and when necessary to prioritize interoperability and multinational cooperation if the Defense Department demands it.

Get Out of the Way of European Defense Integration

While U.S. military planners and their American defense industry partners need to think more often in multinational terms, American leaders also need to foster—versus obstructing—greater European integration in defense cooperation. In June 2017, the EU launched a European Defence

---

102. Interview with a senior NATO civilian working in armaments cooperation, May 17, 2019.

103. Department of Defense Directive 5000.01, May 12, 2003, Incorporating Change 2, August 31, 2018, 5, www.esd.whs.mil/Portals/54/Documents/DD/issuances/dodd/500001p.pdf?ver=2018-09-28-073203-530

104. Department of Defense Directive 5000.01, 7.

105. Department of Defense Directive 5000.01, 7–8.

Fund (EDF) to promote cooperation among its member states in producing advanced, interoperable defense technology and equipment. Although the preliminary funding level over the next EU budget cycle (2021–27) is expected to be relatively small at roughly €13 billion, the goals of the EDF are quite ambitious in seeking to provide support all along the product life cycle, from research to prototype development to certification.[106] Actual acquisition will be left up to the EU member states and funded through their national defense budgets.

In response to the EDF and a related EU initiative known as Permanent Structured Cooperation, Washington reacted with accusations of defense sector protectionism. Specifically, American officials have suggested that the EU is putting in place intellectual property and export control restrictions that would "effectively preclude participation by any company that uses U.S.-origin technology."[107] Furthermore, the United States has threatened to retaliate by implementing "reciprocally imposed U.S. restrictions."[108] EU officials claim that both initiatives are designed to promote industrial cooperation and overcome persistent fragmentation in the European defense market. More specifically, the EU argues that non-EU-owned companies may receive EDF funding subject to certain conditions such as no transfer of sensitive information outside of the EU and no transfer of intellectual property rights outside of the EU, conditions that "are similar to the ones imposed by the U.S. on EU companies aiming to access publicly funded U.S. defence R&D programmes."[109]

Although the balance of transatlantic defense trade has long favored the United States, if the EDF succeeds and grows sufficiently it is certainly possible that European allies may ultimately choose to purchase American-made military hardware less frequently. From Washington's perspective, this is of course bad news, but it may be bad news the United States must tolerate if it hopes to see its European allies bring more capacity and capability to the fight. Devoting more resources to defense will only be sustain-

---

106. European Commission, "The European Defence Fund: Stepping Up the EU's Role as a Security and Defence Provider," March 19, 2019, ec.europa.eu/docsroom/documents/34509

107. As quoted in Frank Wolfe, "U.S. Officials Consider Retaliation if EU Does Not Relax Draft EDF and PESCO Language," *Defense Daily*, June 17, 2019, www.defensedaily.com/u-s-officials-consider-retaliation-eu-not-relax-draft-edf-pesco-language/uncategorized/

108. As quoted in Paul McLeary, "State, DoD Letter Warns European Union to Open Defense Contracts, or Else," *Breaking Defense*, May 17, 2019, breakingdefense.com/2019/05/state-dod-letter-warns-european-union-to-open-defense-contracts-or-else/

109. Letter from EU officials Pedro Serrano and Timo Pesonen to U.S. officials Ellen M. Lord and Andrea L. Thompson, dated May 16, 2019, int.nyt.com/data/documenthelper/1069-european-commission-reply-to-u/6cdebd319d226b532785/optimized/full.pdf

able over time if there are greater domestic political benefits. In simplest terms this means European defense budgets must be firmly tied to European jobs.[110]

For Americans, this political reality is nothing new. High levels of U.S. defense spending are supported, at least in part, by the defense industry jobs brought to congressional districts across the country. By one measure, U.S. defense spending supports 2.8 million jobs annually.[111] In order to build greater political support for higher defense spending in Europe, European politicians and their citizens need to see the domestic benefits of that spending. This necessarily means that a significant level of the defense-related funding the EU makes available for research, development, testing, evaluation, and certification *must* flow into European factories, labs, and research institutes.

Washington may view this as an unfortunate by-product of European efforts to spur greater defense investments and more European capability. Nonetheless, getting out of the way of European integration and cooperation by promoting instead of obstructing EDF and Permanent Structured Cooperation will ultimately benefit U.S. security. Greater defense integration and collaboration in Europe will enable Europeans to make more efficient use of their existing defense budgets. At present, European defense acquisition is incredibly fragmented—for instance, there are 17 battle tanks produced across the European Union, while in the United States there is just one.[112] Incentivizing greater collaboration in the production of tanks could allow the remaining manufacturers to achieve greater economies of scale and reduce prices, thereby helping European states to acquire more capability and capacity.

110. Sophia Besch and Martin Quencez, "The Importance of Being Protectionist: A Long View of the European Defense Fund," *War on the Rocks*, June 13, 2019, warontherocks. com/2019/06/the-importance-of-being-protectionist-a-long-view-of-the-european-defense-fund/

111. "U.S. Aerospace and Defense Industry Supported Almost 2.8 Million Jobs in 2015," *IHS Markit*, April 21, 2016, news.ihsmarkit.com/press-release/aerospace-defense-security/ us-aerospace-and-defense-industry-supported-almost-28-milli

112. Jean-Claude Juncker, speech delivered at the 54th Munich Security Conference, February 17, 2018, europa.eu/rapid/press-release_SPEECH-18-841_en.htm

EIGHT

Conclusion

This thesis of this book is that several of America's major European allies are each undergoing or have recently undergone important, paradigm-shifting changes, and that these changes will have serious—mostly negative—implications for how, when, and where the United States engages with the rest of the world. In the case of the United Kingdom, it seems patently obvious that regardless of the future UK-EU relationship, Britain's economy will be worse off as a result of the Brexit vote. In the worst-case scenario, Scotland could demand another independence referendum and thereby leave the kingdom. This could prompt Northern Ireland to secede as well. A rump Britain—composed of England and Wales—will undoubtedly have a smaller economy and a correspondingly smaller defense budget. The resulting loss of capabilities and capacity will diminish the UK's ability to be America's right-hand partner in international security matters.

Even without Brexit, years of austerity cuts have already significantly reduced the capabilities and capacity of the UK military. Unfolding defense acquisitions—such as aircraft carriers—may provide the appearance of a rejuvenated British military, but ongoing personnel shortfalls, readiness challenges, and related platform shortages (like F-35s) will likely reduce the impact these acquisitions might otherwise have. Slowly, the security horizon of the United Kingdom will recede once again—as it did 50 years ago when London ended its large and expensive military role "East of Suez" and as the Netherlands has recently experienced over the last decade. As that happens, the so-called special relationship with the United States is likely to become an artifact of a bygone era, perhaps referred to rhetorically but of increasingly little substantive meaning.

In the short run, France is likely to displace the United Kingdom as the partner of first resort for the United States when it comes to managing international security challenges near and far. Franco-American security cooperation has already blossomed significantly since 2013, and arguably the French and American military establishments have never been closer. Most of the cooperation over the last decade has focused on operational matters, but a more strategic alignment appears possible as well.

However, Paris's ability to play a greater role in partnership with the United States and to fulfill its own security objectives is already under pressure thanks to ongoing, highly demanding operational commitments in Africa as well as across the French homeland. At the same time, the political revolution represented by En Marche's dramatic victory in 2017 has yet to bring about a promised economic revolution. Many of the solutions to some of France's most pressing economic challenges remain unimplemented, hamstrung by political disagreements or overcome by the challenge of dealing with the magnitude of the COVID-19 economic downtown. Demographically, France is one of the few major American allies in Europe that will likely see modest growth over the coming decades, and so revitalizing the French economy is absolutely necessary to ensure employment for a growing workforce. A revitalized economy will also increase tax receipts, which will subsequently help the government to avoid relying on defense funds as a bill payer for social safety net programs. In the best case scenario over the next decade, increased tax receipts will then enable France to fulfill its own goals and to play a larger role on the international stage, to continue investing in offensive cyber capabilities and advanced military technology, and to resuscitate its ability to project force across time and distance.

While France may displace the UK in the short run, Washington may come to see Germany as its preferred partner in Europe over the long run. Like other countries, Germany will continue to navigate the peaks and troughs of the business cycle, especially the dislocation created by the COVID-19 pandemic, but Germany supersedes all of its neighbors in terms of its long-term economic growth prospects. Economic policy choices made over the last decade and the willingness of German businesses to embrace—more so than virtually all other countries in Europe—advanced information technology, roboticization, and other aspects of Industrie 4.0 have placed it on a trajectory to continue improving productivity over the next decade even as economic growth rates remain decidedly postindustrial.

Although Germany's hard power capabilities and the will to use them pale in comparison to the United Kingdom and France *today*, these factors are likely to evolve significantly over the next decade. Younger Germans have a very different view toward their country's involvement and role in the world. They favor *greater* involvement and having Germany take on more responsibility in international security, unlike most of their grand-parents. This generational difference is part of an evolution in German attitudes toward the use of force that has unfolded since the end of the Cold War and German reunification. It is likely that German attitudes will continue to change in this regard. Therefore, it is also likely that Germany will become increasingly willing to employ military power in the pursuit of its own interests and those of its allies in Europe and beyond, across all domains. For Washington, a slowly burgeoning international security part-nership with Berlin will take time and patience to cultivate, but investing in it is likely to pay dividends, especially considering the far less positive long-term prospects among most of America's other European allies.

Among those declining partners, Italy is perhaps the exemplar. Over the last decade, Italian capability, capacity, and willpower have all shrunk significantly, mostly as a result of Italy's debt crisis and its inability to mus-ter the political will to fix the country's flawed economic fundamentals. The migration crisis of the mid-2010s exacerbated the dire economic situ-ation confronting the country, magnifying the fiscal calamity facing the government and bringing about a crisis of Italian identity. These twin chal-lenges resulted in populists taking over the Italian government in the late 2010s, which only furthered the trends in terms of capabilities, capacity, and willpower.

Even if political will can be found to fix Italy's many problems and turn around the economy in the face of the COVID-19 economic crisis and still massive debt service load, severe demographic challenges will persist. These challenges will dampen Italy's economic performance through the 2020s and will make it difficult for Rome to build and maintain a robust military force over time. As a result, Italy's strategic horizon will continue to shrink, focusing almost exclusively on instability in North Africa and sub-Saharan Africa as a source of what Italians perceive as unwelcome migration northward across the Mediterranean Sea. For all these reasons, Washington is unlikely to be able to rely heavily on Italy as a defender of Western interests beyond the Mediterranean.

Similar to Italy, Poland is very likely to remain focused on a single threat—namely, the Russian Federation. Unlike Italy, though, Poland's economic dynamism over the last decade has meant that its capabilities and capacity have increased, not decreased. Having endured a painful transition to market capitalism in the 1990s without exposing itself to excessive reliance on international financial markets, the Polish economy was better positioned than practically any other European country to withstand the sovereign debt crisis and the Great Recession. As its fiscally demanding commitments in first Iraq and then Afghanistan wound down, Warsaw tapped its robust economy to initiate a series of impressive military modernization programs. In many instances, this has increased Polish capabilities, but the results are largely focused on territorial defense.

This emphasis reflects Polish threat perceptions as well as Polish interests. Poles are not terribly concerned with a nuclear-armed Iran or China's flaunting of international norms in the South China Sea, and there has been a growing consensus in the Polish national security community that its efforts in far-away Iraq and Afghanistan earlier this century were not necessarily worthwhile pursuits. Instead, Poles are justifiably worried about the perceived existential threat posed by Russia. This makes eminent sense, given Russia's relentless destabilizing military actions across all domains and its offensive military buildup in neighboring Kaliningrad. However, this means that over the next decade Washington will have little success in pulling Polish attention and resources away from northeastern Europe, aside from rhetorical support and token contributions.

Together, this array of changes will mean that the constellation of allies that Washington has relied on over the last 20 years to safeguard national and collective interests will look very different by the end of the 2020s. How the United States responds to this eventuality is of utmost importance at a time of geopolitical flux. The unipolar moment—the period of time from roughly the early 1990s until perhaps the early or mid-2000s—has clearly ended. During this period, the United States was the unchallenged global hegemon, China had yet to achieve significant wealth or military power, and Russia was poor, weak, and dependent on the West.

Today, the situation is quite different. American power—both soft and hard—has been sapped by two lengthy, indeterminate wars that cost trillions of dollars. The fiscal implications of these conflicts were significant—prematurely ending what could have been a period of major budget surpluses and long-term debt reduction—and are likely to last a generation. Specifically, spending so much money on extant operations has not only deepened America's debt but it has also generated massive opportunity costs for the Department of Defense in the form of underresourced technological advances and innovation in the military-industrial sphere. Certainly, war has a way of generating its own innovations as the defense enterprise struggles to meet the urgent operational demands of troops at war.

However, it is difficult *not* to conclude that the Pentagon would be much farther along in developing and fielding unmanned autonomous strike vehicles, hyper velocity projectiles, GPS alternatives, human-machine teaming applications, and a variety of other advanced capabilities across all domains if it had not been spending $45 billion per year in Afghanistan alone.[1] Not only has the unipolar moment faded, but any illusions of pursuing American hegemony are utterly without merit.

Meanwhile, Russia and China have not sat on the sidelines. Russia leveraged a tightening of global oil markets and continued European dependence on Russian gas to at least temporarily arrest its long-term decline and invest in an array of new capabilities, including drones, precision guided weapons, and offensive cyber. When combined with a high degree of risk tolerance in international security affairs, Moscow now presents a far more acute threat, at least in the short run, than it did just a decade ago.

China has arguably gone even further but in a less overtly offensive manner. Beijing has amassed unprecedented sovereign wealth, which it has increasingly converted into hard power over the last several years. It is expected to continue to grow in capacity and capability in the coming decade, despite the COVID-19 economic crisis, potentially displacing the United States as the dominant military power in the Western Pacific. Meanwhile, its persistent, predatory behavior in economic and cyber realms threatens to undermine the long-term vitality of American and other Western societies. China therefore represents a systemic, long-term threat.

In this environment and facing threats of such magnitude, allies are arguably more necessary than ever. It was helpful for the United States to have contributing coalition partners in the effort to manage instability and insurgency in Iraq and Afghanistan over the last two decades. However, these conflicts were not systemic in the way that iterative competition with near-peer or peer adversaries is, nor were they existential. In the unfolding era of great power competition with authoritarian China and revisionist Russia, allies will be *vital*. If democracy, and with it the liberal international economic order, remains in retreat over the next decade—as it has arguably over the last[2]—the United States will face an international secu-

1. Matthew Pennington, "Pentagon Says War in Afghanistan Costs Taxpayers $45 Billion per Year," Associated Press, February 6, 2018, www.pbs.org/newshour/politics/pentagon-says-afghan-war-costs-taxpayers-45-billion-per-year

2. "Freedom in the World 2019: Democracy in Retreat," Freedom House, 2019, freedomhouse.org/report/freedom-world/freedom-world-2019/democracy-in-retreat; Uri Friedman, "Will the World Grow More Authoritarian in 2014?," *Atlantic*, January 6, 2014, www.theatlantic.com/international/archive/2014/01/will-the-world-grow-more-authoritarian-in-2014/282840/

rity environment that it has not seen in many decades. In the worst case scenario, Washington may find itself in a world where China dominates the Eastern Hemisphere and parts of the Western in both geostrategic and economic terms, oligopolistic authoritarianism becomes increasingly common, and international norms are replaced entirely by a "might makes right" approach implemented by those countries so able. In this environment, democratic allies with the capacity, the capability, and the willpower to act will be more necessary than they have since the 1940s.

Unfortunately, the approach of President Donald Trump toward allies and adversaries has raised serious doubt about whether Washington is willing and able to meet the most likely security challenges of the next decade. Certainly, President Trump's National Security Strategy and his National Defense Strategy hit all the right notes when it came to the value of allies and the nature of the strategic competition unfolding with regard to China and Russia. For example, the 2018 National Defense Strategy noted that U.S.-centered alliances remain the backbone of global security, providing the United States with an asymmetric strategic advantage over every adversary and competitor. It also clearly states that alliances ease America's security burden, praising allies for consistently joining the United States in "defending freedom, deterring war, and maintaining the rules which underwrite a free and open international order."[3]

However, President Donald Trump has effectively undermined the rhetoric featured in these critical national security documents by throwing America's commitment to its allies into doubt,[4] suggesting the United States withdraw from NATO,[5] and favoring unilateralism vis-à-vis China over unity of effort.[6] With often deep gulfs between what the executive departments promulgate and implement on the one hand and what the President says or does on the other, Washington appears to have a bifurcated approach toward its own partners. Allies have often been told to "watch what we do, not what we say,"[7] but this contradictory approach

---

3. "Summary of the 2018 National Defense Strategy of the United States," 2018, dod. defense.gov/Portals/1/Documents/pubs/2018-National-Defense-Strategy-Summary.pdf

4. Rosie Gray, "Trump Declines to Affirm NATO's Article 5," *Atlantic*, May 25, 2017, www.theatlantic.com/international/archive/2017/05/trump-declines-to-affirm-natos-article-5/528129/

5. Julian E. Barnes and Helene Cooper, "Trump Discussed Pulling U.S. from NATO, Aides Say amid New Concerns over Russia," *New York Times*, January 14, 2019, nyti.ms/2HaZZrK

6. Peter Baker, "Trump Abandons Trans-Pacific Partnership, Obama's Signature Trade Deal," *New York Times*, January 23, 2017, nyti.ms/2jQSDwo

7. Marc Champion, "For U.S. Allies, 'Mad Dog' Mattis Is the Last Adult in the Room," *Bloomberg*, December 9, 2018, www.bloomberg.com/news/articles/2018-12-09/for-u-s-allies-mad-dog-mattis-is-the-last-adult-in-the-room

confuses Washington's allies, emboldens its adversaries, and leads to strategic instability if both friends and foes have doubts about where the United States stands and what it is willing to fight for.

If the White House can once again fully embrace the necessity and importance of allies during this era of great power competition, there are some policy options that can help ensure there will be capable, willing European partners with sufficient capacity by America's side a decade from now. A successful effort to buttress and support American allies must employ all elements of American power, not simply the military. For this reason—and because so many of the critical issues at the heart of the strategic transformations playing out within European allies are tied to their economic performance—trade and economic measures are arguably most important of all. For example, Washington can help rejuvenate European economies trying to recover from the COVID-19 crisis by supporting agreements designed to increase free trade, which has been shown repeatedly to produce long-lasting, widespread economic benefits. Similarly, supporting greater defense sector integration and the European Defence Fund will help to promote increased defense spending in Europe. This support must include acknowledgment by Washington that political support within Europe for greater defense spending will only occur—and be sustainable over time—if that spending is largely tied to more defense sector jobs *in Europe*.

Diplomatic policy tools were also suggested in chapter 7, including relying on multilateral frameworks as a means of cultivating and solidifying European willpower to act. Working with allies, for instance through NATO, brings a degree of difficulty that can complicate operations and result in interoperability challenges. Nonetheless, America's European allies are far more likely to become engaged internationally if they can do so in the context of an "approved" operation or mission. Additionally, the United States should leverage particular predispositions in the strategic culture of individual European allies. For example, Washington could help to build German willpower to engage internationally by emphasizing the need for Berlin to avoid repeating the mistakes of Germany's mid-twentieth-century past. The United States could also spur greater French capability investment by emphasizing Paris's "strategic" role beyond Europe and Africa and by promoting its development of capabilities designed to achieve this. With regard to Italy, the United States should leverage Rome's "fear of missing out" and its desire to be seen as playing an important role in Europe and beyond.

Finally, chapter 7 includes several military policy tools, such as expanding the Five Eyes intelligence sharing network to include France. Increased intelligence and other information sharing—especially of finished intelligence analysis products and particularly with legislators who typically must approve funding for military operations—will help to build common perspectives on threats confronting the West. Additionally, the United States ought to set aside greater numbers of training positions in U.S. military educational and training programs, to facilitate readiness as well as capability retention among American allies in Europe. Washington might also consider more aggressively building interoperability and multinationality into the earliest phases of its military acquisition programs. Bringing Europeans into the conceptual stage earlier would help to build interoperability by incentivizing European purchases of commonly developed military hardware. Chapter 7 also includes a recommendation for a new burden-sharing bargain between Europe and America, one that sees Europeans meeting their agreed defense spending targets while Americans acknowledge that dual-use infrastructure spending as well as foreign aid and development spending ought to figure into the burden-sharing discussion.

None of these policy options alone will necessarily prevent Washington's major European allies from essentially becoming a coalition of the unwilling or unable, or both. Even in their totality, the recommendations featured in chapter 7 and outlined briefly above may not be enough to turn around what appears to be a fairly gloomy outlook for the future of the U.S.-European security relationship. Despite this, what has effectively become the American way of war—working side by side with European allies—appears likely to persist, at least in terms of what the United States aspires to. Indeed, the case was made above and earlier in this book that the United States *needs* allies to its right and left, given the emerging multipolar structure of the international system, the magnitude of the security challenges ahead, their inimical character, and the iterative nature of near-peer and peer competition over time. As America's most important European allies deal with the dramatic changes of the last few years and navigate the twists and turns ahead, Washington can and should do what it is possible to facilitate their success—this is certainly within the vital national security interests of the United States.

Bibliography

"2019 Military Strength Ranking." GlobalFirepower.com, 2019.

Adamowski, Jaroslaw. "Poland Launches Effort to Help Arm E. European Allies." *Defense News*, October 4, 2015.

"Ageing Tigers, Hidden Dragons." *Voice of Asia*, no. 3, September 2017.

Ali, Idrees, and Phil Stewart. "In Rare Move, French Warship Passes through Taiwan Strait." *Reuters*, April 25, 2019.

Allan, Duncan. "Managed Confrontation: UK Policy towards Russia after the Salisbury Attack." Chatham House, October 2018.

Amaro, Silvia. "Germany Is Vastly Outspending Other Countries with Its Coronavirus Stimulus." CNBC.com, April 20, 2020.

Andersson, Jan Joel, et al. "Envisioning European Defence: Five Futures." EU Institute for Security Studies, Chaillot Paper No. 137, March 2016.

Anthony, Ian. "European Security after the INF Treaty." *Survival* 59, no. 6 (2017).

Archick, Kristin. "The United Kingdom: Issues for the United States." CRS Report for Congress, September 23, 2005.

Armellini, Alvise. "Italy Parliament Approves New Election Law Ahead of Next Year's Vote." *Deutsche Presse-Agentur*, October 26, 2017.

Armstrong, Matthew. "No, We Do Not Need to Revive the U.S. Information Agency." *War on the Rocks*, November 12, 2015.

"'Army Cuts Dangerous' Warns Ex-Chief Lord Dannatt." BBC News Online, May 28, 2011.

Arntz, M., T. Gregory, and U. Zierahn. "The Risk of Automation for Jobs in OECD Countries: A Comparative Analysis." OECD Social, Employment and Migration Working Papers, 2016.

Art, Robert J. "Striking the Balance." *International Security* 30, no. 3 (Winter 2005/06).

Atkinson, Rick. "Court Allows German Troops to Join Missions outside NATO Area." *Washington Post*, July 13, 1994.

Audition du général François Lecointre, chef d'état-major des armées, sur les opérations en cours. Commission de la défense nationale et des forces armées, July 17, 2018.

Audition du général François Lecointre, chef d'état-major des armées, sur le projet de loi de finances pour 2019. Commission de la défense nationale et des forces armées, October 18, 2018.

Auerswald, David. "China's Multifaceted Arctic Strategy." *War on the Rocks*, May 24, 2019.

Baker, Luke. "French Parliament Approves SNCF Reform Bill in Breakthrough for Macron." *Reuters*, June 13, 2018.

Baker, Luke. "Macron's Euro Zone Reforms: Grand Vision Reduced to Pale Imitation." *Reuters*, June 18, 2018.

Baker, Peter. "Trump Abandons Trans-Pacific Partnership, Obama's Signature Trade Deal." *New York Times*, January 23, 2017.

Balmforth, Tom. "Another Worrying Sign for Russia's Dire Demographics." *Radio Free Europe/Radio Liberty*, September 27, 2017.

Barkin, Noah. "Five Eyes Intelligence Alliance Builds Coalition to Counter China." *Reuters*, October 12, 2018.

Barkin, Noah. "The U.S. Is Losing Europe in Its Battle with China." *Atlantic*, June 4, 2019.

Barnes, Julian E., and Helene Cooper. "Trump Discussed Pulling U.S. from NATO, Aides Say amid New Concerns over Russia." *New York Times*, January 14, 2019.

Beach, Jim. "Origins of the Special Intelligence Relationship? Anglo-American Intelligence Co-operation on the Western Front, 1917–18." *Intelligence and National Security* 22, no. 2 (August 2007).

Beale, Jonathan. "The UK's Giant Aircraft Carriers." *BBC News Online*, August 24, 2018.

Becker, Sebastian. "Germany's Fiscal Situation." Deutsche Bank Research, July 19, 2017.

Beckley, Michael. "Economic Development and Military Effectiveness." *Journal of Strategic Studies* 33, no. 1 (2010).

Beehner, Lionel et al. "Analyzing the Russian Way of War: Evidence from the 2008 Conflict with Georgia." Modern War Institute at West Point, March 20, 2018.

Belasco, Amy. "Troop Levels in the Afghan and Iraq Wars, FY2001-FY2012: Cost and Other Potential Issues," CRS Report for Congress, July 2, 2009.

Belin, Celia, and Boris Toucas. "The 'Macron Miracle' Could Transform France into a Global Powerhouse." *National Interest*, April 19, 2018.

Bender, Jeremy. "Ranked: The World's 20 Strongest Militaries." *Business Insider*, April 21, 2016.

Benner, Thorsten, et al. "Authoritarian Advance: Responding to China's Growing Political Influence in Europe." Global Public Policy Institute, February 2018.

Bentinck, Marc. "Why the Dutch Military Punches below Its Weight." Carnegie Europe, February 8, 2018.

Berger, Rick, and Mackenzie Eaglen. "'Hard Choices' and Strategic Insolvency: Where the National Defense Strategy Falls Short." *War on the Rocks*, May 16, 2019.

"The Berlin Pulse: German Foreign Policy in Perspective." Körber Stiftung, November 2018.

Besch, Sophia, and Martin Quencez. "The Importance of Being Protectionist: A Long View of the European Defense Fund." *War on the Rocks*, June 13, 2019.

Biddle, Stephen D. *Military Power: Explaining Victory and Defeat in Modern Battle*. Princeton: Princeton University Press, 2004.

Birnbaum, Michael, and David Filipov. "Russia Held a Big Military Exercise This Week: Here's Why the U.S. Is Paying Attention." *Washington Post*, September 23, 2017.

"Birth Rate Hits 10-Year Low in Russia." *Moscow Times*, January 29, 2018.

Blackburn, Gary. "UK Defence Policy 1957–2015: The Illusion of Choice." *Defence Studies* 15, no. 2 (2015).

Blagden, David. "Britain and the World after Brexit." *International Politics* 54 (2017).

Bodalska, Barbara. "Germany and Poland to Explore Revived 'Weimar Triangle'." *Euractiv*, January 18, 2018.

Boeri, Tito. "Italy's Confidence Crisis: Bad Policies from Bad Politicians." Centre for Economic Policy Research, August 17, 2011.

Boffey, Daniel. "Why Does Donald Trump Oppose Theresa May's Brexit Deal?" *Guardian*, November 27, 2018.

Borger, Julian. "US Military Stretched to Breaking Point: Pentagon Report Says Clear Strategy Is Needed, Rate of Deployment 'Cannot Be Sustained'." *Guardian*, January 25, 2006.

Borghard, Erica D. "What a U.S. Operation against Russian Trolls Predicts about Escalation in Cyberspace." *War on the Rocks*, March 22, 2019.

Borrelli, Silvia Sciorilli. "Salvini Strikes Conciliatory Tone on Migration, Italy's Budget." *Politico*, September 8, 2018.

Bötel, Frank. "Überblick: Die 'Armee im Einsatz'." December 15, 2017.

Brands, Hal. "Dealing with Allies in Decline: Alliance Management and U.S. Strategy in an Era of Global Power Shifts." Center for Strategic and Budgetary Assessments, 2017.

Brands, Hal. "Choosing Primacy: U.S. Strategy and Global Strategy at the Dawn of the Post–Cold War Era." *Texas National Security Review* 1, no. 2 (February 2018).

Brattberg, Erik. "Toward a Transatlantic Renaissance? TTIP's Geopolitical Impact in a Multipolar World." German Marshall Fund of the United States, 2015.

Braw, Elisabeth. "For Not-Quite-Wars, Italy Has a Useful Alternative to Traditional Troops." *Defense One*, April 16, 2018.

Brooks, Risa A., and Elizabeth A. Stanley, eds. *Creating Military Power: The Sources of Military Effectiveness.* Palo Alto: Stanford University Press, 2007.

Brozus, Lars (with Jessica von Farkas). "Germany and R2P: Common but Differentiated Responsibility?" In *The Responsibility to Protect: From Evasive to Reluctant Action?*, ed. Malte Brosig. Johannesburg: Hanns Seidel Foundation, 2012.

Buck, Tobias. "German Military: Combat Ready?" *Financial Times*, February 15, 2018.

Buckley, Noah. "Corruption and Power in Russia." Foreign Policy Research Institute, April 2018.

"Budget de la Défense: L'opération Sentinelle coûte un million d'euros par jour." *LCI*, April 29, 2015.

Bugamelli, Matteo, et al. "Il gap innovativo del sistema produttivo italiano: Radici e possibili rimedi." *Banca d'Italia, Questioni di Economia e Finanza*, no. 121, April 2012.

Bulmer, Simon. "Germany and the European Union: Post-Brexit Hegemon?" *Insight Turkey* 20, no. 3 (2018).

Bulmer, Simon, and Lucia Quaglia. "The Politics and Economics of Brexit." *Journal of European Public Policy* 25, no. 8 (2018).

Bundesministerium der Verteidigung. "Entwicklung und Struktur des Verteidigungshaushalts." 2018.

Burns, Robert. "Pentagon: Chinese Carrier Likely to Join Naval Fleet in 2019." Associated Press, May 2, 2019.

Bussoletti, Francesco. "L'Italia in futuro potrebbe avere una Forza Armata cyber." *Difesa & Sicurezza*, September 27, 2018.

Calingaert, Michael. "Italy's Choice: Reform or Stagnation." *Current History* 107, no. 707 (March 2008).

Campbell, Duncan. *Unlikely Allies: Britain, America and the Victorian Origins of the Special Relationship.* London: Bloomsbury Academic, 2008.

"Can Merkel's Diplomacy Save Europe?" *Der Spiegel Online*, February 14, 2015.

Capaccio, Anthony. "China's Stealth Jet May Be Ready This Year, U.S. Commander Says." *Bloomberg*, May 1, 2019.

Carney, Stephen A. *Allied Participation in Operation Iraqi Freedom.* Washington, DC: Center for Military History, 2011.

Carraud, Simon, and Michel Rose. "France's Armed Forces Chief Resigns after Clash with Macron over Budget Cuts." *Reuters*, July 19, 2017.

Catalano, Michele, and Emilia Pezzolla. "The Effects of Education and Aging in an OLG Model: Long-Run Growth in France, Germany and Italy." *Empirica* 43, no. 4 (2016).

Chalmers, Hugh, and Malcolm Chalmers. "Relocation, Relocation, Relocation: Could the UK's Nuclear Force Be Moved after Scottish Independence?" Royal United Services Institute, August 2014.

Chalmers, Malcolm. "Would a New SDSR Be Needed after a Brexit Vote?" Royal

United Services Institute for Defence and Security Studies briefing paper, June 2016.

Champion, Marc. "For U.S. Allies, 'Mad Dog' Mattis Is the Last Adult in the Room." *Bloomberg*, December 9, 2018.

Chan, Szu Ping. "Britain's 'Post-Crisis Hangover' Will Depress Tax Receipts for Years to Come." *Telegraph*, October 16, 2014.

Chappell, Laura. "Poland in Transition: Implications for a European Security and Defence Policy." *Contemporary Security Policy* 31, no. 2 (2010).

Chassany, Anne-Sylvaine. "Emmanuel Macron Pushes through French Labour Law Reforms." *Financial Times*, September 22, 2017.

Chassany, Anne-Sylvaine. "France to Increase Military Spending." *Financial Times*, February 8, 2018.

Chassany, Anne-Sylvaine. "Macron Slashes France's Wealth Tax in Pro-Business Budget." *Financial Times*, October 24, 2017.

Chazan, Guy. "Germany's Record Budget Surplus Triggers Calls for Tax Cuts." *Financial Times*, August 24, 2018.

Chien, YiLi. "What Drives Long-Run Economic Growth?" *St. Louis Fed on the Economy* blog. Federal Reserve Bank of St. Louis, June 1, 2015.

China Power Team. "How Much Trade Transits the South China Sea?" CSIS, August 2, 2017.

Chivvas, Christopher S. *Toppling Qaddafi: Libya and the Limits of Liberal Intervention.* Cambridge: Cambridge University Press, 2014.

Chollet, Derek and James Goldgeier, *America between the Wars: From 11/9 to 9/11.* New York: Public Affairs, 2008.

Christie, Edward Hunter. "Does Russia Have the Fiscal Capacity to Achieve Its Military Modernisation Goals?" *RUSI Journal* 162, no. 5 (2017).

Chuter, Andrew. "UK Restarts Frigate Competition—but Will Anyone Take Part?" *Defense News*, August 17, 2018.

Clarke, Stephen, Ilona Serwicka, and L. Alan Winters. "Will Brexit Raise the Cost of Living?" *National Economic Institute Review*, no. 242 (November 2017).

Coates, David, and Joel Krieger. *Blair's War.* Cambridge: Polity Press, 2004.

Coates, Sam, and Oliver Wright. "Hard Brexit Could Cost £66bn a Year: Leaked Treasury Papers Reveal Lost Revenue." *Times* (London), October 11, 2016.

Cohen, Ariel, and Robert Hamilton. *The Russian Military and the Georgia War: Lessons and Implications.* Carlisle, PA: U.S. Army War College Press, 2011.

Coleman, Katharina P. "The Legitimacy Audience Shapes the Coalition: Lessons from Afghanistan, 2001." *Journal of Intervention and Statebuilding* 11, no. 3 (2017).

Conference Board Total Economy Database™ (adjusted version), April 2019.

Connolly, Kate. "German Troops to Join War Effort in Berlin." *Guardian*, November 6, 2001.

Constitution of the Italian Republic, 1947.

"Contratto di governo Lega-M5s: Ecco il testo." *L'Espresso*, May 18, 2018.

Corbet, Sylvie. "French President Pushes for New Changes as Criticism Grows." Associated Press, August 22, 2018.

Cornish, Paul. "United Kingdom Hard Power: Strategic Ambivalence." In *A Hard Look at Hard Power: Assessing the Defense Capabilities of Key U.S. Allies and Security Partners*, ed. Gary J. Schmitt. Carlisle, PA: U.S. Army War College Press, 2015.

Coticchia, Fabrizio, Andrea Locatelli, and Francesco N. Moro. "Renew or Reload? Continuity and Change in Italian Defence Policy." *EUI Working Paper* RSCAS 2016/01, Robert Schuman Centre for Advanced Studies, January 2016.

Coughlin, Con. "Britain Is Shamed by Its Impotence over Syria and Ukraine." *Telegraph*, February 11, 2015.

"Could Striking French Rail Workers Bring France to a Standstill Once Again?" *The Local*, March 15, 2018.

Cowell, Alan. "Germans Plan Combat Troops outside NATO, a Postwar First." *New York Times*, December 14, 1996.

Crowe, Steven. "10 Most Automated Countries in the World." *Robot Report*, February 7, 2018.

Cyr, Arthur I. "Brexit and Transatlantic Security." *Parameters* 48, no. 1 (2018).

"Czy Polska potrzebuje Marynarki Wojennej?" *Polskie Radio*, July 5, 2018.

Dalsjo, Robert, Michael Jonsson, and Christofer Berglund. "Don't Believe the Russian Hype." *Foreign Policy*, March 7, 2019.

Darling, Daniel. "Poland's Harpia Fighter Acquisition Program Tops Project Queue." *Defense and Security Monitor*, March 12, 2019.

Davies, Michael C., and Frank Hoffman. "Joint Force 2020 and the Human Domain: Time for a New Conceptual Framework?" *Small Wars Journal*, June 10, 2013.

Day, Matthew. "Poland to Establish 46,000-Strong National Guard in the Face of War in Eastern Ukraine." *Telegraph*, January 25, 2016.

Defence and National Security Strategic Review (France). 2017.

Defense Intelligence Agency (U.S.). "China Military Power: Modernizing a Force to Fight and Win." 2019.

Defense Intelligence Agency (U.S.). "Russian Military Power." DIA-11-1704-161, 2017.

Defense Intelligence Agency (U.S.). "Russia Military Power: Building a Military to Support Great Power Aspirations." 2017.

De Hoop Scheffer, Alexandra, and Martin Quencez. "U.S. 'Burden-Shifting' Strategy in Africa Validates France's Ambition for Greater European Strategic Autonomy." German Marshall Fund of the United States, January 23, 2019.

De Hoop Scheffer, Alexandra, and Martin Quencez. "The U.S.–France Special Relationship: Testing the Macron Method." German Marshall Fund of the United States, April 18, 2018.

Delaporte, Murielle. "From Paris to Orbit: France's New Space Strategy." *Breaking Defense*, January 03, 2019.

Delcker, Janosch. "Germany's €3B Plan to Become an AI Powerhouse." *Politico*, November 14, 2018.

Delcker, Janosch. "Inside Amazon's German AI Research Program." *Politico*, May 20, 2019.

Dempsey, Noel. "Turnout at Elections." UK House of Commons briefing paper CBP 8060, July 26, 2017.

Dempsey, Noel. "UK Defence Expenditure." House of Commons Library briefing paper no. CBP 8175, November 8, 2018.

Deni, John R. *NATO and Article 5: The Transatlantic Alliance and the Twenty-First-Century Challenges of Collective Defense*. Lanham, MD: Rowman and Littlefield, 2017.

Deni, John R. *Rotational Deployments vs. Forward Stationing: How Can the Army Achieve Assurance and Deterrence Efficiently and Effectively?* Carlisle, PA: U.S. Army War College Press, 2017.

Deni, John R., ed. *Current Russia Military Affairs: Assessing and Countering Russian Strategy, Operational Planning, and Modernization*. Carlisle, PA: U.S. Army War College Press, 2018.

Department of Defense (U.S.) Directive 5000.01, May 12, 2003. Incorporating Change 2, August 31, 2018.

Dewan, Angela, Livia Borghese, and Milena Veselinovic. "Italy's Foreign Minister Gentiloni Appointed Prime Minister-Designate." *CNN Online*, December 11, 2016.

Dhingra, Swati, et al. "The Consequences of Brexit for UK Trade and Living Standards." London School of Economics and Political Science, Centre for Economic Performance, March 2016.

Di Bella, Gabriel, Oksana Dynnikova, and Slavi Slavov. "The Russian State's Size and Its Footprint: Have They Increased?" *IMF Working Paper*, WP/19/53, March 2, 2019.

Dicke, Rachel, et al. "NATO Burden-Sharing in Libya: Understanding the Contributions of Norway, Spain and Poland to the War Effort." *Polish Quarterly of International Affairs* 22, no. 4 (2013).

Dickson, Annabelle. "Poland and UK to Sign Joint Defense Treaty as May Visits Warsaw." *Politico*, December 12, 2017.

Dixon, Tim, et al. "Attitudes towards National Identity, Immigration and Refugees in Italy." *More in Common*, July 2018.

Dockrill, Saki. *Britain's Retreat from East of Suez: The Choice between Europe and the World? 1945–1968*. 2nd ed. Basingstoke, UK: Palgrave Macmillan, 2002.

Doeser, Fredrik. "Historical Experiences, Strategic Culture, and Strategic Behavior: Poland in the Anti-ISIS Coalition." *Defence Studies* 18, no. 4 (2018).

Doeser, Fredrik, and Joakim Eidenfalk. "Using Strategic Culture to Understand

Participation in Expeditionary Operations: Australia, Poland, and the Coalition against the Islamic State." *Contemporary Security Policy* 40, no. 1 (2019).

Doffman, Zak. "China's Spies Accused of Stealing EU Tech Secrets, Just as China and EU Agree Stronger Ties." *Forbes*, April 11, 2019.

Donadio, Rachel. "President of Italy Nominates Center-Left Official as Premier." *New York Times*, April 24, 2013.

Donadio, Rachel, and Elisabetta Povoledo. "Berlusconi Steps Down, and Italy Pulses with Change." *New York Times*, November 12, 2011.

Drozdowicz-Bieć, Maria. "Reasons Why Poland Avoided the 2007–2009 Recession." Research Institute for Economic Development, Warsaw School of Economics, 2011.

Drummond, Nicholas. "The Challenger 2 Life Extension Programme—Is It Worth It?" *UK Land Power* blog, June 23, 2018.

Dumbrell, John. "The US–UK Special Relationship: Taking the 21st-Century Temperature." *British Journal of Politics and International Relation* 11, no. 1 (2009).

Dumbrell, John. *A Special Relationship: Anglo-American Relations in the Cold War and After*. London: Macmillan, 2001.

Dunn, David H. "Poland: America's New Model Ally." *Defence Studies* 2, no. 2 (2002).

Dura, Maksymilian. "Dlaczego Polska potrzebuje Marynarki Wojennej?" *Defence24*, August 15, 2016.

Dustmann, Christian, et al. "From Sick Man of Europe to Economic Superstar: Germany's Resurgent Economy." *Journal of Economic Perspectives* 28, no. 1 (Winter 2014).

"Dutch Army to Sell All Leopards and Cougars." Defencetalk.com, April 8, 2011.

Dutch Ministry of Foreign Affairs. "International Security Strategy: A Secure Netherlands in a Secure World." June 21, 2013.

Dutch Ministry of Foreign Affairs. "Working Worldwide for the Security of the Netherlands: An Integrated International Security Strategy 2018–2022." May 14, 2018.

DuVal, Will, and Adam Maisel. "It's Time to Bring Back This Cold War Agency and Stop Ceding the Propaganda War to Russia." Modern War Institute, August 15, 2017.

Ebell, Monique, and James Warren, "The Long-Term Economic Impact of Leaving the EU." *National Institute Economic Review*, no. 236 (May 2016).

"Economists' Views on Brexit." Ipsos-MORI, May 28, 2018.

Eder, Florian. "Brussels Playbook." *Politico*, December 6, 2018.

"Effectifs, coût, efficacité . . . ce qu'il faut savoir sur l'opération Sentinelle." *LCI*, August 9, 2017.

Ekström, Markus. "Rysk operativ-strategisk övningsverksamhet under 2009 och 2010." FOI-R-3022-SE, Swedish Defence Research Agency, October 2010.

Elgie, Robert. "The Election of Emmanuel Macron and the New French Party

System: A Return to the éternel marais?" *Modern & Contemporary France* 26, no. 1 (2018).

"Elisabetta Trenta: 'Entro un anno le truppe italiane via dall'Afghanistan,' Moavero risponde: 'Non ne ha parlato con me'." *Huffington Post*, January 29, 2019.

Elizabeth Bryant. "In France, Maverick Macron Sets His Movement En Marche." *Deutsche Welle*, May 1, 2016.

"Embattled German Industrials Pursue the Factory of the Future." *Bloomberg*, June 9, 2017.

"Emmanuel Macron Wants to Change the Beloved Baccalauréat." *Economist*, February 8, 2018.

Erlanger, Steven. "Macron Had a Big Plan for Europe: It's Now Falling Apart." *New York Times*, April 19, 2018.

Erlanger, Steven. "Migrant Crisis Gives Germany Familiar Role in Another European Drama." *New York Times*, September 2, 2015.

"Estonia Says Russian Plane Again Violates Airspace." *Radio Free Europe/Radio Liberty*, June 21, 2018.

European Commission. "Digital Economy and Society Index (DESI) 2018 Country Report Poland." 2018.

European Commission. "EU Remains the World's Leading Donor of Development Assistance: €75.7 Billion in 2017." October 4, 2018.

European Commission. "European Cohesion Policy in Poland." 2009.

European Commission. "European Cohesion Policy in Spain." 2009.

European Commission. "The European Defence Fund: Stepping Up the EU's Role as a Security and Defence Provider." March 19, 2019.

European Commission. "European Economic Forecast." Institutional Paper 096, February 2019.

European Commission. "European Structural and Investment Funds—Poland." April 2016.

European Commission. "Joint Communication to the European Parliament and the Council: Elements for a New EU Strategy on China." June 22, 2016.

European Commission. "Joint Communication to the European Parliament, the European Council and the Council: EU-China—a Strategic Outlook." March 12, 2019.

European Commission. "Poland: 'Initiative for Polish Industry 4.0—The Future Industry Platform'." February 2018.

European Commission. "Trade SIA on the Transatlantic Trade and Investment Partnership (TTIP) between the EU and the USA." May 2016.

"European Foreign Policy Scorecard, 2015." European Council on Foreign Relations, January 2015.

European Investment Bank (EIB). "EIB Group Survey on Investment and Investment Finance Country Overview: Poland." 2018.

European Investment Bank. "European Investment Survey: Poland." 2018.

European Parliament. "Regulation of the European Parliament and of the Council

Establishing a Framework for the Screening of Foreign Direct Investments into the Union." February 20, 2019.

Eurostat. "Employment Rate by Sex, Age Group 20–64." August 17, 2018.

Eurostat. "Fertility Rates by Age." Data as of April 3, 2019.

Eurostat. "Harmonized Indices of Consumer Prices." 2019.

Eurostat. "People in the EU—Population Projections." November/December 2017.

Ewing, Jack. "A Populist Win Could Dull Europe's Appetite for Free Trade." *New York Times*, May 22, 2019.

Faiola, Anthony. "Italy's Berlusconi Agrees to Resign." *Washington Post*, November 9, 2011.

Fanta, Alexander. "Chinas fleißigster Lobbyist: Wie Huawei um seine Rolle im 5G-Ausbau kämpft." Netzpolitik.org, February 8, 2019.

Farmer, Ben. "Obama to Cameron: Maintain UK Defence Spending or Weaken Nato." *Telegraph*, February 10, 2015.

Federal Ministry for Economic Affairs and Energy (Germany). "What Is Industrie 4.0?" 2018.

Federation of German Industry. "Germany in World Trade." June 27, 2016.

Filippetti, Andrea, and Antonio Peyrache. "Productivity Growth and Catching Up: A Technology Gap Explanation." *International Review of Applied Economics* 31, no. 3 (May 2017).

Finch, Sean C. "U.S. Army Europe Soldiers Help Train Polish Troops for Deployment to Iraq." U.S. Army Europe Public Affairs Office, December 19, 2007.

Fiorenza, Nicholas. "Poland Gives Details of New, Fourth Division." *Jane's Defence Weekly*, September 10, 2018.

Flouroy, Michèle A., and Robert P. Lyons III. "Sustaining and Enhancing the US Military's Technology Edge." *Strategic Studies Quarterly* 10, no. 2 (Summer 2016).

Foerster, Schuyler, and Ray Raymond. "The US-UK 'Special Relationship' at a Critical Crossroads." Atlantic Council Issue Brief, July 2017.

Follain, John, and Rosalind Mathieson. "Italy Pivots to China in Blow to EU Efforts to Keep Its Distance." *Bloomberg*, October 4, 2018.

Fonte, Giuseppe. "Italy PM Unveils Sweeping Austerity Package." *Reuters*, December 3, 2011.

Fouchaux, Dorothée. "French Hard Power: Living on the Strategic Edge." In *A Hard Look at Hard Power: Assessing the Defense Capabilities of Key U.S. Allies and Security Partners*, ed. Gary J. Schmitt. Carlisle, PA: U.S. Army War College Press, 2015.

Fox, Benjamin. "EU Unveils Increased Foreign Aid Budget for 2021–27." Euractiv.com. June 14, 2018.

Freedberg, Sydney J., Jr. "FVL Helicopters: How to Avoid F-35 Snafu." *Breaking Defense*, September 08, 2014.

"Freedom in the World 2019: Democracy in Retreat." Freedom House, 2019.

"French Government Strikes Deal to Cut Lawmakers Number by Almost a Third." *Reuters*, April 4, 2018.

"French Navy Frigate Conducts FONOP in South China Sea." Navy Recognition, March 23, 2018.

Friedman, George. "Germany's Role in Europe and the European Debt Crisis." *Stratfor*, January 31, 2012.

Friedman, Uri. "Will the World Grow More Authoritarian in 2014?" *Atlantic*, January 6, 2014.

"From the Baltic to Alaska: More Russian Air Provocations Reported." Warsaw Institute, January 30, 2019.

Funke, Manuel, and Christoph Trebesch. "Financial Crises and the Populist Right." *DICE Report* 15, no. 4 (December 2017).

Galeotti, Mark. "Heavy Metal Diplomacy: Russia's Political Use of Its Military in Europe since 2014." European Council on Foreign Relations, December 19, 2016.

Gamble, Andrew, and Ian Kearns. "Recasting the Special Relationship." In *Progressive Foreign Policy: New Directions for the UK*, ed. David Held and David Mepham. Cambridge: Polity Press, 2007.

Ganguly, Sumit, et al. "History Begins (Again) for the Pentagon." Foreign Policy Research Institute, February 22, 2018.

Garamone, Jim. "Dunford Describes U.S. Great Power Competition with Russia, China." Defense.gov, March 21, 2019.

Garamone, Jim. "U.S., Poland Sign Special Ops Memo of Understanding." American Forces Press Service, February 19, 2009.

Garner, Godfrey, and Patrick McGlynn. *Intelligence Analysis Fundamentals*. Boca Raton, FL: CRC Press, 2019.

Garnero, Andrea. "Why Labor Protests in France Won't Stop Macron's Reforms." *Harvard Business Review*, May 22, 2018.

Gauck, Joachim. "Germany's Role in the World: Reflections on Responsibility, Norms and Alliances." Speech at the opening of the Munich Security Conference, January 31, 2014.

"German Army Facing 'Big Gaps' as Spending Cuts Bite." *AFP*, February 20, 2018.

"German Budget Surplus Hits a Record." *Deutsche Welle*, August 25, 2017.

German Federation of Industry. "Partner and Systemic Competitor—How Do We Deal with China's State-Controlled Economy?" January 10, 2019.

"Germany's Lack of Military Readiness 'Dramatic,' Says Bundeswehr Commissioner." *Deutsche Welle*, February 20, 2018.

Giegerich, Bastian, and Christian Mölling. "The United Kingdom's Contribution to European Security and Defence." International Institute for Strategic Studies, February 2018.

Gilli, Andrea, Alessandro R. Ungaro, and Alessandro Marrone. "The Italian White Paper for International Security and Defence." *RUSI Journal* 160, no. 6 (2015).

Gilpin, Robert. *War and Change in World Politics*. Cambridge: Cambridge University Press, 1981.

Glatz, Rainer L., and Martin Zapfe. "Ambitious Framework Nation: Germany in NATO." Stiftung Wissenschaft und Politik, September 2017.

"Gli italiani e la politica estera." Istituto Affari Internazionali, October 2017.

"Gli italiani lasceranno l'Afghanistan dopo la pace tra Trump e i talebani." *Analisi Difesa*, January 29, 2019.

"The Global Competitiveness Report 2018." World Economic Forum, 2019.

Goettig, Marcin. "Polish Cut in Retirement Age Comes into Force, Bucking European Trend." *Reuters*, October 1, 2017.

Gomułka, Stanisław. "Poland's Economic and Social Transformation 1989–2014 and Contemporary Challenges." *Central Bank Review* 16 (2016).

Goodman, Peter S. "Europe's Economy, after 8-Year Detour, Is Fitfully Back on Track." *New York Times*, April 29, 2016.

Goodman, Peter S. "In Britain, Austerity Is Changing Everything." *New York Times*, May 28, 2018.

Goodman, Peter S. "U.K. Economy Falters as Brexit Looms: Amsterdam Sees Risks, and Opportunity." *New York Times*, February 11, 2019.

Gougou, Florent, and Simon Persico. "A New Party System in the Making? The 2017 French Presidential Election." *French Politics* 15, no. 3 (2017).

Government of Poland. "Ustawa o przebudowie i modernizacji technicznej oraz finansowaniu Sił Zbrojnych Rzeczypospolitej Polskiej." As passed May 25, 2001 and subsequently amended.

Government of the Netherlands. "National Security Strategy and Work Programme, 2007–2008."

Gradzewicz, Michał, et al. "Poland's Uninterrupted Growth Performance: New Growth Accounting Evidence." *Post-Communist Economies* 30, no. 2 (2018).

Gramer, Robbie, and Elias Groll. "With New Appointment, State Department Ramps Up War against Foreign Propaganda." *Foreign Policy*, February 7, 2019.

Grasland, Emmanuel, and Alain Ruello. "Inquiets, les industriels de l'armement demandent audience à l'Elysée." *Les Echos*, March 13, 2013.

Gray, Rosie. "Trump Declines to Affirm NATO's Article 5." *Atlantic*, May 25, 2017.

Greenwald, Michael B. "To Manage Great Power Competition, America Needs a New Economic Patriot Act." *Diplomat*, April 17, 2019.

Guibert, Nathalie. "La France mène des opérations secrètes en Libye." *Le Monde*, February 23, 2016.

Gupta, Vin, and Vanessa Kerry. "Foreign Aid Makes America Safer." *Foreign Policy*, April 11, 2018.

Hall, Thomas W., and John E. Elliott. "Poland and Russia One Decade after Shock Therapy." *Journal of Economic Issues* 33, no. 2 (1999).

Hallam, Andrew. "Poland's Tiger Economy." *European Business Journal* 11, no. 2 (Summer 1999).

Hammond, Phillip. *Framing Post–Cold War Conflicts: The Media and International Intervention.* Manchester: Manchester University Press, 2007.

Hanemann, Thilo, and Mikko Huotari. "A New Record Year for Chinese Outbound Investment in Europe." Mercator Institute for China Studies, February 2016.

Harper, Jo. "Poland Fears Economic Hit as EU Opens Door to Ukrainians." *Deutsche Welle,* January 30, 2018.

Harris, Catherine, and Frederick W. Kagan. *Russia's Military Posture: Ground Forces Order of Battle.* Institute for the Study of War and the Critical Threats Project at the American Enterprise Institute, March 2018.

Harris, Gardiner. "State Dept. Was Granted $120 Million to Fight Russian Meddling: It Has Spent $0." *New York Times,* March 4, 2018.

Hathaway, Melissa, et al. "Italy: Cyber Readiness at a Glance." Potomac Institute for Policy Studies, November 2016.

Hayton, Bill. "How Europe Can Make a Difference in the South China Sea." *Berlin Policy Journal,* February 7, 2019.

"Here Is the First Image of the French Navy Next Generation SSBN—SNLE 3G." *Navy Recognition,* October 3, 2018.

Hernandez, Marcial. "Dutch Hard Power: Choosing Decline." American Enterprise Institute, April 3, 2013.

Hewlett, Nick. "The Phantom Revolution: The Presidential and Parliamentary Elections of 2017." *Modern & Contemporary France* 25, no. 4 (2017).

Hill, Christopher. *The Future of British Foreign Policy: Security and Diplomacy in a World after Brexit.* Cambridge: Polity Press, 2019.

Hill, Christopher. "Turning Back the Clock: The Illusion of a Global Political Role for Britain." In *Brexit and Beyond: Rethinking the Futures of Europe,* ed. Benjamin Martill and Uta Staiger. London: University College London, 2018.

Hille, Kathrin. "China's Army Redoubles Modernisation Effort." *Financial Times,* January 28, 2019.

HM Treasury. "The Long-Term Economic Impact of EU Membership and the Alternatives." Presented to Parliament by the Chancellor of the Exchequer by Command of Her Majesty, April 2016.

Hodder-Williams, Richard. "Reforging the 'Special Relationship': Blair, Clinton and Foreign Policy." In *New Labour's Foreign Policy: A Moral Crusade?,* ed. Richard Little and Mark Wickham-Jones. Manchester: Manchester University Press, 2000.

Hodges, Ben, Janusz Bugajski, and Peter B. Doran. "Securing the Suwałki Corridor." Center for European Policy Analysis, July 2018.

Hoffman, F. G. "The Future Is Plural: Multiple Futures for Tomorrow's Joint Force." *Joint Forces Quarterly* 88, no. 1 (2018).

Hollinger, Peggy, Tobias Buck, and Laura Pitel. "A400M: The €20bn Military Aircraft That Has Bedevilled Airbus." *Financial Times,* July 3, 2018.

Horowitz, Jason. "Italy's Populist Parties Agree on a Common Agenda to Govern." *New York Times,* May 18, 2018.

Horowitz, Jason, and Jack Ewing. "Italy May Split with Allies and Open Its Ports to China's Building Push." *New York Times,* March 6, 2019.

House of Commons Defence Committee. "Shifting the Goalposts? Defence Expenditure and the 2% Pledge." HC 494, April 12, 2016.

"How Will France's Growing Naval Presence in Asia Affect Its China Ties?" *World Politics Review,* June 3, 2019.

Hoyo, Verónica, and William M. Chandler. "Emmanuel Macron Just Won a Majority in France's National Assembly: Here Is Why It Matters." *Washington Post,* June 20, 2017.

Hurst, Ian, et al. *A Preliminary Assessment of the Possible Economic Impact of the Coronavirus Outbreak: Update.* London: National Institute of Economic and Social Research, 2020.

Iasiello, Emilio J. "Russia's Improved Information Operations: From Georgia to Crimea." *Parameters* 47, no. 2 (2017).

"ifo Umfrage: Direktinvestitionen aus China werden kritischer betrachtet als die anderer Länder." ifo Institut, May 20, 2019.

"The Impact of the Financial Crisis on European Defence." Directorate-General for External Policies of the Union, European Parliament, April 2011.

Inman, Phillip. "UK Growth Will Slow to 1.3% amid Brexit Uncertainty—KPMG." *Guardian,* September 10, 2018.

Insinna, Valerie. "Inside America's Dysfunctional Trillion-Dollar Fighter-Jet Program." *New York Times,* August 21, 2019.

Institut National de la Statistique et des Études Économiques. "Comptes nationaux trimestriels—Résultats détaillés du 3ème trimestre 2018." December 21, 2018.

Institut National de la Statistique et des Études Économiques. "Au quatrième trimestre 2019, le PIB baisse légèrement (−0,1 %)." January 31, 2020.

International Monetary Fund. "2017 Article IV Consultation—Press Release, Staff Report, and Statement by the Executive Director for the United Kingdom." IMF Country Report No. 18/42, February 2018.

International Monetary Fund. "2018 Article IV Consultation—Press Release, Staff Report, Staff Statement, and Statement by the Executive Director for the United Kingdom." IMF Country Report No. 18/316, November 2018.

International Monetary Fund. "Italy: Selected Issues." IMF Country Report No. 11/176, July 2011.

International Monetary Fund. "Italy: Selected Issues." IMF Country Report No. 17/238, July 2017.

International Monetary Fund. "Republic of Poland: 2018 Article IV Consultation." Country Report No. 19/37, February 2019.

International Monetary Fund. "Republic of Poland: Detailed Assessment of Observance of Basel Core Principles for Effective Banking Supervision." IMF Country Report No. 12/232, August 2012.

International Monetary Fund. "Republic of Poland: Selected Issues." Country Report no. 19/38, February 2019.

International Monetary Fund. "World Economic Outlook," April 2019.

Interview. A civilian defense policy advisor at the Polish mission to NATO, May 17, 2019.

Interview. A civilian NATO expert in the German Ministry of Defence, September 11, 2018.

Interview. A civilian strategist within the Germany Ministry of Defence, September 13, 2018.

Interview. A European security expert at Johns Hopkins University, December 4, 2018.

Interview. A field grade U.S. officer based in Europe with extensive knowledge of U.S.-Italian mil-to-mil ties, March 20, 2019.

Interview. A field-grade Italian military officer based in Rome, March 3, 2019.

Interview. A field-grade U.S. officer based in Washington who works on U.S.-Italy military-to-military relations, March 4, 2019.

Interview. A former civilian political advisor to U.S. military forces in Europe, June 16, 2017.

Interview. A former senior civilian employee within the Office of the Secretary of Defense, December 2, 2018.

Interview. A former senior political appointee within the U.S. Department of Defense, July 23, 2019.

Interview. A French defense expert at a Paris-based think tank, February 25, 2019.

Interview. A French field-grade army officer, April 11, 2019.

Interview. A French field-grade army officer, February 11, 2019.

Interview. A German think tank expert on Europe security and transatlantic relations, May 9, 2019.

Interview. A Polish civilian employee of the Ministry of Defense and a Polish field-grade military officer assigned to the General Staff, March 2, 2016.

Interview. A Polish defense and national security expert at a Warsaw-based think tank, April 15, 2019.

Interview. A Polish expert on transatlantic relations and national security at a Warsaw-based think tank, April 26, 2019.

Interview. A senior civilian official within the Polish Defence Ministry, March 2, 2016.

Interview. A senior field-grade U.S. officer based in Washington and expert in Franco-American military relations, February 28, 2019.

Interview. A senior NATO civilian working in armaments cooperation, May 17, 2019.

Interview. A U.S. Department of Defense employee based in Europe with extensive knowledge of security cooperation between the U.S. Army and the British Army, November 13, 2018.

Interview. A U.S. field grade officer based in Washington who works on U.S.-Italy military-to-military relations, March 4, 2019.

Interview. A U.S. field grade officer based in Washington who works on U.S.-Poland military-to-military relations, April 5, 2019.

Interview. A U.S. field-grade officer assigned to U.S. European Command, January 15, 2019.

Interview. A Washington-based U.S. field grade officer expert on military relations with France, February 28, 2019.

Interview. An American civilian employee of U.S. Army Europe with extensive experience in military-to-military programs across Europe, November 13, 2018.

Interview. An expert at the American Institute for Contemporary Germany Studies, December 4, 2018.

Interview. An expert on French national security at a Paris-based think tank, February 4, 2019.

Interview. An expert on Polish national security and strategy at a think tank in Warsaw, May 1, 2019.

Interview. An expert on U.S. and European security at a DC-based think tank, December 4, 2018.

Interview. Two civilian defense experts assigned to U.S. European Command, August 9, 2016.

Irish, John, and Marine Pennetier. "France Says It Could Help North Korea Denuclearize if It Sees Real Commitment." *Reuters*, October 15, 2018.

Irwin, Douglas A. "Trade under Trump: What He's Done So Far—and What He'll Do Next." *Foreign Affairs*, November 6, 2018.

Irwin, Neil. "How Germany Prevailed in the Greek Bailout." *New York Times*, July 29, 2015.

Isernia, Pierangelo, and Gianluca Piccolino. "Italians Are Tired of Living under Austerity: That Could Be a Big Problem for Europe." *Washington Post*, July 25, 2018.

Istat (Italian National Institute of Statistics). "The Demographic Future of the Country." April 26, 2017.

Istat (Italian National Institute of Statistics). "Demographic Indicators." February 7, 2019.

"Is the U.S Military Overstretched?" *Voice of America*, October 30, 2009.

"Italian Leader Urges End to EU Sanctions on Russia during Moscow Visit." *Radio Free Europe/Radio Liberty*, October 25, 2018.

"Italian Troops to Remain in Afghanistan Pending Consultation with Allies—Official." *Kuwait News Agency*, February 22, 2019.

"Italy and Cyber Defense." SLDinfo.com, May 8, 2018.

"Italy Army Clearing Naples Rubbish." *BBC*, May 9, 2011.

"Italy Heads for Fresh Elections: Italian Politics." *Economist*. December 29, 2017.

"Italy Hit with 10 Percent Defense Cuts." *UPI*, May 28, 2010.

"Italy Minister Says Defence Spending Set to Fall Further Next Year." *Reuters*, July 26, 2018.

"Italy." Operation Inherent Resolve website, March 16, 2016.

"Italy: Rome Trains Its Sights on Defense Spending Cuts." *Stratfor*, October 4, 2018.

"Italy's Monti Defends Austerity Measures." *Wall Street Journal*, December 11, 2012.

Ito, Katsuya. "Dutch Disease and Russia." *International Economics* 151 (2017).

Jacobs, Jennifer, et al. "Poland and U.S. Closing In on Deal to Build 'Fort Trump,' Sources Say." *Bloomberg*, April 16, 2019.

Jagers, Jan, and Stefaan Walgrave. "Populism as Political Communication Style: An Empirical Study of Political Parties' Discourse in Belgium." *European Journal of Political Research* 46, no. 3 (May 2007).

Janning, Josef, and Almut Möller. "Leading from the Centre: Germany's New Role in Europe." European Council on Foreign Relations, July 2016.

Jasiński, Tomasz, and Paweł Mielcarz. "Consumption as a Factor of Polish Economic Growth during the Global Recession of 2008/2009: A Comparison with Spain and Hungary." *Contemporary Economics* 7, no. 2 (2013).

Jędruchniewicz, Andrzej. "Monetary Policy and Investments in the Polish Economy." *Oeconomia Copernicana* 6, no. 3 (2013).

Jermano, Jill. "Economic and Financial Sanctions in U.S. National Security Strategy." *PRISM* 7, no. 4 (November 2018).

Johnson, Paul, and Ian Mitchell. "The Brexit Vote, Economics, and Economic Policy." *Oxford Review of Economic Policy* 33, no. S1 (2017).

"Joint Statement of Intent by Mr. Jean-Yves le Drian, Minister of Defence of the French Republic, and the Honorable Ashton Carter, Secretary of Defense of the United States of America." November 28, 2016. dod.defense.gov/Portals/1/Documents/pubs/Joint-Statement-of-Intent-between-the-US-and-France.pdf.

Juncker, Jean-Claude. Speech delivered at the 54th Munich Security Conference, February 17, 2018.

Kagan, Robert. "Power and Weakness." *Policy Review*, no. 113 (June/July 2002).

Kaim, Markus, and Hilmar Linnenkamp. "The New White Paper 2016—Promoting Greater Understanding of Security Policy?" Stiftung Wissenschaft und Politik, November 2016.

Kaminski, Matthew. "The Weekend Interview with Leszek Balcerowicz: The Anti-Bernanke." *Wall Street Journal*, December 15, 2012.

Kanniainen, Vesa, and Juha-Matti Lehtonen. "Joint Procurements in Building National Defence: Why Are There So Few?" Helsinki Center of Economic Research, Discussion Paper No. 427, March 2018.

Karnitschnig, Matthew. "For NATO, China Is the New Russia." *Politico*, April 4, 2019.

Karnitschnig, Matthew, and Jacopo Barigazzi. "EU and Turkey Reach Refugee Deal." *Politico*, March 18, 2016.

Kaya, Ayhan, and Ayşe Tecmen. "Europe versus Islam? Right-Wing Populist Discourse and the Construction of a Civilizational Identity." *Review of Faith & International Affairs* 17, no. 1 (2019).

Kazianis, Harry J. "US Intelligence Officials: North Korea Will Sell Nuclear Tech to Iran." *The Hill*, June 29, 2018.

Keck, Zachary. "France and Germany Have a Plan to Build a Stealth 6th-Generation Fighter." *National Interest*, June 22, 2018.

Keller, Patrick. "German Hard Power: Is There a There There?" In *A Hard Look at Hard Power: Assessing the Defense Capabilities of Key U.S. Allies and Security Partners*, ed. Gary J. Schmitt. Carlisle, PA: U.S. Army War College Press, 2015.

Kelly, Lidia. "Poland Signs $4.75 Billion Deal for U.S. Patriot Missile System Facing Russia." *Reuters*, March 28, 2018.

Kelly, Lidia. "Poland to Spend $55 Billion More on Defense amid Russia Fears." *Reuters*, August 23, 2017.

Keohane, Daniel. "Constrained Leadership: Germany's New Defense Policy." Center for Security Studies, ETH Zurich, no. 201, December 2016.

Keohane, Daniel. "The Defense Policies of Italy and Poland: A Comparison." Center for Security Studies, ETH Zurich, no. 219, December 2017.

Kierzenkowski, Rafal, et al. "The Economic Consequences of Brexit: A Taxing Decision." OECD Economic Policy Papers, April 2016.

Kington, Tom. "Italy Delays Vehicle, Helicopter Buys." *Defense News*, July 9, 2012.

Kington, Tom. "Italy Plans to Slash Half a Billion Dollars from Defense in 2019." *Defense News*, October 24, 2018.

Kington, Tom. "Italy's New Defense Minister Commits to F-35, Butts Heads with France." *Defense News*, June 29, 2018.

Kirchgaessner, Stephanie. "Italian PM Matteo Renzi Resigns after Referendum Defeat." *Guardian*, December 5, 2016.

Kirkup, James. "Cancelling Aircraft Carriers Would Have Cost Taxpayers £690 Million." *Telegraph*, November 4, 2010.

Knight, Sam. "Theresa May's Impossible Choice." *New Yorker*, July 30, 2018.

Knodell, Kevin. "The British Army Can't Find Enough Soldiers: Who Will Fight the United Kingdom's Wars?" *National Interest*, January 29, 2017.

Koeth, Wolfgang. "Leadership Revised: How Did the Ukraine Crisis and the Annexation of Crimea Affirm Germany's Leading Role in EU Foreign Policy?" *Lithuanian Annual Strategic Review*, vol. 14, 2015–16.

Kofman, Michael. "The August War, Ten Years On: A Retrospective on the Russo-Georgian War." *War on the Rocks*, August 17, 2018.

Kovalev, Alexey, and Matthew Bodner. "The Secrets of Russia's Propaganda War, Revealed." *Moscow Times*, March 1, 2017.

Krugman, Paul. "Those Depressing Germans." *New York Times*, November 3, 2013.

Kuhn, Raymond. "French Revolution? The 2017 Presidential and Parliamentary Elections." *Parliamentary Affairs*, 2018.

Kulish, Nicolas. "Monti, in Berlin, Calls for Growth Policies in Europe." *New York Times*, January 11, 2012.

Kunz, Barbara. "The Real Roots of Germany's Defense Spending Problem." *War on the Rocks*, July 24, 2018.

Küpper, Daniel, et al. "The Factory of the Future." Boston Consulting Group, December 6, 2016.

Lamandé, Emmanuelle. "Florence Parly, FIC: La France passe à la 'cyber' offensive." *Global Security Mag*, January 2019.

Lamandé, Emmanuelle. "Général Olivier Bonnet de Paillerets, COMCYBER: Le recrutement de cyber-combattants représente un défi colossal pour le ministère des Armées." *Global Security Mag*, February 2019.

Lamigeon, Vincent. "Budget des armées 2019: Qui sont les gagnants?" *l'Opinion*, September 27, 2018.

Lane, Philip R. "The European Sovereign Debt Crisis." *Journal of Economic Perspectives* 26, no. 3 (Summer 2012).

Lanzone, Liza, and Dwayne Woods. "Riding the Populist Web: Contextualizing the Five Star Movement (M5S) in Italy." *Politics and Governance* 3, no. 2 (2015).

Lapo, Amanda. "Italy: Renewed Focus on Overseas Deployments." International Institute for Strategic Studies Military Balance blog, April 9, 2018.

Larrabee, F. Stephen, et al. *NATO and the Challenges of Austerity*. Santa Monica, CA: RAND Corporation, 2012.

Lavery, Scott, Lucia Quaglia, and Charlie Dannreuther. "The Political Economy of Brexit and the Future of British Capitalism First Symposium." *New Political Economy*, 2018.

Lavrov, Anton. "Russian Military Reforms from Georgia to Syria." CSIS, November 2018.

Le Cain, Blandine. "Pourquoi l'armée a du mal à fidéliser ses troupes." *Le Figaro*, July 10, 2017.

Lecointre, François. "Allocution de Bienvenue." Proceedings from the 15th University of Defense, September 2017.

Lees, David. "A Controversial Campaign: François Fillon and the Decline of the Centre-Right in the 2017 Presidential Elections." *Modern & Contemporary France* 25, no. 4 (2017).

Lenti, Renata Targetti. "Sviluppo e declino del sistema economico Italiano." *Il Politico* 76, no. 3 (2011).

Liebermann, Oren, Frederik Pleitgen, and Vasco Cotovio. "New Satellite Images Suggest Military Buildup in Russia's Strategic Baltic Enclave." *CNN Online*, October 17, 2018.

"Limited Number of Weapons in German Military Ready for Action: Report." *Deutsche Welle*, February 27, 2018.

Lindsay, Frey. "Ukrainian Immigrants Give the Polish Government an Out on Refugees." *Forbes*, September 19, 2018.

Lippi, Francesco, and Fabiano Schivardi. "Corporate Control and Executive Selection." *Quantitative Economics* 5, no. 2 (July 2014).

Lledó, Victor, et al. "Fiscal Rules at a Glance." International Monetary Fund, March 2017.

Lopinot, Quentin. "What Does 'European Defense' Look Like? The Answer Might Be in the Sahel." *War on the Rocks*, March 19, 2019.

Lubecki, Jacek. "Poland in Iraq: The Politics of the Decision." *Polish Review* 50, no. 1 (2005).

Lubold, Gordon, and Matthew Dalton. "U.S.-French Operation Targeted Elusive North African Militant, U.S. Says." *Wall Street Journal*, November 27, 2016.

Lucas, Edward R. "Countering the 'Unholy Alliance': The United States' Efforts to Combat Piracy and Violent Extremism in the Western Indian Ocean, 2001–2014." Paper presented to the International Studies Association International Conference, Hong Kong, June 15, 2017.

Luxmoore, Matthew. "Rising Mortality Rates Challenge Russia's Efforts to Kick-Start Population Growth." *Radio Free Europe/Radio Liberty*, April 4, 2019.

Lynn-Jones, Sean M. "Realism and America's Rise: A Review Essay." *International Security* 23, no. 2 (Fall 1998).

Lyons, Gerard, and Patrick Minford, eds. *The Economy after Brexit: Economists for Brexit*. 2016.

MacAskill, Ewen. "British Forces No Longer Fit for Purpose, Former UK Service Chiefs Warn." *Guardian*, November 14, 2017.

Mackenzie, Christina. "France Orders $2.3 Billion Upgrade for Rafale Warplanes." *Defense News*, January 14, 2019.

Mackenzie, Christina. "French Defense Chief Touts Offensive Tack in New Cyber Strategy." *Fifth Domain*, January 18, 2019.

Mackenzie, James. "Italian PM Letta Wins Confidence Votes, Vows Reforms." *Reuters* , December 11, 2013.

"Macron Accepts Resignation of French Military Chief." *France 24*, July 19, 2017.

"Macron Aims to Put Summer Scandal behind Him with New Reform Drive." *France 24*, August 22, 2018.

Macron, Emmanuel. *Revolution*. Translated by Jonathan Goldberg and Juliette Scott. London: Scribe, 2017.

"Macron Signs French Labor Reform Decrees." *Reuters*, September 22, 2017.

Magda, Iga, Aneta Kiełczewska, and Nicola Brandt. "The 'Family 500+' Child Allowance and Female Labour Supply in Poland." Institute for Structural Research, Working Paper 01/2018, March 2018.

Major, Claudia, and Christian Mölling. "The Framework Nations Concept." Stiftung Wissenschaft und Politik, December 2014.

Mallet, Victor. "Paris Vows to Extend Labour Reforms despite Gilets Jaunes." *Financial Times*, January 23, 2019.

Malley, Robert, and Jon Finer. "The Long Shadow of 9/11: How Counterterrorism Warps U.S. Foreign Policy." *Foreign Policy*, July/August 2018.

Malloch-Brown, Mark. "Is This the End of Global Britain?" *Financial News*, June 28, 2018.

Manasse, Paolo. "The Roots of the Italian Stagnation." Centre for Economic Policy Research, June 19, 2013.

Manasse, Paolo, and Thomas Manfredi. "Wages, Productivity, and Employment in Italy: Tales from a Distorted Labour Market." Centre for Economic Policy Research, April 19, 2014.

Mance, Henry. "UK Armed Forces' Personnel Shortage Is 'Largest in a Decade'." *Financial Times*, April 17, 2018.

Manibog, Claire, and Stephen Foley. "The Long and Winding Road to Economic Recovery." *Financial Times*, August 10, 2017.

Marrone, Alessandro, Olivier De France, and Daniele Fattibene, eds. *Defence Budgets and Cooperation in Europe: Developments, Trends and Drivers.* Institute for International Affairs (Italy). January 2016.

Martin, Adam. "NSA: Germany Was 'a Little Grumpy' about Being Left Out of Spying Club." *New Yorker*, November 2, 2013.

Martin, Peter, and Alan Crawford. "China's Influence Digs Deep into Europe's Political Landscape." *Bloomberg*, April 3, 2019.

Martin, Pierre. "Un séisme politique: L'élection présidentielle de 2017." *Commentaire*, no. 158, 2017.

Martinelli, Giovanni. "Bilancio Della Difesa 2016: Quando le apparenze ingannano." *Analisi Difesa*, no. 172, February 2016.

Martinelli, Giovanni. "Il Bilancio Della Difesa." *Analisi Difesa*, no. 184, February 2017.

Martinelli, Giovanni. "Il Bilancio Difesa 2019." *Analisi Difesa*, February 25, 2019.

Matelly, Sylvie. "Defense Innovation and the Future of Transatlantic Strategic Superiority: A French Perspective." German Marshall Fund of the United States, 2018.

Mateos y Lago, Isabelle, and Hans-Werner Sinn. "Should Merkel Embrace Macron's Vision for Eurozone Reform?" *Financial Times*, June 27, 2018.

Maull, Hanns W. "Germany and the Use of Force: Still a 'Civilian Power'?" *Survival* 42, no. 2 (2000).

McAuley, James. "In France, Are Soldiers outside the Eiffel Tower and the Louvre Really Worth It?" *Washington Post*, June 4, 2016.

McCann, Philip. "The Trade, Geography and Regional Implications of Brexit." *Papers in Regional Science* 97 (January 2018).

McCombie, John S. L., and Marta R. M. Spreafico. "Brexit and Its Possible Implications for the UK Economy and Its Regions: A Post-Keynesian Perspective." *Papers in Regional Science* 97 (2018).

McCourt, David M. "What Was Britain's 'East of Suez Role'? Reassessing the Withdrawal, 1964–1968." *Diplomacy & Statecraft* 20, no. 3 (2009).

McDermott, Roger. "Moscow Deploys Latest Electronic Warfare Systems in Kaliningrad." *Eurasia Daily Monitor* 15, no. 174 (December 11, 2018).

McGrath, Bryan. "NATO at Sea: Trends in Allied Naval Power." American Enterprise Institute, 2013.

McLeary, Paul. "State, DoD Letter Warns European Union to Open Defense Contracts, or Else." *Breaking Defense*, May 17, 2019.

Mearsheimer, John J. *The Tragedy of Great Power Politics*. New York: W. W. Norton, 2001.

Mehta, Aaron. "Poland Wants to Play in Franco-German Tank Program." *Defense News*, August 3, 2016.

Meisel, Collin, and Jonathan D. Moyer. "Preparing for China's Rapid Rise and Decline." *War on the Rocks*, April 15, 2019.

Melander, Ingrid. "'No Kid Left Behind': Macron Tries to Fix France's Education System." *Reuters*, July 5, 2018.

Menon, Anand, Jonathan Portes, and Matthew Bevington, eds. *The Brexit Score-card*. London: University College London, 2019.

Mény, Yves. "A Tale of Party Primaries and Outsider Candidates: The 2017 French Presidential Election." *French Politics*, 2017.

Merchet, Jean-Dominique. "Au Sahel, l'armée française 'se dépêche d'attendre' ses renforts de materiel." *l'Opinion*, July 18, 2018.

Messia, Hada. "Italy Approves Austerity, Berlusconi Resigns." *CNN Online*, November 13, 2011.

Meunier, Sophie. "Is France Still Relevant?" *French Politics, Culture & Society* 35, no. 2 (Summer 2017).

Michelot, Martin, and Milan Šuplata. "Defence and Industrial Policy in Slovakia and the Czech Republic: Drivers, Stakeholders, Influence." Armament Industry European Research Group, December 2016.

Michta, Andrew A. "Polish Hard Power: Investing in the Military as Europe Cuts Back." In *A Hard Look at Hard Power: Assessing the Defense Capabilities of Key U.S. Allies and Security Partners*, ed. Gary Schmitt. Carlisle, PA: US Army War College Press, 2015.

The Military Balance. London: International Institute for Strategic Studies, 2000.

The Military Balance. London: International Institute for Strategic Studies, 2008.

The Military Balance. London: International Institute for Strategic Studies, 2014.

The Military Balance. London: International Institute for Strategic Studies, 2016.

The Military Balance. London: International Institute for Strategic Studies, 2018.

The Military Balance. London: International Institute for Strategic Studies, 2019.

"Military Cuts Mean 'No US Partnership,' Robert Gates Warns Britain." *BBC News*, January 16, 2014.

Miller, Russell A. "Germany's Basic Law and the Use of Force." *Indiana Journal of Global Legal Studies* 17, no. 2 (Summer 2010).

Ministère des Armées. "11e rapport thématique du Haut Comité d'évaluation de la condition militaire." June 10, 2017.

Ministry of Defence (France), "Discours de Florence Parly, ministre des Armées_ Intelligence artificielle et defense." April 5, 2019.

Ministry of Defence (Italy). "Iraq—Prima Parthica Operation/Inherent Resolve." 2016.

Ministry of Defence (Italy). "Libro Bianco 2002." 2002.

Ministry of Defence (Italy). "Operation Strade Sicure (Safe Streets)." 2015.

Ministry of Defence (Italy). "White Paper for International Security and Defence," July 2015.

Ministry of Defence (UK). "The Defence Training Estate." December 12, 2012.

Ministry of Defence (UK). "UK Armed Forces Quarterly Service Personnel Statistics 1 January 2020." February 20, 2020.

Ministry of Economic Development (Italy). "MISE: Costituita la Task Force Cina." August 20, 2018.

Ministry of National Defense (Poland). "3 miliardy złotych na cyberbezpieczeństwo." February 28, 2019.

Ministry of National Defence (Poland). "The Defence Concept of the Republic of Poland." May 2017.

Ministry of National Defence (Poland). "Defense Strategy of the Republic of Poland." 2009.

Ministry of National Defense (Poland). "Plan Modernizacji Technicznej—mapa drogowa rozwoju Wojska Polskiego." February 28, 2019.

Miskimmon, Alister. "Falling into Line? Kosovo and the Course of German Foreign Policy." *International Affairs* 85, no. 3 (2009).

Mody, Ashoka, Damiano Sandri, and Refet S. Gürkaynak. "The Eurozone Crisis: How Banks and Sovereigns Came to Be Joined at the Hip." *Economic Policy* 27, no. 70 (April 2012).

Mölling, Christian. "Defense Innovation and the Future of Transatlantic Strategic Superiority: A German Perspective." German Marshall Fund of the United States, 2018.

Mölling, Christian, and Torben Schütz. "Responsible Defense Policy." Deutsche Gesellschaft für Auswärtige Politik, October 11, 2018.

Mölling, Christina, and Torben Schütz. "Verteidigungspolitische Verantwortung: Mehr Geld bedeutet nicht mehr Effizienz." Deutsche Gesellschaft für Auswärtige Politik, August 2018.

Moravcsik, Andrew. "Taking Preferences Seriously: A Liberal Theory of International Politics." *International Organization* 51, no. 4 (Autumn 1997).

Mulholland, Rory. "Head of French Armed Forces Resigns over Budget Cuts Row with Macron." *Telegraph*, July 19, 2017.

"Mullen: Debt Is Top National Security Threat." *CNN*, August 27, 2010.

"Munich Security Conference Chief: Trump Pushes Germany toward Russia and China." Euractiv.com, September 4, 2018.

Nakashima, Ellen. "U.S. Cyber Command Operation Disrupted Internet Access of Russian Troll Factory on Day of 2018 Midterms." *Washington Post*, February 27, 2019.

National Audit Office (UK). "The Equipment Plan 2018 to 2028." Report by the Comptroller and Auditor General, November 5, 2018.

National Security Strategy of the United States of America, December 2017.

"National Strategy for Counterterrorism of the United States of America." October 2018.

NATO. "Defence Expenditure of NATO Countries (2011–2018)." Press release PR/CP(2018)091, July 10, 2018.

NATO. "Financial and Economic Data Relating to NATO Defence." Press release M-DPC-2(92)100, December 10, 1992.

"NATO's Helo Woes." Military.com, November 28, 2007.

"New Russia Missiles in Kaliningrad Are Answer to U.S. Shield: Lawmaker." *Reuters*, November 21, 2016.

Nichiporuk, Brian. *Security Dynamics of Demographic Factors*. Santa Monica, CA: RAND Corporation, 2000.

Nienaber, Michael. "German Real Wages Rise despite Higher Inflation." *Reuters*, September 20, 2018.

Nienaber, Michael, and Holger Hansen. "German Jobless Rate Hits Record Low in May." *Reuters*, May 30, 2018.

Noack, Rick. "Afraid of a Major Conflict? The German Military Is Currently Unavailable." *Washington Post*, January 24, 2018.

"'No More Missions for Germany's Navy,' Warns Armed Forces Ombudsman." *Deutsche Welle*, February 11, 2018. p.dw.com/p/2sTQ9

Norman, Laurence. "EU, in Major Shift, Moves to Confront China's Growing Assertiveness." *Wall Street Journal*, March 13, 2019.

Norton-Taylor, Richard. "BAE Warned Cameron over £5bn Cost of Cancelling Aircraft Carrier Contract." *Guardian*, November 4, 2010.

"Number of Refugees to Europe Surges to Record 1.3 Million in 2015." Pew Research Center, August 2, 2016.

Nye, Joseph. "Protecting Democracy in an Era of Cyber Information War." *Governance in an Emerging New World*, November 13, 2018.

Nye, Joseph S., Jr. "Get Smart: Combining Hard and Soft Power." *Foreign Policy*, July/August 2009.

Nye, Joseph S., Jr. *Soft Power: The Means to Success in World Politics*. New York: Public Affairs, 2004.

O'Brien, Fergal. "$170 Billion and Counting: The Cost of Brexit for the U.K." *Bloomberg*, January 10, 2020, www.bloomberg.com/news/articles/2020-01-10/-170-billion-and-counting-the-cost-of-brexit-for-the-u-k

O'Brien, Matthew. "The Big Secret of Poland's Economic Success—and What It Means for Us." *Atlantic*, December 17, 2012.

Organization for Economic Co-operation and Development (OECD). "Development Aid Stable in 2017 with More Sent to Poorest Countries." April 9, 2018.

OECD. "Employment Outlook 2018: How Does France Compare?" July 2018.

OECD. "OECD Economic Outlook: Statistics and Projections." November 2018.

OECD. "OECD Economic Surveys: Poland 2010." 2010.

OECD. "OECD Economic Surveys: Poland 2012." 2012.

OECD. "OECD Economic Surveys: Poland 2014." 2014. dx.doi.org/10.1787/eco_surveys-pol-2014-en

Office of the Secretary of Defense. "Annual Report to Congress: Military and Security Developments Involving the People's Republic of China 2019." May 2, 2019.

Oliker, Olga. "Russian Influence and Unconventional Warfare Operations in the 'Grey Zone:' Lessons from Ukraine." Statement before the Senate Armed Services Committee Subcommittee on Emerging Threats and Capabilities, March 29, 2017.

Olsen, Gorm Rye. "Transatlantic Cooperation on Terrorism and Islamist Radicalisation in Africa: The Franco-American Axis." *European Security* 27, no. 1 (2018).

Ozzano, Luca. "Religion, Cleavages, and Right-Wing Populist Parties: The Italian Case." *Review of Faith & International Affairs* 17, no. 1 (2019).

Pailliez, Caroline. "You're Hired! France's Macron Targets Apprentices in Labor Market Shake-up." *Reuters*, November 3, 2017.

Pannier, Alice. "France's Defense Partnerships and the Dilemmas of Brexit." German Marshall Fund of the United States, May 30, 2018.

Pappas, Takis S. *Populism Emergent: A Framework for Analyzing Its Contexts, Mechanics, and Outcomes*. European University Institute, January 2012.

Parker, Sam, and Gabrielle Chefitz. "China's Debtbook Diplomacy: How China Is Turning Bad Loans into Strategic Investments." *Diplomat*, May 30, 2018.

Partington, Richard. "Brexit Vote Has Cost Each UK Household £900, Says Mark Carney." *Guardian*, May 22, 2018.

Partington, Richard. "Pound Gradually Climbs despite Brexit Uncertainty." *Guardian*, September 27, 2018.

Pawlak, Justyna, and Kacper Pempel. "In Training with Poland's Volunteer Militia." *Reuters*, October 18, 2018.

Payne, Keith B., and John S. Foster. "Russian Strategy Expansion, Crisis and Conflict." *Comparative Strategy* 36, no. 1 (2017).

Pedder, Sophie. *Revolution Française: Emmanuel Macron and the Quest to Reinvent a Nation*. London: Bloomsbury Continuum, 2018.

Pelkmans, Jacques, et al. "The Impact of TTIP: The Underlying Economic Model and Comparisons." *Centre for European Policy Studies*, no. 93 (October 2014).

Pellegrino, Bruno, and Luigi Zingales. "Diagnosing the Italian Disease." *NBER Working Paper Series*, October 2017.

Pena, Elizabeth. "US, Polish SOF Enhance Abilities through Culmination Exercise." U.S. Air Force Public Affairs, January 2, 2019.

Pennetier, Marine. "Russia, Ukraine 'Damocles Sword' Hangs over French Military Deployment." *Reuters*, March 28, 2017.

Pennington, Matthew. "Pentagon Says War in Afghanistan Costs Taxpayers $45 Billion per Year." Associated Press, February 6, 2018.

Permanent Court of Arbitration. "Press Release: The South China Sea Arbitration (The Republic of the Philippines v. the People's Republic of China)." July 12, 2016.

Perraudin, Frances. "Numbers in UK Frontline Army Units Down by up to a Third." *Guardian*, April 1, 2019.

Perry, David. "A Return to Realism: Canadian Defence Policy after the Great Recession." *Defence Studies* 13, no. 3 (2013).

Persson, Gudrun, ed. *Russian Military Capability in a Ten-Year Perspective—2016.* Swedish Defence Research Agency, December 2016.

Peters, Anne. "Between Military Deployment and Democracy: Use of Force under the German Constitution." *Journal on the Use of Force and International Law* 5, no. 2 (2018).

Pickering, Jeffrey. "Politics and 'Black Tuesday': Shifting Power in the Cabinet and the Decision to Withdraw from East of Suez, November 1967–January 1968." *Twentieth Century British History* 13, no. 2 (January 1, 2002).

Poggetti, Lucrezia. "Italy Charts Risky Course with China-Friendly Policy." Mercator Institute for China Studies, October 11, 2018.

"Poland." Economist Intelligence Unit, August 16, 2018.

"Poland and Sweden Expand the Military Cooperation." *Defense24*, September 15, 2015.

"Poland's ORKA Submarine Competition Limping Along." *Submarine Matters*, September 27, 2018.

"Polish-Led Exercise Anakonda 2016 a Huge Success." SHAPE Public Affairs Office, June 17, 2016.

"Polish Manufacturers Embrace Industry 4.0." *Industry Europe*, September 17, 2018.

Polish National Security Bureau. "White Paper on National Security of the Republic of Poland." 2013.

Pothier, Fabrice. "Macron, l'américain?" *Survival* 60, no. 3 (2018).

Poushter, Jacob, and Alexandra Castillo. "Americans and Germans Are Worlds Apart in Views of Their Countries' Relationship." Pew Research Center, November 26, 2018.

Poushter, Jacob, and Christine Huang. "Climate Change Still Seen as the Top Global Threat, but Cyberattacks a Rising Concern." Pew Research Center, February 10, 2019.

"Pouvoir d'achat : Un sentiment de baisse pour 3 Français sur 4." *Elabe*, October 31, 2018.

Presidency of the Council of Ministers. "National Strategic Framework for Cyberspace Security." December 2013.

"President: No More Far-Off Military Missions." Polish Press Agency, August 15, 2019.

Pronczuk, Monika. "Ruling Party Hopes Child Benefit Scheme Will Woo Poland's Voters in Biala Podlaska." *Financial Times*, February 5, 2019.

"Prospects for the UK Economy." *National Institute Economic Review*, no. 250 (November 2019).

Puzzanghera, Jim. "Trump Says Merkel Meeting Was 'Great,' Then Blasts Germany for NATO Bills." *Los Angeles Times*, March 18, 2017.

Radin, Andrew, and Raphael S. Cohen. "Russia's Soft Strategy to Hostile Measures in Europe." *War on the Rocks*, February 26, 2019.

Rahn, Wesley. "South China Sea: France and Britain Join the US to Oppose China." *Deutsche Welle*, June 27, 2018.

Rayburn, Joel D., and Frank K. Sobchak, eds. *The U.S. Army in the Iraq War—Volume 1: Invasion—Insurgency—Civil War, 2003–2006*. Carlisle, PA: U.S. Army War College Press, 2019.

Reilly, James. "China's Economic Statecraft in Europe." *Asia Europe Journal* 15 (2017).

Reiter, Chris. "How Germany Is Defusing a Demographic Time Bomb." *Bloomberg*, May 23, 2018.

Rempfer, Kyle. "Green Berets Train Polish, Latvian Resistance Units in West Virginia." *Army Times*, July 8, 2019.

Republic of Poland. "National Security Strategy of the Republic of Poland." 2014.

Reynolds, David, *Britannia Overruled: British Policy and World Power in the Twentieth Century*. London: Pearson Educational, 2016.

Rhodes, Matthew. "Central Europe and Iraq: Balance, Bandwagon, or Bridge?" *Orbis* 48, no. 3 (2004).

Robert, Aline. "France's Budget Deficit Could Skyrocket to 7% of GDP in COVID-19 Aftermath." *Euractiv*, March 20, 2020.

"Rosyjskie drony wlatują do Polski." *Gazeta Olsztyńska*, December 9, 2016.

"Rosyjskie śmigłowce wtargnęły nad Polskę i . . . cisza: Nic się nie stało?" Kresy24.pl, April 18, 2016.

Rowley, Emma. "Italy's Austerity May Have Saved the Euro, Says Mario Monti." *Telegraph*, November 17, 2012.

"Royal Navy Could Lose Its Two Amphibious Assault Ships in Cuts." *Guardian*, October 5, 2017.

"Ruling Party Presents Five Major Proposals for 2019 Election Year." Polish Press Agency, February 23, 2019.

"Russian A2/AD Capability Overrated." Swedish Defence Research Agency, March 4, 2019.

"Russia's Global Image Negative amid Crisis in Ukraine." Pew Research Center, July 9, 2014.

"Russia's Population Declines in 2018 for First Time in a Decade." *Moscow Times*, December 21, 2018.

Rüssmann, Michael, et al. "Industry 4.0: The Future of Productivity and Growth in Manufacturing Industries." Boston Consulting Group, April 9, 2015.

Sabak, Juliusz. "Unexpected Russian Air Force Exercise in the Kaliningrad Area." Defense24.com, November 2, 2015.

Sabatino, Ester. "The Innovations of the Italian White Paper: Defence Policy Reform." Istituto Affari Internazionali, Working Paper 17/34, December 2017.

Sabatino, Ester. "The Italian White Paper on Defence: Common Ground with Germany?" Friedrich Ebert Stiftung, November 2017.

Sachgau, Oliver, and Piotr Skolimowski. "Germany's Jobless Rate Drops to Record Low as Economy Booms." *Bloomberg*, January 3, 2018.

Salisbury, Daniel. "Will North Korea Sell Its Nuclear Technology?" *The Conversation*, September 25, 2017.

Sampson, Thomas, et al. "Economists for Brexit: A Critique." London School of Economics and Political Science, Centre for Economic Performance, May 2016.

Samuel, Henry. "France to Boost Defence Spending in 'Unprecedented' Move to Meet Nato Commitments." *Telegraph*, February 8, 2018.

Sanders, Lewis. "Germany Creates DARPA-Like Cybersecurity Agency." *Deutsche Welle*, August 29, 2018.

Sanders, Lewis. "How France's Emmanuel Macron Wants to Reform the EU." *Deutsche Welle*, March 16, 2018.

Schmitt, Gary J. "Italian Hard Power: Ambitions and Fiscal Realities." In *A Hard Look at Hard Power: Assessing the Defense Capabilities of Key U.S. Allies and Security Partners*, ed. Gary J. Schmitt. Carlisle, PA: U.S. Army War College Press, 2015.

Schmitt, Olivier. *Allies That Count: Junior Partners in Coalition Warfare*. Washington, DC: Georgetown University Press, 2018.

Schrieberg, David. "Emmanuel Macron's France Rebounds, yet His Popularity Suffers." *Forbes*, February 18, 2018.

Schulze, Matthias. "Germany Develops Offensive Cyber Capabilities without a Coherent Strategy of What to Do with Them." Council on Foreign Relations, December 3, 2018.

Schwabe, Michał. "Competitiveness of the Polish Economy: Lessons Learned for the Years 2014–2020." *Polish Review* 61, no. 2 (2016).

Sciutto, Jim. "'The Shadow War': How a Chinese Spy Stole Some of the Pentagon's Most Sensitive Secrets." *CNN*, May 14, 2019.

"Scotland in Numbers." *BBC News Online*, November 25, 2013.

Seck, Hope Hodge. "British Pilots Look Forward to Flying P-8 Sub-Hunter in UK." Military.com, July 14, 2016.

Sedghi, Ami. "UK Defence Spending to Be Kept at 2% of GDP." *Guardian*, July 8, 2015.

Segreti, Giulia. "Italy Eases Austerity as Economy Picks Up." *Financial Times*, April 12, 2015.

Seibert, Bjoern H. "A Quiet Revolution." *RUSI Journal* 157, no. 1 (2012).

Serrano, Omar. *The Domestic Sources of European Foreign Policy: Defence and Enlargement*. Amsterdam: Amsterdam University Press, 2014.

Sevastopulo, Demetri. "US Army 'Stretched Thin' by Iraq War." *Financial Times*, February 18, 2008.

Shambaugh, David. *China's Future*. Cambridge: Polity Press, 2016.

Sharkov, Damien. "Donald Trump Scares Germans More Than Terrorism, Eurozone Crisis, and Climate Change." *Newsweek*, September 6, 2018.

Sheehan, James. "US Gives Lift to French Forces." U.S. Army, February 13, 2019.

Shotter, James. "Military Backlash against Defence Cuts Grows." *Financial Times*, February 9, 2011.

Shugart, Matthew Soberg. "The Electoral Cycle and Institutional Sources of Divided Presidential Government." *American Political Science Review* 89, no. 2 (June 1995).

Shurkin, Michael. *The Abilities of the British, French, and German Armies to Generate and Sustain Armored Brigades in the Baltics*. Santa Monica, CA: RAND, 2017.

Simionescu, Mihaela, Yuriy Bilan, and Grzegorz Mentel. "Economic Effects of Migration from Poland to the UK." *Amfiteatru Economic* 19, no. 46 (2017).

Simmons, Katie, Bruce Stokes, and Jacob Poushter. "NATO Publics Blame Russia for Ukrainian Crisis, but Reluctant to Provide Military Aid." Pew Research Center, June 10, 2015.

Simón, Luis. "Europe, the Rise of Asia and the Future of the Transatlantic Relationship." *International Affairs* 91, no. 5 (2015).

SIPRI Military Expenditure Database 2019. Stockholm International Peace Research Institute, 2019.

"SIPRI Yearbook 2018 Online." Stockholm International Peace Research Institute, 2018.

"Six in Ten Britons Think Their Standard of Living Won't Be Affected by Brexit." Ipsos-MORI, May 31, 2016.

Skidelsky, Robert. "Germany's Current-Account Surplus Is Partly to Blame for Eurozone Stagnation." *Guardian*, July 24, 2014.

Sloan, Stanley R. *NATO, the European Union, and the Atlantic Community: The Transatlantic Bargain Reconsidered*, Lanham, MD: Rowman and Littlefield, 2002.

Smith, Martin A. *NATO in the First Decade after the Cold War*. Dordrecht, the Netherlands: Kluwer Academic Publishers, 2000.

Springford, John. "The Cost of Brexit to September 2018." Centre for European Reform, January 27, 2019.

Staudenmaier, Rebecca. "German Issues in a Nutshell: 'Agenda 2010'." *Deutsche Welle*, June 6, 2017.

Stavridis, James. "Putin's Big Military Buildup Is behind NATO Lines." *Bloomberg*, October 20, 2018.

Stearns, Jonathan, and Alexander Weber. "China Threat to Telecoms Cited in EU Parliament Draft Resolution." *Bloomberg*, March 11, 2019.

Steinmeier, Frank-Walter. "Rede von Außenminister Frank-Walter Steinmeier anlässlich der 50." Münchner Sicherheitskonferenz, February 1, 2014.

Stokes, Bruce. "NATO's Image Improves on Both Sides of Atlantic." Pew Research Center, May 22, 2017.

"Strength of British Military Falls for Ninth Year." BBC.co.uk, August 16, 2019.

Strzałkowski, Michał. "Poland Seeks to Protect Its Ukrainian Connection." Euractiv.com, February 22, 2019.

Szary, Wiktor. "Poland Counts the Cost of Losing Millions of Its Workers." *Reuters*, December 5, 2014.

Taggart, Paul. "Populism and Representative Politics in Contemporary Europe." *Journal of Political Ideologies* 9, no. 3 (2004).

Taylor, Adam. "How Brexit Ravaged the Once-Mighty British Pound." *Washington Post*, August 15, 2019.

Taylor, Paul. "Salvini's Sophia Soapbox: Why Rome May Pull the Plug on the EU's Military Mission in the Mediterranean." *Politico*, March 12, 2019.

Tellis, Ashley J., Janice Bially, Christopher Layne, and Melissa McPherson, *Measuring National Power in the Postindustrial Age*. Santa Monica, CA: RAND Corporation, 2000.

Tertrais, Bruno. *The Demographic Challenge: Myths and Realities*. Paris: Institut Montaigne, 2018.

Terzi, Alessio. "An Italian Job: The Need for Collective Wage Bargaining Reform." *Bruegel*, July 6, 2016.

"Thales to Work on French Navy's Future Ballistic Missile Submarine Sonar Tech." *Naval Today*, February 7, 2018.

Thrall, A. Trevor, and Erik Goepner. "Step Back: Lessons for U.S. Foreign Policy from the Failed War on Terror." CATO Institute, Policy Analysis No. 814, June 26, 2017.

Tigner, Brooks. "National Calls Growing for Stronger EU Military and Defence Policies." *Jane's Defence Weekly*, August 31, 2016.

Timmer, Marcel P., et al. "Productivity and Economic Growth in Europe: A Comparative Industry Perspective." *International Productivity Monitor*, Spring 2011.

Toosi, Nahal. "Tillerson Spurns $80 Million to Counter ISIS, Russian Propaganda." *Politico*, August 2, 2017.

Toosi, Nahal. "'Why Germany?' Trump's Strange Fixation Vexes Experts." *Politico*, July 11, 2018.

Torode, Greg, and Ben Blanchard. "Exclusive: Images Show Construction on China's Third and Largest Aircraft Carrier—Analysts." *Reuters*, May 7, 2019.

Tovey, Alan. "Fears over UK Military Budget as MoD Cuts Back Apache Order." *Telegraph*, June 18, 2017.

Tran, Pierre. "France Places C-130 Order." *Defense News*, February 1, 2016.

Tran, Pierre. "French Official Details Intelligence-Sharing Relationship with Five Eyes." *Defense News*, February 5, 2018.

Tran, Pierre. "Macron Signs French Military Budget into Law: Here's What the Armed Forces Are Getting." *Defense News*, July 16, 2018.

Traub, James. "Macron Has Changed France's Political DNA." *Foreign Policy*, June 5, 2018.

Trofimov, Yaroslav. "Turning Muslims Away, Poland Welcomes Ukrainians." *Wall Street Journal*, March 26, 2019.

"Trump Takes Aim at Germany and NATO." *Der Spiegel Online*, July 13, 2018.

Tsang, Amie. "U.K. Auto Industry Already Feeling the Brexit Pinch." *New York Times*, January 31, 2019.

"TTIP and Jobs." European Parliament's Directorate-General for Internal Policies, 2016.

"TTIP and the Fifty States: Jobs and Growth from Coast to Coast." Atlantic Council of the United States, the Bertelsmann Foundation, and the British Embassy in Washington, 2013.

Tucker, Patrick. "Analysts Are Quitting the State Department's Anti-Propaganda Team." *Defense One*, September 12, 2017.

Tucker, Patrick. "NATO Getting More Aggressive on Offensive Cyber." *Defense One*, May 24, 2019.

Tucker, Patrick. "Poland Is Preparing for 15 Years of Rising Tension with Russia." *Defense One*, June 1, 2017.

Tucker, Patrick. "Russia Building Up Military Sites on Poland's Border before Trump-Putin Meeting." *Defense One*, July 9, 2018.

Tyler, Patrick E. "U.S. Strategy Plan Calls for Insuring No Rivals Develop." *New York Times*, March 8, 1992.

UN Refugee Agency. Online Italy portal. data2.unhcr.org/en/situations/mediterranean/location/5205

"Urban and Rural Population: Russian Federation." UN World Urbanization Prospects 2018.

"U.S. Aerospace and Defense Industry Supported Almost 2.8 Million Jobs in 2015." IHS Markit, April 21, 2016.

U.S. Census Bureau. "U.S. International Trade in Goods and Services (FT900), Exhibit 20—U.S. Trade in Goods and Services by Selected Countries and Areas—BOP Basis." October 2018.

U.S. Department of Defense. Summary of the 2018 National Defense Strategy of the United States of America, January 2018.

"US Nato General Fears Rapid Russian Troop Deployments." *BBC Online*, June 20, 2016.

Van Reenen, John. "Brexit's Long-Run Effects on the U.K. Economy." *Brookings Papers on Economic Activity*, Fall 2016.

Varadarajan, Tunku. "Move over Britain, France Is America's 'Special' Friend." *Politico*, April 30, 2018.

Vick, Karl, and Simon Shuster. "Chancellor of the Free World." *Time*, December 2015.

Vinocur, John. "German Lion Emerges from Merkel's Sunset." *Politico*, October 12, 2018.

Vinocur, Nicholas. "5 Key Points from Macron's Big Labor Reform." *Politico*, August 31, 2017.

Von der Leyen, Ursula. Speech on the occasion of the 50th Munich Security Conference, January 31, 2014.

Von Hlatky, Stéfanie. *American Allies in Times of War: The Great Asymmetry*. Oxford: Oxford University Press, 2013.

Wagner, Thomas. "Mehr klicken, weniger schrauben." *Deutschlandradio*, December 11, 2018.

Walker, Peter, Heather Stewart, and Patrick Wintour. "Theresa May Rebukes Trump as Opposition to State Visit Grows." *Guardian*, November 30, 2017.

Wallace, William, and Christopher Phillips. "Reassessing the Special Relationship." *International Affairs* 85, no 2 (March 2009).

Walsh, Mary Williams. "Edging toward Combat, Germans Boost Bosnia Role." *Los Angeles Times*, July 1, 1995.

Walter-Franke, Marie. "Two Years into the EU-Turkey 'Deal': Impact and Challenges of a Turbulent Partnership." Jacques Delors Institut—Berlin, March 15, 2018.

Waltz, Kenneth. *Theory of International Politics*. Reading, MA: Addison-Wesley, 1979.

Waterfield, Phee. "South Korea and Germany Lead 'Automation Index'." *RCR Wireless News*, April 25, 2018.

Wei, Lingling, and Bob Davis. "How China Systematically Pries Technology from U.S. Companies." *Wall Street Journal*, September 26, 2018.

"Weissbuch 2016 zur Sicherheitspolitik und zur Zukunft der Bundeswehr." July 2016.

Werkhäuser, Nina. "German Army Launches New Cyber Command." *Deutsche Welle*, April 1, 2017.

Westerlund, Fredrik. "Force or Modernization?" In *Current Russia Military Affairs: Assessing and Countering Russian Strategy, Operational Planning, and Modernization*, ed. John R. Deni. Carlisle, PA: U.S. Army War College Press, 2018.

Western, Jon. *Selling Intervention and War: The Presidency, the Media, and the American Public*. Baltimore: Johns Hopkins University Press, 2005.

"What Are Italy's Fresh Austerity Measures?" *Telegraph*, November 11, 2011.

"What Does Xi Jinping's China Dream Mean?" *BBC Online*, June 6, 2013.

"What Italy's Foreign Policy Will Look Like under New Rulers." *Stratfor*, June 18, 2018. worldview.stratfor.com/article/italy-foreign-policy-under-five-star-league

White House. "Joint Declaration on Defense Cooperation Regarding United States Force Posture in the Republic of Poland." June 12, 2019.

White House. *A National Security Strategy of Engagement and Enlargement*. July 1994.

White House. The National Security Strategy of the United States of America. September 2002.

White Paper on Defence and National Security (France). New York: Odile Jacob, 2008.

White Paper on Defence and National Security (France). 2013.

Whitlock, Craig. "NATO Allies Grapple with Shrinking Defense Budgets." *Washington Post*, January 29, 2012.

Whitman, Richard G. "Avoiding a Hard Brexit in Foreign Policy." *Survival* 59, no. 6 (2017).

Whitney, Craig R. "German Soldiers Head for Somalia." *New York Times*, July 23, 1993.

Whittaker, Matt. "Ending Austerity?" Resolution Foundation, July 2017.

Wiegold, Thomas. "Schwund beim Eurofighter: Eine Pilotin erklärt ihre Kündigung." Augen Geradeaus, May 1, 2018.

Wilber, Del Quentin. "China 'Has Taken the Gloves Off' in Its Thefts of U.S. Technology Secrets." *Los Angeles Times*, November 16, 2018.

Wilk, Remigiusz. "Poland Relocates Leopard 2A5 Tanks to the East." *Jane's Defence Weekly*, April 20, 2017.

Wilk, Remigiusz. "Poland Unveils Military Acquisition Road Map." *Jane's Defence Weekly*, November 21, 2018.

Wilk, Remigiusz. "Polish Territorial Defence Force Expanded to 53,000 Personnel." *Jane's Defence Weekly*, November 17, 2016.

Wilson, Graham. "Brexit, Trump and the Special Relationship." *British Journal of Politics and International Relations* 19, no. 3 (2017).

Wither, James K. "Brexit and the Anglo-American Security and Defense Partnership." *Parameters* 48, no. , (Spring 2018).

Wodak, Ruth. *The Politics of Fear: What Right-Wing Populist Discourses Mean.* London: SAGE Publications, 2015.

Wolfe, Frank. "U.S. Officials Consider Retaliation if EU Does Not Relax Draft EDF and PESCO Language." *Defense Daily*, June 17, 2019.

World Bank. World Integrated Trade Solution. "Product Exports by Country and Region 2016." 2016.

World Bank Group and World Trade Organization. "Trade and Poverty Reduction: New Evidence of Impacts in Developing Countries." 2018.

Wren-Lewis, Simon. "The Austerity Con." *London Review of Books* 37, no. 4 (February 19, 2015).

Wu, Wendy. "European Militaries 'Will Do More to Counter Assertive China' in Indo-Pacific." *South China Morning Post*, March 19, 2019.

Yglesias, Matthew. "How a Chinese Infrastructure Bank Turned into a Diplomatic Fiasco for America." *Vox*, April 1, 2015.

Young, Brigitte, and Willi Semmler. "The European Sovereign Debt Crisis: Is Germany to Blame?" *German Politics and Society* 29, no. 1 (Spring 2011).

Za, Valentina. "Italy Key Bond Yield Soars to 11-yr High at Auction." *Reuters*, July 28, 2011.

Żemła, Edyta, and Kamil Turecki. "Poland Offers US up to $2B for Permanent Military Base." *Politico*, May 27, 2018.

Zenko, Micah. "America's Military Is Nostalgic for World Wars." *Foreign Policy*, March 13, 2018.

Zissis, Carin. "China's Anti-Satellite Test." Council on Foreign Relations, February 22, 2007.

Index